THE Womanist IDEA

Picking up where *The Womanist Reader* left off, Layli Maparyan presents a systematic analysis of womanism in *The Womanist Idea*. Emphasizing womanism as worldview, she situates spirituality at the heart of womanist thought and praxis, grounding a metaphysically oriented approach to social and ecological activism. Womanism, she argues, is *spiritual movement*, not just social movement. Case studies of five diverse spiritual activists from around the world—Sister Chan Khong (Vietnam/France), Immaculée Ilibagiza (Rwanda), Kiran Bedi (India), Pregs Govender (South Africa), and Wangari Maathai (Kenya)—illustrate womanism in action. The animating impulse of womanism is LUXOCRACY, or "rule by Light," an aspirational form of human social organization that recognizes the innate divinity of all human beings and, indeed, all life on Earth and the entire cosmos. Womanism, thus, invites *a luminous revolution*.

Layli Maparyan is Associate Professor of Women's Studies and Associated Faculty of African American Studies at Georgia State University. In 2006 (as Layli Phillips), she published *The Womanist Reader*, an anthology documenting the first quarter century of womanist thought from an interdisciplinary perspective. Since 2006, she has worked collaboratively with the University of Liberia to develop its inaugural Gender Studies Program, serving as a Fulbright Specialist in 2010. In 2009, she was awarded a Contemplative Practice Fellowship by the Center for Contemplative Mind in Society to study and teach womanist spiritual activism internationally.

THE Womanist IDEA

LAYLI MAPARYAN

GEORGIA STATE UNIVERSITY

Routledge
Taylor & Francis Group

NEW YORK AND LONDON

First published 2012
by Routledge
711 Third Avenue, New York, NY 10017

Simultaneously published in the UK
by Routledge
2 Park Square, Milton Park, Abingdon, Oxon OX14 4RN

Routledge is an imprint of the Taylor & Francis Group, an informa business

© 2012 Taylor & Francis

Library of Congress Cataloging in Publication Data
Maparyan, Layli.
  The womanist idea / Layli Maparyan.
  p. cm. — (Contemporary sociological perspectives)
  Includes bibliographical references and index.
  1. Spiritual life. 2. Womanism. 3. Mysticism. 4. Social change. I. Title.
  BL624.M3444 2011
  204'.4082—dc23
  2011030148

ISBN: 978-0-415-88682-6 (hbk)
ISBN: 978-0-415-88683-3 (pbk)
ISBN: 978-0-203-13593-8 (ebk)

Typeset in Premier Garamond, Helvetica, and Univers 59 Ultra Condensed
by EvS Communication Networx, Inc.

FOR

Aliyah Karmil Phillips
"My Little Womaness"
(1986–2009)

CONTENTS

PART 1: THE METAPHYSICAL ARCHITECTURE OF THE WOMANIST IDEA

1 Luxocracy: Rule by Light 3

Luxocracy—"rule by Light"—is the animating idea of womanism and a vision for the future of humanity. It is predicated upon acknowledgment of the innate divinity and sacredness of all humans and, indeed, all creation and the entire cosmos. In order for Luxocracy to unfold as a liberating form of social organization on Earth, three conditions are necessary: commonweal, planetary identity, and luminous revolution.

2 Womanist Origins: Reading Alice Walker, Chikwenye Okonjo Ogunyemi, and Clenora Hudson-Weems 15

Womanism is the ongoing outgrowth of womanists' everyday thought and praxis. Although the womanist idea in its unnamed form has existed for centuries, if not millennia, contemporary womanism has been shaped by three notable spokespersons: Alice Walker, Chikwenye Okonjo Ogunyemi, and Clenora Hudson-Weems. This chapter examines originary writings on womanism by these three authors in order to locate the core ideas and tendencies of womanism, and also acknowledges the role of everyday women in constructing womanism by interpolating these three perspectives.

3 Womanist Worldview/Womanism as Spiritual Movement 33

This chapter explores womanist metaphysics through an examination of womanist cosmology and ontology, womanist epistemology, womanist logic, and womanist axiology. This systematic approach produces two interrelated and novel conclusions: first, that womanism is a worldview (as distinct from a theory or ideology) and, second, that womanism is a spiritual movement (as distinct from a social movement).

4 Womanist Methodology: Transforming Consciousness,
Changing the World   51

Some womanist methods of social and ecological transformation are explained in detail in order to show the womanist idea in action. These methods include: self-care, spiritual practices, harmonization and coordination, dialogue, arbitration and mediation, mothering, hospitality, mutual aid and self-help, "standing in," and "fly-over." Illustrations of womanist methodology in action from around the world are presented.

5 A Spiritual Archaeology of the Womanist Idea   86

This chapter explores the idea that the womanist idea is coconstituted by multiple spiritual and religious strands that converge at a point of dynamic coordination. Narratives of personal spiritual journeys are used to illustrate the eclectic, synthetic, holistic, personal, visionary, and pragmatic aspects of the spirituality that animates the womanist idea and, in turn, undergirds womanism as social/ecological transformation praxis.

6 Spiritual Activism: A Womanist Approach   114

Womanists take "the invisible realm" as axiomatic, and it forms a basis for a unique type of social and ecological change work. This chapter explores applied mysticism, applied metaphysics, and applied spirituality from a womanist perspective, with an emphasis on how these modalities of praxis can affect and effect social justice and ecological healing in the world.

PART 2: WOMANIST SPIRITUAL ACTIVISM: FIVE CASE STUDIES

7 Transforming War into Peace: Sister Chan Khong
and *Learning True Love*   145

Sister Chan Khong is a Vietnamese Buddhist nun, master of mindfulness, and lifetime peace activist. This chapter offers a close reading of her memoir, Learning True Love: Practicing Buddhism in a Time of War, *with a focus on love-based, nondualistic, and mindful approaches to ending conflict and creating cultures of peace.*

PART 3: BEYOND WOMANISM

What happens when a womanist loses a daughter? How does such a life-changing event impact one's engagement with womanism, spirituality, and social change? This autobiographical chapter explores the outer limits of the womanist idea and ultimately concludes that womanism is a vehicle for moving beyond itself.

In this chapter, the womanist idea is recapped in terms of 13 key themes.

PREFACE

....

When I began to study womanism some twenty years ago, I discerned something within it which, while clearly being embraced by people claiming womanism, was not being expressed in the discourse about womanism, whether by feminists (Black or otherwise) or even womanists themselves. My sense about this "unarticulated something" was that it was quite important and that it was, indeed, the thing that distinguished womanism from feminism or any other prominent social change discourse of the time. This same "unarticulated something" allowed womanism to exist "under the radar" of contemporary feminist histories of consciousness and even to proliferate under these conditions of obscurity, like a seed beneath the soil that is quietly taking root before sending a tightly curled leaflet above the surface in search of the light of day. Without defining this thing, I simply named it in my own mind as "the womanist idea." Like a blueprint enfolded within a seed's DNA that eventually becomes the architecture of the mature plant, I viewed "the womanist idea" as a kind of underlying architecture of womanism, hidden beneath a lack of language to adequately express it and perhaps also beneath social conditions that were incompatible with its idea-istic structure. The more I reflected on this architecture, however, it increasingly appeared to me not so much as a "theory" or "philosophy" but rather as a worldview, a metaphysics, a methodology, a movement, and a spirit. And as I reflected, the more I came to conclude that "the womanist idea" is actually a potent and necessary intervention upon many of the widely lamented shortfalls of this age in which we live (and, as we so often bemoan, might die).

This book, *The Womanist Idea*, offers a new and different account of womanism and womanists, one that seeks out and elaborates the "metaphysical architecture" of womanism, examines and analyzes the practical wisdom and social change genius of womanists, and imagines womanism "out of bounds"; that is, beyond the confines of womanism as identity and womanism as theory. I build on the foundation that was laid in my introduction to *The Womanist Reader* (2006), to further elaborate on the theme of womanism as a form of spiritualized politics that encompasses humans, the environment/nature, and the spiritual realm. In so doing, I refigure spirituality as a foundation for social change—activism—and provide case studies of five women from around the globe whose spiritual activism has been documented in memoirs, biographies, films, news stories, and other media. I subject these women's life stories, thought, and praxis to a close womanist reading that produces new insights about womanism as a thoughtform that operates even in sites where the label womanism is never invoked. This reading allows me to highlight previously elusive features of womanism and demonstrate that the womanist idea is not only part of a zeitgeist but can also effect positive social and ecological change whether or not it is named. This approach makes this book suitable to womanists and nonwomanists alike, researchers as well as students, academics as well as activists, and interested readers of all genders, ethnicities, spiritualities, and political persuasions. Such is the power of the womanist idea to gather us together and transform, even transport us beyond this curious historical moment in which we are all living.

What is this moment? In one of my favorite books—Chela Sandoval's *Methodology of the Oppressed*—Foucault's notion of the self-deconstitution of "Western man" frames an unsentimental and adroit understanding about the end of an age. "Western man" is not a person but a consciousness, a thoughtform, the blueprint inside the seed that matured into our current world civilization. This way of life that once seemed glorious and unstoppable is undoing itself because it has reached the material and spiritual limits of its logic. Foucault's terminology invokes the language of the "limit situation" that I first encountered in another of my favorite books, *Writings for a Liberation Psychology* by Ignacio Martín-Baró. This social psychologist and Jesuit priest translated liberation theology into liberation psychology and with it turned his lens on the mindset that produced the invidious "low intensity conflict" of the 1980s in Central America. The editors and translators of a posthumous collection of his writings, Adrienne Aron and Shawn Corne, wrote: "In speaking of himself as living in a limit situation, Martín-Baró meant that he stood, alongside the people of El Salvador, at an important boundary that marked the limits of human possibility: limits not in the sense of an end of possibility; limits rather as markers of the place where all possibilities begin."[1] They continue, "This is not the division line between being and nothingness; it is the frontier which separates *being* from *being more*."

Chela Sandoval argues that there is a way out, over, or through such a limit situation—in this case, the coming demise of the "Western man" way of life and its generative mindset. This "way out/over/through" has been illuminated by an "eccentric cohort" of women of color who, situated at the interstitial crossroads of multiple vectors of oppression and multiple social justice movements, devised a form of spiritual, psychic, and political mobility called *differential* consciousness and social movement that ultimately becomes a necessary tool of survival for all "refugees of a world on fire" (to quote Cherríe Moraga), regardless of gender, race, ethnicity, nationality, social class, religion, sexual orientation, ability, disability, age, or (insert your vector of difference here, ad infinitum). In other words, as this world system collapses, vulnerability is democratized and everyone must "adapt or die." Those who already learned to adapt as their own worlds were brought down through the very inevitable violences of the dying system at its apex are now the scribes of a future of survival and rebirth. These very same scribes are among those who identified and named "womanism."

Although womanism is not mentioned much in *Methodology of the Oppressed*, when it is mentioned, it is mentioned powerfully and pregnantly: "'womanism': the political hermeneutic for constructing 'love' in the postmodern world"; "the differential (or 'womanist,' 'mestiza,' 'Sister Outsider,' 'third force,' 'U.S. third world feminist'...it has generated many names) mode of oppositional consciousness and social movement"; and " 'womanism' (a democratizing, moral vector)."[2] As we hurtle toward the brick wall that is the limits of our current *dominant* world system, is there some way that we might catapult ourselves over it, into another, better reality? This is the possibility that I saw, however faintly at first, in the womanist idea. Seeing this, I was compelled to press further, to go deeper, to find the language for the womanist idea.

During the mid-1980s, then again in the early 1990s, womanism emerged as a fad that ultimately got swallowed up into Black feminism, but only in the way that Jonah was swallowed by the whale, because, by the mid-2000s, womanism reemerged and reasserted itself "on its own." In *The Womanist Reader* (2006), I attempted to capture this momentum and document its history by presenting a diverse array of originary womanist articles from a wide spectrum of academic disciplines within which womanism had been employed as an interpretive framework between 1979 (the year that Alice Walker debuted the term *womanist* in published writing) and 2004 (the end of the first quarter century of published womanist writing). This document contained womanist writings from theology and religious studies, literary studies, history, theater and film studies, communication and media studies, psychology, anthropology, education, social work, nursing science, sexuality studies, architecture and urban studies, and Africana studies. Two fields that should have been included were inadvertently left out: ecology and disability studies. Although the volume did not sample womanist writing from outside the academic sphere, where it also has a substantial presence, it marked womanism as a bridge between academic and nonacademic communities. My point in creating this document was not

to exhaustively encompass womanism (because something so prolific and pro-
tean as womanism cannot actually be encompassed), nor was it to suggest that
womanism was a new idea (in spirit and in act, womanism predates Walker's
coining of the term *womanist*), nor was it to define womanism, per se (it resists
definition at the same time as it invites embodiment and engagement). Rather,
simply, my goal was to lay the groundwork for articulating womanism's distinctiveness as a thoughtform, and most especially, social and ecological change
modality. Such articulation is the aspiration of the current volume.

In the current volume, my goal is to build upon the foundation laid in *The
Womanist Reader* by taking a deep look at the womanist idea and elaborating
on what I perceive to be its unique attributes and potentials. *First* and foremost,
I take an unabashed look at what I perceive to be the central role of spirituality
in womanism. This emphasis on spirituality provides an opportunity to reframe
understandings about "theory" and "activism" from a womanist standpoint.
Second, I closely examine the role of women's personal spiritual journeys, my
own included, in the construction of the womanist idea. I offer both anecdotes
and case studies, from scholarly as well as popular sources, even some autobiographical and esoteric material, to advance the argument that women's personal
walks with spirituality, however defined, are the origin point of womanist logic
and womanist praxis. *Third*, I attempt some codification of womanism in both
historical and philosophical terms. While I have always been of the opinion
that womanism inherently defies codification, at this point in its "history of
consciousness," a systematic treatment of its chief attributes and tendencies is
warranted (even if they are still subject to change). My point is that the womanist idea has an internal logic that distinguishes it from other critical and social
change perspectives, and until now, this internal logic has not been given a systematic, interdisciplinary scholarly treatment.

Given these aims, a few words about the form of this text must be said. First,
this text can only be described as an intellectual–spiritual hybrid. That is, it has
some attributes of a typical scholarly or academic text as well as some attributes
associated with the genre known as inspirational literature. Inspirational literature is a branch of the self-help genre that bridges spiritual and religious themes
or perspectives with personal motivation and self-improvement. Such literature
often has a first-person character, where the author's personal experience figures
prominently and provides a platform for commentary designed to inspire and
illuminate others. Such a positionality is consistent with the womanist emphasis on self-authored, even divinely inspired, knowledge as well as praxis aimed
at uplifting individuals and society simultaneously. What is lacking in a great
deal of the inspirational or self-help literature, yet is present in womanism, with
its links to the scholarly critical disciplines (such as women's and gender studies,

Africana and other ethnic studies, queer/sexuality studies, and cultural studies) is a critical analysis of systems of oppression and a social/ecological justice orientation. In this sense, womanism forms a bridge between aspiritual (or antispiritual) social change paradigms and spirituality-oriented thought that typically gives short shrift to systemic conditions that limit people's lives and well-being as well as ecological sustainability. It is because of this very bridging that I view womanist thought and praxis as such a significant intervention upon the challenges of our times.

CHAPTER-BY-CHAPTER OVERVIEW

The Womanist Idea begins with a manifesto. This manifesto, "LUXOCRACY: Rule by Light," expresses what I see as the generative seed at the heart of womanism. LUXOCRACY, a neologism not to be confused with the adjective *luxocratic* (another neologism that is occasionally invoked to refer to the spectacular excesses of the superrich; I distinguish my usage in this book through capitalization) refers to *the potential of human spirituality to constitute a highly illumined form of social organization that does not require external mechanisms of control.* The word LUXOCRACY references discourses about Light in numerous world spiritual traditions, borrowing from the Latin word for light, which is LUX. Beyond merely the visible light spectrum, the LUX of LUXOCRACY evokes the notion of Divine Light and that higher octave of consciousness toward which the world's spiritual traditions assist humans to strive. LUXOCRACY asks the question: What if we put spirituality at the center of human life? What would the impact of this reprioritization be on politics, ecology, and everyday human well-being? The discourse created by LUXOCRACY distinguishes spirituality from religion (which is at times related, but is by no means coterminous) in a way that allows religious, nonreligious, and "spiritual but not religious" people, even atheists and agnostics, to be caught up in a common embrace and to engage in a common dialogue.

This impulse is womanist precisely because, as I wrote in my introduction to *The Womanist Reader*, womanists make change through "harmonizing and coordinating." Harmonizing and coordinating involves "figuring out how to make disparate elements work together" and "mak[ing] positive connections between elements that might have seemed unrelatable before." Thus, the womanist social change method of harmonizing and coordinating "is associated with creativity, ingenuity, improvisationality, and the proverbial 'making a way out of no way'"—particularly when that place out of which a way must be made is the morass of social and environmental problems facing humankind today. Furthermore, womanist emphasis on love-based technologies of change means that womanists hone in on and bootstrap from the "Divine Light" (aka spirit, soul, higher self, etc.) that they discern in people and, indeed, all creation. This, as I see it, is the organizing principle of womanism, the animating impulse of the womanist idea. What has been needed in the scholarly literature on womanism (and beyond) is to *name* this organizing principle, this animating impulse, this faculty of seeing, this inspirational foundation for action. The name I have given it is LUXOCRACY, and the manifesto in question serves as chapter 1 of this volume.

Chapter 2, "Womanist Origins: Reading Alice Walker, Chikwenye Okonjo Ogunyemi, and Clenora Hudson-Weems," circles back to the intellectual evolution of the womanist idea and the intertwined roles of three founding foremothers. In this chapter, I argue that the womanist idea represents the interpolated and interpellated perspective of all three of these originary thinkers in combination with the contributions of all the everyday women who have ever engaged and claimed womanism as participants in the larger conversation. In this chapter, my goal was to demonstrate that the womanist idea is both "something in the air" that various thinkers have each characterized (and elaborated) in their own way, but also that womanism is constantly "under construction." In other words, it is an ever-evolving outgrowth of a kind of social dialogue that never ends. Examining closely the contributions of three early thinkers for whom the terms *womanist* and *womanism* have served as a kind of liberating utterance or sign enables us to approach something distinctive about womanism's internal dynamics and logic; namely, their self-authored, self-affirming, and even prophetic character. It also provides us with a platform for respecting (even *seeing*) the distinctive womanist spirit that informed the thought and activism of women (and sometimes men) who came before womanism was itself named. Thus, this chapter highlights the value of three formative constituencies: those whose unnamed womanism "came before," those who created the names *womanist* and *womanism*, and those who, after the fact, have engaged both that which was named *and* its unnamed historical referent.

Chapters 3 and 4 constitute parts one and two of a treatment of womanism from a philosophical angle. This treatment rests upon an assertion that womanism operates as a worldview, that is, holistically and comprehensively. Chapter 3, "Womanist Worldview/Womanism as Spiritual Movement" is a chapter about womanist metaphysics. Borrowing a model from African-centered psychologist Linda James Myers, who published the classic article "Expanding the Psychology of Knowledge Optimally: The Importance of Worldview Revisited" in 1991, I examine dimensions of womanist ontology, epistemology, logic, and axiology. I come to the conclusion that a distinguishing feature of the womanist worldview is a concept of *spiritual* movement, which is distinct from more familiar (and more materialist) notions of social or political movement. This notion of spiritual movement, in turn, provides a distinctive basis for understandings about and approaches to social and ecological change activism. Thus, I devote chapter 4, "Womanist Methodology: Transforming Consciousness, Changing the World," to a consideration of womanist method (reflecting Myers's fifth category of philosophical analysis, namely, methodology), including various modalities of activism. Although there are many modalities of womanist activism, what I find most distinctive and what I essentially focus on for the remainder of the book is womanist spiritual activism.

In chapter 5, "A Spiritual Archaeology of the Womanist Idea," I focus on the way in which womanism is informed by multiple spiritual traditions and the personal spiritual journeys that traverse them. Although womanism has largely been associated with Christianity and, especially, the Black Church, my own close reading of womanist thought suggests that womanists are spiritually eclectic and that womanism can only be understood as an outgrowth of womanists' spiritual explorations. To drive this point home, I draw from narratives about personal spiritual journeys from thinkers whose work exhibits what I consider womanist sensibilities (whether or not these authors self-define as womanist). I choose this relatively more organic approach to viewing the inner workings of womanist spirituality, rather than a more scholastic approach emphasizing academic literature on religion and spirituality. I take this approach because of womanism's inherent vernacularity and my sense that womanists are as likely to produce knowledge directly from "Divine download" as to utilize more accepted rational-logical methods. Alice Walker, Akasha Gloria Hull, Toni Cade Bambara, Gloria E. Anzaldúa, M. Jacqui Alexander, and Barbara A. Holmes all provide valuable descriptions of their own eclectic and synthetic spiritual journeys, demonstrating the spiritual curiosity, spiritual eclecticism, and spiritual self-authorship that I see as defining womanist spirituality. I also include anecdotes and reflections from my own spiritual journey to highlight the autobiographical and inspirational quality of womanist spiritual thought. The womanist spirituality of which I write in this chapter in turn undergirds womanist thought and praxis, womanist spiritualized politics, and womanist spiritual activism, which collectively offer important new tools for social and ecological change activity.

In chapter 6, "Spiritual Activism: A Womanist Approach," I venture into metaphysical territory to explore the possibilities of applied spirituality, applied metaphysics, and applied mysticism. My goal is to demonstrate how "invisible" forms of activism can impact material reality. In order to make this case, I draw from literature oriented toward practitioners—that some would refer to as esoteric, mystical, wisdom traditions, New Age, divinatory, and so on—that is designed to teach people how to understand and engage the "invisible realm." Such literature rests on the assumption that the invisible realm is real, palpable, and manipulable under particular conditions—an assumption that I see as consonant with, if not implicit within, womanism (see chapter 5). From a scholarly perspective, an innovation of this chapter is bringing this "esoteric" type of literature into conversation with prevailing scholarly/critical discourses about social change, social justice, and activist praxis, which tend to focus on strictly materialist approaches to change. From a spiritual perspective, an innovation of this chapter is an analytical dissection of activities heretofore referred to only in such inaccessible and forbidding terms as *magic* and *miracles*. Thus, one practical purpose of this chapter is to advance the democratization of causative spiritual power by treating it as something that anyone can learn and apply with proper preparation. Even though this chapter constitutes only the beginning of such a conversation, it intentionally pushes the envelope with regard to the types of practices than can produce social and ecological change.

In concert with chapters 4 and 5, chapter 6 sets the stage for chapters 7 through 11, in which I present case studies of five women whose spiritual activist praxis reflects and informs the womanist idea. These women are Sister Chan Khong, a Buddhist nun from Vietnam who now works in France; Immaculée Ilibagiza, a survivor of the Rwandan genocide who now works as a motivational speaker; Kiran Bedi, a legendary prison reformer in India; Pregs Govender, an antiapartheid, labor, women's, and peace activist who became part of South Africa's first democratically elected postapartheid parliament; and Wangari Maathai, a Kenyan biologist who won the Nobel Peace Prize for leading the Green Belt Movement. Each of these women has published a memoir detailing her life and work, and I perform a close womanist reading of each text in order to discern additional nuances of the womanist idea and distil womanist praxis in action. None of these women self-identifies as a womanist (or, except for one, as a feminist), a fact that achieves significance precisely because I argue that the womanist idea circulates both within and outside womanist identity as such. That is, the womanist idea, which is essentially a spirit and a walk rather than a theory or ideology (see chapter 3) is perfectly effective regardless of whether people "claim it" or call it by name. This means that womanism has the potential to be, as Alice Walker once alluded, "universalist." It is a perspective born of Black women's ways and observations, but not limited to Black women's enactment. Rather, it is a gift from Black women to all humanity.

Chapter 12, "Witness to a Testimony: Womanist Reflections on the Life and Loss of a Daughter," is a highly personal reflection on the death of my daughter Aliyah Karmil Phillips, who transitioned from this life at age 22 in

November of 2009. This completely unexpected event shattered my sense of security in the world and forced me to marshal all of the spiritual, social, emotional, intellectual, and physical resources I had to make it through to the other side of this devastating tragedy. Aliyah was "my little womaness"—a brilliant, spirited girl with an unbelievably bright future ahead of her. An unprecedented and fast-acting mental illness led to her demise, and yet I found myself unwilling to accept this as the ultimate explanation for her life or death. In chapter 12, I explore other possible meanings, using womanism as a platform for the consideration of otherworldly realities and their connection to our experience on Earth. Womanism as a thoughtform and as a worldview begs us to comprehend that this "sensible," earthly reality is not all there is; it coaxes us into seeking knowledge about other realms and other realities so that our experience of this one might be enhanced and empowered. My daughter's passing forced me to stare these questions in the face and ask whether an ontological understanding that had been primarily intellectual up to that point might actually be embodied. Chapter 12 is one reflection on the answers. I conclude with this reflection because I wish to acknowledge the ways in which our most wrenching life experiences, such as a loved one's transition and the accompanying grief, sometimes bring the most clarity, political and otherwise, at the same time as they expand our consciousness beyond its known limits.

Chapter 12 creates a segue to the epilogue, "Beyond Womanism: The Soul of the Womanist Idea," in which I explore the limits of the womanist idea itself. My purpose in writing this book was not to canonize womanism or "fix" its characteristics in time and space, but rather to illuminate its dynamic internal logic and highlight some of its most valuable features so that they might be more effectively employed and deployed at a time when we desperately need to transform our relations with each other, ourselves, Earth, and the larger cosmos. Thus, in the epilogue, I summarize the major ideas of *The Womanist Idea*, but I also suggest that if, one day, we fulfill its promise, we will no longer need to speak its name. Womanism, a love- and spirit-based worldview and transformational perspective, born of Black women's historically situated struggle, now speaks to the struggles of all humanity and planet Earth. It is in this spirit that I penned and now offer this book.

Layli Maparyan, Ph.D.
July 11, 2011
Decatur, Georgia

ACKNOWLEDGMENTS

All things tangible take birth from seeds of vision and love, and *The Womanist Idea* is no exception. It took me years to be brave enough or coherent enough or schooled enough to write this book. Like any growing thing, it took root in the darkness long before it sprouted forth into the light of day. I have many to thank for its ultimate emergence, without any of whom this volume would still be an unsprouted seed. To begin with, I would like to thank Steve Rutter at Routledge whose unexpected and spontaneous enthusiasm about my initial book proposal was the very thing that gave me the courage and impetus to sit down and actually write it. Even though the book changed "a little" (as they invariably do) from proposal to finished product, the supportive encouragement and periodic check-ins of Leah Babb-Rosenfeld kept me on task. Finally, Rosetta Ross of Spelman College provided valuable comments and collegial challenges in her review of the book that helped me refine the final product.

I offer a heartfelt *pranam* to my dispersed yet supportive international network of spiritually inclined womanist/feminist colleagues, many of whom have blazed the trail for me and given me guidance along the way. These include AnaLouise Keating, Gloria E. Anzaldúa (in print and from the other side), M. Jacqui Alexander, Yi-chun Tricia Lin, Melanie L. Harris, Monica A. Coleman, Jafari Sinclair Allen, Susannah Bartlow, and Xiumei Pu.

A similarly beloved set of colleagues has deepened my journey in ways both profound and immeasurable, including Joyce E. King and Hassimi Maïga, Faye V. Harrison and William Conwill, Derrick Alridge, Lee D. Baker, Carolyn Fluehr-Lobban, Meg Harper, and Laurie Patton.

I must offer heartfelt thanks to all members of my department, the Women's Studies Institute at Georgia State University, for untold support over the years, particularly during the challenges and triumphs of Fall 2009 and Spring 2010: Susan Talburt, Amira Jarmakani, Megan Sinnott, Julie Kubala, and Andy Reisinger. I would also like to thank my colleagues in the Georgia State Department of African American Studies who also offered notable gestures of support at various points over the years: Charles Jones, Akinyele Umoja, Jonathan Gayles, and Cora Presley. A host of other GSU colleagues have played important roles: Carol Winkler, Shirlene Holmes, Sarah Cook, Kameelah Martin-Samuels, Murugi Ndirangu, Farrah Bernardino, Dawn Foster, Doris Derby, and David Smith Jr. Felita Williams in the University System of Georgia Board of Regents office and Yves-Rose Saint Dic of Georgia College and State University also deserve special mention.

Atlanta has a uniquely rich network of women's studies scholars and related folk whose diverse areas of interest spawned valuable and stimulating conversations about womanism over the years, not to mention other forms of intangible support. I would like to single out the following individuals for thanks: Isa Williams, Elizabeth Hackett, Beverly Guy-Sheftall, M. Bahati Kuumba, Al-Yasha Williams, Chris Cuomo (and Janet), and Dianne Stewart Diakete. I would also like to thank some very special colleagues who are farther afield, including Kim Vaz, Gary Lemons, Matt Richardson, Bonnie Thornton Dill, Claire Moses, Ann Snitow, Valerie Kaalund, Dionne Stephens, and Susan M. Glisson.

In the community, where my connections have only grown stronger in recent years, I would like to thank Angela Harrington Rice and the staff of Atlanta Interfaith Broadcasters (AIB-TV) as well as my other "Sisters of *The Circle*"; Sandra Barnhill and the entire Foreverfamily family; the leadership of the Women, Faith, and Philanthropy Initiative of the Atlanta Women's Foundation as well as the supportive women of the Women's Funding Network; Bisi Adelisi-Fayemi, Abigail Burgesson, and Rosalynn Musa of the African Women's Development Fund in Ghana; Bernedette Muthien of Engender in South Africa; Deborah Holmes and Kanyere Eaton of the Black Women's Donor Action Group; Erika Williams of Albireo Group Community Development Solutions; the Fulbright Commission and the Council for the International Exchange of Scholars (CIES); the University of Liberia, especially President Emmet Dennis; Dehab Ghebreab and Binta Massaquoi of the Public Diplomacy Section of the Embassy of the United States in Monrovia; Yvette Chesson-Wureh of the Angie Brooks International Center Secretariat; Mama Tormah of Traditional Women United for Peace in Liberia; Melinda Joss of Women and Children's Development Association of Liberia (WOCDAL); John Mulbah, MD, of the Fistula Rehab Center in Liberia; and Wilhelmina Jallah, MD, of JFK Hospital in Liberia. Associated with my work in Liberia, I would also like to thank my colleagues at the University of Georgia in the College of Agricultural and Environmental Sciences: special gratitude goes to Ed Kanemasu and Victoria Collins McMaken, as well as Melvin Crawford of DMA-USA. I also thank Earl and Opal Picard (of GSU and Spelman College, respectively) in this capacity.

For supporting my movement into spiritual scholarship, I extend deepest gratitude to the Center for Contemplative Mind in Society, especially Beth Wadham, Sunanda Marcus, Mirabai Bush, Arthur Zajonc, and Jill Schneiderman, particularly for the Contemplative Practice Fellowship that I enjoyed during 2009-2010. Through that fellowship, I was able to develop the course called Womanist Perspectives on Spiritual Activism, which contributed substantially to the content of this book. As a result of that fellowship, I was also able to spend time studying mindfulness, Buddhism, and nature at Plum Village in France. At Plum Village, I would like to thank Thich Nhat Hanh, Sister Chan Khong, Sister An Nghiem, and all the nuns who hosted me at New Hamlet, as well as Tina Wild and Mathilde Pieneman whom I met there—a lotus for all of you! Thanks are also due to the Fetzer Institute for hosting the final gathering of my CPF cohort. In this same vein, I would like to thank the staff, organizers, and fellow guest lecturers of the Salzburg Global Seminar, especially Lynn McNair, Larry Yarbrough and Amy Hastings, Astrid Koblmüller, and Rebecca Kneale Gould, who made my experience in Austria discussing "One World, Diverse Faiths" vis-à-vis sustainability and peace one of the most memorable to date. None of this would have been possible without the wheels that were set in motion at the 2007 meeting of the International Feminist University Network (IFUN) in Kleinmond, South Africa, which included a deep engagement with feminism vis-à-vis spirituality, especially contemplative practice. Big thanks go out to Irma McClaurin, and it is with special affection that I thank Peggy Antrobus, Pregs Govender, Best "Bessie" Lovai Kilavanwa, Margo Okazawa-Rey, and Amina Mama. The synergies of that meeting have had a long half-life.

Over the past several years, several spiritual teachers have played a prominent role in my life. I would like to thank them by name for opening doors of insight and illumination as well as for entertaining my persistent questions and remaining patient throughout my slow and fitful growth: Charles Finch III, Will Coleman, Baruti KMT-Sisouvuong, Kofi Kondwani, Josephine "Hathor" Hood and the House of Khamit, and Kristina Buck. Going back to my childhood, I must thank a cherished elder, Mary Fridie Wilson, the kindest person I ever met, still going strong in her nineties. If there is one thing I have learned from these teachers and many others unnamed, it is that this journey is long and I am just at the beginning.

Friends are the bread and butter of one's well-being, the honey of one's day-to-day existence. I bow deeply before the light and love in my sistah-mentors and all-around world change collaborators, Deborah J. Richardson, Cynthia Blandford Nash, Maryalice Moses, and Connie Bracewell. Friends along the path of my burgeoning work in Liberia who are owed a debt of gratitude include Rev. William B. G. K. Harris (and Sister Queeta), Rev. Ralph Phillips, Wilfred Harris and Marilyn Grigsby-Harris, and Amelia Tokpa-Addy. Big thanks to my collaborator-friend who goes way back, W. Imara Canady. The home-girl contingent gets my undying love and devotion: The New Moon crew (Jonelle Shields, Katina Grays, Retha Zollicofer Ashe, Delores Williams, Lisa Frazier, and LaMiiko Moore), the Full Moon crew (Yvonne Miller Vinson, Valarie Sewell, Grace Lynis, Shemeah Richardson, and whoever else we manage to round up), the Spiritual Salon crew (Jef Blocker [and Jeff McCord], Kimberly Hicks, Joan Murray, Cindy Elsberry, Marissa McNamara, and all the rest of y'all), the "we go way back" crew (Vanessa Jackson, Francis E. Wood, Deborah Grayson, and Kimberly Wallace Sanders), the "we go way, *way* back" crew (Lyz Jaeger, Debbie Roberts, and Carla Thompson), and a few other friends who have just been special in a very unique way, including Yolo Akili, Emelia Sam, Asia Thomas, Julie Surya Hill, Lisa Campbell, Dee Dee Chamblee, Imara Canady, Sharon Saffold, Sharon Kennedy-Vickers, Sarah Vitorino, and Meadow Overstreet.

Any teacher owes more than can be expressed to her or his students. Among the current or former students I must thank for their material and spiritual contributions to this journey and, in particular, for their engagement with the womanist idea, are: Jillian Ford, Derrick Lanois, Rondee Gaines, Ahmon Keiler-Bradshaw, Donna Troka and Jes Hand, Lashawnda Lindsay Dennis, Tiffany Simpkins Russell, Shomari Robinette Olugbala, Chanel Craft, and Shani Settles. My Womanist Perspectives on Spiritual Activism class of Spring 2010 deserves special applause and credit: Melody Benjamin, Te Gonçalves, Milton Hall, Emilia Kaiser, Quinchele "Zuri" King, Krista Miller, Kate Morales, Lamont Sims, Hilary Smith, Megan Tedesco, Alex White, Millie Coleman, Rachel Cook, Michelle Hudson, Alexandrea Rich, and Julia Wallace. Our class discussions helped me work through important intellectual questions, your many insights shaped my thinking, and your courageous openness to contemplative practice inside and outside the classroom inspired me deeply. I would also like to thank my 2010 Maymester independent study abroad students, Malika Redmond, Latisha Oliver, and Christi Ketchum, for undertaking an important journey into applied womanism and spiritual activism in Liberia with me. Finally, I would like to thank Tobias Spears, Adenike Harris, Loron Benton, Erin George, Onyekachi Ekeogu, Dionne Lewis, and Ivis Wonleh, as well the leadership of the Progressive Organization of Liberian Students (POLS), past and present. If I have overlooked anyone, know that it is the mind and not the heart that forgets. To those of you in this long list whom I can now count as personal friends, I offer additional thanks. The journey continues!

The virtual world has become a real world for connections that cross the boundaries of friendship, professional networking, and spiritual collaboration. I offer a heartfelt *Namaste* to all of the following individuals: Alexis Escalante, Tricia Mills Baehr, Cherina Jones, Adisa Ajamu, Ibrahim Gaye, Sonja Ebron, Stephen Efejuku, Matema Hadi, Muthoni Njogu, Mel Lewis, Beth McIver Faulk, Stephanie McIver, Jacquie Robertson, Shannon Sylvers, and Linda Romera. You have all taught me that kindred spirits will find each other, beyond the dimensions of time and space.

Three of my daughter's college friends—Stephen Fragaszy, Janene Yazzie, and Keondra Prier—are worthy of mention for so valiantly keeping the flame of her spirit alive in this world. The same goes for her high school friends, too many to name, who will always be like daughters to me. My mother's love extends to you all eternally. Let's keep the "Love Train" in motion!

It is with supreme delight that I express my gratitude to the entire Maparyan clan—my new family—especially my sisters-in-law MaNowai Yarr, MaNowai Maparyan, Cecilia Gour, Baby Maparyan, Queeta Nomiah, Lorpue Kemen, and Edith Norris, as well as my big niece and translator, Mercy Maparyan. You all are my womanist inspirations! My brothers-in-law have my love and thanks as well. I must also thank the paternal clan, the Dumbletons; the maternal folk, the Worthy/Jackson/Meadows/Geer clan; my parents, Mary N. Worthy and the late Duane D. Dumbleton; as well as my children: Thaddeus Hilliard Phillips IV, Moses Maparyan, Jonathan Maparyan, and Seboelyn Maparyan, because you are the future. Aliyah, you are now our "baby ancestor" holding this whole family together on the other side with your angelic love and assistance. In addition to you, dear daughter, I light a candle of love for those of our folk who ascended during the writing of this book, including: Mama Maparyan, Debbie Dumbleton, and Marguerite Dumbleton. The legacy continues.

Last and utmost, I thank the love of my life, the one who completes my spirit and gives me wings to fly, my foundation, my daily inspiration, and my perpetual refuge, Seboe N. Maparyan. I welika maa!

ACKNOWLEDGMENTS OF SOURCES

"Pedagogies of the Sacred: Making the Invisible Tangible," in *Pedagogies of Crossing*, M. Jacqui Alexander, pp. 287–332. Copyright, 2005, Duke University Press. All rights reserved. Reprinted by permission of the publisher.

Reprinted from *Learning True Love: Practicing Buddhism in a Time of War* (2007) by Sister Chan Không with permission of Parallax Press, Berkeley, California, www.parallax.org.

Excerpts from the book *Left to Tell: Finding God Amidst the Rwandan Holocaust* by Immaculée Ilibagiza, copyright 2006 by Immaculée Ilibagiza, are reprinted with permission of Hay House, Inc., 1-800-654-5126, www.HayHouse.com.

Excerpts from the book *It's Always Possible: One Woman's Transformation of India's Prison System* by Kiran Bedi, copyright 2006 by The Himalayan International Institute of Yoga Science and Philosophy of the U.S.A., are reprinted with permission of Himalayan Institute, 1-800-822-4547, www.Himalayan Institute.org.

Excerpts from the book *Love and Courage: A Story of Insubordination* by Pregs Govender, copyright 2007 by Jacana Media (Pty.), LTD., are reprinted with permission of the publisher, Jacana Media, www.jacana.co.za.

From UNBOWED: A MEMOIR by Wangari Muta Maathai, copyright © 2006 by Wangari Muta Maathai. Used by permission of Alfred A. Knopf, a division of Random House, Inc.

THE METAPHYSICAL ARCHITECTURE
OF THE WOMANIST IDEA

LUXOCRACY:
RULE BY LIGHT

Where there is no vision, the people perish.

—Proverbs 29:18

All good enterprises begin with a vision, a telos, fueled by intention. As I begin this project, I am impelled to assert outwardly a vision, a telos, an intention that stirs me inwardly. This vision, this intention, is my guide star, my pole star, my teleology; it is that organizing principle around which everything else coheres, it is that originating fount from which all else springs, it is my creative center. It encapsulates my understanding of what is possible for the world, for humanity, for Earth. It is that toward which we are collectively tending, even if, in these times, it seems improbable, impossible, or even unthinkable. I assert it now only because my feeling, my unshakeable sense is that time is short and the stakes are high, and the possibility of rerouting human destiny far outweighs the risk of being deemed preposterous or absurd. As a scholar, I am aware that I am going out on a limb, but if that limb forms a bridge across a river we must cross, then my choice is to proceed intrepidly.

The name of this vision, this intention, is LUXOCRACY, which means "rule by Light." Light in this instance refers to the Inner Light, the Higher Self, the Soul, the God Within—what I will hereafter refer to as Innate Divinity—as described by mystics and others across cultures, across faiths, and across the centuries, if not millennia. As more and more people recognize this Inner Light in themselves and others, by whatever name they call it, as this recognition becomes universal, structures of governance as we know them today will become unnecessary; as aptly stated by Ayi Kwei Armah, "An awakened soul does not need to follow a leader."[1]

Humanity is in the process of evolving toward global society and planetary identity based on global, even cosmic citizenship, yet none of the existing or traditional forms of social organization is suited to fully encompass this emerging reality. Not only is humanity evolving as a whole, but also individual humans are experiencing an expansion of consciousness on a scale unprecedented in previous historical periods. A critical mass, the dimensions of which are only beginning to be visible, is building in size and momentum. What is needed at this juncture are new languages to encompass emerging possibilities: Enter LUXOCRACY.

LUXOCRACY represents the higher octave of many of the better known systems of social organization in discourse today. Like democracy, LUXOCRACY is egalitarian; unlike democracy, LUXOCRACY rests on a foundation of spirituality. Like anarchy, LUXOCRACY eschews formal, hierarchical structures of governance; unlike anarchy, LUXOCRACY is thoroughly benevolent and nonviolent. Like theocracy, LUXOCRACY is spiritualized and spiritually centered; unlike theocracy, LUXOCRACY rests on internal, personal notions of spirituality rather than on external, organized religion. While, in today's world, these systems of social organization seem mutually contradictory and in conflict, another perspective is that a dynamic synthesis is in process, the ultimate upshot of which is LUXOCRACY. In other words, the conflicts between these perspectives today will ultimately help people to understand and be drawn toward LUXOCRACY.

In today's world, many people look toward politics for liberation. Politics or political activism is assumed to be the answer to human misery, strife, and injustice. Yet, the limitations of this strategy are rendered invisible by belief systems that, at best, separate the material world from the spiritual realm or, at worst, negate the spiritual realm altogether. The political is earthbound. If politics is not undergirded by a sense of the spiritual, the sacred, it is a dead end. This is equally true of politics on the right and politics on the left. Politics as it is understood and enacted today is incapable of delivering humanity to its own potentiality. Yet, outside politics, this potentiality is gaining expression and momentum in the larger global society among people from all walks of life who are awakening to the power and reality of their own spirituality as well as the spirituality of others and the spirituality of the world around them. As people come to apprehend their own Innate Divinity directly, as well as the Innate Divinity of others, Earth, and all aspects of Creation, they think, speak, and act differently; they expect different things from their world, and they begin to live in a different reality altogether, regardless of what is going on around them.

Debates—and wars—over which political system would be better are nullified by the reality that only a political system that is informed by spiritual considerations would be significantly better. One important caveat, however: spirituality is not to be confused with religion. Religions exist to deliver people to spiritual knowledge and its application, although they have historically been compromised by the interference of politics. Thus, religions themselves are no more related to LUXOCRACY than is politics. While religious expression and participation is a matter of choice that would be supported within a luxocratic system, religion itself could not serve as the basis for LUXOCRACY. Similarly, while awareness of multiple religious traditions and teachings could facilitate the consciousness necessary to enact LUXOCRACY on a global scale, these traditions and teachings alone would not be enough to make LUXOCRACY feasible. It is only the *universal* recognition of innate human divinity *and* the immanent spiritual nature of the lifespace in which humans exist—above and beyond all religions—that would make LUXOCRACY possible.

Indeed, I prefer the term *lifesystem*[2] to the term *religion* because it encompasses religious expression and personal, internal spirituality simultaneously, and it is impartial to all particular forms this may take. Historically, religion has been the province of institutionalized structures, while spirituality as such has been the province of mysticism and metaphysics. Yet, the two are connected and interpenetrating in ways that, again, require new language. For womanists, spirituality is an acknowledged relationship with the divine/transpersonal/cosmic/invisible realm, while religion is a culturally organized framework for experiencing that relationship. The term *lifesystem* allows Hinduism, Judaism, Zoroastrianism, Buddhism, Christianity, Islam, the Baha'i faith, and all other "institutionalized" religions to be on equal footing with African traditional and African-derived religions, Native American religious traditions, Aboriginal religious traditions, and all other "indigenous" spiritual systems. This language, the language of lifesystems, also creates space for numerous initiatic traditions from around the globe; so-called New Age spirituality; Wiccan, pagan, and other Earth-spirit based traditions; and various humanistic, secular, and agnostic traditions. Womanists embrace many paths to the same destination, and the term *lifesystem* affirms this value. Furthermore, the term *lifesystem* acknowledges the simultaneous interaction between cosmology, metaphysics, culture, practices, traditions, histories, and social networks in the operation of human life around spiritual questions and the spiritual dimension. Womanists accept the contemporary reality of highly eclectic and synthetic approaches to spiritual experience. Thus, the term *lifesystem* is a great equalizer, badly needed in this day when, globally, people are not only becoming more aware of one

5

another's traditions, but also are becoming personally attracted to, and involved in one another's traditions on an unprecedented scale.[3] This movement makes a concept like LUXOCRACY cognitively and socially necessary.

My own personal terminology for the common spiritual architecture and energy underlying and animating all lifesystems is SOURCE. For me, SOURCE is both the Origin Point (i.e., the Creator of All That Is, whether it is called God, Mind, the Unified Field, or something else) and the totality of the emanation from that Origin Point (i.e., Creation, the Cosmos, etc., especially the spiritual mystery that all religions make reference to and seek). For me, SOURCE is the one true "religion" and the object of the quest of all lifesystems. SOURCE is like the ocean from which all rivers originate, as well as the water that flows in these rivers. When we stand by or in the river, we see the ocean, if only we know what we are looking at. And, if we are motivated, we can walk or swim or float like a leaf on the river all the way back to SOURCE.[4] Humanity collectively is now swimming back to SOURCE and is caught in some rocky rapids along the way.

The two things most facilitative of LUXOCRACY coming into being are education and health. True education fosters the discovery and development of the Inner Light, while the promotion of health and vitality provides its necessary physical substrate. As goes a famous Latin quotation, "Mens sana in corpore sano";[5] that is, "sound mind in a sound body." A society that centers on education and health as vitality would necessarily evoke LUXOCRACY as a form of social organization once a certain level of universality was attained with regard to these conditions. As a Baha'i passage states, "Man is the Supreme Talisman. Lack of a proper education hath, however, deprived him of that which he doth inherently possess.... Regard man as a mine rich in gems of inestimable value. Education can, alone, cause it to reveal its treasures and enable mankind to benefit therefrom."[6] The education we are talking about here cannot merely be "education for domestication," however, it must be "education for liberation."[7] That is, it must reflect the true meaning of education—e (out from) ducare (to lead), literally, to lead the Inner Light out from within. This type of education would go far beyond the acquisition of information and knowledge, which are currently emphasized, into the realms of wisdom, and ultimately, onward toward enlightenment in a process I refer to as the Ladder of Learning (see chapter 3). Health would move far past notions of "freedom from disease" through "wellness" onward toward "vitality" and indeed the "luminous body" in a process I refer to as health empowerment.

LUXOCRACY takes as fundamental that all persons are unique manifestations of the One, the All, the Creator, SOURCE. As such, each person's Inner Light guides the manifestation of that uniqueness across the span of a lifetime. The optimal purpose of society is to foster, facilitate, nurture, protect, and coor-

6

dinate the expression of every person's Innate Divinity simultaneously. In the past, various structures of governance have used the principle of the commons to try to maximize the number of people who can experience such self-expression and development. The principle of the commons, through its goal of maximization, assumed implicitly that the good could not be optimized for all persons. LUXOCRACY, on the other hand, assumes that this right of optimal well-being has now been extended to all and has become universal and categorical. Thus, the principle of the commons has now been transcended to encompass everyone because LUXOCRACY rests upon the broader concept of commonweal.

Humanity is shifting into a new age. This new age represents an evolutionary shift in the human being as well as human society. Numerous writers and thinkers argue that the human being, currently known as *Homo sapiens sapiens* or "very wise man," is moving toward what has alternately been called *homo illuminatus* or *homo noeticus*—both of which essentially mean the illumined, enlightened, or superconscious human.[8] These authors argue that we are currently in the midst of a period of what evolutionary scientists would call rapid evolution, and even though we may be centuries if not millennia away from the full flowering of these emerging forms of humanity, the initial signs of emergence, of a true turn in the nature of what it means to be human, are clearly visible now.

The difference between wisdom and illumination is complete and unequivocal recognition of the Inner Light and its relationship to spiritual realities that go far beyond Earth. LUXOCRACY is simply the willingness, or even just the tendency, to organize human society around such knowledge and its embodiment. As we evolve, so must our social structures.

How does LUXOCRACY relate to womanism? LUXOCRACY is inherent within the womanist idea, as well as its upshot. I know this because womanists recognize the Innate Divinity in all humans and all creation, as well as the principle of interbeing.[9] In addition, womanists distinguish spirituality from religion, which opens up new possibilities. Thus, LUXOCRACY is implicit within womanism and must be recognized in order to draw out both the highest aspiration and most profound architecture of womanism. People do not expect LUXOCRACY to emanate from Black women's thought, yet Black women have kept this flame of Innate Divinity and the Inner Light eternally lit across history, culture, and geography, as documented in Black women's religious thought, spiritualized social change leadership, and personal spiritual practice.[10] This preservation of the flame of Innate Divinity has not been limited to Black women—indeed, other women of color, and other people of all genders from a variety of backgrounds—have also done so. The *womanist idea* is really about a practice and a perspective more than an ethnic group or a gender, even

7

though it is undeniable that Black women have had a special role to play in its propagation and promulgation. What is perhaps most important to recognize at this point in time is that once womanism has done its work, it will disappear and no longer be relevant, but that time has not yet come.

THE THREE RECOGNITIONS: A FORMULA

There are three fundamental principles that underlie or enable LUXOCRACY. I call them "The Three Recognitions." They are: Recognize your own sacredness. Recognize the sacredness of everyone. Recognize the sacredness of all created things. And then act accordingly—inwardly and outwardly. Sacredness refers to the higher dimension of a thing, that essence which evokes awe. When we become aware of sacredness, our mindset changes and we become capable of operating within a frame of reverence, and reverence evokes our most generous and respectful feelings and behaviors. This fundamental change in how people think and feel is what is needed to dislodge current conflicts on Earth—those seemingly intransigent and intractable forms of violence that some unimaginatively refer to as "human nature." But human nature is only debased when we think of human beings as debased; when we think of human beings as sacred, human nature becomes sacred, and the establishment of the "humans are sacred" thoughtform within the collective consciousness fundamentally alters our collective sense of what is possible, probable, and necessary for us as a species. When we expand this reverential, sacred thinking to other life forms (i.e., "livingkind")[11] and from there to all creation, then we end up with a qualitatively different kind of life on Earth. This is the simple formula for change that LUXOCRACY proposes.

INNATE DIVINITY

The next stage of human evolution is the universal recognition of the Innate Divinity of human beings. Innate Divinity means that the fundamental essence of human existence, of the human condition, is a spiritual one, is energic rather than material, and is constituted by a "seed of light" connecting all embodied beings to the Great Light, otherwise known as Divine Intelligence, God, or the All. Through this Innate Divinity, this seed of light, all human beings are interconnected with each other, with all creation, and with the Creator. All that exists, all that appears materially, is an emanation of this fundamental essence, a reflection of the ability of the seed of light to manifest as the Great Light does and, in so doing, to create the world, indeed, worlds.

Recognition of Innate Divinity is comparable in magnitude on the scale of evolution to the recognition of mind as a fundamental human attribute. Civilization is an artifact of the human mind and its creative ability and reason, as indeed is human society as we know it and have known it historically and prehistorically. Heretofore, human society has been governed by faculties of mind, most notably reason and emotion. Once humanity collectively recognizes Innate Divinity as a governing principle of human functioning at both individual and collective levels, society will evidence a quantum leap and will reform along new lines of organization and governance.

The times in which we are living now are the times of transition between an old order based on mind and a new order based on the recognition of Innate Divinity. At the same time as we are witnessing the limits of civilization based on mind, we are also observing the emergence of social formations based on collective consciousness of Innate Divinity. Prior to the present period, such forms of consciousness have been largely limited to individuals and small collectives—sages, adepts, and recondite spiritual communities. Today, however, such consciousness is becoming democratized and epidemic. We are observing a phase shift in human life. Many of us sense it. Some people call it the Age of Aquarius, while others simply call it the Shift, and still others speak of the Sixth Sun.[12] Regardless of nomenclature, these terms all refer to the democratization and universalization of systems of knowledge and ways of being that acknowledge the Light Within and teach us how to use it as a foundation for collective well-being and flourishing on Earth.

Innate Divinity is the basis of human equality. It is the only uncomplicated foundation on which human equality can coexist with human difference—the infinite difference of individual human beings from one another and of human cultures from each other. When human beings are understood in terms of Innate Divinity, difference is then understood as an expression of Innate Divinity. Difference then becomes not a ground for conflict but rather a text through which to explore and understand new perspectives on life and creation. The recognition of Innate Divinity, the seed of light illuminates difference through the lenses of splendor and wonder and allows it to be received with love rather than fear. It also refigures how we think about concepts like justice and sustainability.

In this infusion of the world with love emanating from the recognition of Innate Divinity, the logic of boundaries and oppression will dissolve. As a consequence, the logics of domination and violence will also dissolve, relegating war, exploitation, hatred, and dehumanization to a forgotten epoch, relics of a past era of human evolution. Global human society, situated on a borderless planet, will finally materialize, setting the stage for humans to rediscover not only their own spirituality, but also the living, breathing spirituality of the Earth itself, as well as their connection with other energies in the Universe.

In this time of transition, both worlds coexist—the dying world that is buckling beneath its own limits and the limitless world that is being born. The imperative of this moment is to choose: In which world do I live and work? Of which world am I a citizen? Into which world's tomorrow do I figure? And that choice will determine everything else that follows.

COMMONWEAL

Commonweal is both a value and objective of womanism. Commonweal involves both a state of collective well-being and a modality of collective thought/action that does not compromise individual well-being or freedom. Commonweal is not unlike the concept of the noosphere[13]—the telepathic unification of human mind and Earth—insofar as it rests upon a universal acceptance of the integral oneness of the human collective and its integration with its Gaiaic medium of survival (i.e., Planet Earth) and only understands human individuality within this paradigm. This is different from the collectivism/individualism duality insofar as humanity and individual humans are not viewed as oppositional. Rather, this notion of commonweal is more related to concepts like Thich Nhat Hanh's Interbeing and the African metaphysical principle "I am because We are and We are because I am."[14] Commonweal springs from a heart-centered intelligence that implicitly understands, and acts upon the knowledge of, how one's own life holistically integrates with the rest of creation, human or nonhuman. If I am operating from the intelligence of commonweal, for example, I am constantly thinking about (and feeling) how my choices, actions, thoughts, words, and the like impact other people, the natural environment, and the energetic field in which I exist; my moral compass in this universe impels me to "do good by the whole" out of love and desire, not fear, thus grounding a very pleasure-based ethics of care and self-actualization.[15] Commonweal requires an understanding of the whole *within* each individual. Each individual simultaneously recognizes both the necessity of coordinating with the whole and the role of one's own freedom and self-expression in the coconstitution of the whole. When each individual is operating from LUXOC-RACY, commonweal eventuates by default. However, full-fledged commonweal is not possible until its prerequisites are achieved: (1) universal recognition of the organic wholeness of humanity (and creation), (2) universal recognition of Innate Divinity (including the "Three Recognitions"), and (3) a universalization of health and education (sound body and sound mind). If we wish to move toward commonweal, we can begin by turning our attention and action to each of these three areas.

The concept of commonweal that I have described is latent within the metaphysical dimensions of the womanist idea, and my purpose here is to elucidate it. People expect Black women and other women of color ("womanists") to be community- and relationship-oriented, but they don't expect these "everyday" women to apply this idea/proclivity to the whole world. Black women's and other women of color's communitarian tendencies are often viewed in terms of their surface characteristics, with less attention to their architectonic and energetic characteristics and the implications of these. Commonweal is simply one such implication. Commonweal is womanists' culturally and spiritually based tendency applied to the whole world. In postmodern times, Black women and women of color around the globe—the womanist core community, such as it is—think beyond their (our) own communities. Stated differently, we envision the whole world as our community, as our home place. We are not alone in this, but we are consistent in it from a historical and cross-cultural perspective.

PLANETARY IDENTITY AND CULTURE AS WEALTH

In order to fully appreciate the idea of LUXOCRACY and the depth of commonweal as womanists envision it, it is important to understand two concepts simultaneously: *culture as wealth* and the emerging *global transculture*. For womanists, race[16] is not color but culture, and culture is not deficit, but wealth.[17] That is, culture is a repository of wisdom (both material and spiritual, exoteric and esoteric) developed by a people with ancestral, geographic, and historical ties. The emerging global transculture is a global culture that is transcending but not overwriting individual cultures in the face of globalization, the evolution of human consciousness, and increasing awareness of the oneness of humanity. Because of this twofold condition, humans can and often do possess two identities: a cultural identity and a planetary identity. The *planetary identity* is a new development in the history of humanity. The time has come to recognize it and name it. Womanists and kindred thinkers have been encouraging this. For example, the idea is subsumed in Gloria Anzaldúa's futuristic statement "I am a citizen of the universe";[18] it also finds expression in Barbara A. Holmes's bold suggestion that we "view issues of race and liberation from the perspective of the cosmos."[19] An imaginary that extends far, far beyond identity

11

categorizations that have locked humanity into conflict for so long—without negating the cultural wealth that gives the human race such vibrancy—is characteristic of womanists, womanism, and the womanist idea. All who embrace it can consider themselves womanists in name or spirit.

Within this emerging global transculture comprised of people with planetary identities, the wealth of all cultures, historical and contemporaneous, becomes a common human treasure trove. This only works when this cultural wealth is approached from a place of genuine spiritual affinity—not co-optation and exploitation (the old modalities). As we move from historically based, socially ascribed group identities to planetary identity, Earth culture becomes all of ours. For this to work, we have to move away from acquisition and ownership "turf" models toward spiritually based "affinity" models that recognize our fundamental human connecting tendency and respect/revere both individual and collective expressions of divinity that manifest as cultures and subcultures. Although this may challenge a familiar way of life, it is time to accept that spiritual affinities may not match skin tone, language, or geographic origin—stated differently, "love (attraction, affinity, appreciation) knows no boundaries." However, because we are in a transitional period cognitively and culturally, it is appropriate to remain vigilant with regard to processes of cultural co-optation and exploitation.

Womanists implicitly recognize the highly synthetic and multifarious nature of cultural flows. At the same time, womanists guard cultural traditions against the forces of annihilation. Many indigenous and diasporic cultural traditions must be protected, and it is often the women who protect them most diligently. The purpose of this protection is not adherence to a traditional standard, but rather the preservation of robustness in the human knowledge base as well as the preservation of human dignity. It is important to spell these purposes out because the preservation of traditional knowledge is often equated or confused with backwardness and anti-intellectualism. Part of what womanism is out to prove (often through the scholarship of recovery but sometimes simply through personal practice) is that everyday women of color (and similar people of all genders and colors) who do this labor are not backward; rather, they are incredibly forward-thinking and integral to humanity's survival, despite their compromised visibility on the world stage and in the academy. Reference to, recovery of, and reinvigorated application of ancient wisdom traditions by womanists is one way that this takes place; preservation of cultural artifacts and practices is another. Indeed, I might invoke the term *remixing* to adequately characterize this process.

The womanist approach to cultural protection and preservation makes me think about the Svalbard global seed bank in Norway. This seed bank was constructed in 2006 (opened in 2008) in the Arctic permafrost (1,120 kilometers/700 miles from the North Pole) to collect and warehouse seeds from around the world to protect Earth's biological heritage against global catastrophe, whether man-made or astrophysical in origin. The fact that genetic modification of seeds during the last half century has flooded the world with nonreproductive seeds adds another dimension of significance to the Svalbard project. According to an online encyclopedia article on the Svalbard facility, "a feasibility study determined that the vault could preserve seeds from most major food crops for hundreds of years. Some seeds, including those of important grains, could survive far longer, possibly thousands of years."[20] The establishment of this seed bank is premised upon three core ideas: (1) biological diversity must be preserved; (2) the world's seeds are the world's heritage; and (3) given global trends that portend massive changes in life on Earth, human beings must be proactive in their preparation for the future. On a more local level, individuals all over the world, many of them "everyday people," collect and preserve heirloom seeds for similar reasons, often establishing informal or semiformal networks to facilitate this work.

These three core ideas run parallel to womanist ideas and practices surrounding the protection and preservation of cultures, and could be restated thus: (1) cultural diversity must be preserved; (2) the world's cultures are the world's heritage; and, again, (3) given global trends that portend massive changes in life on Earth, human beings must be proactive in their preparation for the future. Like the seed collectors of Svalbard, womanists recognize that cultural diversity is under assault. In particular, many indigenous cultures—and the languages, worldviews, practices, artifacts, and knowledge they have developed over centuries if not millennia of human history—are in jeopardy, and many groups, cultural or subcultural, which have been marginalized by existing politico-economic systems and structures are subject to ongoing forces of annihilation. Certain forms of cultural globalization are not unlike genetic modification of seeds in terms of their impact on the ability of the world's cultures to survive and reproduce. Because most academic research tends to parallel the interests of the dominant politico-economic system, womanists do not count on researchers or any "official" channels to preserve culture; rather, they take it upon themselves. The preservation of culture is an informal, group effort comprised of individuals from a variety of social sectors using a variety of practices. All who participate form an affinity group.

From a womanist perspective, the question of culture, whether cultural preservation or cultural identity, is not "either-or"; that is, it is not a decision between adopting global culture/planetary identity *or* maintaining one's ancestry/culture of origin. Rather, it is about recognizing that one can *simultaneously*

maintain a connection to one's roots, adopt a planetary identity with its identification with global transculture, *and* incorporate aspects of other cultures
with which one feels spiritual affinity. The womanist solution to questions of
culture is definitively a holistic, synthetic, *both–and* solution. However, adop-
tion of such a strategy requires the development of a highly mobile form of
consciousness—called differential consciousness by Chela Sandoval[21]—that
can maintain and cognize multiple affiliations at multiple levels at once. This
type of mobile consciousness, for a variety of historical reasons, is "natural" to
womanists—and it is becoming more "natural" to others who are increasingly
subjected to similar life conditions as those that womanists have historically
experienced. In this way, a global shift in consciousness, which looks womanist
but is ultimately human, is taking place. Thus, womanists can be considered
part of the vanguard.

THE LUMINOUS REVOLUTION

Why is LUXOCRACY crucial now? What we are facing is a crisis of materiality.
By materiality, I mean focus on the material world. What we are observing all
around us in the alarming social and ecological conditions that threaten our
survival is that we have hit the limit of what is possible within a materialistic
frame of understanding. There are no more solutions within this frame. Indeed,
the world that was created within this frame is self-deconstituting, externally
and internally. There is only one way out, and it is a luminous revolution.
Indeed, the luminous revolution is that which will establish a new universal
understanding around Innate Divinity, or the inherently luminous nature of
humans and all creation. Thus, the most important work any of us can do right
now is to bring awareness of Innate Divinity, of the Inner Light, and make
it stick. There are so many ways to do this, so many paths, so many voices in
which this message must be spoken to reach all humanity. Thus, we are in a
necessary and underappreciated period of intense polyvocality, through which
Spirit—SOURCE—speaks to and through multiple populations simultaneously, sometimes in mutually unintelligible tongues. Seeing ourselves and all
creation differently is the solution to our current crisis, and whatever facilitates
this is needed now. All channels of Light must be open, and there are many.
Womanism is but one portal and there are others; ultimately, it is the amicable
confluence of these portals back to SOURCE that will liberate humanity and
save Earth. The vision of LUXOCRACY offered here is a door between where we
are now and an optimistic future—indeed, between who we are now and who
we are capable of becoming. Open it, and the journey begins.

WOMANIST ORIGINS:
READING ALICE WALKER, CHIKWENYE OKONJO
OGUNYEMI, AND CLENORA HUDSON-WEEMS

What are the origins of the womanist idea? Although most feminist scholars in the United States (and some outside it) trace womanism back to Alice Walker exclusively, contemporary womanism is actually coconstituted by a number of distinct strands of womanist discourse pioneered by different authors. In addition to U.S. writer Alice Walker,[1] Nigerian literary critic Chikwenye Okonjo Ogunyemi[2] and U.S. Africana studies scholar Clenora Hudson-Weems[3] introduced and developed original womanist perspectives. In this chapter, I offer an account of how contemporary womanism evolved from these three perspectives in interrelationship. I begin by discussing each author's perspective separately. I then demonstrate how, through a process of interpolation, these three perspectives form a discursive space within which the formation of womanist thought is completed—to the extent that womanism can ever by complete— by the participation of everyday folk. My focus is on what each of these three "founding mothers" has contributed to the womanist idea and, in particular, to contemporary applications of womanism, illustrating how contemporary womanism coordinates, harmonizes, and synthesizes—indeed, metaphorically, braids—three autonomous yet interrelated perspectives.

A word about terminology: In this chapter, indeed, in this entire book, I use the words *womanist*, *womanism*, and *the womanist idea* relatively interchangeably for reasons of semantic efficiency, with the understanding that most womanists retain a preference for "their perspective" not to be concretized into an "ism," namely, womanism. The title of this book is *The Womanist Idea* because this phrase captures more effectively the fluidity and "non-pin-down-ability" of womanism, disidentifying this thing—"womanism" or "the womanist idea"—from both theory and ideology as such and highlighting its underlying architecture (see chapter 3). As my readings of the three major progenitors of womanism will ultimately demonstrate, womanism or "the womanist idea" as an organizing principle is much more of a "spirit" or a "way" or a "walk" or even a "vibrational level" than it is a theory or ideology. I also define it as a "mindset" and a "worldview." My position is that womanists who use the word *womanism* basically know that it is not really an "ism," but in the interest of simplicity, they use the word anyway.

The womanist idea has been in existence now for over three decades, as exemplified by the circulation of the terms *womanist* and *womanism*. During this span, the term and the perspective it represents have been embraced, debated, dismissed, and conflated with other terms and perspectives by feminists, Africana studies scholars, critical theorists, and activists. In the 1980s, womanism gained popularity. During the 1990s, womanism came to be conflated with Black feminism within academic women's studies, and for this reason, fell below the radar of feminist histories of consciousness. Yet, womanists were still doing womanist work, and this was a time of proliferation within the disciplines, as more and more womanists explored how the womanist idea relates to diverse bodies of knowledge. By the second half of the first decade of the 2000s, through the sheer weight of this quiet proliferation in multiple locations, womanism had again resurfaced as a unique perspective. Three intellectual generations of womanist scholars in the theological and religious disciplines, in particular, kept the thread of womanist thought unbroken and evolving across these three decades.[4] In 2006, the publication of *The Womanist Reader* firmly established womanism "on its own" and displayed the interdisciplinary reach that womanist thought had achieved over its first quarter century, documenting the emergence of womanism not only the theological and religious disciplines, but also virtually every other discipline in which womanism had been employed in print in English.[5] In the introduction to this text, I attempted to present a long overdue treatment of womanism as a distinct and innovative social theory and praxis, pioneered by women of African descent but in no wise limited to women of African descent any longer. *The Womanist Reader* showed definitively that womanism has grown beyond its original Black female base to include women, men, and even transpeople of other ethnic and cultural backgrounds from a variety of countries around the world. Such is the power of the womanist idea!

In many respects, this chapter on womanist origins encompasses much that I would have liked to say in the introduction to *The Womanist Reader*, given unlimited space. Situated here, in *The Womanist Idea*, it serves as a point of departure for a completely new take on womanism, womanists, and the womanist idea—one that continues my quest to go both beneath and beyond the manifest surface of womanism to discover its metaphysical depths and mystical possibilities for social/ecological change on a global level, and to capture and convey what I see (and feel) as the spirit of womanism, that fundamental animating impulse that has captivated and motivated the hearts of so many people worldwide.

ALICE WALKER'S WOMANISM

Alice Walker first used the term *womanist* in her 1979 short story "Coming Apart," initially published in a 1979 issue of *Ms.* magazine as "A Fable" and almost immediately thereafter in Laura Lederer's 1980 book, *Take Back the Night: Women on Pornography*.[6] In this story about a Black husband and wife arguing over the effect on their marriage of the husband's consumption of pornography, there is a line where Walker writes: "The wife has never considered herself a feminist—though she is, of course, a 'womanist.' A 'womanist' is a feminist, only more common." This line in the text is footnoted by the author. The footnote reads: "'Womanist' encompasses 'feminist' as it is defined by Webster's, but also means *instinctively* pro-woman. It is not in the dictionary at all. Nonetheless, it has a strong root in Black women's culture. It comes (to me) from the word 'womanish,' a word our mothers used to describe, and attempt to inhibit, strong, outrageous or outspoken behavior when we were children: 'You're acting *womanish!*' A labeling that failed, for the most part to keep us from acting 'womanish' whenever we could, that is to say, like our mothers themselves, and like other women we admired." She continues in this footnote: "An advantage of using 'womanist' is that, because it is from my own culture, I needn't preface it with the word 'Black' (an awkward necessity and a problem I have with the word 'feminist'), since Blackness is implicit in the term; just as for white women there is apparently no felt need to preface 'feminist' with the word 'white,' since the word 'feminist' is accepted as coming out of white women's culture."

This comment comes at a point in the story where her husband has just finished gay-baiting his wife by referring to one of the women whom she has been reading as part of her consciousness raising, namely Luisah Teish, as a dyke. The wife's response: "Another one of your sisters." The line indexing "womanist" is followed by a passage during which the husband has questioned the wife's race loyalty: "So she is surprised when her husband attacks her as a 'women's liber [sic]' a 'white women's lackey,' a 'pawn' in the hands of Gloria Steinem, an incipient bra-burner! What possible connection could there be, he wants to know, between her and white women—those overprivileged hags, now (he's reluctantly read in *Newsweek*) marching and preaching their puritanical horseshit up and down Times Square!" A few lines down, the husband wonders where his wife's new connections to "dykes and whites" will leave him, a Black man: "the most brutalized and oppressed human being on the face of the earth"?

By invoking the concept of womanist, the wife in the story is able simultaneously to maintain her "connection" with "whites and dykes" while also mending her relationship with her husband and raising his consciousness about gender oppression and sexuality issues. Thus, the invocation of womanism—a new concept, a new framework, at the time—has allowed the symbolic protagonist to resolve the situation by harmonizing and coordinating antagonistic social groups and political positions, all from a location of gendered, cultural self-authorship. Walker's act of joining the terms *woman* and *common* at the border of feminist/not feminist in her definition of "womanist" situated a particular mode of women's resistance activity squarely within the realm of the "everyday," thereby defying both academic and ideological claims on the definition, labeling, and elaboration of women's resistance activity under the exclusive and limited label "feminist." In two simple yet pregnant sentences, Walker opened up a new way of talking about the relationship between women, social change, the struggle against oppression, and the quest for full humanity. Yet, this "way" itself was not new—only the terminology. Womanists walk and work with a knowing about the ancestral depth of the womanist way of being and doing—a topic I explore in greater depth in chapter 5.

Walker uses the term *womanist* for a second time in her book review essay "Gifts of Power: The Writings of Rebecca Jackson," originally published in *The Black Scholar* in 1981.[7] This book, edited by Jean McMahon Humez, recovers and interprets the life work of a Black Shaker woman, Rebecca Jackson, who, after leaving a husband who didn't support her calling, lived and evangelized for many years with her white Shaker companion, Rebecca Perot. In one section of this otherwise glowing review, Walker contests the following statement by Humez: "Perhaps, had she been born in the modern age, she would have been an open lesbian." Walker writes: "There is only one point at which I stopped ... to question her obviously deep knowledge of her material." She continues:

Though women ministers who worshipped and lived with other women were perceived by the male leaders of the early churches as "closeted lesbians," because they followed their own inner voices rather than the "fathers" of the church, there is nothing in these writings that seems to make Jackson one. It would be wonderful if she were, of course. But it would be just as wonderful if she were not.... What I am questioning is a nonblack scholar's attempt to label something lesbian that the black woman in question has not.

Walker goes on to write:

The word "lesbian" may not, in any case, be suitable (or comfortable) for black women, who surely would have begun their woman-bonding earlier than Sappho's residency on the Isle of Lesbos. Indeed, I can imagine black women who love women (sexually or not) hardly thinking of what Greeks were doing.... [W]omen who love other women, yes, but women who also have concern, in a culture that oppresses all black people (and this would go back very far), for their fathers, brothers, and sons, no matter how they feel about them as males.

She then asserts:

My own term for such women would be "womanist." [She clarifies:] A word that said more than that they choose women over men. More than that they choose to live separate from men. In fact, to be consistent with black cultural values (which, whatever their shortcomings, still have considerable worth) it would have to be a word that affirmed connectedness to the entire community and the world, rather than separation, regardless of who worked and slept with whom.

Thinking strictly in terms of sexuality, one is reminded of Gloria Wekker's discussion of mati-ism in the African-descended women of Dutch Surinam.[8] Wekker challenges the view that lesbianism is the only way to view Black women's homosocial and homosexual orientations and behavior, and she presents mati-ism as another view. The word *mati* means "friend," and matisma (pl. of mati) often maintain domestic or sexual relationships with women and men simultaneously or, at least, sequentially. Matisma are group-centered rather than couple-centered, and children remain important, particularly as a marker of womanhood and adult status. Matisma typically choose not to talk much about or even label their sexual and affectional practices, despite the existence of mati terminology. As Astrid Roehmer, who is quoted by Wekker, states, "There are, after all, things which aren't to be given names—giving them names kills them. But we do have age-old rituals originating from Africa by which women can make quite clear that special relations exist between them." According to Wekker, the differences between Black lesbians and matisma are cosmological and not just sexual or social. Mati-ism is a direct outgrowth of an African-centered cosmology in which community integration, cooperation, and wholeness remain supreme values and the person or "self" is largely an epiphenomenon of invisible spiritual forces that are larger than one, such as ancestors or divinities. Within this worldview, "lesbianism" as such makes little sense and is not embraced, even though no stigma is placed on domestic, affectional, or sexual relationships between women. Thus, in the mati idea, not unlike the womanist idea presented by Walker in "Gifts of Power," we encounter an orientation toward harmonization and coordination, synthesis and mutual supportiveness, among disparate and sometimes contradictory or adversarial social groups, a "certain something" that makes the heterogeneous elements work together dynamically yet amicably. This is, or at least has been up to now, the mystery of womanism—a mystery that is partially illuminated by having recourse to an underlying African cosmology.

The third and most famous use of the term *womanist* by Alice Walker appears in the preface to her 1984 book, *In Search of Our Mothers' Gardens: Womanist Prose* (as well as throughout the text).[9] In the preface, Walker "defines" the womanist, invoking a dictionary-definition style of presentation. Here she writes: "Womanist 1. From *womanish*. (Opp. of "girlish," i.e., frivolous, irresponsible, not serious.) A black feminist or feminist of color." She continues, for four paragraphs, to expand upon the term, albeit in a fashion that is characteristically poetical and impressionistic. In this definition, we find residues of her earlier uses of the term—for example, her reference to the comment "You acting womanish" and her statement "A woman who loves other women, sexually and/ or nonsexually"—but also significant new content. For instance, in paragraph two, she writes: "Sometimes loves individual men, sexually and/or nonsexually" and "Not a separatist, except periodically, for health." At a time when feminism was still indelibly associated with separatism in the popular imagination, not to mention the Black community specifically, Walker's stance on this issue was a significant rhetorical move that opened up new doors for the participation of everyone who found herself or himself backing away from feminism on the basis of an aversion to separatism, or alternately, a decided love of bringing people together.[10] Furthermore, Walker's identification of a love spectrum that includes but is not limited to sexuality and which has room to contain both women and men removed both homosexuality and heterosexuality from the clutches of dualism (although it did not explicitly do the same for gender), again opening doors to new kinds of identity, relationship, and kinship—political, sexual, or spiritual. Again, this was a discursive move away from dualism and oppositional, resistance-based politics.

In paragraph four of the *Mothers' Gardens* definition, which is actually just a single sentence, Walker presents her most enigmatic characterization of the womanist idea: "Womanist is to feminist as purple is to lavender." Because lavender is a color that has historically been associated with lesbianism, this sentence is often interpreted as a suggestion that womanism is a more intense (literally, more saturated) form of woman-centeredness than is lesbianism. Alternately, given Black women's historical resistance to white women's feminism and lesbianism on the basis of racial exclusion or cultural exclusivity within those arenas, the sentence is sometimes interpreted to mean that womanism is a "Black" form of feminism. I argue that Walker's intended meaning goes much deeper than these interpretations; however. I read her meaning as the suggestion that womanism is a more comprehensive vision of human liberation than feminism, lesbianism, or even humanism—at least as these were defined up to and until the early 1980s when Walker penned the line. This is not because womanism inherently contains better ideas, per se, but because womanism, its gendered name notwithstanding, embodies and enacts a version of liberation that does not bootstrap itself from systems of human classification, rooted in Cartesian dualism, reinforced by Linnean taxonomism, and exploited by sexism, racism, capitalism, and the like; that is, from the partitioning impulse itself. Rather, it proceeds directly from the recognition of humanity's basic commonality and fundamental, if not woefully underrealized, oneness.

Walker's literary elusiveness undergirds and feeds this possibility. Embedded within her intentionally poetical and impressionistic definition of womanist is the recognition that it is this partitioning impulse itself that oppresses human beings—not race, gender, class, and the like, which are merely its servants. Womanism recognizes, in a way that has heretofore remained underarticulated, that this partitioning impulse oppresses everyone, not just the people on the downside of any given dichotomy. The partitioning impulse and the dichotomies it generates diminish the humanity of all humanity—a theme that has been echoed by numerous authors. Yet, the womanist version of this notion is not equivalent to traditional poststructuralist discourses; rather than constituting a critique of dualism, it originates in and expands upon African diunital logic—the logic of harmony and wholeness-making. It even bears semblance to certain concepts embedded in the spiritual logics of other communalistic cultures, such as the notion of "Interbeing" articulated by Buddhist monk Thich Nhat Hanh, with whose work and philosophies Alice Walker has had contact.

It is this ontological and fundamentally spiritual move away from taxonomic logic and toward integrative logic, I argue, that makes the womanist idea a whole different thoughtform from feminism in any of its versions.

Collectively, these four paragraphs that provide the "definition" of the term *womanist* have stood as the foundation for the development of woman*ism*, now a vibrant theoretical and activist perspective that ranges far beyond Alice Walker's original design. They help explain why womanism is not a theory or an ideology, but rather a "spirit" or a "way." However, to fully understand Alice Walker as womanist—and even Alice Walker's "womanism"—one must look beyond her origination of the term *womanist* into her "postwomanist" period. It is here, I argue, that we actually find a deeper and more explicit enactment of the very womanist idea that Alice Walker intended, or at least "felt," all the way back to 1979, or certainly by 1983. In many respects, Alice Walker herself embodies womanism in a way that defies words. This theme is explored in Melanie Harris's book, *Gifts of Virtue: Alice Walker, and Womanist Ethics.*[11]

Two other theorists have been central to the construction of the womanist idea, namely, Chikwenye Okonjo Ogunyemi and Clenora Hudson-Weems. Each introduced her writings on womanism slightly later than Alice Walker and both reference Walker. Ogunyemi states that she developed the concept of womanism, which she now calls African womanism, independently at around the same time as Alice Walker, while Hudson-Weems, founder of Africana womanism, claims to have articulated an independent form of womanism that is significantly different from Walker's. Walker's, Ogunyemi's, and Hudson-Weems's versions of womanism all have certain organizing principles in common that shape the infrastructure of contemporary womanism as both social theory and activist praxis. At the same time, Ogunyemi and Hudson-Weems both articulate certain contentious departures from Walker, most notably around lesbianism and the ultimate relationship between Blacks and whites as communities. Rather than creating fissures within the womanist idea, these differences of opinion and perspective generate creative tensions that, paradoxically, allow more people to participate in womanism as a harmonizing and coordinating enterprise.

CHIKWENYE OKONJO OGUNYEMI'S AFRICAN WOMANISM

In 1985, Chikwenye Okonjo Ogunyemi, who is from Nigeria, published the article "Womanism: The Dynamics of the Contemporary Black Female Novel in English," in the leading feminist journal *Signs*.[12] In this watershed article, she writes thus of womanism:

More often than not, where a white woman writer may be a feminist, a black woman writer is likely to be a "womanist." That is, she will recognize that, along with her consciousness of sexual issues, she must incorporate racial, cultural, national, economic, and political considerations into her philosophy.

She further states that "African and Afro-American women writers share similar aesthetic attitudes in spite of factors that separate them." She continues: "[M]y intention is to establish that womanism is widespread and to pinpoint the factors that bind black female novelists together under this distinct praxis." In making these statements, Ogunyemi establishes the link between womanism and an intersectional perspective, characteristically a hallmark of Black feminism, demonstrating that womanism is partially overlapping with Black feminism. She continues by identifying additional features of the womanist perspective:

> While the white woman protests against sexism, the black woman writer must deal with it as one among many evils.... Black women writers are not limited to issues defined by their femaleness but attempt to tackle questions raised by their *humanity*.... [T]he womanist vision is racially conscious in its underscoring of the positive aspects of Black life. The politics of the womanist is unique in its racial-sexual ramifications; it is more complex than white sexual politics, *for it addresses more directly the ultimate question relating to power: how do we share equitably the world's wealth and concomitant power among the races and between the sexes?* [emphasis added]. [The womanist] is not as primarily or exclusively interested in sexism as is the feminist. [She continues] The intelligent black woman writer, conscious of black impotence in the context of white patriarchal culture, empowers the black man. She believes in him; hence her books end in *integrative* images of the male and female worlds. [emphasis added].

Ogunyemi's statement about how womanists support Black men is more direct than Walker's and it anticipates Clenora Hudson-Weems's perspective, which will be described below.

As Ogunyemi asserts in her article, "I arrived at the term 'womanism' independently and was pleasantly surprised to discover that my notion of its meaning overlaps with Alice Walker's." Although Ogunyemi initially identifies areas of overlap with Walker's perspective, she begins calling her version of womanism "black womanism" after mentioning Walker and proceeds to trouble Walker's womanism by introducing elements of Black separatism that seem to imply both the impossibility of reconciliation between white feminists and Black womanists and the permanence of a Black–white racial divide based on the intractability of racism. She also explicitly links Black womanism with religion (rather than spirituality) in a fashion that paves the way for the rejection of Black lesbianism (and I use this word loosely, in full acknowledgment of Alice Walker's critique of the term) that she will express in a later interview conducted in 1997 but published in 2000, also in *Signs*. Finally, she makes this statement: "[T]he black woman writer in Africa and in the United States has finally emerged as a spokeswoman for black women and the black race by moving away from black male chauvinism and the iconoclastic tendencies of feminism to embrace the relative *conservatism* of womanism" (emphasis added). Ogunyemi's suggestion that womanism is relatively conservative stands in stark contrast to the radical politics that undergird Walker's womanism.

By 1996–97, Ogunyemi renamed her perspective *African womanism*.[13] To quote her, "Since feminism and African-American womanism overlook African peculiarities, there is a need to define African womanism." To cite interviewer Susan Arndt, "Only African women may be African womanists in Ogunyemi's sense." According to Arndt, Ogunyemi also dissociates herself from Walker on two grounds: (a) "the African obsession to have children" and (b) "incompatible attitudes toward lesbianism." Arndt states: "The core of Ogunyemi's definition of African womanism is the conviction that the gender question can be dealt with only in the context of other issues that are relevant for African women." According to Ogunyemi, as summarized by Arndt, these issues include "inter-ethnic skirmishes and cleansing,... religious fundamentalism,... the language issue, gerontocracy and in-lawism." In addition, African womanism plays out within an intertextual field in which other autonomous African alternatives to feminism, such as Molara Ogundipe-Leslie's (1994) stiwanism (based on the acronym for "*s*ocial *t*ransformation *i*ncluding *w*omen in *A*frica"),[14] Catherine Acholonu's (1995) motherism,[15] and Mary Kolawole's later womanism (1997),[16] have also been offered.[17] Overall, Ogunyemi's point about the importance of cultural and geopolitical particularities, and, in particular, about the distinctiveness of women's political perspectives and imperatives in different cultural and regional contexts, is apt.

In her 1996 book, *Africa Wo/Man Palava: The Nigerian Novel by Women*, Ogunyemi presents a far more sophisticated and nuanced treatment of African womanism that, in a number of respects, makes significant departures from her 1985 treatment of the topic.[18] In this groundbreaking yet arguably under-utilized text, she situates African womanism within Ifa (Yoruba/Igbo) religion and spirituality, centering on the figure of the Orisa Osun (including her derivative deities, such as Mammywata) as a womanist prototype. This move introduces a level of esotericism into womanism that is discernible but deeply latent in Walker's womanism and largely absent in Hudson-Weems's Africana womanism.

The palava metaphor is central to Ogunyemi's development of the womanist idea. In West African pidgin, the term *wo/man palava* refers to "a problem, partly gender based, involving men and women." This concept is further elaborated by Ogunyemi thus: "In damage control, the desire for a harmonious community entails that each individual, male or female, must be enabled to contribute that difference, without flaunting it, to ensure dynamism in apparent unity." This concept, articulated in Yoruba, is traceable back to the myth of Osun and her brother Orisa, at a time when they had alienated her, to the detriment of the community, and needed to win her back in order to ensure the community's survival. The power was hers to restore the community to harmony, and her brother Orisa were in awe of her power, since, in part, it involved the mystery and suspense of childbirth. Mediation and reconciliation controlled by women are central themes of this myth. "Her ability to do what they cannot do is crucial."

Extending this myth and the theme of wo/man palava beyond the literal, the concept of harmonizing and coordinating difference as it manifests prolifically within the global human collective can be extrapolated. Thus, in African womanism, the wo/man palava concept is a central thematic concept justifying Black women as leaders in organizing, mediating, reconciling, and healing a world overrun with conflict, violence, and dehumanization—the ultimate damage control. In this vein, womanism is not about women's issues; rather, it concerns global reorganization and healing. Indeed, Ogunyemi writes, "Nigerian women writers [who embody African womanism in her view], in particular, do not view the twentieth-century problem as a 'woman palava,' that is, simply, feminism. Rather, *their perspective encompasses all oppressed people*, men included; as *a human problem*, the Nigerian dilemma must be resolved by the collaborative efforts of men and women, rather than being treated as gender specific" (emphasis added).

According to Ogunyemi, "Osun's story encapsulates several principles: motherhood, gender problems, woman's independence, fe/male interdependency, woman's career [Osun was a hair braider], economics, aesthetics, domesticity, sustenance, fertility to ensure the future, interest in the environment [Osun is associated with water, especially rivers], quarrel and mediation, *siddon look* tactics, that is, 'sit down and cogitate,' a belligerent form of pacifism."[19] The parallels with Walker's "responsible, serious, *in charge*," Harriet Tubman-esque womanist figure are immediately apparent. Ogunyemi continues: "Osun inspires women to be a mother with a career, to bring order in the face of anarchy, to engage debate across gender lines, to cancel oppositionality." The thread of Africanity linking Walker's and Ogunyemi's rich womanist concepts is now clearly visible despite their separation in time and space. Ultimately, Ogunyemi's African inflections on womanism add a significantly new dimension to the womanist idea that invites more people to the table and makes the banquet richer.

CLENORA HUDSON-WEEMS'S AFRICANA WOMANISM

Unlike Walker's and Ogunyemi's womanist perspectives, which originated within arguably feminist contexts, Clenora Hudson-Weems's Africana womanism arose within a nationalist Africana studies context. Her 1993 book *Africana Womanism: Reclaiming Ourselves* presents an overview of the Africana womanist perspective. In this book, Hudson-Weems reports that she introduced the concept and terminology of Africana womanism in 1988 at the National Council of Black Studies (NCBS) conference, and that she began formulating the concept in two earlier papers, namely, "The Tripartite Plight of Black Women," presented as part of a panel she organized called "Black Womanism vs. Black Feminism—Racism First, Sexism Last: The Survival of the Black Race" at NCBS in 1988, and "Black Womanism vs. Black Feminism: A Critical Issue for Human Survival," presented at several Black studies conferences between 1987 and 1988 and later published as "Cultural and Agenda Conflicts in Academia: Critical Issues for Africana Women's Studies" in the *Western Journal of Black Studies* in 1989.[20] Based on these well-substantiated claims, I am situating Hudson-Weems as one of the three founding mothers of womanism since her originary work—unpublished but still public—took place in the 1980s.

Hudson-Weems coined the term *womanist* not as a contrastive to the more widely used term *feminist*, but rather to evoke Sojourner Truth's famous cry, "Ain't I a woman?" In her book *Africana Womanism*, Hudson-Weems rejects feminist identity and politics for Africana women (meaning women of the African diaspora) and establishes an alternative identity and politics for Africana women who want to challenge patriarchy and sexism within Africana cultural contexts. Her basis for rejecting feminism is threefold: First, she argues, feminism is semantically and philosophically rooted within a Eurocentric cultural frame that automatically marginalizes not only Black women but also Afrocentric cultural frames. Feminism cannot simply be "fixed," she argues, by adding women of color and attempting to incorporate their cultural perspectives. Thus, women of color, particularly Africana women, must create and name their own frames that are centered within and semantically linked to their own cultural contexts. Feminism is okay for white women, she argues, but it will never be adequate for Black women.[21] Hudson-Weems even goes so far as to reclaim "proto-feminist" icons such as Sojourner Truth, Harriet Tubman, and Ida B. Wells on the basis that their "feminist" actions were actually spurred by racial rather than gender politics.

Second, Hudson-Weems argues that Africana women must reject feminism on the basis of its historical collusion with racism and white supremacy. The two most prominent examples she cites include white suffragists' link with white supremacist movements at the turn of the twentieth century[22] and contemporary white feminists' capitulation to neoimperialist processes and practices that seek to establish mainstream white feminism as a universally applicable feminism worldwide.[23] In Hudson-Weems's view, any endorsement of white feminism or collaboration with white feminists by Africana women is, by definition, a misguided and self-destructive act that will harm both the Africana woman herself and the larger Africana community in which she is embedded by immersing her in a toxic consciousness and making her and her community vulnerable to exploitation. By way of analogy, Hudson-Weems argues that, "Feminism is to Africana women as post-Mandela apartheid is to Black South Africans."

Third, Hudson-Weems argues, the relations between Black women and Black men are significantly different from the relations between white women and white men, necessitating a different gender-based politics between the two racial groups. White women's feminism, she argues, is based on "an age-old battle with her white male counterpart for subjugating her as his property." Black women, on the other hand, do not perceive Black men as their enemy, but rather, to quote Joyce Ladner, whom Hudson-Weems cites in *Africana Womanism*, "the enemy is considered to be oppressive forces in the larger society which subjugate black men, women, and children." On this basis, Africana women do not privilege sexism among their many oppressions, according to Hudson-Weems. Indeed, Hudson-Weems is quite clear that, in her view, Africana womanists privilege racism and class-based oppression over gender-based oppression, because the racism and economic injustice affect the whole community, while sexism only affects half the community.[24] This is, by most accounts, one of her two most controversial points (the other being her stance on Black lesbianism). Yet, she contends repeatedly, Africana womanists do not countenance any female subjugation, maltreatment of women, or violence against women within Africana contexts.

Generally speaking, Hudson-Weems' Africana womanist project establishes a gendered discursive framework for Black women that challenges but does not contradict or subvert the major tenets of Afrocentric/Africentric or Black Nationalist[25] discourse. In line with other African-centered perspectives, a fundamental tenet of Hudson-Weems's perspective is the primacy of the group as the unit of analysis. On one level, the group is the Black race as a collective, encompassing all people of African descent. On another level, the group is the Black family comprised of mother, father, children, elders, and other extended kin. On yet another level, the group is the entire human collective. With the collective in the forefront and the individual in the background, the politics of Africana womanism at times appear to facilitate certain forms of women's subjugation. Yet, arguably, voluntary subordination to the collective is ontologically not the same thing as involuntary subjugation to some particular segment of that same collective. Although this argument is not well-drawn out in Hudson-Weems's text, it seems implicit.

Regardless, Hudson-Weems's perspective contains other tenets that are less easy to reframe. Most notably, Hudson-Weems endorses heteronormativity and denies the legitimacy of same-sex relationships for people of African descent. Thus, while Hudson-Weems seeks to elevate women as speakers and participants within Afrocentric discourse, she still manages to discipline and police women's difference within the community of women of African descent around issues of sexuality, feminism, and even cultural orientation. Nowhere is this more clear than in Hudson-Weems's overt disassociation from Alice Walker's womanism, ironically, on the contention that it is too closely affiliated with feminism and thus too accommodating to racism. Hudson-Weems also argues that Walker's womanist perspective focuses too exclusively on women's sexuality and women's culture—an oblique critique of Walker's endorsement of lesbianism.

Hudson-Weems maintains a posture of Black separatism that is highly consonant with traditional Black nationalist discourses, on the assumption that white racism is intractable and fundamentally threatening to Black cultural integrity. What is hard to swallow, but at the same time valuable in its unapologetic nature, is Hudson-Weems's hard line on Western racism and her refusal to accede that Black people can be healthy or function normally under its entrenched conditions. Although I would argue that Hudson-Weems's reading of both mainstream feminism and Black feminism lacks both depth and adequate contemporaneity (even given the time at which it was written), her argument about racism, or more specifically white supremacy, as a destructive social force with which feminism has not yet adequately dealt (and perhaps cannot adequately deal on its own), even in the face of valiant efforts, holds water.

WOMANISM AS DYNAMIC INTERPOLATION

Taken together, Walker, Ogunyemi, and Hudson-Weems can be viewed as three weight-bearing pillars of the womanist idea, each with different yet equal strengths. Walker's womanism is expansive and inclusive; spiritually, sexually, and emotionally open and fluid; sassy, pragmatic, and autonomous. Ogunyemi's African womanism is maternal and cooperative, diplomatic and nurturant, pragmatic and communal. Hudson-Weems's Africana womanism is strident and uncompromising, protective and warriorlike, traditional and conservative. If the pillars were Orisa, Walker's would be Osun, Ogunyemi's would be Yemaya, and Hudson-Weems's would be Oya. All three perspectives are pragmatic, with an emphasis on everyday people, healing the wounds of oppression, restoring communities, and bringing order and balance to the world. When all three are interpolated, we get a dynamic and magnetic discursive space into which an infinity of Black women and others can enter, participate, and mold the "what it is" of womanism. This unnamed infinity of Black women and others becomes a fourth leg of the stool if we continue with this analogy, or perhaps it becomes the body seated stably on the stool itself.

The distinct yet overlapping perspectives of Walker, Ogunyemi, and Hudson-Weems reflect a common womanist architecture. Womanism in its wholeness cannot be apprehended unless all three "versions" of womanism are *simultaneously* maintained, contradictions and all. Real-world womanists enact a type of interpolation that utilizes all three perspectives at once and acknowledges the deeper reality that the womanist idea "goes way back"—further than Walker, Ogunyemi, or Hudson-Weems—to an unidentifiable past.[26] Indeed, both the womanist idea and womanist praxis have evolved out of Black women's unique situation as multiply oppressed yet infinitely resourceful and hopeful beings. The womanist idea is visible in the ideas and actions of many people whose lives and works predate the articulations of Walker, Ogunyemi, or Hudson-Weems. It is also visible in the ideas and actions of many people who did not or do not refer to themselves as womanists. Although some people today claim a womanist identity, womanism is something bigger than an identity. It is a way of understanding the world that is predicated on taking action which harmonizes the elements—people, spirits, nature—that make up the world. Indeed, as I argue in the next chapter, womanism is a worldview.

Each of the three authors I have discussed contributes something unique to the womanist idea. Walker contributes an express connection to the "everyday" woman whose life is not constrained by the artificial strictures of hardline ideologies but who remains committed, nonetheless, to making better lives for herself and the people around her however she can (aka "by any means necessary"). Walker also contributes the assertion of commitment to the survival and wholeness of the entire community, male and female, as if to settle that question once and for all. Walker recognizes the necessity and salutary benefits of moving between separatist and integrated social spaces and takes pains to articulate as much. She also recognizes "women of color" as a space where women are both united by marginality and made distinctive by valued lines of culture and ethnicity. Walker illuminates the nuances of women's relationships with one another, sexual and nonsexual, as well as many subtleties of women's emotionality. In so doing, she both challenges the heterosexism and homophobia of the Black community and challenges the racism and ethnocentrism of the white community. Walker acknowledges the spirituality that many women of color quietly live by, making it possible for women of color to quit apologizing for that spirituality and the ways in which it informs, fuels, and sustains their politics. In so doing, she erases one of the primary splits between academic and everyday populations and undermines one means by which people outside the academy are dismissed and oppressed by those in the academy. Finally, she acknowledges feminism, but decenters it for women of color, thus allowing women of color to center themselves and share their visions of social change and human well-being with the rest of the human community autonomously.

Ogunyemi "represents" for the African continent, highlighting the ancestral and cultural connections that many women of African descent around the world feel with their kindred on the continent. Thus, Ogunyemi writes from a place that is both continental and diasporic. In so doing, she overwrites the limiting construct of nation that imperfectly resonates for many people of African descent, on and off the African continent. At the same time, she firmly asserts global African people's concern with all humanity and universal human issues, not merely with Black people and Black issues, as is commonly assumed. This elevates the existential footing of Black women in the community of thinkers and opens the door for a different kind of political discourse and discursive participation than is usually permitted to or recognized of Black women. By mentioning the intersectionality of race, class, and gender, Ogunyemi demonstrates that womanism overlaps with but is underdetermined by Black feminism. But by adding the term *African* to the word *womanist*, she reminds her Black sisters that the African American experience cannot be conflated with the experience of all people of African descent, and she highlights specific issues that are prominent in the African context to drive this point home.

Hudson-Weems contributes a needed hard-line stance on racism and white supremacy to the womanist enterprise. Even in a world where racial politics are changing, where new, hybrid, and even transracial forms of identity are emerging and becoming mainstream, racism still functions virulently and white supremacy still lurks beneath the surface. Her stance disallows denial or disavowal of racism and white supremacy as destructive forces that hinder human development at the individual level and human society at the collective level. Racism and white supremacy contribute to all forms of ill-being, from physical and mental health problems, to interpersonal violence and war, to environmental problems and spiritual malaise. They also continue to infect feminism, despite valiant efforts across many decades to redress this historical reality. Thus, there is no getting around the need to address and eliminate racism and white supremacy. These things are, to use the words of Carlos Castaneda's teacher Don Juan, a type of "foreign installation" that needs to be removed from human consciousness and Planet Earth.[27] Thus, the philosophical heterogeneity that is womanism contains an element of unabashed and unapologetic "no-ness" to pernicious toxic thoughtforms such as these, at the same time as it brings an even stronger "yes-ness" to its better known and more freely admitted loving and luminous values such as love and spirit.

As I have already stated several times, womanism operates at a point of interpolation between the perspectives of Walker, Ogunyemi, and Hudson-Weems. Each of these authors represents—articulates—in academic form, a particular kind of Black women's viewpoint that already exists "out there" in the "everyday" world of Black women. In the "real world," these perspectives and positionalities are in constant tension and dialogue, forming a network of meanings and methods that defines a particular worldview and approach to social change. Ironically, as I mentioned above, this creative tension means that more, rather than fewer, people can participate in womanism as a harmonizing, coordinating dialogue. The womanist idea moves beyond recognizing difference toward creating an architecture—indeed, an energy framework—in which difference can be amicably and productively sustained.

A GIFT TO THE WORLD

My approach to examining womanism in this chapter is unique because it focuses on a triad of founding mothers rather than working exclusively within the frame established by Alice Walker or any other single progenitor. My intent has been to show that womanism is a dynamic and ever-evolving product of a process of interpolation that gained significant momentum from the articulations of these three women and now invites all who are attracted to the womanist idea to the table of discourse and action. Although it is true that the triad of womanist progenitors whom I have named as founding mothers in this chapter can be described in one way or another as "academic women," academic women did not create or invent womanism and academia cannot contain womanism. Womanism—the womanist idea—circulates "out there" in the "real world" and is a means by which "everyday" women, whether they work inside or outside the academy, transform "everyday" settings and the political consciousness of "everyday" people in line with a particular vision of human well-being, social justice, and commonweal. Womanism—the womanist idea—is a gift to the world from women of color, particularly women of African descent. Like the three kings mentioned in both the Bible and the Qur'an, these three womanists have brought something of great value from a great distance, and now that it has been laid before a great being, namely the human collective, it is time to open it.

WOMANIST WORLDVIEW/WOMANISM AS SPIRITUAL MOVEMENT

It is important to understand that womanism is a worldview not just a theory or an ideology; that is, it is an "overall perspective from which one sees and interprets the world" and "a collection of beliefs about life and the universe held by an individual or group."[1] In addition, womanism is a "spirit," a "walk," or a "way of being in the world." The womanist worldview and its associated social movement is rooted in the lived experience of survival, community building, intimacy with the natural environment, health, healing, and personal growth among everyday people from all walks of life, and articulated primarily but not exclusively by women of color from around the world, and now a gift to all humanity. Womanism is not argument based, it does not privilege rationality, and it does not rest its case on academic intelligibility. Rather, it privileges the experience of inspiration, a heightened, nonrational spiritual state that makes the seemingly impossible possible—materially, socially, politically, economically, ecologically, psychologically, and relationally—and contributes to an ongoing sense of inner well-being and power that defies, and in turn, transmutes external conditions. Womanists know this state personally and they draw from it to do their social change work. The collective accumulation of this inspiration-based energy and its multiple effects upon personal, political, and environmental conditions in the world today is what we call womanist social movement, or more specifically, womanist *spiritual* movement.

This chapter is dedicated to the presentation of a systematic overview of womanist worldview and to the development of the idea of womanism as spiritual movement. The concept of spiritual movement must itself be defined and explained, as it is not the exclusive domain of womanism and womanists.

TABLE 3.1 BASIC PHILOSOPHICAL QUESTIONS PERTINENT TO ANY WORLDVIEW

Cosmology	What is the creation story?
	What is the origin of the universe?
Ontology	What exists? What is real?
	What is the nature of being?
Epistemology	What is good knowledge?
	How do we know what we know?
Logic	What is the form of our knowing/reasoning?
	What process do we use to make judgments?
Axiology	What is good and why is it good?
	What do we value and why do we value it?
Methodology	What are our methods?
	What is our body of practices?
Basis for Identity & Self-worth	Who are we?
	How do we become ourselves?
	What is the basis of our value as human beings?

Borrowing a method that Linda James Myers used to develop her theory of optimal psychology, I systematically examine multiple layers of womanist worldview through the lenses of various philosophical questions posed by cosmology, ontology, epistemology, logic, axiology, and methodology (see Table 3.1).[2] I then discuss the implications of this worldview for *spiritual* social movement.

WOMANIST ONTOLOGY AND COSMOLOGY

Womanism assumes an immanent spiritual reality. What this means is that "spiritual stuff" is the substrate of all reality and that it pervades everything. Everything is a manifestation of spirit; nothing is without spirit, a perspective I call "Innate Divinity." Spirit, aka divinity, is present and active in all things. Because spirit is alive, everything is alive. Stated differently, spirit is what is "real"; it is at the bottom of things or what is behind everything. In addition to being the basis of life, that is, alive, spirit is full of power, beauty, and splendor, and its qualities transcend or exceed what is typically visible or manifest at the mundane level of life. Seership, a capability valued by womanists, which also goes by names such as *la facultad* and *conocimientos*,[3] is the ability to see through the mundane to the divine, and to understand the truth of things based on their spiritual essence.[4]

This spiritual universe is energetic and vibrational. That means spirit is energy, energy is spirit. Spirit is an efflux of the Creative Presence, whether called God or Mind or Allah or Source or YHVH or Olodumare or Divine Intelligence or the Unified Field or Brahma or Self. In its infinite dynamism reflecting the unbounded expressivity of this Creative Presence, spirit exists at different levels and rates of vibration, making it possible to talk in terms of a transcendent spiritual reality alongside the immanent one (a both/and relationship). All things, including humans, mirror this Creative Presence, a reality encapsulated in the Hermetic aphorism, "As within, so without; as above, so below," as well as by quantum scientists in notions such as the implicate order and the holographic universe.[5] All things manifest in a way that reflects their rate of vibration, and vibration is manipulable by humans and others. Humans are not assumed to be the only kinds of volitional beings in the universe, and all things exist in energetic interrelation. As Barbara A. Holmes has written, "The reasonable assumption is that God is in relationship not only with humankind, but also with a divine community."[6] In addition to plants, animals, and other flora and fauna, "higher beings" whose rate of vibration, and thus whose power exceeds that of humans, are also assumed to exist and play a role in human affairs as well as environmental phenomena. Some even posit the existence of "lower beings" (i.e., energetically negative or destructive beings)—a logically consistent extension of this cosmology. Humans may act as arbiters of the relationships between various types of beings (humans included), but humans are not necessarily the only arbiters. Thus, the "political universe" of womanists is not limited to human society; it also includes a host of "spiritual beings" as well as plants, animals, and Gaia (i.e., Mother Earth) herself.

In my introduction to *The Womanist Reader*, I mentioned that womanism sits upon a three-legged stool supported by what I called the womanist "triad of concern." That is, womanists are simultaneously concerned with rectifying the relationships between humans and other humans, humans and nature, and humans and the spirit world (see Figure 3.1).

Within this triad, Spirit, Source, Divinity, the Creative Presence *by any name* pervades everything: human beings, "nature," and the spirit world itself. Although I did not mention it in that earlier publication, even the nature–spirit world connection is important in its own right. This spiritualized sense of interrelationship must be understood as a cosmological and ontological foundation of the womanist idea.

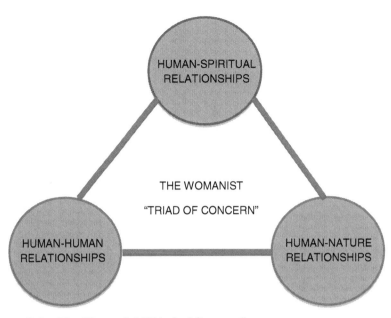

Figure 3.1   The Womanist "Triad of Concern"

Clearly, then, reality, the universe, or existence, whatever one wishes to call it, from the womanist perspective has both visible and invisible dimensions. For womanists, invisible dimensions and all they contain are no less real than visible dimensions and all they contain; indeed, the invisible realm is far more vast and influential than the visible realm. Human affairs, world conditions, and the like, are as much a product of forces operating on the invisible side of reality as they are a product of forces operating on the visible side of reality. Indeed, the human condition sits at the interface of the visible and invisible realms. Thus, womanists are prepared to entertain—and influence—both sides of the equation. Such involvement requires "spiritual" methods and various forms of education in methods of energy manipulation.

Womanism, while intently and unapologetically spiritual, is not aligned with any one particular religion, faith, or lifesystem. Its spiritual perspectives are amenable to a host of spiritual traditions and are flexible enough to accommodate the doctrinal differences in diverse "pathways to infinity."[7] Indeed, because the language of spirituality can be translated into the language of the sublime or the transcendental, womanist spirituality even relates to some forms of atheism and secular humanism, bringing these decidedly antireligious perspectives into a common conversation with both orthodox and nonorthodox forms of religion. Melanie L. Harris, for example, writes on "womanist humanism."[8] Because womanists view interconnectedness as a foundational feature of reality, it is unthinkable that such spiritualized politics could exclude any humans regardless of belief or creed. Womanist ontology with its related cosmology is not a commentary on religion but rather a commentary on the nature of the reality that undergirds all human experience. The bottom line is this: human beings are sacred, other beings are sacred, Earth and the rest of the Cosmos are sacred, and a politics based on this view would necessarily result in the realization of most utopias, whatever their source.

How do we understand human beings within this scheme of creation? First, human beings are divine. We are made of "star-stuff," that is, condensed light, the same material as the stars and planets and elements of Earth, animated by a vibrational spectrum that is uniquely human, making us alive (in the conventional sense), emotional, cognitive, and moral. Second, human beings are energy transforming machines; that is, instruments of vibrational tuning and agents of transformation, channels of creativity and will. We are able to change the energetic quality of other human beings, animals and plants, "inanimate" objects, and environments. In fact, this "change agent" quality of ours is one of our distinguishing features as well as a characteristic that we are responsible for refining. Third, human beings are "part of nature." We are not separate from the rest of creation; even though we have unique qualities and roles in the larger scheme of things, we are not "a species apart" or designed to exercise dominion as domination. Our optimal state is harmony with and embeddedness within the rest of nature, that is, the ecosystem.

WOMANIST EPISTEMOLOGY

For womanists, good knowledge is knowledge that helps people and other living beings, promoting both balance and well-being within Creation. Therefore, good knowledge is practical and beneficial—back to basics! Within a womanist framework, humans, and indeed all things, exist to grow and evolve, to realize their power, beauty, sublimity, and splendor, as well as their balanced interrelationship with all elements of Creation, visible and invisible. Good knowledge, then, facilitates this growth, evolution, and balanced interrelationship. When there are problems, good knowledge facilitates problem solving; when there are hurts and harms, good knowledge facilitates healing, health, wellness, and vitality; when all is well, good knowledge promotes self-development, self-expression, and the expansion of consciousness at individual and collective levels. Divine Self[9]-actualization becomes a right afforded not only to each and every human, but each and every human community as well as to each and every nonhuman entity.

Because spirit pervades everything, knowledge is ubiquitous. That is, it is everywhere present and available. Rationality—thinking, reasoning, deducing, inducing, analysis—is one approach to knowledge. Another approach to knowledge is intuition—direct perception or apprehension, gained by sudden insight, focused contemplation, deep meditation, or even dreams. Knowledge may come from internal or external sources, but the verification and validation of knowledge is inherently and ultimately an internal and personal process. Education is literally, the process of drawing forth that which already exists internally or immanently, and it is ideally a process of bringing external and internal dimensions of knowledge into full and complete alignment. Thus, womanists value education highly, but only true education as defined above and explicated below.

THE LADDER OF LEARNING

Womanists recognize implicitly that true education reflects a Ladder of Learning that ascends from information to knowledge to wisdom to enlightenment. Current understandings and operationalizations of education typically more accurately reflect the concept of schooling, which emphasizes the acquisition of facts, socialization into dehumanizing social hierarchies, and domestication of creative energies.[10] Schooling as such is largely limited to the first rung of the Ladder of Learning, namely, information (the acquisition of isolated facts), peaking at its highest levels (and in its most privileged settings) at the second rung, knowledge (theoretically organized or empirically confirmed facts). A multigenerational history of marginalization from formal school systems, combined with a legacy of sustained wisdom acquisition (mother-wit, survival genius, etc.), has infused womanist sensibilities with an appreciation for the third rung on the Ladder of Learning, namely, wisdom (applied knowledge, practical or esoteric, experientially verified). Because wisdom can be gained outside school, and because, in the absence of book learning, bookish knowledge is typically sidestepped in favor of "street smarts" (another kind of wisdom), womanists have often held wisdom in a privileged place of distinction. However, striving to obtain formal educational opportunities for children and youth has been a major preoccupation of women of color ever since such opportunities have been denied to enslaved, colonized, or economically, culturally, or racially marginalized people as a whole, demonstrating a recognition that book knowledge and wisdom work best in tandem.

Enlightenment as such is a topic that has not received extensive treatment among womanists, yet which is latent in womanist discourse. Enlightenment, sometimes referred to as illumination, is the target of mystical knowledge systems, ancient wisdom traditions, deep thought traditions, initiatic traditions, and the "inner teachings" of most religions, faiths, and lifesystems. Moving up the Ladder of Learning past wisdom, womanists enter seership, oraclehood, prophecy, *la facultad, conocimientos,* and other forms of extraordinary perception and communication rooted in sustained contact with the "higher realms" and their powerful, transformative energies.[11] Womanists approach this topic in discourses on revolutionary love,[12] priestesshood,[13] and spiritual quests[14]; it is also somewhat apparent in magical realist fiction and film.[15] All of these discourses refer in some way to a supernatural realm, the experience of nonordinary reality and phenomena, the expansion of consciousness, a merger with higher energies, and the relationship between human life and the invisible world. The quest for what has variously been called Higher Consciousness, Cosmic Consciousness, God-realization, Nirvana, Gnosis, dissolution of the Ego, Infinity, and so on, is a universal theme across spiritual traditions. From my perspective, it is a logical extension of womanist thought and one which increasing numbers of womanists are relating to their own lives and thought, particularly as more and more people synthesize traditions and practices in the development of personal spirituality.[16] The recognition and achievement of illumination and enlightenment on a mass scale, the upshot of many such personal journeys, is part and parcel of what is variously referred to as the Shift, the Age of Aquarius, the Sixth Sun, and the noosphere, as mentioned in chapter 1.

Once acquired, knowledge is verified and validated any number of ways. As mentioned above, internal verification and validation, based on a feeling of resonance ("it feels right"), is chief. There is an assumption here that Spirit is intelligent and that the more direct, conscious, and intentional one's relationship with Spirit, the more intelligent and ethical one's determinations of truth and right will be. This modality is based on Self-knowledge, in line with the ancient dictum "Know thy Self," and is sometimes referred to as the "Book of Humanity."[17] A second modality is social: Knowledge is verified and validated through community consensus (based on dialogue among peers) as well as the authentication of elders and other acknowledged authorities. This might include oracular, divinatory, or even textual authorities, presumed to speak on behalf of higher beings on the invisible plane, for example, the Bible, the Qur'an, the Vedas, or the Ifa Odu. Despite a valuation of existential equality in the political sphere, womanists respect and utilize certain humanizing types of hierarchical relationships, based on the accepted model of literal or figurative mother–daughter relationships and other intergenerational connections.

A third modality of knowledge verification and validation involves recourse to the observation of nature, sometimes called the "Book of Nature," including natural (nonhuman) phenomena and natural laws and cycles, based on *both* an assumed metaphorical relationship between humans and nature and an assumed literal two-way causative relationship between the forces of nature or the cosmos and human thought, behavior, and experience.[18] Between this observation of nature and the methods of communication with various higher powers described above, womanists know through signs, symbols, patterns, and messages, which may be conveyed idiosyncratically (i.e., of meaning only to the individual) or collectively (i.e., recognized by an entire group). This process of knowing is called discernment, sign-reading, or divination, and it rests on the previously mentioned principle, "As above, so below; as within, so without," as well as the African (Bantu/Baganda) principle of Ntuology, or interconnected spiritual networks.[19]

A fourth modality of knowledge verification involves the body, or "bodily intelligence." This modality assumes that the body is like a tuner capable of distinguishing between different energy frequencies and that it resonates with "truth" or "good knowledge." Other language to refer to this modality includes "gut knowledge," "instinct," or "sixth sense." Womanists trust the body to comment on the veracity or value of information. Finally, deductive or inductive reasoning (i.e., the formal scientific method) might also be employed along with one of the methods named above, but these would rarely if ever be used by themselves to provide the last word on truth. In the womanist sphere, knowledge is inherently social and all but the most foundational, esoteric truths are rooted in human interest, thus are implicitly relative, malleable, and subject to interpretation. What truly distinguishes womanist epistemology is the ability to sustain paradox comfortably, one aspect of which is the ability to respect different truths and the people who hold them simultaneously and without succumbing to discord, animosity, or conflict.

It is important to state that in the womanist spiritual worldview, a dynamic divine order is presumed to exist. This assertion patently contradicts a purely social constructionist perspective on human affairs, insofar as it acknowledges organizing forces that are outside/beyond humans. Yet, in the womanist view, humans play an agentive role in the unfolding and maintenance of this order; they (we) cocreate it. This presupposition of a divine or cosmic order does not conversely imply an essentialist or idealist position. Rather, womanism maintains a third position that I call *spiritual constructionism*. This view stems from the concept of Ntuology, which, as indicated above, asserts that "all sets are interrelated through human and spiritual networks,"[20] fundamentally through the effluxive spirit of the Creative Presence. Because the Creative Presence is creative, "construction" is always going on; because humans are creators that mirror or express the Creative Presence, humans, too, are always engaged in "construction." However, the Creator has established a lawful universe that shapes the creative process, and this lawful universe has a structure and an order that is knowable.

Unlike philosophical essentialism, which assumes that all phenomenal (material) things possess a noumenal (ideal) essence, spiritual constructionism maintains that there is a structure to the *process* of creation as well as to the vibrational spectrum that organizes spirit/energy. This third position articulates that all outward manifestations of form, from identity to society to materiality, are expressions of inner states of consciousness in both individuals and various collectivities.[21] Furthermore, they may be influenced by nonhuman entities. The cosmos is lawful but dynamic; its fundamental substance is mind, and like the Creator, humans and other volitional entities are always already creators. This position is not earth-bound like social constructionism, nor is it removed from quotidian reality like philosophical essentialism or idealism; rather, it is always directly linked with and embodied within humanness, understood in its full spiritual multidimensionality.

WOMANIST LOGIC

The logic of womanism is experiential, narrative, ecological, moral, emotional, communal, and mystical. The validity and value of arguments and knowledge claims is assessed according to these criteria. Personal experience and personal reality are the ultimate arbiters of truth, because one trusts the Self to know. Truth obtained through dialogue and in relationship with others constitutes a second avenue of validation, because one respects one's fellows and values the process of sharing knowledge and experience. Womanist logic is narrative because arguments are often presented in or evaluated through stories, personal or allegorical, where context is as important as, if not more important than, syllogistic form. Furthermore, womanist logic is ecological, which means that truths are understood within networks: networks of truth, networks of people, ecological networks within nature or linking humans and nature, or even supernatural networks of signs. Truth is assessed according to the impact of one thing (for example, an argument or an action) on other things within the network/ecosystem. Things that cause disruption, disharmony, or destruction within the system are considered invalid.

Womanist logic also has a moral quality. This is very similar to Patricia Hill Collins's notion of the "ethic of personal accountability." She writes: "[P]eople are expected to be accountable for their knowledge claims.... [E]very idea has an owner and ... the owner's identity matters."[22] Furthermore, "Knowledge claims made by individuals respected for their moral and ethical connections to their ideas will carry more weight than those offered by less respected figures."[23] Integrity matters, wisdom matters, love matters, moral consistency matters. Within womanist logic, hypocrites, "haters," and people who harm others are afforded less credibility than others. Related, then, is the emotional dimension of womanist logic. Truth is vibrationally verified in womanism; that is, that which yields higher vibrations is truth (from one's particular point of observation or standpoint), and that which yields lower vibrations is not. Emotional validation of truth is often communally expressed when a person makes a bid to the community for additional validation. For example, in church (or daily life), when someone says, "Can I get a witness?", "Can I get an Amen, church?", or "Well!", it is a form of communal truth validation, couched within call-and-response form, that circles womanist logic back to its social, dialogic dimension. Because the human feeling mechanism can both detect and generate vibrations, womanist logic is very "heart" or "soul" based, rather than "head-centered," per se; it also has a "body" logic dimension. Good vibrations include happiness, peace, love, joy, tranquility, certitude, gratitude, awe, wonder, enthusiasm, as well as social accord, health and vitality, insight, efficacy, and so on; bad vibrations include fear, anger, jealousy, hatred, anxiety, discomfort, despair, as well as social conflict, interpersonal rancor, confusion, disempowerment, certain forms of physical illness and loss of vigor, and the like.

Finally, truth can be validated through sacred, mystical, and metaphysical channels. One's personal knowledge, whether individually or collectively expressed, is optimally always dynamically aligned with the divine order. That divine order, in turn, expresses itself through epiphanies and signs. Truth can also be mystically validated by nature, through the law of cause and effect (examining nature for the positivity or negativity of the results of one's actions or thoughts), or examining the vibrational quality of one's environment (e.g., pets, houseplants, garden, even the weather). Clearly, this is a very different type of logic than that which undergirds the Western academic, scientific, and political mainstream, hence, the importance of articulating it forthrightly in this discussion of womanist worldview.

WOMANIST AXIOLOGY

Axiology is the basis of both aesthetics and ethics. Offering a set of precepts about what is good, valuable, or right, allows people to make decisions about what is helpful, beneficial, desirable, acceptable, and even beautiful—or not. I do not profess to encapsulate here all of the womanist values that could be listed; however, I focus on a few that are particularly salient to me. These are values that I see as central to the womanist idea. I see these values as falling under four interrelated domains, namely, personal, community, environmental, and spiritual, which correspond to key points on the womanist triad of concern. At the personal level, these values include self-actualization, wellness, and self-care. At the community level, these values include amity, harmony, and common-weal. At the environmental level, these values include reverence, balance, and nurturance. At the spiritual level, these values include reverence, inspiration, consciousness, memory, and love. I detail each below.

Self-Actualization

Self-actualization is the foundation of positive social change because free, creative, expressive, self-loving individuals make the most altruistic political actors and the most responsible and accountable servants of humanity. Thus, investment in self-actualization is investment in the social good. Self-actualization begins with the recognition of the Innate Divinity or inner light of all people; that is, seeing the highest and best in people. It continues with the nurturance of children, including the provision of their basic physical, emotional, intellectual, social, environmental, and spiritual needs. Individuals and the collective must contribute to the raising of children. Self-actualization is furthered when the expanding autonomy and agency of youth is respected and cultivated. It is cemented when adults not only treat one another as valued peers, thus acknowledging their fundamental existential equality, but also respect and support the incredible diversity of interests, perspectives, objectives, and modes of self-expression that come with the exploration and pursuit of one's best and highest self within the context of fascinating choices and opportunities provided by life. A special flourish is added when people respect and assist the elders of their society, whose long life of varying experiences is worthy of honor and has much to teach younger generations. As should be evident, the process of self-actualization presents an alternative to the dehumanizing domestication process that currently passes as socialization, breeding conformity and dumbing people down to the ultimate peril of themselves and the larger society. Preconditions for self-actualization are self-knowledge (which requires both exploration and introspection), self-love (which is fortified when people receive significant love and validation from others), freedom to explore, express, and create from the place of one's own vision or inner light (which is closely related to the quality of the educational system and people's access to it), and a baseline of physical health. Liberation psychology points out the crucial role of society in creating and maintaining just and humane institutions and processes in order to support the self-actualization of all members of society, because a dehumanizing social context places limits on self-actualization.[24]

Wellness

Wellness is understood as encompassing physical, emotional, mental, spiritual, social, and environmental dimensions. It is a subjective state of energetic integrity and vitality that is independent of, yet facilitated by, external conditions. From a womanist perspective, all people have a right to live in conditions that are not merely physically, emotionally, mentally, spiritually, socially, and environmentally *adequate*, but rather are positively *superlative*. With the constant emphasis on basic human rights, current standards encourage people to be satisfied with minimums. Of course, social actors who are wrestling with their own lack of self-actualization will be less inclined to pursue high standards of living on behalf of others, which is part of a chicken-and-egg problem. However, womanists value provision of the best, not just the minimum. This value goes back to a historical tradition of hospitality—providing generously for the stranger—that is found in many cultures and demands provision of the best one has to offer.

Self-Care

Wellness also encompasses self-care. This means pausing to take care of the self, even when others fail to do so. This womanist value relates to women's, especially women of color's history of overwork and exhaustion on the behalf of others, often others who do not afford or even recognize the need for breaks and self-replenishment. Womanists claim the right to self-care and extend it to others of any race, ethnicity, culture, class, or gender. Self-care is a way of maintaining both wellness and balance in the energetic economy of social and economic intercourse. Activists and caretakers who do not attend to self-care are vulnerable to burnout, and burnout in turn can breed alienation from both issues and communities. Failure to engage in self-care can also compromise physical and mental health, and impact personal relationships. Self-care and care of others needs to be balanced.

Amity, Harmony, and Commonweal

At the level of community, amity refers to good feeling and a sense of accord among people in a social group; that is, peaceful, friendly relations. The etymological root of "amity" is the Latin verb *amare*, which means "to love," giving some indication of amity's overall tenor. The Buddhist concepts of *bodhicitta* (friendly goodwill) and *metta* (lovingkindness) also resonate with amity.[25]

Harmony as a womanist value refers to positive and mutually enhancing interrelationships among various subgroups or entities comprising a community or ecosystem. These diverse groups are able to recognize their own and others' relationship and contribution to the larger whole. It is this respectful and accommodating *consciousness* of shared relationship to the whole that distinguishes the womanist notion of harmony, predicated upon a universal definition of that whole as humanity in toto. Indeed, it could even extend to the entire cosmos. No longer do any notions of the partitionability of the human race exist in the womanist sphere; *Homo sapiens sapiens*[26] is a single kind.[27] As such, it is able to recognize and realize its interrelationship with other "kinds" and communities, such as plants, animals, and higher beings. Taliba Olugbala[28] has coined the term *livingkind* to refer to this larger, interrelational sphere; it warrants a type of democratics[29] more expansive than typically conceived when the concept of political, economic, and social equality is applied to humans alone.

Commonweal, as I have written elsewhere, refers to "the state of collective well-being"; that is, "the optimization of well-being for all members of a community."[30] Who is "the community"? From a womanist perspective, community is conceived as a field of overlapping circles of varying scales—from a family to a group of friends to all people who share a certain identity or affinity to all humanity, conceptually centered at the level of humanity as a whole, but which may actually function in smaller or larger units. Movement, whether mental or physical, between and among various communities (for example, family, nation, thought community, etc.) is part of the human experience and need not lead to tension or conflict as long as positive aims guide this movement. I am reminded of Alice Walker's assertion that a womanist is "Committed to survival and wholeness of entire people ... [and] not a separatist, except periodically, for health."[31]

Reverence

Reverence as a womanist value relates to both the environmental and spiritual domains. As a feeling, reverence combines awe, respect, love, and veneration. Reverence in its environmental connection refers to reverence for life as a sacred energetic force, reverence for all forms of life (human as well as non-human), reverence for Planet Earth (variously referred to as Mother Earth or Gaia) as a living organism, and, ultimately, reverence for all aspects of creation as a powerful and sublime expression of something "larger than ourselves" yet coextensive with ourselves. This attitude of reverence translates into behaviors that reflect nonviolence (also known as harmlessness or *ahimsa*), nurturance, caretaking, honoring, celebrating, and, where necessary, healing. In this connection, the existential equality defining the relationship between and among humans extends to the relationship governing human and nonhuman entities. This reverence is rooted in the recognition that everything is made of the same sacred "stuff," whether it be called God, Spirit, Mind, or even the Unified Field.[32] Reverence reflects an awareness that this energy, or more accurately its primordial Source, has given birth to us all; thus, to revere each other is to revere that Source.

Balance

Balance refers to respect for and maintenance of the dynamic equilibrium of the Universe and its subentities. In the context of the natural environment, for womanists, balance refers to recognizing Earth as a delicate and dynamic system in which humans are neither dominant nor inferior, but rather an integral part of the system. Receiving sustenance from and giving sustenance to this system can and should be a conscious, intentional process from a womanist perspective. People have the ability to observe, monitor, and adjust the impacts of their actions on Earth and its various ecosystems, nonhuman as well as human; as described earlier, humans are "energy transforming machines." Recognizing that Earth and its natural ecosystems are a great source of inspiration to humans, there is the inclination to protect these ecosystems as a source of spiritual power and physical sustenance. Protection also involves participation, however; womanists have historically enjoyed a particular intimacy with the Earth through agriculture, gardening, herbalism, spiritual ceremonies, and nature-based recreation.[33] At this juncture in history, Earth's dynamic ecological balance is severely threatened by excesses in human activity as well as a mindset that has valorized "control of nature" and "domination of nature." Womanists supplant such violent and exploitative notions with a spirit of loving collaboration and cooperation with nature.[34]

Nurturance

Nurturance is the spirit of caretaking, a motherly stewardship concerned with the optimal development of some entity for which one has assumed responsibility. It resonates with Patricia Hill Collins's notion of "ethic of care"[35] as well as Chikwenye Okonjo Ogunyemi's notion of "community mother."[36] Nurturance does not imply superiority or dominance of the caretaker over the one being cared for, but rather it implies the type of "humanizing hierarchy" mentioned previously in this chapter. That is, caretakers may possess resources, knowledge, or feelings that make a caretaking role or practice logical or desired. With regard to the natural environment, womanist caretaking emanates from two sources: first, the fact that Earth has been damaged by human activity, morally mandating human efforts at repair; second, the fact that, even in an optimally balanced relationship, a certain amount of caretaking is required to uphold the human half of the equation. Thus, the nurturer takes responsibility for assisting with the healing or self-actualization of the entity in her or his care, in this case the Earth, its ecosystems, its human creatures, its nonhuman creatures, and its mineral substrate. Practical implications of this value for nurturance include, but are not limited to, such actions as: not using more than one needs; obtaining maximum use from those things that one does need ("reduce, reuse, recycle"); respecting the integrity of ecosystems; working with the cycles of nature; respecting animals and plants[37] as sentient, volitional creatures; actively promoting the optimal well-being of animals, plants, and even mineral[38] aspects of the environment; using minimally processed materials and goods whenever possible; supporting holistic healing practices that utilize natural remedies and emphasize prevention of disease; using technology to support and align with nature rather than to dominate and control nature; developing communal strategies for solving common problems (e.g., public transportation); and, simply, living simply.[39]

Inspiration

For womanists, inspiration is the fuel of life. Inspiration is a vibrationally heightened state infused with spiritual energy that makes one capable of great thoughts and feats (see chapter 6). Inspiration is that state that enabled the survival of our ancestors against all odds, in the face of opposition, and despite a lack of resources, to "make a way out of no way." Inspiration is that state that enables us, to paraphrase Patanjali, to "break all our bonds."[40] That is, it is a state of mental and sometimes physical freedom in which we can envision and enact "the impossible." Academia relegates inspiration to the realm of religion, separating it from rationality and knowledge production. Mystics and others who are located within the traditions of wisdom and deep thought view inspiration as the primary vehicle for direct knowledge. Inspiration as such can be received spontaneously or it can be cultivated. In the mystery schools of the ancient past, the scholastic pursuit of knowledge and the cultivation of inspiration and the knowledge it yields were not separated.[41] Today, the type of knowledge conveyed and inculcated in the mystery school tradition has been rerouted to the esoteric region of many faiths (both institutionalized and "traditional" or "indigenous"), initiatic orders, and the like, where it is decidedly separate from academic knowledge production and validation, except in those cases where particular scientists and artists merge the two in their own private lives. The Ladder of Learning, described at the beginning of this chapter, may aid the reconvergence of these lines of knowing. Regardless of the site of inspiration, it is a central value of womanists and a supporting pillar of the womanist idea. Indeed, womanist practice unapologetically involves rejoining inspired, academic/scientific, and even social (discursive) approaches to knowledge production and validation, as well as democratizing mystical knowledge.

Consciousness

Consciousness here is used to capture knowledge/awareness in its broadest sense, as per the Ladder of Learning discussed above. Because womanists value all levels on the Ladder of Learning, womanists implicitly value not only consciousness in and of itself, but also the development or evolution of consciousness. Consciousness relates to spiritual Self-awareness, awareness of the larger cosmos, and awareness of the relationship between (essential unity and interconnectedness of) the two. My choice of the terms *consciousness* and *evolution* here reflects an intentional move toward linking existing womanist discourse, which has previously relied primarily on academic (materialist) and religious (exoteric) vocabularies, with the more esoteric vocabularies of metaphysics and the wisdom traditions. Even further, my intention is to widen the portal through which vocabularies of global spiritual diversity may enter into this conversation. My internal sense is that these departures/extensions are in line with the spirit of womanism from its beginnings and will expand the power of womanism to articulate its vision and perspectives.

Memory

Implicit within the womanist notion of consciousness is reference to the mystical idea that all that is knowable in the universe can be known by the human being through one method or another. The human soul, spirit, or Higher Self is the vehicle through which knowing is reached; this apparatus links physically embodied humanity with the infinite informational stores of the universe[42] and enables communication between they physically embodied human and unknown yet knowable dimensions of existence. Thus, no question that a human being might pose is too great for the human knowledge faculty, even if we must expand, refine, and exercise this faculty to operate at maximum capacity. Monica A. Coleman writes about memory from a womanist perspective in "Learning from the Past: The Role of the Ancestors," in which she argues that connection with ancestral memory and ancestors is one way to "remember our past and incorporate it into our process of becoming."[43] For womanists, memory is infinite and encompasses past, present, and future.

Love

Like inspiration and consciousness, love is an invisible vibrational phenomenon of great power. The concept of love as it is intended here goes far beyond everyday romantic meanings, resonating with notions such as Chela Sandoval's "revolutionary love"[44] and Audre Lorde's "erotics."[45] Stated differently, love is a transformative and highly motile energy that pervades personal, interpersonal, and transpersonal realms or dimensions of human experience. Self-love, interpersonal love, revolutionary love, and spiritual/cosmic/transcendental love are all interrelated and manifestations or emanations of the same underlying energy. This energy, intimately identified with the immanent energy of the Creator, is what does the real work of social change. Indeed, it is also the result of social change. It is what makes social change "stick." Love is not just a feeling, but it is an energy with associated technologies, that is, modalities of application, not unlike light. The difference between love and light is that light is visible, while love is invisible. Love, then, can be thought of as a higher octave energy that can be felt but not seen and, like light, its denser more visible counterpart, is effective in the literal sense of the word. That is, it produces effects, and these effects can be guided, shaped, and steered. In fact, love is the bridge between womanist axiology and womanist methodology, insofar as love-based technologies of social and ecological transformation constitute the prototype for all forms of womanist activism. Stated differently, love-based technologies, the ultimate "magic," are at the heart of the womanist idea, connecting womanist metaphysics with LUXOCRACY—a vital love- and light-filled vision of the future. They found the basis of womanist methodology, which is explored next in chapter 4.

WOMANISM IS SPIRITUAL MOVEMENT

At the beginning of the chapter, I made the claim that womanism is not just social movement, but spiritual movement. Spiritual movement means movement of consciousness, which, within the womanist worldview, is the energetic substrate of the material world, including all social institutions, social identities, and political/economic conditions, as well as the material culture of daily existence. As the next several chapters explore, for womanists, the point of intervention for all social and ecological change is consciousness itself, which is different from intervening at the level of materiality (i.e., the outcropping or outmirroring of consciousness).

One thing that makes womanism unique is the way that consciousness change is framed and enacted within the "everyday" sphere, through "everyday practices" by "everyday people." Womanism as spiritual movement does not require arcane spiritual terminologies or jargonistic theoretical formulations to promote consciousness change (even though these modalities are embraced as part of the larger panoply of vehicles for consciousness change on Earth). Rather, womanism privileges accessible and mundane routes of entry. If womanists can shift consciousness by baking and serving a cake rather than through an ideological exposition, womanists will. If, as that slice of cake is served, a few suggestions for political change are thrown in, all the better. If womanists can conscientize youth by letting them gather in the driveway or the church parking lot to play basketball, they will. It is all the better if a steady loving presence teaches those youth to walk with dignity and consideration for others. If womanists can speak their minds and illumine folk by circulating at the family reunion, or encourage activists and academics to take care of their mental health by adding a meditation session to the conference program, they will. The strategies—the tactics—are diverse, improvisational, and heart-centered. They pervade everyday life, they crop up everywhere the womanist is, and they leave a trail of energetic vitalization in their wake. Thus, *spiritualized* social and ecological change work is not compartmentalized; like Spirit Itself, it is immanent.

The fruit of womanism as spiritual movement will be known when and in places where consciousness achieves a tipping point; that is, a critical point producing transformation on a mass scale. Whether that "mass scale" occurs in a neighborhood, an academic field, a religious denomination, a nation, or the whole world is irrelevant because, ultimately, the sea change will be universal and humanity will arrive at a place where love, peace, and amity, interconnectedness and cooperation, and environmental vitality prevail. This is the vision that inheres within the womanist idea, and spiritual movement is the process by which that vision shall materialize.

WOMANIST METHODOLOGY: TRANSFORMING CONSCIOUSNESS, CHANGING THE WORLD

You are here to gather Light and spread it to the world.

—*Intenders of the Highest Good*[1]

How do womanists cause or influence social and ecological transformation? What are some of the methods that distinguish womanist change modalities from other kinds of change modalities? In the broadest sense, womanist methodology is about the transmutation of energy—mental, emotional, physical, material, social, and environmental energy. It is on this basis that I described womanism as spiritual movement in the previous chapter. Insofar as thought-forms and the energies of feeling underlie all human phenomena, both as basic architecture and the impetus for creation and maintenance, it stands to reason that this dimension of existence is the optimal locus of social change intervention. Any farmer knows that the quality of seed and soil (and water and light) determines the quality of the eventual crop; any gardener knows that to eradicate a weed, the root must be pulled up, plucking up the plant at the visible, above-ground level won't solve the problem. Any parent or teacher knows that the template laid down early has the greatest influence on ultimate outcomes; any psychologist knows that to address present problems, past conditions must be examined and reconfigured. Why should it be any different for the conditions of the larger society and the natural environment? Tracing the origins of social and environmental problems back to their roots in terms of human thought and feeling leads to the opportunity to rework the ground-level platforms of human experience. Thus, the proverbial "changing of hearts and minds" is the basic womanist modus operandi. Changed hearts and minds then create and sustain different physical, material, institutional, and ecological structures. Womanist methodology is about being able to envision a desired outcome, then going back to the level of thought and feeling to transmute originating conditions in ways that lead to that outcome. And much of this process takes place on planes and in places that can only be described as "spiritual" or "invisible," and it is knowledge and wisdom that "our grandmothers" perpetually maintained in both theory and act.

In the introduction to *The Womanist Reader*, "Womanism: On Its Own," I outlined eight major methods of social and ecological transformation utilized by womanists: (1) harmonizing and coordinating, (2) dialogue, (3) arbitration and mediation, (4) spiritual activities, (5) hospitality, (6) mutual aid and self-help, (7) motherhood, and (8) physical healing. In this chapter, I revisit and elaborate on these methods. I also add, based on observations, reflections, and conversations that took place after that volume was published, two methods that I did not include previously, namely, "standing in" and "fly-over." Next, I provide illustrations of womanist methodology in action by discussing five efforts that, in my opinion, exhibit the distinctiveness of womanist social and ecological change work: the Newtown Florist Club, the Women's Bean Project, LaGender, the Womanist Party of India, and the Womanist Studies Consortium. Each of these efforts manifests different elements of womanist methodology, yet collectively they show the momentum generated by a breadth of local- and personal-scale actions designed to influence untended areas of social change, thereby preparing the ground for institutionally based actions. In these instances, womanist methods work by "opening hearts" and entrenching altruistic and communitarian practices that are infused with love energy into social and ecological transformation projects. This is the womanist idea in action.

FOUNDATIONAL METHODS

Foundational methods are those that begin in self and form the basis of daily praxis. Foundational methods undergird all other methods. These methods insure that the basic integrity (wholeness, wellness, and dynamic interfunctionality) of the person—in this case, the womanist, but ostensibly anyone—is intact and "ready to go." Foundational methods are predicated upon the awareness of innate divinity, namely, the concept that each human being is an expression of, and vehicle for, higher spiritual energies; that is, the energy of the Creator or Source. As Kelly Brown Douglas writes, a womanist "esteems the body as a vessel of divine revelation."[2] That body constitutes the visible manifestation of our earthly personhood. Yet, each person is a *unique* expression of this Divine energy, with unique transformational talents that must be cared for and cultivated. Thus, in this section, I focus on what I see as the three foundational methods: self-care, spiritual practices, and harmonizing and coordinating. These three womanist methods form the basis of all the others.

SELF-CARE: HEALTH, HEALING, AND WELLNESS PRACTICES

Health, healing, and wellness practices are designed to rectify the physical, emotional, mental, and spiritual imbalances that emerge in the process of daily living and also to foster dynamic vitality in the whole organism. As I wrote in "Womanism: On Its Own":

> Bodily well-being is the foundation of other forms of well-being; the lack of good nutrition, fitness, and health make it hard for people to contribute their energy toward higher level concerns. In the current social context, many forms of infirmity are the result of oppressive conditions and processes. Arguably, suboptimal bodily health also relates to violence and hatred. Thus, from a womanist perspective, the most basic forms of health and healing are related to rebalancing the world socially, environmentally, and spiritually.[3]

Vitality, defined here as vibrant health, is a concept that goes far beyond the notion of basic health, typically defined as freedom from illness or disease. Vibrant health, to quote naturopathic physician Norman Walker, "is that kind of health that makes one feel literally intoxicated with life, with the urge to do and to be beyond the capacity and limitations of any day's efforts, with untiring energy, clarity of mind, unquenchable enthusiasm."[4] Vitality, to quote N. Walker again, "comes from a deep-rooted sense of rest, poise, awareness and strength which makes one feel 'on top of the world' and that life is truly worth living every waking moment."[5] The word *enthusiasm*, it should be noted, means literally "to be filled" (*en-*) "with God" (*-thus*), thus supporting the concept of innate divinity as a vitalizing energy which, when activated, enhances the experience of life on all levels, including the propensity for both deep reflection and social or ecological change activity.

Vitality, arguably the human birthright, can be sapped by all sorts of things, and albeit largely forgotten in these times of profound and pervasive unwellness. Those things that sap vitality contribute to disequilibrium, imbalance, and ultimately disease.[6] In the holistic perspective being presented here, disease at the physical level is assumed to be interconnected with (if not caused by) imbalance and disequilibrium at emotional, mental, and spiritual levels, and to also manifest outward socially and environmentally;[7] hence, the importance, indeed the primacy, of self-care. This perspective has profound implications for understanding the nature and origin of the most entrenched human problems—the very problems that "activism" is intended to confront and change. Based on the ntuological perspective of interconnected spiritual and human networks[8] described in the previous chapter, and in keeping with the Hermetic principle, "As above, so below; as within, so without,"[9] the implication here is that *all* social and environmental problems, as well as *all* individual human problems, are simply macrocosmic and microcosmic, or systemic, resonances of the same thing. Thus, impacting any sphere, human, social, environmental, or spiritual, impacts all other spheres. The key is to intercede at the creative source, that is, at the locus of the originating thought and its accompanying feeling (this subject is treated more extensively in chapter 6). For humans, this is the *Self* (conceived as the spiritually infused aspect of physically embodied existence, as opposed to the mundane aspect known as *self*); hence, the primacy of self-care and vitalization of the physical organism as the origin point of all social change activity.[10]

How does a womanist (or anyone) maintain vitality? The basic tenets are well-known but often ignored in the hustle and bustle of daily life. When I am teaching my students about a womanist perspective on attaining and maintaining vitality, I offer them this practical "to-do" list, culled from both scientific and spiritual teachings:

- Drink sufficient pure water
- Consume healthy, high-vitality foods
- Obtain regular, high-quality sleep
- Exercise the body
- Breathe properly
- Avoid toxins in the body and the environment
- Maintain loving relationships and avoid toxic relationships
- Be aware of, monitor, and refine your emotional states
- Engage in mentally stimulating activities and maintain healthy curiosity for the duration of your lifespan
- Spend time in the natural environment
- Have adequate amounts of quiet time
- Meditate regularly
- Maintain one or more sources of spiritual inspiration
- Visualize yourself and your life in optimal condition frequently and in detail

Such activities sound basic and obvious, but when we examine the degree to which people ignore or are barred from participation in these behaviors, we have cause for deep reflection on the grave degree of unwellness plaguing the world's people, at all levels of the economic spectrum. Thus, womanist social or ecological change may begin with cooking a meal or planting a garden or taking a walk. Collectively, I call these activities "health empowerment." The proof of their efficacy is experiential.

SPIRITUAL ACTIVITIES

Womanists engage in a variety of spiritual activities that fall along a spectrum from passive religious participation to high-level energy transmutation practices. These activities are the heart of womanist spiritual activism, which I discuss more fully in the next chapter. Briefly stated, spiritual activism is social or ecological transformational activity rooted in a spiritual belief system or set of spiritual practices or activities. These practices and activities have womanists' everyday, personal spiritual beliefs and behaviors at the core. Womanist spiritual practices may be received passively, trained or taught interactively, developed over a course of intensive study, transmitted directly by spiritual teachers and guides, or simply made up when a womanist is so moved. Usually a combination of methods is involved. Either way, the result is an awareness of "the world beyond (or within) this world," that is, the invisible or spiritual world, as well as some active, communicative relationship with it, which forms the second foundation of womanist social and ecological transformation methodology.

In "Womanism: On Its Own," I wrote:

> Spiritual activities involve communication between the material and spiritual realms, based on the assumption that these realms are actual, interconnected, and interpenetrating. Drawing from a diversity of traditions, womanists may use prayer, rituals, meditation, collective visualization, and a host of other means to draw spiritual energy toward social, political, and even physical problem solving and healing. Spiritual methods of social transformation, which may be exercised by individuals or groups, recognize not only the value of power based in the spiritual realm that can be applied toward human problems, but also the importance of maintaining a harmonious relationship between humans, the environment, and the spiritual realm.[11]

What connects the diversity of spiritual activities in which womanists engage is the common intent of communing with the "invisible realm" and harmonizing oneself with it; that is, one's physical, emotional, mental, social, and environmental energies. For a womanist, the invisible realm is a realm of power and information. Going to it is like going to a river to gather water that is needed for drinking and gardening; in the absence of such water, the organisms—humans, animals, and plants—wither and die. To live without spiritual practices, individually or collectively, is to live in a perpetual state of drought, relying only upon that "water" that happens to trickle down randomly. Such a life lacks vitality; it misses the opportunity to achieve full Self-actualization, full Self-realization, and full Self-expression. From the spiritual realm may be gained intuition, inspiration, and illumination, all of which are vehicles for the betterment of life on Earth.[12]

Spiritual activities as womanist methodology rely on the concept of energy manipulation. Energy is manipulated when it is changed in quantity, quality, or form. For example, changing the energy of liking ("I like you") to the energy of love ("I love you") is a change in quantity, if not quality as well. Changing the energy of hate into the energy of love is a change in quality. Changing the energy of competition into the energy of cooperation, or the energy of individualism into the energy of communality, is a change of quality. Because these changes take place at an invisible level with visible manifestations, we can name them spiritual impacts on the physical world.[13] Such impacts are at the heart of spiritual practice as womanist methodology.

HARMONIZING AND COORDINATING

"Harmonizing and coordinating" is both a disposition and an activity. As I wrote in *The Womanist Reader*,

> "Harmonizing and coordinating" involve figuring out how to make disparate elements work together. It requires a kind of cognitive mobility that Chela Sandoval refers to as "differential consciousness." Differential consciousness permits movement among and between divergent logics (cultural, religious, ideological, etc.) and conceptual schemes (cosmologies, value systems, ethical codes, etc.) and its hallmark is a higher-octave coordinating mechanism ("the differential") that enables them to collectively make sense and work together. It requires the ability to make positive connections between elements that might have seemed unrelatable before; thus, it is associated with creativity, ingenuity, improvisationality, and the proverbial "making a way out of no way." As Sandoval points out, the transcendental-emotive state of love creates

a space within and a mechanism by which limiting rational-analytical logics can be dissolved to make different, paradox-superseding logics possible and active.[14]

Harmonizing and coordinating is foundational because all womanist methods have as their ultimate goal or organizing telos the desire for the reconciliation of human–human conflicts, human–environment conflicts, and human–spiritual realm conflicts. Such reconciliation is only possible when no element or being, human, environmental, or spiritual, is left out, sidelined, or demonized. This is why the womanist idea is "traditionally universalist," "committed to survival and wholeness of entire people," and "just like a flower garden."[15] It is about moving into a new era in which the politics of separation, struggle, battle, resistance, opposition, "the enemy," and all forms of "us vs. them" are behind us. Womanism, therefore, eschews territoriality in the social change arena, as it undercuts the goals of harmonizing and coordinating diverse groups in peaceable ways. We call this "womanist universalism."

What seems to surprise some people, given that the womanist idea arose out of Black women's thought, is that the oneness of humanity is a central operating principle of womanism. Given that Black women focused so intensely on race/class/gender and racism/classism/sexism, indeed masterfully refining the concept of intersectionality and contributing it to the larger progressive discourse during the nineteenth and twentieth centuries,[16] a popular notion seems to be that the intersection of race, class, and gender is Black women's only concern, that Black women only speak to and about Black women. However, this perspective reflects a pigeon-holing of Black women and Black women's thought that womanists seek to undo. Womanists and womanism are not concerned only with the "problems" or "issues" of women of color. Rather, womanism represents what everyday women of color would say or do with regard to any world problem affecting or related to any group inhabiting Earth. It is a "Listen up!" move addressed to a global audience.

From these three foundational methods—self-care, spiritual activities, and harmonizing and coordinating—emanate all other womanist methods of social transformation. We will now turn our attention to a sampling of these additional methods, including dialogue, arbitration and mediation, mothering, hospitality, mutual aid and self-help, standing in, and fly-over. This list of womanist social change methods is illustrative rather than exhaustive, insofar as womanists are, by their very nature, highly creative methodologically, creating new, undocumented methods all the time.

DIALOGUE AND THE POWER OF THE WORD

The simple act of communicating with another being, whether human, animal, plant, mineral, or supernatural, is a basic act of recognition, honoring, and connection. As I wrote in "Womanism: On Its Own,"

> Dialogue is a means by which people express and establish both connection and individuality. Dialogue permits negotiation, reveals standpoint, realizes existential equality, and shapes social reality. Dialogue is the locale where both tension and connection can be present simultaneously; it is the site for both struggle and love.[17]

Dialogue is the first move away from egocentrism and the first move toward universal oneness. As such, dialogue holds the capacity to be the most fundamental vehicle for energy transformation and transmutation, as it carries the power of the word. As condensed thoughtforms or symbols and signals of feeling, designed to encounter and affect the thoughtforms and feelings of their receivers, words are a basic tool of energy transformation. Womanists recognize the power of the word.

The Christian Bible refers to "the Word" (Greek *Logos*) and a Hebrew reading of Genesis focuses on the word *Bereshit*, which, symbolically unfolded, refers to powerful, causative emanations from an original Creative Mind. Other traditions, such as the Hindu Vedas, refer to sound, particularly the sound of the syllable "AUM" or "OM" being the origin of the Universe.[18] KMTic religion refers to MDW NTR, or "Divine speech."[19] Bantu cosmology offers the term *Nommo* to refer to "the magical power of words to cause change"[20] as well as the act of self-naming.[21] Kabbalists refer to *tzimtzum* as the moment when the oneness of Ain, Ain Sof, and Ain Sof Aur generated the Tree of Life.[22] Some quantum physicists refer to the Unified Field or Divine Intelligence as makers of reality as we humans know it.[23] Numerous metaphysical perspectives, from ancient to New Age, link Divine Creativity with the human being through the "I AM" principle.[24] All of these are forms of speech that parallel, albeit at higher octaves, ordinary human speech and communication: in a word, dialogue.

The power of the word may be infused with potent intentionality or may go unrecognized, but its effective power is the same either way. Intended words and unintended words are both effective of realities—and both constitute causes that produce effects, desired or undesired. To recognize, claim, and utilize the power of the word is a basic womanist social change modality. Words carry conceptual content as well as feeling content, and thus are extensions of the energy of the speaker. Words also carry the energy of histories. This power of words is recognized by Buddhists such as Thich Nhat Hanh, who expands upon the power of the word in the Fourth Mindfulness Training thus: "Aware of the suffering caused by unmindful speech and the inability to listen to others, I am committed to cultivating loving speech and deep listening in order to bring joy and happiness to others and relieve others of their suffering."[25] Mindful speech is intentional, conscious speech, and deep listening is intentional, conscious listening. The Fourth Mindfulness Training continues: "Knowing that words can create happiness or suffering, I am determined to speak truthfully, with words that inspire self-confidence, joy, and hope. I will not spread news that I do not know to be certain and I will not criticize or condemn things of which I am not sure. I will refrain from uttering words that can cause division or discord, or that can cause the family or the community to break. I am determined to make all efforts to reconcile and resolve all conflicts, however small." I provide this extended example to show the power of intentional speech to transmute undesirable or harmful social conditions into desirable, beneficial ones.

The power of speech is similarly recognized in African traditions that are founded on an oral tradition and a sacred orature.[26] In these traditions, power, whether good or ill, travels on the word (sound) and through speakers (bodies). It is also sometimes captured in symbols, ideograms, and other forms of expression such as drumming or dance, which retain and convey the power of the word. In most, if not all of these traditions, speech is considered divine, not something to take lightly or abominate. Thus, dialogue between humans, whether dyadic or communal, has sacred dimensions. To abuse the word is to upset the order of things, to cause evil or harm where none existed before. Dialogue, then, is a site of power where energy transmutation is not only intended but also inevitable. This perspective carries over into womanist thought on dialogue.

As I wrote in *The Womanist Reader*,

> The "kitchen table" is a key metaphor for understanding the womanist perspective on dialogue.[27] The kitchen table is an informal, woman-centered space where all are welcome and all can participate. The table is an invitation to become part of a group amicably comprised of heterogeneous elements and unified by the pleasure and nourishment of food and drink. At the table, people can come and go, agree or disagree, take turns talking or speak all at once, and laugh, shout, complain, or counsel—even be present in silence. It is a space where the language is accessible and the ambience casual. At the kitchen table, people share the truths of their lives on equal footing and learn through face-to-face conversation. When the kitchen table metaphor is applied to political problem-solving situations, the relations of domination

and subordination break down in favor of more egalitarian, interpersonal processes.[27]

When two or more people engage in dialogue, the power of the word is amplified and energetic gears of influence upon material reality are automatically set into motion. When the process of dialogue becomes intentional and conscious, energetically directed toward a well-defined and principled end, dialogue becomes a powerful tool for change. Womanist methodology capitalizes on the human love for communication and tethers it to metaphysical principles of energy transmutation. The kitchen table metaphor highlights the value womanists place on accessibility and inclusiveness around language; however, the kitchen table is not the only site that is emblematic of womanist values as they pertain to language. Forms of speech and communication that are taught and exemplified in diverse sacred settings also do this job. Many if not all wisdom traditions teach about the power of the word, the power of sounds and symbols, and the importance of uttering speech judiciously and using words wisely. People who refine their speech through beautification, elocution, and other forms of training (such as those which often occur in churches, temples, mosques, and other religious or sacred settings) bring power to their causes, good or ill, as history witnesses. Womanists who are dedicated to positive social change know the power of dialogue as well as other forms of speech and steward them consciously in order to harmonize and coordinate humans from diverse backgrounds and of diverse interests in the service of universal peace and optimal well-being for all.

ARBITRATION AND MEDIATION: "SIDDON LOOK"

What happens when there is conflict? Womanists eschew allowing conflict to break social bonds, to create social or political fissures, or to divide human beings one against the other. This goes against the familial, communal spirit of womanism and the womanist idea of planetary or cosmic identity; namely, all human beings under a single umbrella. Commonweal is not predicated on homogeneity of identity or ideas but, rather, on harmonious diversity and coordinated difference; yet, because conflict can descend into rancor and violence, it must be dealt with consciously and with intentionality. Furthermore, because dialogue can break down when there is disagreement, there must be methods for preempting or rerouting this energy and its probable negative outcome. Womanists, then rely on various arbitration and mediation methods—formal or, more likely, informal—to transform conflict into peace. As I wrote previously:

Arbitration and mediation involve helping warring parties to calm down and return to positive relationship. The arbiter or mediator is the person who serves as bridge or connector by maintaining simultaneous positive relationships with both parties at once and translating communications in ways that make fresh perspectives possible.[28]

As Alice Walker wrote, the womanist "loves Struggle."[29] Chikwenye Okonjo Ogunyemi described womanists' "siddon look" tactics—which literally means to "sit down and look" or "sit down and cogitate"—as a form of "belligerent pacifism."[30] These methods for dealing with discord, despite their strong language, are embedded within larger, overarching understandings about the indissoluble bonds connecting human beings as well as humans' ultimate divine nature. As I wrote,

> When tension, disagreement, or conflict arises, the goal in arbitration and mediation—unlike war—is not to vanquish, eliminate, or separate one or the other opposing party, but rather to facilitate both parties' return to a state of happy, unhampered, and authentic life pursuit within the context of commonweal. What undergirds the mediation process and gives it moral legitimacy is the appeal to common humanity, expressed as a family relation, answerable to transcendental, spiritual, or ethical imperatives.[31]

Words and actions are both important during processes of arbitration and mediation, but arguably also is the spirit, energy, or vibration that one embodies and emanates. Understanding arbitration and mediation as physical and metaphysical processes as well as a dialogic process allows us to emphasize that the work people do to cultivate a particular energy within their being (referring back to the foundational practices) is also the work that allows them to serve effectively as bridges, translators, harmonizers, healers, and guides in the face of social conflict. At a time when many social conflicts around the world or in the neighborhood have reached a boiling over point, the need for individuals who not only know all the right things to say but also can walk into a room and present a trustworthy, loving, healing, and humble spirit is greater than ever. Womanism as (a) spiritual movement offers both the idea and the practice of this transformational energy work as an innovative social/ecological transformation method with the possibility of mitigating everything from intimate partner violence to world war to environmental destruction. Later chapters in this volume on spiritual activists will illustrate this translation of a "harmonizing and coordinating" mindset into concrete arbitration and mediation activity in diverse spheres of social and ecological change activity.

MOTHERING: LOVE AND LEADERSHIP

Womanists have employed motherhood metaphors to think about a unique and very vernacular form of social change methodology that often flies under the radar. Motherhood is a multidimensional construct that, once extricated from its purely biological associations, is ripe with models for social change praxis. Ogunyemi provides a particularly illuminating taxonomy of possibilities for motherhood drawn from West African cosmologies, most notably the Yoruba and the Igbo, which includes the spiritual mother (Osun or Chi/Ori), the oracular mother (Odu), the childless mother (Mammywata), and the community mother (Omunwa/Iyalode).[32] Each of these mothers produces social transformation in a different way. Furthermore, each of these forms of mothering-as-social-change-leadership is capable of being embodied by a person of any gender or sexual orientation, further detaching this mother-as-activist model from biological constructions of motherhood.

What holds the "mother" construct together and gives it utility in this context is the connection between diverse attributes. These attributes include nurturance that is both physical and emotional, educational leadership that shapes both consciousness and morality, dynamically equitable resource distribution, creative conflict resolution, and modeling a dynamic relationship between self-care and self-sacrifice that balances the interests and needs of the individual and the collective. Ultimately and in its ideal form, a mother takes a person or a group of persons who have a simultaneous array of qualities characteristic of blank slates, preformed beings, and self-authoring beings, and provides a range of inputs and supports that protect the person or people, on the one hand, and shape the person or people on the other. While this is to some extent an idealization, all of the types of mothering listed so far reflect these attributes in some fashion. Motherly power evinces from a combination of love, caretaking, and authority; perhaps most importantly, it is tethered to a sense of unbreakable ties that bind a group of people, however different they each may seem or be. This is why motherhood serves as a trope of womanist social and ecological transformation methodology, and this is what distinguishes it from other forms of social change praxis that are willing to countenance various kinds of fissure in the social fabric. We are all children of a common parent, say womanists, however that "parent" is defined, and most if not all of us have the ability to take turns mothering each other along the paths of individual and collective liberation and evolution. The bottom line is this: The very things that an actual biological mother does with her child or children to facilitate well-being and optimal development can be done by people of any sex, gender, or sexual orientation with people biologically related to them or not (or even nonhuman beings) on behalf of individuals, specific groups, all humanity, or all creation. These things are: love, care, nurture, teach, listen, guide, problem solve, share, and inspire. Mothering is a holistic, package-deal kind of social and ecological change modality.

Motherhood is built upon a sense of deep caring that comes from the sense that another person (or group of people) is one's flesh, and that by protecting and nurturing others, one is protecting and nurturing oneself. It is a kind of loving ecology in which one recognizes one's own agency at the same time as one recognizes one's fundamental interconnectivity with others. It is having a sense of self that is bigger than individuality, yet individually responsible and accountable. As Tamara Beauboeuf-LaFontant points out, cultural constructs of motherhood that have their origins in Africa—West Africa in particular—do not succumb to patriarchal notions of mothers as weak, vulnerable, or oppressed that often plague contemporary Western constructions of or panics about motherhood.[33] A similar perspective is documented by both Mercy Amba Oduyoye and Diedre L. Badejo.[34] The womanist perspective on mothering as social change modality should be distinguished from another perspective, motherism, which maintains that motherhood is the primary motivation for women's activism. For example, Shamara Shantu Riley, citing Ann Snitow, writes, "motherists are women who, for various reasons, 'identify themselves not as feminists but as militant mothers, fighting together for survival.'"[35] She continues, "motherism usually arises when men are absent or in times of crisis, when the private sphere role assigned to women under patriarchy makes it impossible for the collective to survive. Since they are faced with the dictates of traditional work but face a lack of resources in which to fulfill their socially prescribed role, motherists become a political force." Under this formulation, motherists are similar to womanists insofar as they draw from their everyday community roles and caring orientation to enact political action. However, motherists differ from womanists here because womanist mothering as activist method does not require women to have limited roles or men to be away. In fact, womanism offers a kind of role reversal or role expansion in which men and people of any gender who, for whatever reason, are not normally associated with mothering can engage in it as a care-based form of social change alongside women.

Catherine Acholonu has also written on motherism. The motherism she presents is more similar to womanism, insofar as it can include both women and men and it is holistic, advocating a notion of care that encompasses human beings and the Earth. She writes, "The motherist is the man or woman committed to the survival of Mother Earth as a hologrammatic entity. The weapon of motherism is love, tolerance, service, and mutual cooperation of the sexes."[36] Acholonu's motherism also acknowledges the African cultural reality that economic power often supersedes gender, making it possible for economically well-off individuals to be invested with and wield power regardless of their gender. This resonates with Chikwenye Okonjo Ogunyemi's assertion that, in the African context, age and seniority (elderhood) also outweigh gender as a variable defining an individual's social power.[37] Both of these Africanized interventions on the gender/power discourse convey that women's power is not always a function of gender, and that, within an African frame, even though gender duality is prized, power is power, regardless of whether it embodies a female or a male physical frame. This is significant in understanding the womanist idea, because womanism is able to sustain the paradox of women's importance qua women with *both* a cosmological principle of gender *and* a radical notion of gender fluidity based on social construction and personal choice. Thus, mothering does not "belong" to any gender, even if it simultaneously is a women's or womanly activity.

The ability of womanism to suspend paradox is also reflected in some Muslim articulations of womanism, particularly as they relate womanism to motherhood. For example, in an encyclopedia article, Earl Waugh writes:

> Still others react to long-standing Muslim antagonism to the very term feminism, and try to shape a new perspective that will embrace the best within Islamic culture without challenging the basis of the Qur'an's own wording. Dubbed Islamic womanism, this trend regards the distinctive emphasis placed on the "feminine" to be quite foreign to Islam, insisting that the true Islamic understanding of gender is one of complementarity. Theoretically akin to [Nah] Dove's argument for post-colonial Africa, womanist discourse sees "traditional" Muslim society as importantly, but differently, matriarchal, with roles and responsibilities that allow gender to function synergistically in the wider Islamic culture. Womanists see this as anything but a passive discussion; rather they insist upon the gender equality in the Qur'an as the foundation for discourses within Muslim homes and communities, a kind of participatory process of determining true Islamic identity.[38]

This treatment of womanism from an Islamic perspective shows similarities to African cosmological perspectives in which male–female complementarity is axiomatic and motherhood is an accepted, if not valorized, form of social power. This cosmological similarity is not surprising given Islam's origins on the peninsula that links the KMTic region of Africa with Asia, especially since both continents display collectivistic cultural themes in which women and men are viewed as interlocking complements.[39]

Nigerian scholar Chidi Maduka, who overviews an array of African-inspired variations on feminism (or, more accurately, critiques of and substitutes for feminism)—including African feminism, negative feminism, positive feminism, femalism, gynism, stiwanism, and womanism—writes this of womanism: "All the discussions of the African version of feminism (or indeed African feminism) can be subsumed under the concept of womanism, for it succeeds in encoding the essential points raised by the advocates of other varieties of the concept."[40] These "essential points" include male–female complementarity, an emphasis on motherhood, and liberation from the dehumanizing structures of racism, white supremacy, colonialism/imperialism (including its feminist embodiments), and Westernization.

Albeit African-derived, the womanist perspective on motherhood as a socially transformative praxis modality is not limited to people of African descent; rather, it can be embodied and enacted by anyone who resonates with womanist values. As I wrote in "Womanism: On Its Own":

> Anyone—whether female or male [or transgender], old or young, with or without children, heterosexual or same-gender loving—can engage in these behaviors and, therefore, mother. In so doing, every individual has the ability to contribute to the ultimate goals of womanism: societal healing, reconciliation of the relationship between people and nature, and the achievement and maintenance of commonweal.[41]

HOSPITALITY: THE TRANSFORMATIONAL POWER OF WELCOME

The giving spirit associated with mothering infuses another womanist social change method, namely, hospitality. In the introduction to *The Womanist Reader*, I wrote:

> Hospitality as a method refers to taking good care of guests. Guests are those who, by one or more degrees of difference or separation, are not members of one's house or intimate circle, but are welcomed into one's house and treated in ways that respect their existential worth and integrity. By implication, hospitality is a practice that facilitates positive encounter between people who are strangers or "other" to one another, setting the stage for possible friendship or collaboration. Hospitality is fundamental to the management of difference on a global scale.... Hospitality as a method of social transformation emerges out of womanist caretaking sensibilities as they manifest in everyday

life activities and reflects traditions of caring for the friend or stranger that
have long histories in many of the world's cultures and religions. [42]

The ability to treat the stranger as the guest, indeed, like a member of the
family, is central to womanist social change methodology. If the family metaphor is what defines human-human relations, human–nature relations, and
even human–spirit world relations in the womanist worldview, then one must
have a sense of how to welcome, connect with, treat, and form bonds with anyone who is outside one's ordinary ken of relations. One place that attempts at
world peace or global harmony break down is when people feel that there are
certain groups or classes of people that they simply would not admit into association with themselves, or worse that they would ban from the world in which
they live.[43] This attitude impedes bringing the world's peoples under one fold
and it also impedes the formation of a loving, cooperative, reverent relationship with the natural environment. The womanist notion of hospitality does
not imply that one must blithely welcome all individuals into close association.
There are individual variations in affinity that make some people better candi-
dates for hospitality with certain people than others. Rather, one must carry an
attitude that every person on Earth (or every element of nature) can be loved
and respected and that every person on Earth (or every element of nature) has a
place in the human (or planetary, or Cosmic) family.

What are the methods by which one moves through such landmines as fear
of the (so-called) other, mistrust of strangers, romanticization of the other,
unfamiliarity with the other, and so on? Hospitality in its more vernacular
sense offers a host of methods, from the sharing of food, to the sharing of music,
to the opening of one's home, to shared public or private festivities. In many
societies, food is a gift and an offering that demonstrates one person's or group's
openness to welcoming a putative outsider as an insider, whether temporarily
or permanently. The ability to receive such food (such as the time I was offered
a freshly killed hawk as a gift when I visited my husband's native village in Liberia for the first time, even though hawk is not normally part of my diet) is the
dialogic response to that offering that closes the bond of friendship and conveys
trust. Contemporary society offers many opportunities to get to know people
who are very different through web-based activities such as social networking,
online chatting, blogging, tweeting, and Google-searching. I and many of my
friends and family members, for example, now count among our dearest friends
people from around the world whom we have met online but never in person.
The ability to converse about everyday life and even life's more esoteric subjects
with someone who is literally "half a world away" is a unique and enriching
opportunity of these times that prior generations have not enjoyed. This oppor-

tunity for world-encompassing friendships also comes, from a certain kind of ethical perspective, with a responsibility to close longstanding social and cultural fissures and transmute historical enmities into forward-looking amities. The womanist idea is uniquely suited to these times precisely because of opportunities such as these.

There is also a place within the practice of hospitality to use it as a self-care method. As Alice Walker aptly wrote, the womanist is "not a separatist, except periodically for health,"[44] which suggests that there is time for being with one's (self-defined) own as well as a time for bringing together people or groups with self-definitions that differ from one's own. In her book, *Dear Sisters: A Womanist Practice of Hospitality*, author N. Lynne Westfield merges womanist theological insights on the Christian hospitality discourse with cultural attitudes about and the lived experience of hospitality from an African American woman's standpoint. Westfield points out the ways in which gathering, socializing, eating, drinking, and other forms of festivity, serve to fortify the spirits of, and galvanize group cohesion among, members of oppressed or marginalized populations, in this case, African American women, and enables them to meet the challenges of resistance and overcome them with joy and vigor. Such gatherings of people who share a common identity or affinity impact mental health and wellness, facilitate the perpetuation of unique cultural elements, and provide a place of respite that allows group members to reflect and reenergize.

Models of integration designed to undo social and political histories of exclusion (such as those that followed, for decades, the 1954 *Brown v. Board of Education* U.S. Supreme Court decision that desegregated public schools) have historically overlooked the positive possibilities of relationship between "separatist space" and "integrated space," ostensibly out of fear that all "separatist space" would model itself after, or take on attributes of, "racial separatism" (i.e., white supremacy). While this anxiety was not unjustified at that time, it disallowed other perspectives on "birds of a feather flocking together." While the risk remains that some groups will use separatist space to cultivate hate, violence, or domination, the real possibility also exists that, for some people, for some affinity groups, separatist space will make amazing and highly desirable forms of positive social change possible. Such "separatist space" is part of the harmonizing and coordinating process that exists at the core of womanist social change praxis. Even the womanist notion of planetary identity acknowledges that an "emerging global transculture" coexists with specific and distinctive cultures from humanity's long history, which, when maintained, contribute to humanity's physical, intellectual, and spiritual robustness, resilience, and resourcefulness. Hospitality plays a role in womanist social and ecological change efforts by linking joy, pleasure, and fun with group endeavor at any level of inclusiveness.

MUTUAL AID AND SELF-HELP:
THE "DO-IT-YOURSELF" METHODS

As I have stated time and again (and as the activists portrayed in this chapter as well as later chapters demonstrate), womanists rely on themselves and their own ingenuity to get things done in a world where most institutions and many individuals vigorously cling to, if not enforce, a dehumanizing status quo. For womanists, activism, like identity, is self-authored. Womanists don't wait for leaders to show up, rather, they become leaders; womanists don't wait for government to "do something," rather, they "just do it." Once womanists get a social change ball rolling, they welcome any like-minded participants, regardless of identity, to help out and "be a part of it." There is no ideology involved, just the "spirit of womanism." Any method that can work might be employed, in the spirit of "getting it done" and "making a way out of no way." As I wrote previously:

> Mutual aid and self-help are everyday "do-it-yourself" methods that involve coming together as a group at the grassroots level to solve a common problem. Mutual aid and self-help rely on the principles of strength in numbers, wisdom gained from life experience, self-education, and democratic knowledge sharing.... Womanist mutual aid and self-help begins with the survival wisdom of women of color, but it does not end there—ultimately it welcomes and embraces all who can benefit from this body of knowledge without negating its source or denying the social conditions that created it.[45]

The mutual aid/self-help model has a long history within the U.S. African American community, relating to the early post-Emancipation era when formerly enslaved Africans and their children had nominal freedom but no access to established social institutions. Only the Black church and Black initiatic societies (the latter peopled primarily by free Blacks) existed and were functioning independently. All other functions of society, from schooling to health care to burial services, as well as stores for food, clothing, and other merchandise, had to be created de novo by Black people themselves. In this era, women took leadership, building upon their existing social roles as caregivers and providing "the social glue" to create institutions and establish services, first at neighborhood and municipal levels, later at the national level. Examples include Maggie Lena Walker's work with the Independent Order of Saint Luke, a mutual aid society, which included the establishment of the Saint Luke Penny Savings Bank for washerwomen in 1903 as well as a department store called the Emporium, both of which were in Richmond, Virginia; Mamie Phipps Clark's establishment of the Northside Center for Child

Development in Harlem, the first institution of its kind to provide holistic mental health services to African American children in New York City; the work of Callie House, a widowed washerwoman, to birth and steward the national ex-slave reparations movement from her home in Nashville, Tennessee. Even earlier, Harriet Tubman's Underground Railroad and Milla Granson's "midnight schools" exemplify the spirit of mutual aid and do-it-yourself womanist activism.

Later examples include the Combahee River Collective's creation of domestic violence shelters in Boston during the 1970s and the National Black Women's Health Project's effort to bring "by us, for us" health care to Black women in the 1980s and 1990s. Susan Glisson's relatively undocumented efforts to bring racial peace, justice, and amity to Mississippi and the rest of the Deep South in the late postintegration era through a home-style, "walking around" process of racial reconciliation demonstrates unequivocally that a white activist can embody the spirit of womanism. Since the 1990s, Karamah: Muslim Women Lawyers for Human Rights, founded and led by Azizah Y. al-Hibri, has collectively demonstrated the spirit of womanist mutual aid and self-help by linking jurists and scholars to educate Muslim women about human rights as well as their own "transformative power."[46]

An outstanding international example is provided by twentieth century Nigerian activist Funmilayo Ransome-Kuti, who founded a number of organizations to involve women in suffrage, independence, and peace movements in Nigeria during the country's late colonial period, many of which organized illiterate market women. Other international examples can be found in the work of Sister Chan Khong (Vietnam/France), Wangari Maathai (Kenya), Kiran Bedi (India), Pregs Govender (South Africa), and Immaculée Ilibagiza (Rwanda), whose spiritual activist praxis is detailed later in this book. What these many examples demonstrate is that the do-it-yourself quality of womanist mutual aid and self-help activism is something that cuts across social class, economic status, educational level, nationality, geography, and even historical era. As I wrote in *The Womanist Reader*:

> Mutual aid and self-help demonstrate two important things: first, that an underestimated genius for problem-solving circulates among institutionally dispossessed populations and, second, that such marginalized populations will not be forced to succumb beneath institutional neglect, whether benign or malign. Indeed, at times, mutual aid and self-help are the only means by which intellectually marginalized groups can implement superior methods of problem solving that are either rejected or not acknowledged by the mainstream.[47]

This commitment to self-authored and self-initiated solutions to large-scale social and ecological problems (including their local manifestations) is an important dimension of the womanist idea, particularly since many prevailing social movement modalities (particularly the more ideological ones) place the bulk of their effort on changing institutional structures—whether government, big business, or media—through external pressure. Womanism functions differently: it begins with inner psychospiritual change, supported by bodily wellness and all forms of self-care, and proceeds to create outer change through the magnetic and attractive properties of love-based technologies and mindsets, which I have previously referred to as the "politics of invitation." In the womanist scheme, people are then invited to change, and change is made to look attractive, humanizing, enjoyable, and rewarding. It is a "bees to honey" method. Utilizing do-it-yourself methods, womanists create spaces where life is different, spaces where "another world is possible" is being enacted, however messily, and people who wish to reside in these worlds are invited to "just show up." In this fashion, the old, undesirable world is simply abandoned and the new, desirable world becomes inhabited. It is essentially a psychospiritual and vibrational migration, one more reason that womanism can be characterized as (a) spiritual movement.

STANDING IN: CREATING THE MIGRATION WITHOUT LEAVING

After *The Womanist Reader* was published, in which I briefly outlined a number of womanist social change methods, I began to notice other distinctive forms of social change activity that felt resonant with the womanist idea. The first of these, standing in, was inspired by the work of womanist scholars and practitioners in the theological and religious disciplines, whether academic or community focused. What I noticed is that, for many of these women (and a few of the men), a conscious decision had been made to "stay inside" a putatively oppressive institution (for example, a particular church or church denomination) in order to change it from the inside and help it realize its liberatory potential. What I sensed was that these womanists were reading the landscape of their religious communities in order to assess lacunae where interventions could be wedged, as well as subpopulations that were energetically ready for mobilization around a new way of doing business. On the basis of such assessments, they were "standing in" to do the work and be the agent of change, even at some personal risk to themselves. Stated differently, they were standing up, whether quietly or boldly, as representatives and leaders of "another world," positioning themselves to invite others to it, rather than leaving, breaking off to found another, competing institution (such as another church or denomination). Examples of issues where I saw standing in include women's ordination or other involvement in formal institutional power and acceptance/welcoming of lesbian and gay people in the church. What I recognized upon reflection is that standing in as a method also has applicability beyond church settings. I began to look for other examples.

In 2007, I had an e-mail exchange with an audience member from one of my lectures who asked me to clarify what I meant by "standing in." Here is what I wrote:

> The phrase that comes to mind is "standing in." By that I mean being present as a voice of difference in environments where you are both "an insider" and "the opposition"—and not giving into the pressure or temptation to leave when a group is uncomfortable with that difference or your presence. So, in the case of institutionalized religion (which, I agree with you, has some merits), particularly for those who want to stay involved, it is a commitment to "internal struggle" within the institution, the organization, the tradition, the community. Religions tend to fractionate when there is difference; hence, the proliferation of denominations historically. A different, more womanist method, is to defy the fractionating tendency and stay inside, despite the difficulty and risk to oneself, with the larger aim of change from within.[48]

I then provided my correspondent with several examples that reflect my thinking at that time:

> There is a guy named Richard Cizik who was/is a Vice President for Governmental Relations for the National Association of Evangelicals. He got very involved with global environmental issues (global warming, population control, destruction of ecosystems, etc.) after a personal epiphany (not unlike Al Gore) and wanted to bring that to the evangelical congregants, even to get the NAE [National Association of Evangelicals] to endorse these issues as Christian concerns. He took a number of autonomous actions to this end, attending major environmental conferences and summits, forming relationships with prominent environmental organizations and leaders, and so on. He even went so far as to craft a biblical rationale for the church to deal with environmental issues. Despite making significant headway, he ultimately got "disciplined" by some of his elders and powerful peer pastors in the NAE (see the first link in note 47). Their reasons were variable, but basically it boiled down to not wanting the NAE to be in a position to get linked with the political left (where most environmentalists can be found), thus upsetting

the powerful Christian conservative/Republican political formation now in force. There were other reasons as well, but I forget some of them. All this information comes from a radio interview I heard.[49]

From what I understand, after this "disciplining," Cizik took a compromise position and "calmed down" or "backed off" trying to get the NAE to formally back the environmental issues. I use him as an example, because what many individuals would have done is quit the organization over disagreement, thus foreclosing any opportunities for continued transformation from within. Such an action would have sent the message that you can't be both evangelical and pro-environment. Yet, by backing down and taking the personal sacrifice entailed in that, potentially he remained within for the long haul of continuing to bring the NAE around to environmental issues at a more gradual pace, thus continuing to stand up (and "stand in") for the fact that you CAN be both evangelical and pro-environment. He recognizes that there's a new generation, even within the evangelical community, where people can see environmental issues within the Christian purview, and it seems he has proven himself willing to contribute to that evolution of thought and the cultivation of that generation. Given his personal epiphany, it is likely that he remains committed to environmental issues in his heart, and that "heart energy" (from a womanist perspective) emanates outward and transforms the people and ideas around him. This is a kind of activism and I think it speaks to your question.

Another example, also recently brought to my attention by my Arab feminist colleague, Amira Jarmakani, relates to Islamic womanists. They are also demonstrating the "standing in" principle by demonstrating that you can be both Muslim and womanist—rather than splitting off and thus furthering the status quo within that faith community. In particular, you can look at the work of Azizah Y. al-Hibri, an Islamic womanist scholar and activist at the University of Richmond Law School, as well as Karamah, an organization of Muslim Woman Lawyers for Human Rights. Karamah presented a pointed critique of Western feminism based on its neoimperialist attitude toward Islamic women (particularly around issues like veiling or cultural gender segregation, which aren't even often the core issues of concern for Islamic women) and has argued that womanism is a better perspective for allowing gender concerns to be raised by Islamic women who remain committed to their faith community. Al-Hibri wrote a book chapter called "Islamic Law" published in *A Companion to Feminist Philosophy*, edited by Alison M. Jaggar and Iris Marion Young (1998), in which she discusses how womanism can "harmonize and coordinate" (my language) Muslim women from diverse countries around the culture-specific gender oppressions they face. In other words, it's a vehicle for an autonomous, within-group solution that is neither fundamentalist nor non-Islamic. It unifies women in their difference, but honors the banner of Islam under which they all desire to remain.[50]

Another example, although I think it already comes through in my book, is how African American Christian womanists have used the technique of "standing in" around the issue of homosexuality (same-gender-loving advocacy). They have allowed this issue to become visible and have developed a "kitchen table" method for discoursing without disconnecting.

Now, the answers I have given so far only address conflicts that occur within religions based on within-group difference. They are all examples of people who are trying to "heal the institutions," to use your language (great language, I might add). As you say, they preserve the structure for those who want it, but engineer change from within. I'm sure you are also very concerned about inter-religious violence and conflict and how womanism might relate to that. My short answer is that it is about friendship building (like the Black Christian—White Jewish friendship group that formed in Atlanta—I think I mentioned this while at TWU) or "energy manipulation" (like the groups of expert meditators that have formed at various times in various places around the world—Israel/Palestine and Washington, DC, are two examples I know about, but don't yet have the citations). In this latter example, the people used their systematically developed, spiritually-based transformation powers/actions to lower rates of violence in the areas named. (For a reference on how this kind of thing can work, I recommend a book by David R. Hawkins called *Power vs. Force*).[51]

My portion of this e-mail exchange highlights how my understanding evolved about standing in as a womanist social change method and logic. A similar process can take place, for example, in nonprofit organizations or NGOs where a particular structure, process, or ideology predominates in ways that impede the participation or comfort level of certain constituencies. Examples might include: feminist organizations that are racist or classist; racial or ethnic organizations that are homophobic and heterosexist; lesbian and gay organizations that are transphobic; environmental organizations that are imperialist; and human rights organizations that only understand rights from Western or individualistic perspectives and not from collectivist perspectives. The list could go on, as all combinations of variables are possible. The womanist antioppressionist logic is that all forms of oppression, named or unnamed, are unacceptable and derive from a common problem: the dominating impulse, which is, with effort, alchemically transmutable. This same impulse causes the very problems that many activists are fighting, hence the need to identify and eradicate inconsistencies in one's own liberationist mindset and praxis. Standing in helps this process along by insuring that internal dialogue (within organizations) can always take place.

FLY-OVER: FAST-TRACKING CHANGE

In my ongoing ruminations regarding womanist social change methodology, I discerned another distinct method that needed naming: fly-over. The contours of fly-over began to emerge when I examined womanist and feminist thinkers who had begun to move away from womanist and feminist language and identity in the interest of more "universal" or "cosmic" themes and concerns. The neologism itself arose spontaneously in an e-mail exchange with Susannah Bartlow, a young womanist scholar I met at a conference at SUNY-Buffalo in early 2008, where she presented an astute womanist reading of Alice Walker's 2006 novel, *Now Is the Time to Open Your Heart*. In our exchange, Susannah and I discussed how, over the decades, Walker seemed to have moved away from the term *womanist* at the same time as she had unwittingly (or wittingly) continued to enlarge its meaning through her writings and activism. Susannah and I identified a paradox: that the womanist idea contains the seeds of its own demise because it is fundamentally about delivering humanity to a place where labels and identities (such as we understand them today) are no longer relevant due to the fact that a more spiritual or cosmic perspective has replaced them. We asked ourselves, why do some womanists and like-minded feminists basically "remove themselves from the conversation," oftentimes to the chagrin of their greatest admirers who want "more" from them with regard to the perspective in question? And how do we understand this phenomenon? To wit: "I wrote this question in the margin where you wrote of Walker 'moving on' from womanism: 'Do all womanists ultimately "move on"?'"[52] I was thinking not only of Alice Walker, but also of Gloria Anzaldúa between *Interviews/Entrevistas* and "...and now let us shift." As I wrote to Susannah:

> I am developing this new idea called "fly-over" as a womanist activist/praxis method, and what it means—and I think you allude to it in the paper—is jumping over certain discursive steps or layers of an ongoing social conversation in order to arrive more quickly at a needed endpoint, idea, or practice; it is related to transcendence. So, let's say you are talking about intersectionality and you need to get to cosmic humanness or whatever, you just "fly over" the intervening steps of tediously unpacking everything intersectionality *could* mean and you just jump into using the humanness frame right away.... [I]t is

a way of saying "[W]e are not gonna participate in *that* conversation because we want to participate in *this* conversation, even if you don't understand how we got there" because it is emblematic of the new world coming into formation that you need to support through participation *now*.[53]

Susannah responded to me with this comment:

> I think that "fly-over" is an incredible term that I am processing wildly. At Alexis DeVeaux's keynote at NEMLA [Northeast Modern Language Association] on April 11th, she dealt with an offensive question by saying "That is not the conversation I want to have with you tonight. The conversation I am here to have is a conversation about whiteness." (I should say that she and I have never had the "are you a womanist" conversation, so I don't want to place that label here.) The intentionality of this response is very similar I think to the intentionality I am trying to explicate in Walker's embodiment. I think the embodiment is the process that leads up to being able to fly, to choose the conversation.[54]

She then continued:

> With fly-over as leading to a particular end, then, it makes sense that people would have a hard time with Walker's "fly-over"—she leapt over places they have chosen to land. The question for me then becomes, how do "we" (people who care about justice, especially justice for women) find common ground among our necessarily different "fly-over"? What happens if you fly and land somewhere that doesn't have enough coalition to get things done?

My response to Susannah's questions elaborated on the notion of fly-over:

> What happens when people fly over places others have chosen to land? This gets into a very psychological arena: people sometimes (often?) feel offended, insulted, wounded when you "fly over" them! And just barreling headlong into (causing) those feelings isn't very womanist, no? At the same time, I am reminded of/animated by Chikwenye Ogunyemi's description of "siddon look" tactics, translated from pidgin as "sit down and cogitate," i.e., what she calls "belligerent pacifism," you know, the "I love you G*ddammit, now listen to what I'm sayin' and get with it!"... This is like Harriet Tubman very lovingly pulling out her gun and saying we are gonna keep walking folks because we don't have time to sit here and bellyache. Everybody knows that story, that metaphor. Again, it boils down to the energy you bring to it.... How

many forms can Love take? Fly-over is suffused with the love of urgency and impatience and wisdom and just taking a chance. Bottom line, sometimes we have to take risks with each other, especially in situations when the stakes for humanity, for survival, etc., are high. Like right now. Too much pussyfooting when we are all refugees from a world on fire (to borrow from Cherríe Moraga) is...not loving? not womanist? not something...which the womanist is trying to remedy with "fly-over."[55]

This conversation,[56] complete with its messy and casual elements, helps to convey the nature of fly-over as a womanist method of social change. In an age when multiple conversations about multiple topics are going on within a discursive multiverse, it is nearly impossible for people to stick with the paradigm of linear, methodical conversations to create a complete exposition of a topic or position before moving on to something else. Some might call this the "attention deficit disorder" of our hypertextual, media- and telecommunications-saturated age, but another way of thinking about it is as differential consciousness—mobile, able to discern patterns quickly, able to shift frames easily, able to see distant horizons readily, and not be particularly attached to identities.[57] Even for womanists, however, this form of consciousness is not new; rather, it is a form of consciousness that evolves spontaneously out of the necessity to survive amidst unpredictable conditions—the very situation in which colonized peoples have existed for hundreds of years,[58] and the very condition in which prehistoric humans existed for millennia. It is also the situation into which most of humanity is hurtling; a condition Chela Sandoval refers to as the "democratization of vulnerability."[59] This is one more reason why the womanist idea is well suited to these times and potentially applicable to all humanity.

At this point, I have reviewed and elaborated on several modalities of womanist methodology—including self-care, spiritual practices, harmonizing and coordinating, dialogue, arbitration and mediation, mothering, hospitality, mutual aid and self-help, standing in, and fly-over. In the next section of the chapter, I will examine five examples of womanist methodology in action.

THE NEWTOWN FLORIST CLUB

The most succinct description of the Newtown Florist Club comes from the opening paragraph of a profile of the group written by journalist Mary Jo McConahay:

In the 1950s housewives in the African American neighborhood of Gaines-ville, Georgia, started a social service club to collect money for funeral wreaths. Eventually the question loomed: "Why are so many of us dying?" Over the years the women of the Newtown Florist Club, located in a neigh-borhood described as "an industrial fallout zone," have become a force for environmental justice and against racism through legal challenges, lobbying, media coverage, and testing of toxic levels. Youngsters are being groomed as the next generation of grassroots leaders. Members still attend funerals together in community solidarity, bearing roses, wearing crisp white in sum-mer, black in winter.[60]

As it turns out, the residents of Newtown lived in homes that had been built upon the old Gainesville city dump after a tornado destroyed Gainesville's African American neighborhood in 1936—a fact that was not confirmed by city officials until 1993. In addition to the landfill, "13 out of the 16 industries ["chicken feed, hairspray, and chemically treated wood"[61]] emitting toxic pol-lutants in the Gainesville, Georgia, area are located within a five-mile radius of Newtown."[62] Thus, for many years, the residents of Newtown were living what might be considered the worst nightmare of the environmental justice move-ment, namely, undisclosed exposure to deadly toxins on the basis of their deval-ued race and class, leading to waves of debilitating illness—lupus, cancer—and untimely death. Nevertheless, the women of the Newtown Florist Club became "citizen scientists" and "citizen advocates" on behalf of their own community, bringing national attention to their plight and gaining retrenchment from some of the offending industries, most notably the Purina animal feed com-pany. Over time, the Newtown Florist Club became a multi-issue advocacy and self-help organization that addressed challenges as diverse as housing, edu-cation, highway encroachment, and girls' empowerment, in addition to toxic pollution. The organization describes itself by stating that it "promotes youth development and organizes for social, economic, and environmental justice in Gainesville, Hall County, Georgia."[63]

A close examination of the Newtown Florist Club reveals several aspects of womanism, including the use of womanist methodology. First, the Club was founded and built up by everyday women based on their everyday roles as care-takers of the dying and deceased—funerary florists—in the Newtown commu-nity. This role and responsibility became politicized when the women noticed a higher than expected number of people, especially children and adolescents, dying in their community. Their response was twofold: to investigate the causes of death, which landed the women inside the environmental justice movement, and to continue their community support activities with regard to community funerals and aiding the sick and ailing, a form of love and care embedded within community mothering. Thus, the women of the Newtown Florist Club took a two-pronged inner/outer approach to social and environmental change. Over time, recognizing the connections between different issues, the women of the Newtown Florist Club diversified their activism and developed a holistic approach to social and environmental change that remained rooted in the local community. All the while, they maintained a core focus on healing and wellness—of individuals and the whole neighborhood. Ellen Griffith Spear, for instance, writes of Newtown Florist Club member Ruby Wilkins, "who hosted vote-seeking white politicians at her dinner table and counseled a generation of neighborhood youth who played basketball in her side yard."[64] McConahay writes about Faye Bush, a 67-year-old founding member, who, in one fell swoop, provides counseling to a neighbor whose son has been subjected to racial profiling, carries on a meeting about putting an end to a proposed four-lane highway through Newtown, meets with the leader of the club's youth wing, and presents a "birthday cake, pink candles blazing" to a 14-year-old member of the youth empowerment program.[65] In sum, their movement was not ideological, but rather, based on insuring that all members of the community were well, cared for, and empowered.

THE WOMEN'S BEAN PROJECT

I first learned about the Women's Bean Project of Denver, Colorado, when I received one of the project's gift baskets in appreciation of a talk I had given for a women's philanthropic organization. Reading the organization's literature enclosed with the basket and reading the name tags of the women who had prepared the basket, feeling their transmitted energy, brought me to tears. I immediately began doing research on the organization and came to the conclusion that it exemplifies many womanist characteristics. The Women's Bean Project is a women's self-help organization that was founded by Jossy Eyre, a social worker and World War II-era Dutch immigrant living in Denver, to provide transitional employment and workforce education. She became concerned that many women in her community were locked into poverty and unemployment based on criminal backgrounds, histories of drug use, lack of high school diplomas, homelessness, and other factors that made them unemployable within the mainstream economy, so she decided to create a for-profit boutique business to employ the women and help them with other aspects of their lives. Noticing that many of her friends and other health-conscious people in Denver were eating more legumes, she decided to invest $500 of her own money to purchase beans and employ two community women. They created a 10-bean soup recipe that proved to be very popular in area health-food stores. Over time, the Women's Bean Project was able to employ more women and diversify its product offerings, as well as increase the amount of programming offered to the women it employed.

According to Jossy Eyre, her original vision for the Women's Bean Project was "to create a family environment."[66] The Women's Bean Project describes itself as striving "to break the cycle of chronic unemployment and poverty by helping women discover their talents and develop skills by offering job readiness training opportunities."[67] The organization continues, "With this stepping stone toward success, the women will be able to support themselves and their families, and create stronger role models for future generations."[68] In addition to creating bean-based food products and other culinary specialties as well as hand-crafted jewelry for sale, the organization arranges an array of services and educational programs that help women obtain their GEDs, gain workforce skills, manage childcare responsibilities, promote psychological wellness, and procure jobs after their training and apprenticeship at the Project has ended. Some women who have gone through the program are rehired by the organization as members of its staff, inspiring women who are new trainees that there is a future of advancement for them. As the organization proclaims, "The Women's Bean Project does not hire women to make and sell bean products. We make and sell bean products to hire women."[69]

In many respects, the Women's Bean Project seems like a traditional charitable project or small business; however, I argue that its eclectic, creative, and participatory approach to women's empowerment qualifies it as womanist in addition to its original inspiration to "make a way out of no way" for women who were immobilized within and by the mainstream economy. While academic feminism offers a fairly strident, if not well-reasoned, critique of capitalism, womanism welcomes social entrepreneurship and other humanistic, reasonably scaled forms of profit-making into its purview. Womanism is less concerned about whether an economic scheme is capitalist or communist, recognizing that both systems are deeply flawed, and is more concerned about the spirit that pervades economic structures and transactions. Womanism also makes room to imagine and experiment with economic schemes of whatever scale that are unclassifiable within the current economic world system, in hopes that a recognition of the spiritual and energetic dimensions of money, finance, and financial transactions will ultimately refigure them in ways that promote human beings' self-actualization and the realization of LUXOCRACY.

The Women's Bean Project exhibits a mutual aid and self-help focus, and it originated out of a decision to circumvent "the system" by providing jobs for economically marginalized women outside a system that would not provide jobs for such women. Employment is an "everyday" issue. Its use of food as a focal point and connector of communities, particularly cross-class communities, reflects the womanist focus on hospitality and the transformative power of food in social context. The Women's Bean Project's programming reflects a focus on healing and wellness at psychological, economic, and community levels. Finally, its ongoing reliance on community women of all ethnicities assisting each other, particularly through "mother–daughter" transmissions of training and opportunity, illustrates the womanist notion of humanizing hierarchies and love- and inspiration-based technologies of change.

LAGENDER

LaGender is a non-profit HIV/AIDS social service agency catering to the needs of transgender people, with an emphasis on transgender people of African descent.[70] LaGender is based in Atlanta, Georgia, and was founded in 2001 by Dee Dee Ngozi Chamblee, an African American transgender woman. Its services address HIV/AIDS education, intervention, prevention, mental health, substance abuse, intimate partner violence, and access to public social services, particularly health care services, from which transgender people are often barred by discrimination. One highlight of LaGender is a peer counseling program that matches transgender youth from the organization with transgender youth in the community. Transgender youth are often a highly mobile population, being more susceptible than other youth to family rejection, homelessness, commercial sexual exploitation, and hate violence. Capitalizing on the "house" tradition within queer communities of color, LaGender strives to provide a familylike environment for individuals who might otherwise have no family. LaGender also works as a local-, state-, and national-level advocacy organization and research partner for issues pertaining to the transgender community. For instance, LaGender helped organize and participated in two Southeastern Transgender Wellness Conferences (2005 and 2006) that reached over 500 participants per year. In addition, LaGender collaborated with a major research university to gather data on the impact of the HIV/AIDS epidemic on transgender people for the Georgia Department of Human Resources. LaGender has also maintained a speaker's bureau that has been utilized by regional academic institutions. Finally, LaGender has worked with a local church to provide religious programs and access for transgender individuals seeking Christian community.

The work of Dee Dee Chamblee and LaGender inspires the term *transwomanism* to capture the unique dimensions of the intersection of womanism and transgender experience or positionality. Dee Dee Chamblee's activism manifests motherly qualities; for example, the inclusion of HIV/AIDS and safer sex education in cosmetic application training sessions offered by peer counselors, or the way she maintained a safe-house for transgender youth in her own home.[71] Dee Dee Chamblee's activism has also exhibited womanist ingenuity, insofar as much of the work has been carried out without external funding and in the absence of large-scale donations, relying on community members and their allies to help each other "make a way out of no way." LaGender is a purely grassroots organization built on a holistic social activism praxis that braids together political, economic, spiritual, and everyday strands of change work as well as healing work. Dimensions of Africanity are even brought to bear on the transgender experience through Dee Dee Chamblee's own African-centered commitments and interests, insofar as African spirituality is viewed as one vehicle for empowering persons of African descent, regardless of sexuality. Quietly, LaGender is as much a spiritual organization as a political, economic, or social one. Because few womanists have addressed the transgender experience, I feel that it is important to hold up LaGender as a model of womanist praxis and as a pioneer of transwomanist praxis.

THE WOMANIST PARTY OF INDIA

In October of 2003, a group of Indian women led by Varsha Kale, a thirty-something social worker, launched the Womanist Party of India (WPI), also known as Bharatiya Streevadi Paksh, to advance the cause of women's rights and political representation in India, particularly by mobilizing less privileged, grassroots women in both rural and urban sectors. The party purposefully aligned themselves with womanism to distinguish themselves from feminist political actors in India. As one source reports, "The party decided to call itself 'womanist' as they consider the word 'feminist' to carry an upper class connotation in India."[72] To quote Varsha Kale: "When we chose the symbol of our party—hands with bangles—feminist groups said bangles are a symbol of slavery. But, in our culture, bangles are the basic jewellery [sic] women wear. We represent womanism, not feminism."[73]

One news source reports that "WPI's chief agenda is what they call the womanisation of politics. Kale and her associates believe that their brand of 'politics of caring and sharing' is increasingly relevant in the world of 'male' politics of war and terror."[74] Even though WPI admits only women, it exists to balance male–female ratios in politics; for example, the group advocated for a 50% target for women's political and corporate participation on a legislative bill that was only putting forward a recommendation for a 33% target. The WPI has also engaged controversial and neglected populations, for example, by helping form the Bharatiya Bar Girls Union, "[s]eeking recognition, respect, dignity and their right to livelihood as entertainers, [for] about 30,000 women from 'dance bars' all over Mumbai, Thane and other satellite townships."[75] Other projects of the WPI include advocating for the inclusion of women's names on land ownership deeds and implementation of the Maharashtra State Women's Policy.

Critics of the Womanist Party of India accuse its members of being "publicity-mongers who do not possess a serious political or ideological agenda,"[76] a criticism that quite possibly reflects a failure to cognize the unique modus operandi of womanist activism that rejects both ideology and conventional (oppositional/resistant) politics. While the formation of a political party is arguably a rather conventional means of social change, the WPI has seemingly infused its party politics with the interpersonal, inspirational, and community-based methods of changing heart and minds through processes of attraction and invitation that I argue are favored by womanist activists. It is clear that the WPI emerged in response to the political marginalization of poor and neglected women in particular; women whose political needs were "off the radar" even of existing women's mobilization efforts. The available news reports convey a sense that the Womanist Party of India represents "outrageous, audacious, courageous [and] *willful*" women who "appreciate and prefer women's culture, women's emotional flexibility, and women's strength"[77] in their pursuit of social justice society-wide.

THE WOMANIST STUDIES CONSORTIUM

The Womanist Studies Consortium (WSC), a Rockefeller Humanities Fellowships Residency Program, founded and directed by my colleague Barbara A. McCaskill and myself, operated between 1995 and 2000, at the University of Georgia. Our mission was to contribute to social change in the academy by "making room" for womanists and womanism. Targeting institutional structures as well as unofficial practices that marginalized women of color and economically disadvantaged scholars, the Womanist Studies Consortium offered a variety of postdoctoral fellowships, including one for single parents that included provisions for childcare and another for independent scholars working outside the academy. Special consideration was also given to scholars working at community colleges and other institutions for whom the procurement of funding and recognition is often a great challenge. The WSC provided internships for graduate students working in the area of womanism and also published an interdisciplinary journal known as *Womanist Theory and Research* (originally *The Womanist*). The overall goal of the Womanist Studies Consortium was to create a pipeline through which the development, transmission, and dispersal of womanist knowledge production and validation could take place at many levels and in many places simultaneously, all while aiding womanist scholars to advance professionally through networking and the opportunity to pursue their desired research areas in an unhampered fashion. Academia was the targeted site of impact.

During the years of its operation, the Womanist Studies Consortium funded nearly twenty-five residential scholars, including four graduate students, from a diversity of disciplines ranging from the humanities and arts to the social sciences and applied fields. Black, Latina, Asian, white, and Middle Eastern women from the United States and abroad were supported, as well as one male womanist scholar. A consortium of womanist scholars from different academic institutions in the region created a scholarly support network, audience, and social support network for the visiting scholars, and the entire community built a level of momentum that improved the climate for the entire community of womanist scholars. During this time period, supported scholars, as well as other womanist scholars from around the country and the world, published in the WSC's journal. Some of this scholarship formed the foundation of *The Womanist Reader*, which documents the first quarter century (1979–2004) of womanist scholarship from a cross-disciplinary perspective.

While the Womanist Studies Consortium was a time-limited phenomenon, it embodied a number of noteworthy characteristics that help us to understand what womanism and womanist methodology is about. First, the Womanist Studies Consortium embodied the notion of "be where you are"; that is, examine the problems that need fixing and the issues that need addressing closest to home and within the environments where one has most direct influence. For us, "closest to home" meant academia—an environment rarely considered as a target of activism by activists. Our action highlighted the local nature of much womanist activism, particularly when local activism connects with national and global issues—in this case the underrepresentation of women of color, women of color scholarship, and "everyday women" in academia and intellectual discourse. The fact that we went out of our way to design fellowships for underrepresented populations—single-parent scholars, independent scholars, scholars from community colleges, and scholars in need of flexible fellowships—was lauded by our funder. Furthermore, the fact that we operationalized womanism as explicitly multicultural and multigender at a time when womanism was still largely a "black (feminist) thing" was also considered innovative and forward-thinking. The fact that we published our own journal, based originally on the 'zine model, but thanks to the budgetary largesse of the supportive Director of the Institute for African American Studies, R. Baxter Miller, represented very much a do-it-yourself intervention in academic knowledge production. Furthermore, we held weekly womanist "just show up" lunch tables in the faculty dining room where womanist scholars could present their research informally to a hospitable audience. While Barbara and I were young scholars at the time—both untenured junior professors, who were put at risk by such an unconventional program—we demonstrated "outrageous, audacious, courageous [and] *willful*" behavior by moving forward with our program despite opposition from some more conventionally oriented, tenured colleagues. We were "acting womanish."[78]

Barbara and I were motivated by a vision and inspired by a cause larger than ourselves, one that had been set in motion at the first annual "Black Women in the Academy: Defending Our Name" conference held at MIT in late 1994. This conference had invested us with a sense of our power and responsibility as credentialed Black women academics, accountable to larger publics outside the academy as well as to younger scholars in the pipeline and elder sisters struggling against the racialized glass ceiling and fighting with the academy's revolving door. We were not content to simply "publish or perish," or, more aptly, quoting Ignacio Martín-Baró, "publish and perish." In our sensibility, there was "no time like the present" to take action and we were "the ones we have been waiting for." Looking back, we made a few tactical errors and encountered a few unexpected challenges and setbacks, but, in the end, we also made a big difference in many, many womanists' lives, including our own, and the larger academic sphere. It is entirely possible that I would not be writing this book today if it were not for that experience.

CONCLUSION

Womanist methodology (womanist methods for changing the world and the logic behind them) emanates from a deep love and concern for humanity that originates in love and concern for our family, friends, and loved ones, our communities, the natural environment, and the spirit world. Our motivation is the healing and wellness of the world. Our forms of social and ecological transformation are invitational rather than oppositional, although they evince a certain feisty spiritedness. Womanists understand that to change the world requires inner and outer change, rooted in the transmutation of the underlying energies and thoughtforms that create undesirable conditions on earth or in the human heart in the first place. Womanist methods capitalize on everyday interactions in everyday spaces and places, and maintain a grassroots quality regardless of the social status of the actor. At the same time, womanists are not afraid of power and authority. Rather, womanists conceptualize power and authority in inspirational, humanizing ways that enable humans to channel and direct Divine power or the energy of the Universe. Womanism sustains the paradox that while women and women's ways are important, on one hand, gender is both socially constructed and completely irrelevant in certain situations, on the other. Womanist social and ecological change efforts, such as those evidenced by the Newtown Florist Club, the Women's Bean Project, LaGender, the Womanist Party of India, and the Womanist Studies Consortium, show the diversity of possibilities for meaningful and effective womanist activism as well as the distinctiveness of womanist methodology. Ultimately, to paraphrase the epigraph that opened this chapter, "*We* are here to gather light and spread it to the world."

CHAPTER

5

A SPIRITUAL ARCHAEOLOGY OF THE WOMANIST IDEA

All human beings, though they may seem to be walking on divergent paths, are all marching to one goal, and that goal is Self-realization.

—*The Bhagavad Gita*

A spiritually oriented perspective is one of the hallmarks of womanism and arguably its most distinguishing feature as a critical theory and social change modality. In this chapter, I hope to show the depth and breadth of spiritual traditions that shape womanist thought and praxis. My approach will be hermeneutic; that is, interpretive and metatheoretical, interrogating what is behind or beyond the obvious and the overtly stated. My method will be archaeological. To quote Gary Gutting (2003), "The premise of the archaeological method is that systems of thought and knowledge (epistemes or discursive formations, in Foucault's terminology) are governed by rules, beyond those of grammar and logic, that operate beneath the consciousness of individual subjects and define a system of conceptual possibilities that determines the boundaries of thought in a given domain and period."[1] That being said, however, my approach and method will neither be neat, tidy, nor linear; rather, it will be full of twists and turns, stories and sidebars.

The spirituality undergirding womanism is cross-cutting and global, and it serves as the basis for a new kind of universalist politics; namely, spiritualized politics.[2] Spiritualized politics are animated by metaphysical and cosmological understandings and practices, by love for people and other beings as a feeling and a praxis, by inspiration as a higher vibrational state filled with clarity and power, and by an inspired vision illuminating and giving life to future, present, and past realities. On this basis, I argue now as I argued in my introduction to *The Womanist Reader* and in chapter 3 of this volume that womanism cannot be characterized as an ideology;[3] rather, womanism is a spirit of being and a spirit of doing. For womanists, decisions about what to do and how to be and what to expect and what is possible are informed by this ongoing *personal, practical, lived, and alive* engagement with the spiritual and metaphysical strata of existence and human understanding.

How did womanism get to be this way? Womanism exhibits a dynamic heterogeneity of perspective, of method that is distinctive, yet hard to capture within existing academic languages. In order to illuminate the formation and inner dynamics of womanism and spiritualized politics, in particular, I develop a method I call *spiritual archaeology*. Spiritual archaeology is the method of backward-looking spiritual story recovery, the act of digging up the spiritual roots of womanism by looking at the spiritual lives of self-proclaimed womanists and their kindred spirits. Through stories (spiritual life stories) the dynamism that is womanism becomes cognizable (womanist methodology, womanism as spirit, spiritualized politics, womanism as vision, the womanist idea in toto). To support the parallel I am making between personal spiritual journeys and the evolution of the womanist idea, I draw from a diversity of spiritually and metaphysically oriented authors, including Akasha Gloria Hull, Toni Cade Bambara, M. Jacqui Alexander, Gloria Anzaldúa, AnaLouise Keating, Judylyn S. Ryan, and Barbara A. Holmes. I also draw from the story of my own spiritual journey to trace the evolution of the womanist idea and spiritualized politics, naming and interrelating a diverse array of spiritual, cosmological, metaphysical, and philosophical traditions that have influenced my thought and praxis.

Ultimately, I demonstrate that three important characteristics underpin womanist spirituality and in turn give birth to and sustain both womanism and spiritualized politics; namely, spiritual curiosity, spiritual eclecticism, and spiritual self-authorship. Spiritual curiosity gives rise to spiritual eclecticism, which, in turn, necessitates spiritual self-authorship. Spiritual self-authorship in turn radicalizes and revolutionizes one's sense about what exists, how it came into being, who we are, how the world works, how to move in the world, how to effect change, and what kind of change to effect. A fuller examination of these characteristics and understandings yields deeper insight into the nature of womanism, womanists, and the womanist idea. Before I get to this, however, I clarify the terminology we use to talk about spirituality and I discuss six characteristics of womanist spirituality, namely, that it is eclectic, synthetic, holistic, personal, visionary, and pragmatic. I then turn to personal narratives by spiritually and metaphysically oriented women thinkers to illustrate these dynamics in action.

COMING APART

Let us begin in 1979, when Alice Walker published her short story "Coming Apart" containing the now famous quote, "A womanist is a feminist, only more common." Let us call 1979 the birth of the term *womanist* as it is used today. However, as indicated in chapter 2, we will not limit ourselves to thinking that this is when womanism began, nor that Alice Walker invented something new when she penned the word *womanist*. Indeed, she herself has indicated repeatedly that womanism is something we inherited from our foremothers; it is something we learned from them. It is a spirit as well as a practice as well as a set of knowledge*s*. Thus, we can talk in terms of "womanists" who existed before "womanism" was named and "defined," academically or otherwise.[4] We can also imagine what informed, or better yet, *inspired* these originary womanists, if ever there were such a thing, as well as what invisible thread has kept "us" (contemporary womanists) and "them" (our womanist foremothers ... *and* forefathers) connected across time, place, identity, and circumstance.

While many people assume that the Black Church is or has been the primary source of Black women's spiritual knowledge and praxis, Black women and other women of color are now and have historically been informed by a number of traditions, from the institutional to the indigenous. Womanists, by temperament, are spiritual grazers because they see Spirit or spirituality everywhere and in everything. For womanists, all faiths and traditions inherently reference a common spiritual architecture undergirding the entire Universe, which I call Source. Womanists, and in turn, womanism are informed by these many traditions, faiths, and lifesystems in ways that are neither neat, linear, homogeneous, nor even necessarily logical by customary standards. Yet, womanist spirituality can be identified by a distinctive imprimatur: It is eclectic, synthetic, holistic, personal, visionary, and pragmatic.

Before we proceed further into a discussion of these six aspects of womanist spirituality, let us revisit the clarification of basic terminology that distinguishes between religion and spirituality, and subsequently elaborates on a new and more comprehensive term, *lifesystems*.

RELIGION, SPIRITUALITY, AND LIFESYSTEMS

In the interest of full disclosure, my degree is not in religion, yet the study of world religions and spirituality has constituted a large part of my personal "alternative curriculum" for most of my life, having been raised by parents for whom this was also a key area of interest and investigation.[5] I was raised in the Baha'i Faith, which teaches children that all religions come from the same God and exposes children to the general contours of major world religions at an early age. My undergraduate major was philosophy, and my doctorate is in psychology, which traces its roots back to *Psyche*, or Soul—a connection that is generally overlooked today but which is integral to my interest in the field.[6] As a young adult, I suspended my formal participation in the Baha'i Faith, distanced myself from organized religion more generally, and began to explore numerous world traditions, including indigenous, New Age, and divinatory traditions, as well as to study mysticism and esotericism. As a result of these many influences, my mind often finds its musings at this border of psyche, spirituality, religion, and philosophy, articulating with my avid interest in culture, politics, ecology, and social change. It is in this spirit and from this wellspring that all of my work in the arena of womanism proceeds. What follows are my working definitions of religion, spirituality, and lifesystems.

Religion

Religion is a particular system of thought and practice that is created or has evolved to encompass a particular cosmology, ontology, epistemology, axiology, ethical system, moral code, set of rituals, and group identity. In general, religions, particularly orthodox or institutionalized religions, have one or more deities or avatars who are considered superior to (e.g., more powerful or more good than) ordinary humans in some way. Religions are a way to regulate the relationships between humans and these deities or to help humans become more like these avatars. Even though their origins are generally "sacred," often religions evolve over time into forms, agents, or vehicles of social control or into large bureaucracies or governmental systems with secular overtones. Most religions convey or even enforce some sense that theirs is "the only one" or "the best one," to the exclusion or diminishment of others, even if their originating figureheads reportedly spoke words to the contrary. Last but not least, religion is often presented as a justifiable "management system" for "ordinary people," insofar as it maintains a reasonable "common good" for the majority of the population (assuming that there would be greater chaos and destruction in the absence of religion's constraining force, and that this would be bad). Set against these "ordinary people" is typically some more "advanced" group of people who need less management because they have attained greater knowledge, wisdom, consciousness, enlightenment, or simply power and authority. Thus, most religions maintain some kind of hierarchy, with the highest reaches or ranks generally disincarnate.

Spirituality

Spirituality concerns people's search for, aspiration toward, or connection with the sacred, the suprahuman, the supernatural, the unseen, or nonexistence/ emptiness. Spirituality is that recognition that there is "more" beyond our five-sense reality and our mundane pursuits; it is a quest into the mysteries of life. Patricia Hill Collins offers a noteworthy definition: "[S]pirituality is not merely a system of religious beliefs similar to logical systems of ideas. Rather, spirituality comprises articles of faith that provide a conceptual framework for living everyday life."[7] Judylyn S. Ryan writes, "[S]pirituality [is] a combination of consciousness, ethos, lifestyle, and discourse that privileges spirit—that is, life force—as a primary aspect of self and that defines and determines health and well-being."[8] Associated with her notion of spirituality—specifically the spirituality of Black women, inflected by a transnational Africanity —is an "ethos of interconnectedness," a "paradigm of growth," and a "democracy of narrative participation."[9] Leela Fernandes writes:

> When I speak on spirituality, at the most basic level I am referring to an understanding of the self as encompassing body and mind, as well as spirit. I am also referring to a transcendent sense of interconnection that moves beyond the knowable, visible material world. This sense of interconnection has been variously described as divinity, the sacred, spirit, or simply the universe. My understanding is also grounded in a form of lived spirituality, which is directly accessible to all and which does not need to be mediated by religious experts, institutions, or theological texts; this is often referred to as the mystical side of spirituality.[10]

Although none of these cited authors identifies exclusively as a womanist, the resonance of their definitions with the notion of spirituality that animates the womanist idea supports my contention that the womanist idea is nonideological and capable of cropping up nearly anywhere. In this sense, womanism exists as one expression of a particular zeitgeist, one that is arguably expanding at this time.

In sum, where religion is institutional, spirituality is personal. Whether it sits in the foreground or the background of a person's or a group's daily life, spirituality, unlike religion, cannot be quit or abandoned or switched; it is as much a part of our human beingness as body, emotions, or mind, as breath, heartbeat, or digestion. However, from a social/political/cultural/historical standpoint, we may suppress or distort our awareness of spirituality, which has the effect of diminishing our wellness as well as our basic humanity. Alternately, we may choose as individuals or as peoples to emphasize and elevate spirituality, which has the effect of increasing our individual and collective vitality and bringing our human beingness into full expression.

What is the relationship between these two entities, spirituality and religion? For some people, religion is a vehicle for spirituality, insofar as it presents information about sacred, suprahuman, supernatural, invisible, or existential concerns, and offers a community of people similarly engaged. For other people, religion is "too restrictive" to contain this pursuit. For many people, religion is an identity, a label, an historical artifact based on family heritage. It may be a source of pride, confusion, comfort, or antipathy, not unlike race, ethnicity, nationality, or culture, and may or may not relate to spirituality in any deep way. For others, religion is an article of active affiliation, having been the product of a careful and conscious search for a belief system or spiritual community based on affinity and much introspection. For others still, religious affiliation is simply the result of finding a welcoming community, and community itself is spiritual. Thus, there are many ways that religion and spirituality can be intertwined.

In today's world, it is increasingly common to find individuals for whom the statement "I'm spiritual, but I'm not religious," resonates.[11] Or, "I believe in God, but I don't belong to any particular faith." Or, simply, "I think there's something greater than ourselves—I'm just not sure what it is." Another variant is, "I was raised in [fill-in-the-blank faith], but these days I'm checking out a whole bunch of different things and finding a lot of value in many places." Here's another: "I find that I can get all the answers I need from within." Or even, "God is within" or "I AM God; we are all God." These types of beliefs and practices defy conventional religion, yet often make for passionately spiritual people. Such people comprise a kind of informal community on a global scale, and the meaning-making that these people do is, I argue, one thread that informs womanism. This perspective may be variously characterized as nonreligious, antireligious, multireligious, religiously eclectic, religious "sampling" (to pull from a DJ metaphor), or even "everyday mysticism." "All paths lead to One," "All paths lead to Source," "All paths end up in the same place," "It's all good...." These are the kinds of things people say to reference this transcultural yet culturally conscious, sociospiritual mindset.

Taken together, these statements reflect a sentiment that seeks liberation and self-determination (whether individual or collective) as well as connection with the profound and sublime. Such yearnings reveal a deeply rooted dissatisfaction with purely materialist accounts of reality as well as their political outmirrorings in the form of dehumanizing social institutions and processes. They anticipate the uprising implicit in the slogan "Another world is possible," albeit in ways too often inchoate and emotionally untranslatable under the strictures of current materialist languages and grammars. In chapter 1 I intimated that these stirrings and strivings anticipate LUXOCRACY, or "rule by Light," meaning an enlightened form of self-rule and communitarian commonweal requiring no external systems of authority or governance, based on the universal recognition of one's own and others' innate divinity—indeed the innate divinity of the planet and entire cosmos. Although the concept of LUXOCRACY stretches contemporary imaginings about either spirituality or politics, it is, I argue, at the heart of the womanist idea.

Lifesystems

The concept of lifesystems, as coined and elaborated by Baruti KMT and introduced in chapter 1, is a larger, broader, and more dynamic conceptual scheme for thinking about humans in a spiritual context.[12] A lifesystem is both a thought-form and a thought community. As such, it may contain institutions (such as religion), but is not constrained by them. More important is the thought-architecture that ultimately produces those outward manifestations that come to be known as traditions, religions, or faiths. A lifesystem, then, encompasses both institutional and personal expressions of a particular understanding of humans, life, and creation in sacred or transcendental context. Such an understanding is cocreated and shared by a number of people throughout time and across space. The concept of lifesystems is useful here because it allows us to begin imagining how a global network of people who share nothing more than a common thought architecture about spirituality might collectively influence the shape of human society and life on Planet Earth merely by the power of their ideas. An institutional or ideological platform is not necessarily required; it is mass spirituality beyond religion. Amorphous and heterogeneous entities like "womanists" or "womanism," then, can be extremely influential because they translate ideas, such as the womanist idea, into psychological and material reality.

THE IMPRIMATUR OF WOMANIST SPIRITUALITY

As mentioned, womanist spirituality has six identifying characteristics: it is eclectic, synthetic, holistic, personal, visionary, and pragmatic. That is, it draws from many sources; it combines many sources; it dynamically creates a whole from parts; it is defined and determined by the self; it sees a "bigger picture"; and it exists to solve problems and make life better. Let me now address each of these aspects in turn.

ECLECTIC, SYNTHETIC, AND HOLISTIC

Womanist spirituality is eclectic insofar as it is comprised of diverse elements. It is synthetic insofar as these diverse elements are brought together creatively. It is holistic insofar as a new whole is made from what were formerly diverse and distinct elements. As mentioned, many people assume that womanist spirituality is rooted in the Black Church. In one very limited respect, this is a true statement. However, we can unpack the many influences on "the Black Church." We begin with the Black Church because we know that Black women were the first to articulate the womanist idea and introduce the term *womanist* into the popular lexicon. We know that, with a few possible exceptions such as the Copts, Christianity was historically imposed on people of African descent, usually through a colonial process, overwriting, or more commonly, being syncretized with traditional African religions. We also know that Islam followed a similar process with slightly different parameters. When Africans were brought to the New World as part of the Ma'afa,[13] they came as Christians, Muslims, and members of various African religions (which were generally part and parcel of geographic ancestry, aka "tribal membership"). We don't know that they didn't also come as African Jews, insofar as the slave trade did not discriminate in terms of religion. When they came to the Christianized New World, in this case the United States, the Christian church was "authorized" as a place of congregation for New World Africans, even as it served as a vehicle of oppression and external social control. Thus, it became the symbolic and literal meeting ground and marketplace of all the influences shaping the Black experience in the old and new worlds alike.

We know at the very least that these threads were there: African, Christian, Islamic, and maybe Jewish. But what other threads might have been present at that moment of transfusion? And what other threads were interwoven along the way? One thing I love about Julie Dash's film *Daughters of the Dust*, which Barbara McCaskill read as womanist film in one of our early articles,[14] is the way in which it so skillfully depicts the interweaving of not only African, Christian, and Islamic threads, but also Native American Indian threads, in the lives of Black women living in a turn-of-the-century Sea Islands community. This film was in many respects revolutionary at the time it came out in terms of illuminating and memorializing the ancestral multireligiousness of New World Africans' spirituality. Implicitly, the message conveyed was: *Those threads are still here, just like strands of DNA.*

Another factor, present but submerged, informing the womanist spiritual imprimatur at that time, prior to that time, and into the present, is the influence of participation in initiatic societies that typically have a spiritual, metaphysical, or mystical component in addition to social and service components. Derrick Lanois is at work on a dissertation on Prince Hall Masons and the Order of the Eastern Star in the Southeastern United States from 1870 to 1970.[15] One of his central theses is that the level of influence exerted by these organizations on the formation of Black community, identity, and social action praxis was equivalent to that of the Black Church, which is generally awarded primacy in accounts of African American social history. Many such initiatic societies—and this is true on both sides of the color-line—trace their metaphysical components back to ancient KMTic (Egyptian) religion and allied mystical traditions such as Kabbalah, Sufism, and Gnosticism.[16]

I remember my reaction when I first encountered the words of Selena Sloan Butler, best known as the Black cofounder of the PTA, who wrote in 1897, *when she was 24 years old*:

> It is amusing as well as provoking to hear intelligent men and women, speaking on the Negro, begin with the savage period of his life, forgetting or not knowing or ignoring the fact that he once occupied a stage of civilization to which other races bowed before he lapsed into barbarism. How shall we remedy this weakness? Study the past and current history of your race and with pride, tell it to your pupils in the classroom or to your children as you sit around the fireside. If you do not do this, who will? Hang upon the walls of your homes pictures of the men and women of your own race who have given a chapter that deserves to be recorded in the history of the civilized world.... We should appreciate everything that represents the achievement of our people, whether modern or ancient. Then fill your libraries with books that are the product of the Negro brain. Do these things, and I prophesy that almost every child of the succeeding generation will speak with as much pride of his race and the Negro blood in his veins.[17]

These are the words of someone who has been educated outside the mainstream school system of the times. Who was conducting this education? And what was behind this education? We have the initiatic societies to thank for maintaining and transmitting some of the information to which Selena Sloan Butler is referring. This was before Cheikh Anta Diop and Yosef ben-Jochannan and Ivan van Sertima and John Henrik Clarke and Carter G. Woodson and Jacob Carruthers and Charles Finch and LaVerne Gyant—before Black children and white children, girls and boys, were receiving equal education, indeed, only a year after *Plessy vs. Ferguson*![18] It just so happens to also be only one year after erudite Haitian-born and Haitian educated scholar and statesman, Joseph-Antenor Firmin, published his monumental 400+ page tome, *De *l'Egalité des Races Humaines*, or, in English, *The Equality of the Human Races*, in which he wrote, "Egypt was a country of Negroes, of Black Africans. The Black race has preceded all other races in the construction of civilization."[19] It is also a mere five years after Anna Julia Cooper, the first African American woman to receive a PhD (at the Sorbonne), published *A Voice from the South*.[20] However, it was 66 years after Maria W. W. Stewart, the first American woman of any race on record to address a mixed-sex audience, did so inside and at the invitation of a Masonic lodge.[21]

Butler's passage may seem on the surface as though it has nothing to do with spirituality, but her reference to the ancient Egyptians is extremely telling, insofar as one can read into it a familiarity with ancient Kemetic (KMTic) knowledge systems, also known as the Egyptian mysteries. Admittedly, this is detective work, but also the work of archaeology and the work of hermeneutics. It is related to womanist spirituality today insofar as certain knowledges and certain ways of being in the world have been transmitted along this unbroken thread not unlike the threads of Christianity, African traditional religions, Islam, Native American religions, Judaism, and so on. Submerged though they may be, their contributions remain significant. I argue that they are crucial to understanding the womanist idea.

African novelist Ayi Kwei Armah explores these connections in a work of historically grounded metaphysical fiction called *KMT: In the House of Life*.[22] In this story, a twentieth century scholar by the name of Lindela, who is situated in a fictional West African locale, conducts research on a series of KMTic scroll fragments spanning 3,910 years that have been preserved by an isolated community of adepts in her country. These scrolls, which are based on actual KMTic hieroglyphic texts, tell the story of two philosophical camps—the Sharers, whose symbol is the sphere, and the Keepers, whose symbol is the pyramid—in competition for control of society. The Sharers advocate for keeping mystical knowledge public and accessible through the maintenance of community mystery schools, while the Keepers advocate for an elite priesthood that regulates access to the knowledge through a process of gatekeeping and trials. The Sharers, which were the original group in ancient KMT and the authors of the scrolls examined by Lindela, included women and men and were characterized by gender equality and a nonhierarchical political structure. In fact, the majority of the scrolls were composed by women—although this did not occur until after the development of writing, well into the Sharers' history. It was, in fact, the development of writing that allowed the Keepers to evolve first, as a subgroup within the Sharers and, later, the Sharers' chief nemesis. The Keepers, once they established themselves by aligning and ingratiating themselves with political and military power and placing esoteric knowledge in the service of both, rejected female participation and sent the Sharers into exile, which is how they ended up in West Africa. The Sharers, meanwhile, continued to cultivate esoteric knowledge as a means toward peace, healing, scientific discovery, artistic creativity, and personal illumination, inviting all so inclined to join them. As the Keeper-based philosophy gained ascendancy, fewer and fewer people joined or even knew about the Sharers, until their perspective was nearly completely submerged and they had virtually been written out of history.

I link this story to womanism because the Sharers' perspective and practice, as presented in the novel, bears numerous similarities to womanism. Depending on the degree of historical verisimilitude in this text, it is possible that the womanist idea, by whatever name, has roots that are deeper than our current world system, which very much resembles the Keeper system. In the novel, the Sharers were very much about the democratization of esoteric knowledge, viewing it as humans' common birthright and a sine qua non of the full realization of humans' innate divinity. Thus, their horizonal form of social organization was Luxocratic, even though this term was not used. Their implicit aim of gradually producing a Luxocratic society was thwarted by the rapid and violent ascent of the Keepers, who effectively shut down the Sharers. Yet, they survived and, the novel implies, through Lindela's translation and publication of the contents of the scrolls for modern society, the Sharer thoughtform might reestablish itself, just in time to preempt the worst perils precipitated by thousands of years of Keeper influence.

The secret societies associated with initiatic orders that relate their origins to ancient KMT[23] are not the only ones shaping African thought, as numerous societies also existed and continue to exist in West Africa. Sylvia Ardyn Boone, for instance, in her book *Radiance from the Waters*, described in detail certain aspects of the West African Sande society, a women's initiatic society with major influence on the social, metaphysical, domestic, and aesthetic understandings, beliefs, and values of West African women.[24] Presumably, although I have not yet seen it documented in scholarship, these understandings traveled with West African women to the New World and all throughout the African diaspora. One example might be the so-called politics of respectability associated with the Black Women's Club Movement of the early twentieth century,[25] which are remarkably similar to the domestic and aesthetic values associated with Sande society philosophy. Bennetta Jules-Rosette documents some relationship between African women's initiatic or secret societies and the character of charismatic and Apostolic churches in West and South-Central Africa,[26] suggesting that transfer and synthesis do occur when Western and African spiritual systems come into contact.

Personal, Visionary, and Pragmatic

Let us jump ahead to the period from 1979 to 1989, during which the three women whom I name in chapter 2 as progenitors of womanism were publishing their groundbreaking work. Let us first hone in on two of them, namely, Alice Walker and Chikwenye Okonjo Ogunyemi. Each of these women has shaped contemporary womanist spirituality in different yet intertwining ways. The ways in which they have done so reflect past lineages and engender new ones.

Alice Walker's own life and career, embodying womanist thought and activism, have encompassed numerous spiritual traditions.[27] In her writing and activist praxis, we can observe the legacy of the ubiquitous Christianity of the Black Church during the Civil Rights era; Earth-based traditions rooted in numerous indigenous lifesystems, from Native American Indian to Meso-American to African to Oceanic; and Buddhism along with other contemplative traditions, such as Transcendental Meditation (TM). We can trace the threads of these influences through her activism during the 1970s and 1980s, including antinuclear and environmental activism, as well as her creative work and nonfiction writing up to the present.[28]

I like to look at the circuit that has been covered between her inaugural womanist text, "Coming Apart," and her first twenty-first century novel, *Now Is the Time to Open Your Heart*. Although neither of these are considered her most famous or most critically acclaimed pieces, for our purposes, they are among the most illuminating in terms of examining the way that spirituality works in womanism. "Coming Apart" focuses on an African American husband and wife who are struggling around the wife's reaction to her husband's consumption of pornography. The wife is disturbed by the way her husband's feelings toward her are mediated by his magazine induced cathexis on depersonalized nude white women. She wishes to be regarded differently, although she wishes to abandon neither her marriage, in particular, nor "the black man," in general. What moves this story along is the wife's gradual awakening to feminist consciousness through her reading of three real-life black feminist authors who are quoted in the story: Audre Lorde, Luisah Teish, and Tracey A. Gardner. Crucial moments in the story revolve around the wife's establishment of a self-defined and culturally sensitive gender politics that Alice Walker, in a fourth-wall authorial insertion, names "womanist." There is no mention of spirituality in this story; it lurks quietly behind the veil. We know this, because in her next womanist piece, "Gifts of Power: The Writings of Rebecca Jackson," Alice Walker blows the topic up.[29] *That* essay is all about spirituality, pure and raw. So, we have to read backwards and forwards and backwards again to get the full picture.

Fast forward to *Now Is the Time to Open Your Heart*, published in 2004.[30] This meandering novel traverses two geographies: the interior geography of a middle-aged "New Age" African American woman and the exterior geography of her unconventional, midtransformation relationship with a "New Age" African American man who also happens to be feminist/womanist. Kate, the story's female protagonist, goes on a number of "vision quests"—one down the Colorado River, another into the Amazonian rainforest—on a search for the invisible realm, its powerful inhabitants, and the center of her Self. These quests refigure her relationship with Yolo, the man in her life. As in "Coming Apart," spiritual concerns (loosely defined, admittedly) are played out in the arena of sexuality, although at different ends of the spectrum: the partners in "Coming Apart" make love, while the partners in *Now Is the Time* come to terms with celibacy. There is a concealed allusion to the double entendre of the much earlier story, "Coming Apart"—an intricate demonstration of the many ways the threads of spirituality interlace psyches and bind intimate relationships.

Now Is the Time's Kate could be the wife in "Coming Apart" twenty years later, now divorced, having gone deeper into feminism and womanism, having experimented with same-gender-loving experiences, having "gone New Age," and now trying to sort it all out. This nonlinear neo-Odyssean journey with inward and outward directions could define the womanist process of coming into consciousness, moving through consciousness, and ultimately expanding consciousness beyond the usual parameters of political speech, then trying to figure out how to speak again in political contexts and to political problems in contemporary society—all without scripts! Through this story we see how the process of coming at spirituality from a womanist angle is very personal. Indeed, the person *is* the coordinating mechanism, the "differential," to use Chela Sandoval's metaphor, that makes the multilayered multiplicity of experiences and knowledges make sense.[31] Stated differently, holism is made through and by the person.

Now we turn to Chikwenye Okonjo Ogunyemi, who has forcefully infused womanism with a blend of Yoruba and Igbo spirituality that complements and enlarges, if not relocates and refigures, Western-centric formulations of womanism. At the center of this enterprise stands the majestic, alluring, and powerful figure of Osun, whose unique blend of female attributes challenges both feminist *and* feminine ideals of women's power and agency.[32] This work is best elaborated in Ogunyemi's 1996 book, *Africa Wo/Man Palava: The Nigerian Novel by Women*, particularly in the chapters titled, "An Excursion into Woman's (S)(p)ace" and "(En)gender(ing) Discourse: Palaver-Palava," which make up the section called "Kwenu: A Vernacular Theory," in which she constructs womanist theory.[33] *Kwenu* is "a cry for attention, for order, an invitation to modify the tenor of the debate, and, finally, a ratification of what has been determined."[34] It is also "a shrill, urgent call that must be heeded, to recognize and ratify the decision-making process," whose "intent is to silence needless protest or dissidence." Another translation is, "Consent!" in the imperative tense. "Reiterated during a palaver"—or argument, empty words, conversation going nowhere, and maintaining the status quo—"it guarantees submission, integrity, total agreement with the common will, and unity in action." More, "its exhilarative and affirmative effect magically transforms dissonance, which a disintegrating community can ill afford." Thus, it is "a gambit, inviting the audience to say yes to a joint decision."

The "vernacular theory" in question, then, is womanism. And the cry "Kwenu!" that precedes it is thus an invitation to allow womanism to "solve the problem" and "restore order" or "bring peace": To what?—to world affairs, to humanity's ailing psyche, to Planet Earth. This is the foundation for the practicality, the pragmatism, of womanist spirituality.

What does Osun, the water Orisa, the divinity of the rivers, bring to this endeavor? A model of womanhood that is redemptive: A problem-solver. A mediator. A genius. A captivating lover. A mother. A savvy businesswoman. An *Iyalode*. A hair plaiter. A strategist. A woman with *asé*—the "authority to effect a change or make things happen."[35] She gets us "outta this mess." A woman who can "save the world." Her story is telling. Ogunyemi tells it thus:

> In one oral version, Osun, charged with (re)production, was the lone female among seventeen orisa sent by Olodumare, the supreme deity, to establish the world. Since they disrespected her by failing to consult her to make the colony function smoothly, she withdrew from them. In the ensuing postcolonial crisis, the world suffered from the repercussions of the quarrel for, during her strike, she did not permit rain to fall. The drought caused chronic shortages in diverse areas of the productive process, even though, quite tellingly, she was pregnant, a condition which served as her ace. Isolated, she continued to ply her vocation of hair plaiting by the river named after her, firmly establishing her autonomy. As Osun is both orisa and the essence of the river without which there would be no civilization, the male orisa were panic stricken. They appealed to Olodumare for help to right matters. The supreme deity ordered them to reconcile with Osun, who, as hair plaiter, holds a crucial portfolio as she is also in charge of aesthetics and fate, which is ori in Yoruba, the word that doubles for head, the seat of reason and one's destiny. For success and harmony, woman's place in the scheme of things had to be guaranteed. In the ensuing negotiations, she promised that, if she had a son, he would act as a mediator between her and them, but if she had a daughter, she would have

added support in maintaining her difference, and there would be an impasse. The male orisa, marveling at the magic of the womb, stunned by the silence of the womb which they could not hear, the darkness of the womb which they could not read, the mystery of the womb which they could not decipher, prayed fervently for a son.... The conciliatory moves became fruitful when Osun gave birth to the male child Osetura, the name the babalawo use for Esu. Still autonomous and different, Osun had saved the world.[36]

It is not insignificant that that "male" child was Esu, Orisa of the crossroads, of the border between light and dark, the human and the divine, sometimes depicted as an androgynous or bisexual figure, as one who is indeterminate or beyond/outside gender. He, like his mother, is the bridge and the mediator, the connector and the go-between—yet he is the "male version," not unlike Yolo in Walker's *Now Is the Time*. The relationship between Osun and Esu helps us to explore and understand how diarchy, masculinity, and feminism can all work together in unexpected ways. This is a spiritual gift from the Yoruba/Igbo/Ifa lifesystem.

Both Osun and Esu, as well as Ogunyemi's treatment of womanism generally, help us see the eclectic, synthetic, holistic, and personal nature of womanist spirituality. On one level, we can think about the global spread of Ifa-based religion from Africa to all sectors of the African diaspora, even beyond people of African descent (if there is such a thing), and we can observe how Ifa melded with and transmuted other religions, creating new lifesystems. On another level, we can think about how Ogunyemi bridged and interwove Yoruba, Igbo, and Western/postcolonial thought frames in her construction of womanist theory, or how African descent women in the West have integrated Yoruba, Igbo, and Ifa spirituality into their own lives as a means of spiritual emancipation—a topic treated by Shani Settles.[37] On another level, we can think about how Osun and Esu are feminine and masculine mirrors of one another, interrelated as parent and child, reflecting Osun's maternal power and Esu's filial feminism.[38] On another level, we can consider how Ogunyemi's womanism interpolates with that of Walker and also Clenora Hudson-Weems. Although spirituality does not figure prominently in Hudson-Weems's Africana womanism, it is, once again, behind the scenes, shaping historically and psychically the (pan-)Africanity that she does reference overtly. Individual womanists all over the world draw from and holistically synthesize these threads in highly individualized and profoundly personal ways, re-creating womanism all over again each and every time they do so. Womanism, thus, is the sum total of all these personal re-creations.

Womanism is triply visionary: It envisions the resolution of human–human conflict; it envisions the healing of the Earth, and more specifically, the reconciliation of humanity and Earth; and it envisions a restoration of harmony and acknowledged relationship between humans and the spiritual/transcendental realm. This is the "womanist triad." These "big problems" are both *simple* and *critical*, and they are what womanists concern themselves with; they are what the womanist idea addresses. Womanists, then, focus on "the bigger picture" and actively define horizons. At the same time, however, womanists focus on the immediate, the everyday, seeing the relation between "above" and "below," "within" and "without." This perspective is nascent within so many different lifesystems that it is nearly impossible that a worldview as global and encompassing as womanism would not reflect it in manifold ways.

How does womanist spirituality relate to this? Spirituality is a *means* of transformation; spirit is the *root* or *foundation* of transformation itself. To change the world is to change spirit first, and to change spirit is to change self. Thus, self-change is the heart and the mechanism of social change. Spiritual practice *is* activism, because it changes the energy of things and initiates a chain reaction eventuating in a transformed outcome. As indicated in chapter 1, change begins with vision, whether that vision is conscious or unconscious. Womanism incorporates this perspective, implicitly and explicitly.

To deal in the invisible world—to see it, to communicate with it, to work it—is the logical upshot of both womanist spirituality and spiritual activism. In this sense, womanism reflects a system of beliefs and practices that some would call magical. What if "magical realism" were real? This is the question implicitly posed by womanism. "Magic" simply refers to energy manipulation of the unseen forces and powers of the universe, and manipulation of the material world by means of these unseen forces and powers (see chapter 6). For many womanists, it *is* real. Magic as such is generally denigrated (and I use this word intentionally) by academics as irrational, primitive, empirically nonverifiable, unsystematic, and intellectually immature. From a womanist perspective, it is another way of thinking, another way of cogitating, another way of understanding; one that does not compete with rationality, but, rather, overlays it. It is another kind of logic, and a highly systematic one at that. Indeed, one must be schooled in it to be proficient. Womanists do not own it, but they circulate in this thought system.

I should state that womanists generally do not use the term *magic* to refer to what they do. Indeed, I hesitate to use the word *magic*, although sometimes it is the quickest entrée into this topic; that is, how womanists move energy for social change and problem solving. As I state in *The Womanist Reader*,

"Spiritual activities involve communication between the material and spiritual realms, based on the assumption that these realms are actual, interconnected, and interpenetrating."[39] We all know the terminologies—prayer, meditation, ritual, visualization—so ubiquitous are they in everyday life. As I also write, the purpose of these methods is "to draw spiritual energy toward social, political, and even physical problem solving and healing."[40] What is different about womanism, as compared to other critical theories and social movement modalities, is that it *encourages* the use of these methods for the *explicit* purpose of social change, beginning with healing ourselves and the Earth. As I write, "Spiritual methods of social transformation, which may be exercised by individuals or groups, recognize not only the value of power based in the spiritual realm that can be applied toward human problems, but also the importance of maintaining a harmonious relationship between humans, the environment, and the spiritual realm."[41] Social change, for womanists, begins with healing. Womanist spirituality and womanism generally is wellness-oriented, with an emphasis on people and nature instead of ideologies and institutions. In a social movement arena that is accustomed to confrontation, struggle, "war," and a host of battles, womanism is simply another way of thinking about and doing activism and being in the world.

THE ROLE OF THE PERSONAL SPIRITUAL JOURNEY

In her book *Soul Talk: The New Spirituality of African American Women* (2001), Akasha Gloria Hull uses Toni Cade Bambara's classic novel, *The Salt Eaters*, as a point of departure to discuss an emergent form of synthetic spirituality that she has observed among many of her peers:

> What is different in this book is the profound and wholly respectful attention accorded to these more traditional racial aspects, as well as to astrology, past lives and reincarnation, Tarot cards, the metaphysical extensions of quantum physics, chakras and energy, Sufi tales, psychic telepathy, numerology, ancient black Egyptian wisdom traditions, Eastern philosophies of cosmic connectedness, and so forth—in short, an array of alternative knowledge systems founded on the belief that this visible "phenomenal" world is the external reflection of an underlying "noumenal" reality that can—and indeed, should—be tapped for the full and optimum functioning of life in material form. In other words, *The Salt Eaters* validated largely unknown or discredited (by black people and whites), *non*-rational ways of knowing—and

promoted the idea that *we will function more effectively if we use the unseen energy that surrounds us.*[42]

Although she does not call it womanist, the eclectic, synthetic, holistic, self-authored spirituality she describes bears a great deal of resemblance to womanist spirituality as I have described it. The women she describes and interviews for the book are all "politically conscious" in ways defined by the progressive left since the 1960s (they include Alice Walker, Lucille Clifton, Dolores Kendrick, Sonia Sanchez, Michele Gibbs, Geraldine McIntosh, Masani Alexis DeVeaux, Namonyah Soipan, and the now late Toni Cade Bambara). All of these women have been political activists or politically inspired artists; all have expressed strong African-centered cultural affinities; and all were raised in the Black Church. Yet, at the time of the writing, all had redefined their spirituality on the basis of new information, new insights, or new experiences that could no longer be contained within the old mold, whether politically or in terms of religion. All of these women, including Hull herself, had experienced revelations and epiphanies, some subtle, some stark, which turned into transformations of their spiritual and political selves. Hull writes:

> For all of us, 1980 was a turning point. It was the year we each independently began exploring radically different spiritual teachings and paths, avenues that were less traditional for African American women and that brought us in confluence with the rapidly accreting New Age—even as we instinctively played out the realities of race and gender that defined us and gave shape and meaning to our lives.... [W]e simultaneously applied our new learning to black subject matter, found spiritual transcendence in black revolutionary struggle, and sought metaphysical origins in Africa.[43]

These things included acceptance of supernatural phenomena, spiritual study of diverse traditions (including divination), the development of "astral proficiency," and increasing meditation practice. Over time, it led to the conclusion that "*being spiritual* is also a legitimate way to participate in social struggle."[44] Stated differently, "Many contemporary African American women take spiritual development seriously, understanding it as one more tool in the arsenal we use to help ourselves and the wider world."[45] To the point, "We are beginning to envision a new kind of politics fundamentally grounded in spirituality and not simply strengthened by it,"[46] that is, "a more spiritually informed vision of what is necessary to achieve revolution."[47]

Hull's interviews and reflections give substance to the tenets of womanist spirituality described above as well as to the more specific concept of spiritualized politics. On the one hand, "African American women orient toward useful and daily spiritual practices—those that they weave into their household environment and activities, those that are simple but effective ways of affirming divine connection."[48] The women in her informal and highly personal study tended to "do something spiritual" every day. On the other hand, these women develop a firm grasp on the big picture, namely, that "there is an order larger than this visible one that holds everything together."[49] According to Hull, "Because it is normally not stated and because it makes space for both 'religious' and 'scientific' paths to the divine, this is the root, the defining reality of spirituality that I always try to emphasize."[50] Her assertion alludes to similar understandings within other wisdom traditions about multiple pathways to the same Divine/Cosmic point of union, such as the *bhakhti* (devotion) and *gnani* (wisdom) paths in Vedanta/Hinduism[51] and the red rose (devotion) and white lily (intellectual) paths in the Qabalistic Tarot.[52] This suggestion in turn illuminates contemporary debates about esoteric/religious vs. scientific paths to ultimate understandings about the nature and origins of the Universe or God. Within the view proposed by Hull and common to womanists, all these paths end up in the same place—SOURCE—and all are open, and all are valuable.

Hull's text focuses on African American experiences, demonstrating some of the culturally specific pathways to spiritual conscientization for members of the U.S. Black community. Toni Cade Bambara, for example, speaks of the role of Black community bookstores, particularly those with "special black gnostic books" and "sometimes little study groups" that focused on such books.[53] Through such exposure, participants gain "a sense of spirituality as both metaphysics-religion and world activism."[54] As Hull commented about her own path, "I learned beyond a shadow of a doubt that the spiritual universe is another, inner world, complete with its own inhabitants, occurrences, and laws..." and "I was learning the wisdom handed down through the ages about the constitution and operation of the spiritual universe. I was gaining enough theoretical and experiential understanding about spirituality to write this book.... All that time, this was my real 'research' and preparation, not the old tried-and-true spinning of scholarly wheels." Ultimately, Hull concludes, "Black people's spirituality—if acknowledged and consciously used—could be an awesome force" because of "the metaphysical role people from the African continent and the triangular slave trade have played in the spiritualization of the globe."[55] For purposes of this discussion, the womanist idea obtains a unique quantum of potency from its original location within African-based spiritual understandings, globally flung, transculturally synthesized, then reinterpreted and rearticulated through the visionary pragmatism of Black women whose focus is the well-being of all people and the Earth.[56] Although it is important to reiterate that womanism is now the province of all humanity, Black women's originary Afro-spiritual influence on womanism formed its basic blueprint, and the eclectic spiritual journeys of contemporary Black women and other women of color, whose cosmologies are often markedly similar, have given womanism its distinct cultural-spiritual-political flavor.[57]

Numerous authors, many of them academics and activists have documented their journeys of spiritual and political transformation or written powerfully on spiritualized politics. Examples include Gloria Anzaldúa, M. Jacqui Alexander, AnaLouise Keating, and Barbara A. Holmes. In her essay, "Pedagogies of the Sacred: Making the Invisible Tangible" which appears in *Pedagogies of Crossing*, for example, M. Jacqui Alexander writes of her own journey to and through African-based spiritualities associated with Yoruba/Ifa and Bantu-Kongo cultures—such as minkisi, Ifa, Orisa, Lucumi, Santeria, Vodun, Winti, and Espiritsmo—and the way that it opened up not only her research, but her life.[58] She writes of a particular time in her scholarly life when she had writer's block and how the embodiment of her research "subject" Thisbe, self-renamed as Kitsimba, spoke through her:

In 1989, I had embarked on a project on the ways in which African cosmologies and modes of healing became the locus of an epistemic struggle in nineteenth-century Trinidad, the period marking the establishment of the slave plantation economy and the consolidation of the colonial state. My intent was to use an array of documents surrounding the trial, torture, and execution of Thisbe, one of those captured and forced into the Crossing, who was accused of "sorcery, divination and holding frequent concourse with the devil." I wanted to show the ways in which the body had become central in the contest between European and African systems: positioned as moveable property—chattel—and as repository of sin, or understood as the direct instrument of the Divine, mediator between the world of the living and the world of the dead. I used this approach in order to move beyond the more dominant understanding of African spiritual practice as cultural retention and survival, to get inside of the meaning of the spiritual as epistemological, that is, to pry open the terms, symbols, and organizational codes that the Bantu-Kongo people used to make sense of the world. I had surmised that cosmological systems housed memory, and that such memory was necessary to distill the psychic traumas produced under the grotesque conditions of slavery. How, why, and under what conditions do a people remember? Do spiritual practices atrophy? Or do they move underground, assuming a different form? What is the threat that certain memory poses?[59]

As we see, all of these are very intellectual questions, methods, and processes. Yet, for Alexander, they resulted in a psychic and scholarly impasse that manifested as writer's block. She continues:

> What once seemed a legitimate set of questions to understand the plantation figure Thisbe were entirely inadequate to the task of knowing Kitsimba, who was waiting to be discovered. I first had to confront the limits of the methodology I had devised to know her. While legal and missionary documents gave me proximate access to daily life, they were unable to convey the interior of lived experience, the very category I needed to inhabit in order to understand how cosmological systems are grounded and expressed. Reading against the grain to fill in the spaces of an absent biography was not sufficient. I couldn't rely on the knowledge derived from books, not even on the analytic compass that I myself had drawn. Moreover, I had to scrutinize my own motivations for embarking on the project, as well as to figure out why I had been delegated to go in search of Thisbe's life. In short, I had to begin to inhabit that unstable space of not knowing, of admitting that I did not even know how to begin to know. Divested of the usual way of posing questions, I became vulnerable and experienced the kind of crisis that is named "writer's block."[60]

This is when and where Alexander's epiphanic breakthrough took place. She writes:

> It was this that led me to examine the recalcitrance that masked an unacknowledged yearning for Spirit. Propelled to seek a different source, I began to undertake linguistic spiritual work with a Bakongo teacher so that I could follow Thisbe from a plantation located about seven miles from the Mojuba crossroads of my childhood back to the Mayombe region of Central Africa to discover Kitsimba, who refused to be cluttered beneath an array of documents of any kind, whether generated by the state, the plantation owners, or by me. It was in that basement in the Bronx, New York, that she manifested her true name, Kitsimba—not the plantation name Thisbe—and placed it back into the lineage that she remembered and to which she belonged. From then I began the tentative writing of a history that was different from the one I had inherited, knowing that I could no longer continue to conduct myself as if Kitsimba's life were not bound inextricably with my own.[61]

In case it is unclear what happened here, Alexander's scholarly subject, a historical figure known as Thisbe, "showed up" in the spiritually dedicated space of the Bronx basement of a Bantu-Kongo priest who was teaching Alexander, renamed herself Kitsimba (her precrossing African name), and began delivering direct knowledge of her history to Alexander. Alexander's days of scholarly conjecture and speculation on Thisbe were instantly morphed into a directly narrated autobiographical account of Kitsimba by Kitsimba. From there forward, Alexander was in a spiritually (un)mediated relationship with her historical subject, and, as she later relates, the relations between author and subject arguably even became subverted, as Kitsimba began, at times and in ways, to narrate and author Alexander's life. This experience refigured Alexander's understandings not only of Thisbe/Kitsimba, but also of scholarship, of spirituality, and of self.

This chapter, "Pedagogies of the Sacred," which serves as the concluding chapter in Alexander's highly regarded and groundbreaking text *Pedagogies of Crossing: Meditations on Feminism, Sexual Politics, Memory, and the Sacred,* functions as something of a spiritual coming out story. I define a "spiritual coming out story" as a narrative in which a person discloses the depth and breadth of her or his spiritual commitments or experiences to an audience likely to view these with skepticism, possibly to the point of discrediting the individual to whom they belong. Coming out spiritually is a risk, particularly to academics and activists (how much more so to corporate or governmental actors?) who circulate within and whose currency is built upon a materialistic world/view in which five-sense realities and rationalistic empiricism dominate to the exclusion of other epistemic possibilities. To say, "I know because I received the knowledge directly from a spiritual source" in a social arena where the highest form of knowledge is considered to be logical deduction or scientific induction, both of which are probabilistic and speculative, is to expose oneself to a very real kind of danger.[62] Yet, more and more people are "coming out" because what they find in these "spiritual realms" brings a level of clarity about and liberation from—not to mention power to transform—the ails and perils of the logico-scientific world that simply cannot be replicated within the currently dominant paradigm. As more and more people come out in this fashion, a groundswell is forming and a consciousness shift is perceptibly occurring. Womanism is one visible manifestation of this shift and movement, which is why, in chapter 3, I characterized womanism as *spiritual* movement.

Womanism, unlike many other academic or social change modalities, is unafraid of these audacious spiritual forays. Indeed, it welcomes them and is enriched by them. Let me provide a few additional illustrations to give substance to this point. One text where this relationship of enrichment really becomes apparent is *Interviews/Entrevistas*, a compendium of interviews with Gloria E. Anzaldúa edited by AnaLouise Keating, who herself makes an appearance in the text as meta-interviewer and interpreter. The very introduction to this text sets the tone with the title "Risking the Personal." As I have discussed with Keating on more than one occasion, this book is more often read for its content about borderlands, lesbianism, queer politics, and Chicana feminism than for its content about spirituality—a fact that underrecognizes how spirituality undergirds all of these things for Anzaldúa. Concepts such as *nepantla, conocimiento, nagualismo, la diosa,* and *la facultad* all resonate with deep spiritual and cosmological meaning and method in ways that deserve closer investigation. Anzaldua herself was aware of this when she stated:

> The "safe" elements in *Borderlands* are appropriated and used, and the "unsafe" elements are ignored. One of the things that doesn't get talked about is the connection between body, mind, and spirit. Nor is anything that has to do with the sacred, anything that has to do with the spirit. As long as it's theoretical and about history, about borders, that's fine; borders are a concern that everybody has. But when I start talking about *nepantla*—as border between the spirit, the psyche, and the mind or as a process—they resist."[63]

What are these "unsafe" elements of which she speaks? *Interviews/Entrevistas* is replete with them. To repeat Keating's summary, "near-death experiences, meditations, astrological signs, spirits, and extraterrestrial beings." I might also add to this list accounts of esoteric reading material, explorations into quantum physics, and occult or divinatory practices, such as Tarot card reading, I Ching throwing, and visits to psychics. Even her own life story is "unsafe" in many respects, with her accounts of being forcibly inhabited by a succession of spirits, some of them extraterrestrial, beginning in infancy, and the impact this had on her consciousness—spiritual, political, and sexual. The full details of Anzaldúa's life story are beyond the scope of this chapter; however, they should be examined closely for full impact and illumination. To give a sense of what Anzaldúa's personal journey was like, I draw from some of her interviews: "When I was young, I went to several churches to see what they were doing.... My religion was the stories my mother and father would tell, which had to do with spirits, with devils.... My religion was more like the earth religions of the Indians, which people now call witchcraft. I believed that certain people have powers, like the curanderas."[64] "I became involved with spirituality [around 1974]. I went to some lectures given by a Buddhist. I started doing the I Ching, the Tarot, and psychic readings.... I was reading *Seth Speaks* [note: she also read Sri Aurobindo and Satprem].... I was really quite into the occult...I was also studying surrealism, avant garde literatures, and Spanish ... I use my coins. I used to have divination rocks. Or I meditate and the answer comes."[65] Anzaldúa also admits that having a vision (possibly entheogenically stimulated) was a turning point.[66] These snippets give the flavor of a far-ranging spiritual curiosity, courageous levels of exploration, and a creatively synthetic yet purposeful tendency.

Although she only saw the first few years of the twenty-first century, Anzaldúa felt certain that a shift would gain momentum early in the new millennium. She predicted:

> Once the century turns, more people will believe in the existence of something greater than the physical world. If you think of reality as a continuum or a spectrum, the reality we see with our eyes, hear with our ears, smell with our nose, and touch with our fingers—that spectrum is a skinny little territory. Parts of a person are unknown to that person or to the culture but are known through dreams, imagination, spiritual experiences, or intuitive feelings. If science is going to continue as the reigning paradigm, it will have to change its story, change the way it controls reality, and begin acknowledging the paranormal, intuition, and subjective inner life.[67]

The result of all this spiritual exploration and eclectic practice is profound. It is a transformative understanding about human beings, identity, society, and justice:

> I'm a citizen of the universe. I think it's good to claim your ethnic identity and your racial identity. But it's also the source of all the wars and all the violence, all these borders and walls people erect. I'm tired of borders and I'm tired of walls. I don't believe in nationalism. I don't believe that we're better than the people in India or that we're different from people in Ethiopia.... [P]eople talk about being proud to be American, Mexican, or Indian. We have grown beyond that. We are specks from this cosmic ocean, the soul, or whatever. We're not better than people from Africa or people from Russia. If something happens to the people in India or Africa—and they're starving to death and dying—then that's happening to us, too.[68]

As she says, "I've always had a planetary vision, not just a regional or even a national one."[69] This theme of universal, or cosmic, citizenship, is taken even further in Anzaldúa's final published article, "... and now let us shift," in *This Bridge We Call Home*, which I discuss in greater detail in the next chapter. Nevertheless, her personal spiritual journey eventuated in a place that is consistent with themes I identify with womanist vision and the metaphysical architecture of the womanist idea; namely, planetary identity and a sense of self that expands to encompass not only all humans, not only all livingkind, but also the entire universe—and the inner light.

FROM COSMOLOGY TO THE COSMOS: WHEN SCIENCE IS PART OF THE SPIRITUAL JOURNEY

Like Anzaldúa, Barbara A. Holmes, a feminist/womanist theologian and legal scholar, has incorporated cosmic themes into her discussions of identity, community, and social change, however, from a distinctly different angle—that of quantum science. Holmes has written a provocative book entitled *Race and the Cosmos: An Invitation to View the World Differently*,[70] in which she situates our most entrenched human–human and human–environment conflicts into a spiritual context that explicitly embraces science. Her text reflects how deep study of quantum physics, theoretical physics, and astrophysics (aka cosmology) has been part of her personal spiritual journey. She writes, for example:

> I am suggesting that we view issues of race and liberation from the perspective of the cosmos, and that we begin to incorporate the languages of science into our discussions of liberation. This is a reasonable choice given the reality that the universe is an integral aspect of any human endeavor, even when it is a taken-for-granted backdrop for our activities. I am challenging all justice seekers to awaken to the vibrant and mysterious worlds of quantum physics and cosmology. Recent discoveries on cosmic and quantum levels are as dramatic as the realization that the sun does not rotate around the earth. Now, at the beginning of the twenty-first century, all the narratives that frame reality have been unsettled by Hubble's unblinking eye and strangely responsive but unseen quantum elements. From cosmic and quantum levels, we learn that we are connected to one another in unexpected ways. Theoretical physics suggests that even when separated, entities that have once been in contact will react to changes in the other....

In an age of astounding scientific findings that allude to a world that is holistic, relational, and intrinsically diverse, most of us are conducting business as usual. We pay homage to fallen leaders of the liberation movements on dates of their demise or birth, and we reminisce about valiant skirmishes for justice during the 1960s. Nostalgic strains of freedom songs loop in our collective memories as symbols of the struggles, optimism, and determination of the era. But the energy for liberation has dissipated and the impetus for justice has stalled.[71]

In case the implications of this science/spirituality/social change interface are unclear, she writes:

> To consider our lives within the scope of a planetary system that is billions of years old would put our race/class/gender scuffles into perspective. To realize the rarity of blue/green life sustaining planets in the cosmos would put ecology on the top of the priority list. The awakening begins when we finally sneak a peek upward or inward. In those moments, it's difficult not to "know" that we are connected to vast mysteries.[72]

Furthermore:

> Difference can then be viewed as variations on a theme. What we shall be has not yet appeared, because images of human embodiment don't subsume human potential. Although people appear to be black, white, or brown; gay, straight, or bi; male or female; able or disabled, these are resonances that reflect a universe that appreciates and solicits difference. Sexuality, gender, class, and race are not deterministic categories; rather, they are fugues and etudes in a larger and more complex symphony. As a consequence, those who exhibit particular ways of embodiment should be neither assigned static moral value nor divested of it. We are beings of light and dark and difference. We are dying and transcending death. The complexities seem almost musical to scientists.[73]

Finally,

> Any community that we construct on earth will be only a small model of a universe whose community includes billions of stars and planetary systems. Are we alone? We don't know, but if we don't know how to become a community with our own species, how shall we find harmony in the cosmos? Our ideas of community begin with fragmentation, difference, and disparity seeking wholeness. Our beloved community is an attempt to hot glue disparate cultures, languages, and ethnic origins into one mutually committed whole. The universe tells a completely different story—that everything is enfolded into everything.[74]

Holmes's perspective is interesting and important for several reasons. For one thing, it represents a twist on the "spiritual coming out story," insofar as Holmes, a theologian, reveals that her spiritual perspective is heavily influenced by a nontheological domain, namely, hard science. Other authors, such as Hull and Anzaldúa, have mentioned that reading about quantum physics has shaped their thought, but none has gone as far with the discussion as Holmes, who made it a central organizing principle of her spiritualized social theory and social change perspective. I argue that inclusion of the cosmos in this way is consistent with, if not illustrative of, the womanist idea. Womanism is essentially a cosmic perspective: it "reaches for the stars" in more ways than one, whether through its evocation of ancient African cosmologies to which "the stars" are central (such as the Dogon of Mali, the Borana of southern Ethiopia and Northern Kenya, or the Shona of Zimbabwe),[75] its unapologetic embrace of "celestial" knowledge systems/divination methods such as astrology, or its consciousness of the emerging Age of Aquarius,[76] which portends the previously mentioned "shift" in both consciousness and social organization for human beings as well as a cosmic rebalancing of the gender energies on Earth.

The spiritual archaeology of womanism is basically about tracing the progression of eclectic spiritual source material through the process of synthesis and the creation of new spiritual holisms that are both visionary and pragmatic through the personal spiritual journeys of "outrageous, audacious, courageous [and] *willful*" women who "love Spirit" and "love the Folk" and love themselves, "regardless."

The spiritual archaeology of womanism is basically about looking backwards through the personal spiritual journeys of "outrageous, audacious, courageous [and] willful" women who "love Spirit" to observe how diverse spiritual influences have shaped the womanist idea. This exercise also allows us to consider the notion of Source; that is, the possible unified underpinnings of all lifesystems and a future in which universal acceptance of the Inner Light, Innate Divinity, guides humanity toward a new form of social organization, namely, LUXOCRACY, or "rule by Light." As I see it, these are two contributions of the womanist idea to the broader humanity and to humanity's future at this time of crisis.

THE WOMANIST SPIRITUAL JOURNEY: "WANTING TO KNOW MORE AND IN GREATER DEPTH THAN IS CONSIDERED 'GOOD' FOR ONE"

A distinguishing attribute of the womanist as defined by Alice Walker in her famous 1983 definition is "wanting to know more and in greater depth than is considered 'good' for one."[77] This phrase is perhaps the best characterization of womanist spirituality and the womanist spiritual attitude. The phrase implies *intense* curiosity as well as a willingness, if not a compulsion to "turn over rocks," dig through attics, convene in cellars, sneak around in libraries, sit with elders, converse with babies, wander through forests, listen to the ocean, analyze dreams, call down spirits, play with cards, visit psychics, meditate, and pray to Jesus/Buddha/Muhammad/Krishna/Moses/Baha'u'llah/Osun/Isis/Ma'at/Mary/Kuan Yin/Coatlicue-Cihuacotal-Tlazolteotl-Tonantzin-Guadalupe[78]/the altar of Myself to pursue life's mysteries, get answers, and generate new questions.

"Received religion" doesn't usually work for womanists unless they have "put it through the fire" and mixed it up with other things that also seem to make sense and make life better. This attribute is womanist spiritual curiosity, and it inevitably leads to womanist spiritual eclecticism, which has already been elaborated. Womanist spiritual eclecticism manifests through philomathic reading and media grazing, blending practice and spiritual experimentation, fluid community life and diverse spiritual relationships, communion with nature and spiritualizing the human-made environment, and numerous other ways. Spiritual eclecticism fueled by spiritual curiosity eventually crosses the threshold into spiritual self-authorship, defined by the affirmation "I AM the organizing principle of my [spiritual] life."[79] This affirmation reminds us that sense is not made for us; rather, we are the sense-makers, the meaning-makers, the authors of reality. Even when attempts have been made to talk us out of that right, we can always, in any given moment, reclaim it. The womanist idea is fundamentally about claiming such self-authorship, spiritual or otherwise, and allowing ourselves to be guided by our own Inner Light to truth, goodness, freedom, and, ultimately, commonweal.

The journey I describe in this chapter is partly my own journey. In the spirit of "Know thy Self" and "As within, so without," I have used my own life as a jumping off point for reflecting on womanism and its underlying architecture, the womanist idea. How did it come to be as it is? What gives it its unique character? Why does it sometimes defy articulation? What are its possibilities? The recognition that many are on the same quest has let me know that "something bigger is happening" and its possibilities are vast. As I have shown in this chapter, womanists intrepidly blend globe-spanning spiritual offerings into new spiritual thoughtforms and praxis, and the womanist idea, indeed womanism, would not be possible without those whose spirits dared to defy convention, peer behind veils, and discover keys to long locked doors.

SPIRITUAL ACTIVISM:
A WOMANIST APPROACH

This is the way of peace: Overcome evil with good, and falsehood with truth, and hatred with love.

—Peace Pilgrim

Over the last few years, my interest in spiritual activism—putting spirituality to work for positive social and ecological change—has increased markedly, particularly as a result of intense personal study across multiple religious, mystical, and divinatory traditions as well as my engagement with a spectrum of associated contemplative and meditative practices. The political conscientization that I call the second phase of my education (the first phase being my "standard" education that deposited in me the "official narratives" of my culture), was grounded in exposure to critical social theory and social movement praxis as both student and participant, which provided one avenue of understanding about changing the world. The spiritual and metaphysical education that came with the third phase, which involved deep study of texts and work with a variety of teachers outside academia, provided another. What I am now experiencing and writing about is merging these interests for a more powerful, effective, and visionary social change praxis that meets the exceptional demands of the challenges now facing humanity and Earth. In this chapter, I explore the idea of spiritual activism, with emphasis on what it is, how it works, and how it can be used in the interest of womanist social change objectives.

OPENING LIBATION: INFLUENCES

My thinking about spiritual activism has been influenced by a distinct set of authors who have also addressed the spirituality/activism interface. Most prominent among these are the late Gloria E. Anzaldúa, who pioneered the use of the term *spiritual activism* within the discursive field of women's studies, and AnaLouise Keating, who has expanded and clarified Anzaldúa's work through both cultural and philosophical lenses, building bridges between diverse audiences that might not otherwise have considered the possibilities for spirituality in activism. Anzaldúa's *Borderlands/La Frontera* (1986) as well as her now legendary essay "now let us shift ... the path of conocimiento...inner work, public acts" (2002) have had the greatest impact on me, in addition to her joint project with Keating, *Interviews/Entrevistas* (2000), which ranks as one of the most intriguing women's studies books that I have ever read. Keating's edited volume, *EntreMundos/AmongWorlds* (2005), although putatively focused on Gloria Anzaldúa's legacy, stands on its own as a watershed in women's studies' treatment of spiritual issues and themes, and reflects Keating's own distinctive "spiritualized politics" imprimatur. More than any other academic writers I have read, these two authors have bravely and boldly—if not systematically—explored how deep spirituality, including metaphysics, mysticism, and the supernatural, as well as orthodox and indigenous forms of religion, interrelate with social/ecological transformation.

I have also been influenced by the more recent works of M. Jacqui Alexander and Akasha Gloria Hull, whose feminist writing was deeply transformed by their personal spiritual quests into African spirituality and other ancient wisdom or New Age traditions. These two writers widen a path that was earlier laid down by Luisah Teish in *Jambalaya* (1985). Alexander's groundbreaking essay, "Pedagogies of the Sacred: Making the Invisible Tangible" (2005) dissolves the wall separating academic and mystical forms of consciousness and experience, opening a door that other spiritually inclined scholars can now freely enter; Hull's *Soul Talk* (2001) similarly breaks through the wall separating activists and artists from a frank and public acknowledgment of their active spiritual lives.

Two authors whose work is less frequently cited within women's studies—Judylyn S. Ryan and Barbara A. Holmes—inspired me to proceed intrepidly with my refiguration of how Black women's spirituality relates to the whole of humanity and possesses/embodies transformative, redemptive, and liberatory dimensions that have been underexplored, academically or otherwise. Ryan's book, *Spirituality as Ideology in Black Women's Film and Literature* (2005), with its nomenclature of "paradigm of growth"[1] and "democracy of narrative participation,"[2] is one of the freshest accounts of Black women's spirituality and its latent, transnational Africanity that I have read to date. Holmes's *Race and the Cosmos* (2002) simply dares to ask questions that no one else (except, perhaps, in a different way, novelist Octavia Butler) has dared to ask. In this same vein, Chela Sandoval's impact on my thinking about spirituality, activism, politics, culture, gender/sex, and liberation, as transmitted through *Methodology of the Oppressed* (2000), is notable. The fact that Sandoval was able to merge a serious treatment of love as social change praxis with a high theory deconstruction of high theory itself speaks for itself.

Finally, two trade books and two limited circulation texts should be mentioned that heightened my appreciation of mainline religious activism by women as well as some unique ways that putatively nonspiritual radical/progressive political communities are incorporating spiritual tools into their toolkit,. The first is Katharine Rhodes Henderson's *God's Troublemakers: How Women of Faith are Changing the World* (2006), a highly readable examination of twenty "socio-ethical entrepreneurs," or religiously/spiritually motivated women who are "changing the world as leaders in the public arena."[3] The second is a mapping study called *Healers of Our Time: Women, Faith, and Justice* (2008) produced by The Sister Fund, a philanthropic organization that donates to projects linking spirituality or faith, women, girls, and social change, in collaboration with the Institute for Women's Policy Research and the Women in Theology and Ministry of Emory University's Candler School of Theology.[4] This report documents and analyzes social change activity by committed Christian, Jewish, or Muslim women in the United States, showing the impact of orthodox faiths on social change work. The third is Paul Hawken's popular book, *Blessed Unrest: How the Largest Social Movement in the World Came into Being and Why No One Saw It Coming* (2007).[5] Hawken discerns a global convergence among democratic, indigenous, and environmental movements that is producing a new supermovement as well as a new social movement paradigm. Although he doesn't discuss spirituality as a feature of this new paradigm, to my ear, it calls out from behind the scenes. Finally, the Center for Contemplative Mind in Society produced a handbook called *The Activist's Ally: Contemplative Tools for Social Change* (2007), which offers "how-to" modules drawn from a culturally diverse array of contemplative traditions designed to "bring contemplative practice to people who are working to improve our world."[6] This includes people who are working on "civil rights, equal rights, environmental justice, economic justice, welfare and poverty, education and the arts, health care including AIDS/HIV, labor, criminal justice, free speech and media reform, immigration, and housing and homelessness." The exercises provided are offered to help activists avoid burnout, improve conflict resolution, reinvigorate their organizational dynamics, and take time for self-care.

While the authors and texts listed here do not constitute the universe of authors and texts I could have named, the ones that I have identified stand out as pioneers of *spiritual movement* and spiritual movement praxis, especially within academia or activist contexts. Their insights have shaped the way that I understand and talk about spiritual activism, a supporting pillar of the womanist idea and a portal to the realization of the womanist vision of LUXOCRACY.

NAMING THE SITE OF INTERVENTION

Where is the pivotal site of intervention in any situation? What is the root cause of societal, environmental, even individual problems? The tendency has been to look outside ourselves, but in so doing we have only acted on effects, not causes. The root cause of our outward reality is the nexus of our thought and our feeling—"heart and mind," as we say. So, how do we intervene upon that, and what kinds of interventions do we use? Spiritual activism is a set of practices designed to change "hearts and minds" in ways that promote optimal well-being in individuals, communities, humanity as a whole, all livingkind, and ultimately Planet Earth.[7]

That the heart–mind nexus is the most effective locus of social or ecological change activity is the first premise of spiritual activism. The second premise is that everything is energy, and all social or environmental change is fundamentally changing energy. Spiritual activism acknowledges that we—humans—are energy changing machines, energy changing instruments, energy transformers. Spiritual activism is about manipulating energy—invisible energy and its visible manifestations—which can be called anything from magic[8] to vibrational medicine[9] to spiritual technologies.[10] All of these are the same thing, in different languages, different vocabularies: everyday life, New Age spirituality/ integral medicine, and academic theory, respectively. Recognizing their fundamental identity is critical to overcoming the barriers of communication that have foreclosed dialogue between people engaged in similar activities in different spheres but for largely coordinated purposes. What has been lacking, unfortunately, in both the academic mainstream and the arena of progressive activism, is any reference to or acknowledgment of the incredible bodies of knowledge that have been built up over millennia about how to do this (i.e., manipulate energy). While spiritual activism is in no wise a new phenomenon, what is new—arguably post-postmodern—is the articulation and definition of spiritual activism as a distinct mode of praxis germane to progressive social justice and ecological activism. While this articulation cannot be traced to womanists exclusively, womanism is connected to this discourse and stands to add unique dimensions to its development. Beyond exploring these connections, my goal in writing this chapter is to mainstream spiritual activism.

Womanists have already been mainstreaming spiritual activism by insisting upon (re-) connection to indigenous knowledge bases, ancient wisdom and deep thought traditions, and metaphysical sources in which information about energy manipulation is *central*. The "everyday" has been and continues to be a powerful arena for the "schooling" of this knowledge because it is not regulated by the academic disciplining tactics of rationalism, positivism, or the scientific method or theory. Thus, womanist academics (and others) have had to keep "dipping" into the "everyday" arena to keep their (our) reality system (i.e., cosmology) and lifework alive. Some of this lifework involves transforming energy in the academy itself; acknowledging the fact that the academy can be a target for activism, for social change, and is not always the point of emanation. But much of it also involves social and ecological transformation outside the academy.

In this chapter, I intend to show how spiritual activism is a logical extension of womanism and women of color activism more generally, and also how womanism, with its spiritually activist praxis, is part of a larger set of interconnected discourses and practices bridging people from numerous, diverse communities. What these communities have in common is a similar vision for the future of humanity and the Earth, as well as a similar set of ideas about how to realize that vision.

BASIC DEFINITIONS, CONCEPTS, AND PRINCIPLES

Womanist activism takes many forms. As I wrote in the introduction to *The Womanist Reader*, "Womanism is a social change perspective rooted in Black women's and other women of color's everyday experiences and everyday methods of problem-solving in everyday spaces, extended to the problem of ending all forms of oppression for all people, restoring the balance between people and the environment/nature, and reconciling human life with the spiritual dimension."[11] Spiritual activism occupies a privileged position in the womanist pantheon of social change methods because Spirit and spirituality are foundational to womanism. If existence is sacred and life is sacred and humans are sacred and self is sacred, then social change activity must, by association, also be sacred or capable of serving as a conduit for the transmission of sacred energy or the transmutation of energy from a less to a more sacred form. As I have written previously, womanist politics are *spiritualized* politics; therefore, womanist political interventions are necessarily informed by spiritual belief, practice, and community as well as notions of *spiritual power*. However, outside theological contexts and beyond authors like those already named, spiritual power is not something commonly considered in progressive activist discourses; hence, the development of a vocabulary and the identification of practices that link spiritual power to progressive social and ecological change constitutes a unique contribution of womanism.

SPIRITUAL ACTIVISM

Spiritual activism is social or ecological *transformational activity* rooted in a spiritual belief system or set of spiritual practices. As stated at the beginning of this chapter, spiritual activism is *putting spirituality to work for positive social and ecological change*. Spiritual activism can be as basic as putting one's faith or ethical system into action by simply doing all the good things it recommends. At the other end of the spectrum, spiritual activism can involve the active application of metaphysical knowledge toward material ends. Stated differently, spiritual activism can take the form of what I call applied mysticism or "performing miracles." Akasha Gloria Hull uses the language of "applied spirituality."[12] Spiritual activism rests on the idea that the tenets of faith, religion, or metaphysical/ esoteric knowledge systems are not simply abstract bodies of knowledge meant to be studied and banked, but rather, they have experiential implications and applied uses, which are, in this case, brought to life by womanist pragmatism and womanist understandings, if not embodiments, of everyday (vernacular) spirituality.

AnaLouise Keating writes: "Spiritual activism is a visionary, experientially based epistemology and ethics, a way of life and a call to action ... [that] posits a metaphysics of interconnectedness and employs relational modes of thinking."[13] Gloria Anzaldúa writes about spiritual activism in terms of conocimiento: "The work of conocimiento—consciousness work—connects the inner life of the mind and spirit to the outer worlds of action. In the struggle for social change I call this particular aspect of conocimiento spiritual activism."[14] She also writes, "This work of spiritual activism and the contract of holistic alliances allows conflict to dissolve through reflective dialogue.... You dedicate yourself, not to surface solutions that benefit only one group, but to a more informed service to humanity.... When one person steps into conocimiento, the whole of humanity witnesses that step and eventually steps into consciousness."[15] Conocimiento—which she describes as both "a consciousness raising tool" and "the awareness of facultad that sees through all human acts whether of the individual mind and spirit or of the collective, social body"[16] is the consciousness that makes spiritual activism possible. I have also long been enamored of the Judaic concept of *tikkun olam*, translated as "the healing and repair of the world," which, to me, speaks directly of spiritual activism.

PUTTING SPIRITUALITY INTO PRACTICE

All of the world's major spiritual traditions have some version of "The Golden Rule." Most faiths also have a host of highly specific directives, however highly contested, designed to increase social order and cause good to prevail over evil. Most faiths also have concrete examples within their holy scriptures or lore of people or "higher beings" who were especially virtuous or amazingly helpful to others. Simply attending to these principles and emulating these exemplars to a greater degree than we currently do would generally cause the kinds of positive social change most of us seek. Thus, this is an entry point for spiritual activism.

Above and beyond this, however, virtually all of the world's religions and faiths also have an associated mystical tradition. I call this the mystical side of faith. Christianity, for example, is associated with the Essene tradition, Gnosticism, and various forms of Western mysticism (including Rosicrucianism, Freemasonry, etc.), and has, in recent times, spawned a variety of "New Age" perspectives like mental science, theosophy, and A Course in Miracles (ACIM). Judaism is well known for its esoteric Kabbalah (variously transliterated as Cabala and Qabala) tradition. Islam is associated with Sufism, which has multiple cultural/regional forms including Middle Eastern and West African, although at least one author suggests that Sufism predates Islam and that it may have birthed certain Western esoteric traditions.[17] Hinduism has Vedanta and yoga, not to mention the spiritual lineages of myriad gurus. Virtually every branch of Buddhism—Tibetan, Zen, Theravada, Mahayana, Pure Land, even Engaged—is associated with some form of mysticism. African religions such as Ifa, Yoruba, Akan, Bantu-Kongo, and so on, as well as ancient KMTic religion and numerous initiatic and divinatory traditions associated with different African ethnic groupings—for example, Sande and Poro, to name just two—contain significant mystical and esoteric content; the same can be said of African derived New World traditions, such as Orisa, Voudoun, Santeria, Candomblé, Lukumi, and the like. Native Americans and numerous other indigenous, First Peoples, and Fourth World societies in North America, South America,

Oceania, Australia, and elsewhere, have evolved religions and traditions with mystical dimensions. Earth-based religions, such as Paganism and Wicca, offer esoteric knowledge systems to their adherents and practitioners. New Age religion, beyond what has already been mentioned, is basically an amalgam of all of the above. Thus, the threads of mystical knowledge are many and prolific, ancient as well as modern, and global.

These mystical knowledge systems, sometimes called wisdom traditions, offer a largely unexplored metaphysical treasure trove to humanity. Historically, access to these knowledge bases has been highly regulated on the assumption that "the masses" were ill-equipped to comprehend or ethically employ the information they contain; however, a feature of this historical moment, which has been referred to as the dawning of the Age of Aquarius, the Shift, the Awakening, is the democratization of this knowledge and the increased access that has come from both intensified, multidirectional, global cultural flows and advances in information technology. It can be said that a door that was once cracked is now wide open for those who choose to walk through it.

APPLIED MYSTICISM/APPLIED METAPHYSICS

Applied mysticism (which could just as easily be called "applied metaphysics," particularly for those who are less theistically inclined) refers to putting this esoteric knowledge to use for desired ends, which, in some cases, may be material or political in nature. Anecdotally, we are familiar with the language of "performing miracles"; however, in general, this language externalizes the action associated with so-called miracles and mystifies the means by which "miracles" are produced. Spiritual activism requires the demystification of the performance of miracles—which I define here as the conscious and intentional transformation of energy to produce desired and sometimes surprising outcomes—and reconnects everyday people with the possibility of performing or manifesting them. Historically, Black women have performed everyday miracles as encapsulated in the oft-repeated phrase "making a way out of no way." In today's world of interlinked and potentially catastrophic crises of global proportions, miracles are often exactly what is needed. Thus, if ever there were a time when it would be germane to democratize the performance and production of miracles, it would be now.

What metaphysical and mystical knowledge bases teach us is that there is a science to "performing miracles." We have first to understand that we can learn and use the information contained in mysticism, which has often been relegated to a small set of specialists we refer to as mystics, prophets, or adepts. Womanist spiritual activism is about opening this up to everyday people and democratizing the performance of miracles! In the next section, I offer my understanding of how spiritual activism works, in an effort to make the performance of "miracles" accessible as well as to open up discussion about the possibilities of spiritual activism, particularly applied mysticism, for social and ecological transformation on Planet Earth. My overview is by no means exhaustive or conclusive, but rather constitutes an invitation to deeper study of these methods and their social and ecological change possibilities. I begin with a basic, but essential, definition that undergirds other understandings.

THE CONCEPT OF VIBRATION

Spiritual activism begins with the concept of vibration, the defining characteristic of all energy. Everything is energy: every natural element, every manufactured object, every human being, all our thoughts and emotions and ideals, the sounds, smells, tastes, textures, and light patterns that make up our world, and, by extension, all of those entities, beings, archetypes, and ideals or forms that occupy the so-called spiritual or transcendental realm. Everything has a vibration.[18] For purposes of this discussion, consider that all the vibrations that are possible exist on a spectrum in the universe (whether it is seen or unseen, known or unknown, dimensions) and that the things that make up the human world are generally composites of multiple sets of vibrations. Thus, the "vibrational universe" is rich and diverse and dynamic, manifesting characteristics of both simplicity and complexity.

Vibration is governed by laws that answer to an elegant mathematics that is largely predictable and knowable. Within this universe, change happens—things impact other things—leading to a state of constant motion and only apparent stasis. One such effective force is that of human consciousness and will. Scientists have documented that thoughts impact matter.[19] The natural implication of this finding is that thoughts, when applied with intentionality, can change things in predictable and desired ways, for the better or the worse. This is the basic foundation upon which spiritual activism rests. In a nutshell, spiritual activism is the conscious transformation of vibration. Therefore, the principles of vibration can be used to make social and ecological change.

What is needed to make this happen is, initially, recognition that it is possible. Individually and collectively, we must embrace the notion that we can make change energetically. In fact, we do it all the time, usually unconsciously (and, hence, haphazardly), so the awareness that we can direct the process is necessary. This recognition must be followed by ever-deepening awareness, through study and practice, of *how* this is possible. That is, we must learn the principles of vibration and one or more methods of energy transmutation. Last but not least, we must learn how to coordinate our practice of vibrationally based change with that of others, to increase the power of what we do, of our actions and intentions.

THE PRINCIPLES OF VIBRATION

As previously stated, everything has a frequency—sound, light, thoughts, feelings, objects, ideas, principles, substances. Frequencies run from low to high—the material world is on the low end and the invisible world is on the high end. By the principle of entrainment, grouped frequencies tend to synchronize around the dominant one. High frequencies trump low frequencies; strong frequencies trump weak frequencies. As we control vibration, so we control events and ourselves. Actually the place of origin for spiritually based social change work lies within us. The principles of vibration can be used to make social change, particularly at the levels of heart and mind energy.

One researcher whose work has been influential in my thinking is David R. Hawkins. Using an applied kinesiology method, Hawkins devised a logarithmic scale of human emotions, thoughts, and states of mind that he named the "Levels of Consciousness."[20] On this scale, emotions, thoughts, and states of mind that we generally consider negative fall at the low (dense) end of the scale, while emotions, thoughts, and states of mind that we generally consider positive fall at the high (light/luminous) end of the scale. The idea of such a scale is not new, but what is new is the idea that these nonmaterial forms of energy have lawful mathematical properties. The Hawkins model, for instance, lets us know that a vibration of "love" at 500 on the logarithmic scale is 10^{350} times more powerful than a vibration of "anger" at 150 on the logarithmic scale. In principle, this means that a vibration of love is capable of entraining a vibration of anger but not vice versa. When multiple people come together with the same vibration, the strength of that vibration becomes even more powerful and influential, whether that vibration is positive (e.g., love) or negative (e.g., anger). In theory, one should be able to calculate (or at least approximate) what kind of thought or emotion would be needed to transmute another less desirable thought or emotion, whether within oneself or out in the world. I don't agree with everything Hawkins has written, but I have found his "Levels of Consciousness" model to be useful and efficacious in both self-change and social change contexts, as well as to align with similar models of understanding from other sources (e.g., the notion of Kundalini rising through the chakras or consciousness ascending the Tree of Life).[21]

Biologist Rupert Sheldrake's widely cited notion of morphogenetic fields ("M-fields") buttresses both Hawkins's notion of "levels of consciousness" and the principle of vibration more generally.[22] M-fields can be defined as "attractor sites" that "organize energy" by creating an energy pattern within a field of entropy.[23] Once patterns are created, m-fields continue to entrain energies—whether physical or psychological, thus maintaining the pattern until it reaches a critical point (of growth or stress) and transforms into a new pattern. This notion of patterns is also critical to the quantum theory of physicist David Bohm, who maintains that phenomena reflect both an implicate (enfolded) and an explicate (unfolded) order.[24] In holographic fashion, implicate and explicate orders mirror each other as microcosmic/macrocosmic. The implication for spiritual activism is that human beings, as spiritually infused energy transformers, both respond to and create morphogenetic fields. These morphogenetic fields are coconstituted by our inner states or energy patterns and the energetic characteristics of the environments in which we live. By honing the abilities that enable us to control vibration—move up and down the scale of consciousness at will as well as counter vibrational influences from the environment—we become able to use this ability toward social change ends. This is why, in chapter 3, I characterized human beings as "energy transforming machines."

This idea that vibrations can be grouped and made more effective during mass actions has been explored and documented by practitioners of Transcendental Meditation (TM). According to John Hagelin in *Manual for a Perfect Government*, TM scientists have figured out a precise mathematical formula for assembling advanced meditators in a geographic area to influence a variety of types of events, from crime rates to conflict to weather.[25] Such a paradigm for social change may seem unthinkable given prevailing emphases on materialist understandings of effective political and environmental action; however, research and continued experimentation with methods such as these may expand our understandings of what is possible as well as what is effective.

A vivid illustration of the impact of vibrational frequency on matter can be found in the work of independent researcher Masaru Emoto, who has studied the impact of words, music, and environmental agents on ice crystal formation.[26] Emoto discovered that when water is brought into sustained contact with words and ideas that we generally consider negative (e.g., "I hate you"), as well as certain forms of music (e.g., heavy metal) and certain environmental agents (e.g., microwaves), ice crystal formation is impeded or deformed. In contrast, when water is brought into sustained contact with words and ideas that we generally consider positive (e.g., "I love you"), as well as certain forms of music (e.g., classical music) and certain environmental agents (e.g., organic fruits and vegetables), then beautiful, harmonious, well-formed ice crystals result. While the beauty of an ice crystal is certainly subjective, the harmony and completeness of the crystal formation is not. One implication of this research is that, since the human body is 50 to 90% water (depending on the age and health of the person), vibrational impacts on water also influence the human organism in corresponding ways.

Most of us have had serendipitous encounters with vibrational entrainment, such as when someone with a very positive attitude reroutes the dynamics in a meeting or someone who offers us a smile or a joke when we are down shifts our mood. The opposite thing can also happen when someone with a forceful personality enters a room with negative energy and entrains the attitudes or feelings of others in the room. Similar entrainments happen in the mass media through advertising, music, and other kinds of imagistic interventions carefully designed to shape consciousness in a particular direction. Applied mysticism is about examining everyday examples such as these more deeply in a way that facilitates their translation into replicable social change methodologies for challenges of increasing scope and scale, while also augmenting people's sense of personal power to make change in situations that demand it.

HOW TO PERFORM MIRACLES AND MAKE THE WORLD A BETTER PLACE

There are two basic steps to performing miracles and changing the world:

- Step 1 Change yourself (the inner work)
- Step 2 Change the world (the outer work)

Because these two steps evolve in parallel and mutually determine each other's success, these two activities must always mirror each other. One cannot exist without the other if social or ecological change is to prove enduring. Changed beings require a changed environment, and a changed environment is unsustainable without changed beings. Gloria Anzaldúa refers to the interdependence of inner and outer work in several places, including the title of "now let us shift" which includes the phrase "inner work, public acts." As she writes in this essay, "The work of conocimiento—consciousness work—connects the inner life of the mind and spirit to the outer worlds of action."[27] She also states, "You make the inner changes first, and then you make the outer changes.... Sometimes you can do both at the same time: work to create outer change through political movement, at the same time that you're ... developing yourself."[28] This understanding—that social and ecological change work must necessarily involve both inner and outer—is central to what distinguishes the womanist perspective on activism. Below, I discuss each of these steps in detail.

BECOMING THE CHANGE WE WISH TO SEE: THE INNER WORK

Distilled, there are three basic aspects to inner work: (1) purification of the body; (2) purification of the emotional self; and (3) purification of one's mental realm (thoughts and beliefs). Purification refers to the process of removing elements that are contrary to intended states of being. For example, if a person desires to be peaceful but feels aggressive, then purification is elimination of the aggression from the emotional system. At the bodily level, purification involves removing or ceasing to consume substances that harm the body or downgrade its functioning, such as unhealthy foodstuffs or environmental toxins, with the assumption that emotional and mental states and capacities are influenced—and potentially limited or enhanced—by the state of the body. At the mental level, purification involves the removal of thoughts and beliefs that are false, unproductive, or out of alignment with intended states of consciousness. For example, if a person believes in justice but rationalizes a sense of entitlement, purification involves eliminating the belief in entitlement in order to open the way for more a complete understanding of justice. Purification removes resistance to achieving our goals and thus promotes and produces self-mastery, defined here as a maximum state of intentionality and agency.

Inner work is also supported by purification of one's immediate environment. While this is the beginning of Step 2, changing the world, the intimate relationship between the environments in which we spend the most time every day—home, workplace, school, vehicles, even clothing—and our bodily, emotional, and mental well-being is so strong that purification of the immediate environment can be considered a "bridge" activity, linking one's inner world with the more public realm. Purification of one's environment involves removal of elements that are antithetical to the purification of one's body, emotions, or mind and enhancement with elements that support one's intended bodily, emotional, and mental states. To continue with our previous example, if one desires to be peaceful emotionally, one would facilitate this process by removing stimuli that instigate feelings of aggression or discomfort, such as images depicting violence, furniture that habitually makes one uncomfortable, or sources of agitating sound, and replacing these things with items that make one feel inspired, relaxed, compassionate, and so on. Across time and place, ideas such as these have been collected in such familiar bodies of knowledge as feng shui, vashtu, and even classical or neoclassical architecture, which offer recommendations for increasing peace, power, prosperity, health, and the like within physical spaces.

One method for assessing one's immediate environment is to conduct what I call a "vibrational inventory"; this is an examination of the physical, symbolic, social, and intrapsychic elements of one's lifespace in order to determine the degree to which these elements raise or lower one's vibration. Elements to be examined include such things as one's home environment; one's office or workplace; one's books, music, films, or games, the ideas and images that one consumes; one's relationships, particularly with intimate partners, family members, friends, coworkers, and close community associates; what one puts into one's body (food, beverages, fumes, chemicals, etc.); and, last but not least, one's mind (particularly habitual thoughts and emotions). One might also examine the condition of the animals and plants in one's environment, if relevant. Such an inventory allows us to observe and transform the way that our environments support (or fail to support) our intended and desired states of being, as well as gaining a sense of our impact on the environments in which we circulate. Transformation of our immediate environment makes the inner work easier because it creates an energetic or vibrational match between ourselves and our environment. Just like people often feel better when they "clean up the house," they often feel better when they have "cleaned up" their energetic or vibrational environment.

When I am talking with my students or others who have come to me for consultation about improving the quality of their lives, I often suggest simple vibrational refinements that offer instant inner or outer shifts, such as smiling, breathing deeply, drinking water, focusing on love, stating positive affirmations, focusing on giving, or meditating—all of which have been validated in psychological or metaphysical sources as having positive transformational value.[29] I recommend to my students or consultees that they notice and subsequently reduce or eliminate vibration-lowering practices such as frowning, shallow breathing, being dehydrated, focusing on fear, holding negative expectations, focusing on receiving, or staying cognitive/logical "24/7." Experiencing success with these simple, easy practices opens the door to exploration of larger scale transformational practices within bigger, higher stakes situations, including social and ecological change situations. I encourage students and consultees by reminding them that self-refinement leads to self-mastery, that is, bringing one's self-as-experienced into alignment with one's intended self, as well as gaining the power to execute one's intended actions with more efficacy.

The bottom line is that, based on mystical/metaphysical information common to multiple traditions, purification of the body, emotions, and mind make it possible to expand consciousness and awareness, experience more voluntary control of our emotions and actions so that they achieve their desired ends, and to enjoy better states of health, vigor, and, sometimes, greater longevity. All of these outcomes improve the efficacy of social and ecological change work and demonstrate how self-change is linked to changing the world, as encapsulated in Mahatma Gandhi's famous quote, "You must be the change you wish to see in the world." These purification exercises enable us to receive more Light, channel more Light, and manipulate more Light, as I sometimes put it. "Light" here refers to higher vibrating invisible energies, the divinity factor; Innate Divinity or our connection to invisible realms that are imbued with greater power and filled with more information. My argument vis-à-vis spiritual activism is that we can power up our social change work by bringing in the divinity factor, and spiritualizing our politics through the recognition of the invisible substrate of material life and our elemental interpellation with it. Womanism comes in as both an advocate and an originator of such methods, particularly as they rise up out of the everyday experience and practice of women of color and other culturally and spiritually grounded people worldwide.

To summarize, self-mastery is the gateway to higher powers and performing miracles, and self-mastery begins with a process of inner purification. We ourselves, as agents of change, become the bridge[30] between inner and outer conditions; we *become* "the change we wish to see in the world" by refining our ability to transform war and conflict into peace, violence and aggression into love and care, poverty into abundance and well-being, illness into health and vitality, and ecological destruction into ecological restoration and sustainability—first within ourselves, then in the world. Womanists worldwide demonstrate that, no matter what our religious tradition or affiliation, there are three important things that we can do to guide our outer work: (1) recognize *our own Innate Divinity*; (2) recognize the *Innate Divinity of others*; and (3) recognize the *Innate Divinity of all creation*, including the natural environment. Stated differently, for those preferring less theistic wording, (1) recognize *our own sacredness*; (2) recognize the *sacredness of others*; and (3) recognize the *sacredness of all creation*, including the natural environment. These statements mirror the "Three Recognitions" introduced in chapter 1.

APPLYING SPIRITUAL ACTIVISM IN THE
PUBLIC SPHERE: THE OUTER WORK

Outer work is all the things we do to change the visible, material world or the natural environment as well as the conditions of humans living in it. Existing social change methods primarily address this outer realm, and hence, this domain is already familiar. What is being newly articulated (although perhaps not newly practiced) from a womanist perspective is the conscious and explicit application of spiritual belief, spiritual practice, and spiritual power to these pursuits. This work begins with the understanding that we are "always already" working with Divine beings or a Divine creation, and always doing whatever it takes to return ourselves to this understanding. It also involves operating based on principle rather than expediency, because principle is vibrationally stronger than expediency. In so doing, we minimize the vulnerability of our actions, programs, and projects to external assault. When we design social or ecological change activities, we do so in ways that help participants or beneficiaries tap into their own Divinity and power, thus creating spiritual sustainability. Finally, we create campaigns that change the social architecture by impacting hearts (how people feel) and minds (how people think) in order to remove injustice and oppression from society, recognizing the power and necessity of mass media and telecommunications in shaping or mobilizing collective consciousness on a multiplicity of scales.

RELANGUAGING

One concrete example of spiritual activism applied to the symbolic or representational realm is relanguaging. From a metaphysical perspective, every word we speak is an act of creation with a particular vibrational frequency (Cf. "the power of the Word," as discussed in chapter 4). When we relanguage our targets of social change by substituting high-vibrating words and desirable outcomes for low-vibrating words and undesirable outcomes, we open up more inviting and sustainable possibilities for positive change. Some examples that bootstrap from current areas of concern include, for example, relanguaging "ending poverty" with creating prosperity, wealth, economic empowerment, or economic security; "fighting violence against women" with ensuring women's safety, security, or freedom of movement; "antiwar protest" with peace action; and "fighting disease (cancer, HIV/AIDS, etc.)" with promoting, ensuring, or universalizing health, wellness, and vitality. Relanguaging is an act of activism that alters people's thoughtforms, which is key to changing outer (material) conditions. Even the language of everyday life shapes our overarching political reality, making even the most seemingly insignificant utterances productive of some outcome, desirable or undesirable. "Watching our language"—choosing our words with intentionality and awareness of outcomes, and paying attention to linguistic virtues such as parsimony, kindness, and truth—is an act of spiritual activism, advocated in sites as diverse as monastic codes from around the world, etiquette books, and old-school grandmothers. All of these sources embody a common idea: Language is power, and speech is a creative act.

GETTING TO KNOW THE INVISIBLE REALM

The practice of spiritual activism at the level of applied mysticism or metaphysics requires the cultivation of an understanding about the structure and dynamics of the invisible world. M. Jacqui Alexander refers to "making the invisible tangible." The first prerequisite is an understanding that the invisible world exists, that it is real. The second prerequisite is an understanding that the invisible world is lawful and knowable. The third prerequisite is ongoing study of that world, through a variety of possible pathways, with the recognition that not unlike the visible realm, one can study the invisible realm for lifetimes without coming to know it completely. In this section, I share three understandings that I have gained through study about the invisible world, which has been aided by a variety of teachers and guides. Each of them has both shaped my womanist thought and refined my practice of spiritual activism. I provide these three as examples only, acutely aware of the vast set of possibilities from which this subset was chosen, yet with a conviction that there are fundamental and noteworthy commonalities between virtually all such formulations. Additionally, I emphasize that I am still studying all of these systems on an ongoing basis.

AN EXAMPLE FROM KABBALAH: THE FOUR WORLDS

For several years, I have had the good fortune to study Kabbalah with Will Coleman, PhD, a multilingual theology scholar, student of ancient doctrines, ordained minister, and preeminent Kabbalist. Kabbalah is a study of energy dynamics associated with the Tree of Life, a metaphysical configuration that captures the structure of reality, with emphasis on the interconnected nature of visible and invisible realms. Over the course of this study, I have also engaged

Kabbalistic scholarship by a variety of other authors. One Kabbalistic lesson which has proved particularly useful in my formulation of spiritual activist practice is known as "The Four Worlds" (see Table 6.1). These four worlds present a model of reality that contains four nested "layers," "spheres," or "dimensions," each with more generative power than the one that succeeds it.[31]

At the most powerful dimension, there is the "World of Emanation," or Atziluth. At this level, the Creator sets things in motion and the archetypes or spiritual seeds of all that exists can be found. At the next dimension, there is the "World of Creation," or Beri'ah. In this sphere, *we imagine it*—archetypes become translated into thoughtforms that are cognizable by human beings. We could call this dimension the mental blueprint. This is our "world of possibility." It is encapsulated in language and symbol; change at this level involves "stretching our imaginations." In many Kabbalistic formulations, it is referred to as the higher mental plane. At the next dimension, there is the "World of Formation," or Yetzirah. In this sphere, *we think it and feel it*—the desire energy which translates thought into action can be found. We could call this the dimension of drive; it is known as the lower mental plane. Finally, at the densest, least powerful dimension, albeit the level with which we are most familiar, there is the "World of Action," or Assiah. In this sphere, *we do it*—this is where the material result, brought into being by spiritual seed energy translated into thought and given life by emotional impetus, manifests. Thus, it can be said that Assiah is the world of effects, less so the world of causes. Yet, it is in Assiah that we live our daily lives; it is the quotidian realm. It is the realm within which the politico-economic and ecological problems that we

TABLE 6.1   THE FOUR WORLDS

THE FOUR WORLDS	WHAT HAPPENS THERE
World of Emanation (Atziluth) i.e., the spiritual plane	The Creator sets things in motion
World of Creation (Beri'ah)* i.e., the creative plane	We imagine it (mental blueprint)
World of Formation (Yetzirah)* i.e., the emotional/intellectual plane	We think it and feel it (drive)
World of Action (Assiah) i.e., the physical plane	We do it (material result)

Each world is more power-filled than the one below it. Most social and environmental problems occur at the lowest (material) dimension, however, they are created—and best solved—at the dimensions(s) above. Thus, spiritual activists study how to work with the higher dimensions (*) in order to become more effective problem-solvers.

are trying to solve through activism exist. What the Four Worlds paradigm teaches us is that, to solve problems at the level of Assiah, we must relocate our problem-solving effort to one of the profounder, more causal dimensions. That means relocating our problem solving efforts to the realm of hearts and minds or imagination, and even invoking (the) Transcendent Being(s) as collaborators in the problem-solving process. It means creating what Gloria Anzaldúa calls "spiritual-imaginal-political vision[s]."[32]

This model provides a rubric for evaluating social or ecological problems, as well as ourselves as agents of transformation, spiritual activists in the world. If the material effect that we find unacceptable is viewed as the endpoint of a causal chain, we can work our way up the chain of causality to find increasingly effective loci of intervention. For example, if our problem of interest is the buildup of toxic waste and pollution in our communities, we can simply clean up the waste and pollution (a solution at the "World of Action" level), knowing that it will likely recur and we will have to do it again because the root causes have not been addressed and people will keep polluting. We can then address what kinds of intellectual and emotional conditions are producing the waste buildup (a solution at the "World of Formation" level), from ideas and feelings associated with consumption and easy disposability, to the feelings of (and rationalizations for) entitlement linked to the idea that someone else should clean up our messes, to the psychological stresses that manifest outwardly in the form of a disordered and "stressed" environment (i.e., pollution). In that sense, interventions that transform emotions of greed, need, entitlement, or stress, as well as the ideas that normalize these emotional conditions and hold them in place, would interrupt the causal chain that produces environmental toxicity and waste accumulation. Moving higher up the scale, we could look at what kinds of thoughtforms or ideas (including forms of ignorance) produce the thoughts, feelings, and ultimately material effects mentioned above (a solution at the "World of Creation" level). For example, certain kinds of ideas about self vis-à-vis others or the natural world, particularly egoistic notions that are rooted in the idea that we are disconnected individuals or that we are deficient in some way that must be addressed consumeristically, or even a lack of scientific awareness about our bodies or the bodies of animals and plants (e.g., susceptibility to toxicity), or ideas about "living in the moment" without regard for future generations, have a causal role in the accumulation of toxins and waste in the environment. We could look at how our language around these things has limited our imaginations with regard to a different world.[33] Basic ideas about interconnectedness vs. separateness fall within this sphere.

From a Kabbalistic perspective, average individuals do not have access to the World of Emanation level of intervention (a full discussion of which is beyond the scope of this chapter); however, through processes of contemplation, reflection, and meditation, as well as other spiritual practices, it is possible for people to glean some insight with regard to the causal factors at this level. For example, Kabbalists regard the Law of Cause and Effect as a universal principle that operates at all levels of the Four Worlds, set in motion at the time of Creation by the Elohim, and the regularity and predictability of this principle is considered both just and merciful insofar as it invariably creates conditions that maintain equilibrium in the highly dynamic universe.[34] Thus, bad conditions ultimately self-destruct due to their own inherent limitations, even if, by human standards this requires a long and painful process. We might view global climate change as an example that represents a higher octave of the toxic waste and pollution buildup example presented above.

AN EXAMPLE FROM IFA: THE 400+1 AND 200+1 OF THE IFA COSMOS

I must thank M. Jacqui Alexander, Omo Yemayá, for guiding me to Kola Abimbola's text, *Yoruba Culture: A Philosophical Account*, which provides a very clear account of Ifa metaphysics. I can thank numerous practitioners and scholars for contributing to my overall understanding of Ifa through lectures, personal accounts, and additional book suggestions. My journey to and through Ifa and related African and African-derived religions is ongoing, yet my evolving understanding of the Ifa cosmos has been one of the most influential on my womanist spiritual activist thought. To quote from Abimbola's concise summary:

> [T]he cosmos is divided into two halves; the right-hand and the left-hand. We have 400 primordial powers on the right, and 200 primordial powers on the left. The powers on the right hand side are the Orisa (i.e., divinities). They are benevolent, but they sometimes punish humans who corrupt society.
>
> Inhabitants of the left-hand side are the Ajogun (the "Anti-gods") and they are irredeemably malevolent. The word Ajogun literally means "warrior"; hence the Ajogun wage war against both humans and the Orisa....
>
> There are, however, two supernatural forces that straddle both sides of the left-right divide. These are the Aje (who are usually improperly translated as witches)[35] and Esu (the universal policeman). Esu is the neutral element in

the sense that he is neither good nor bad. He is simply the mediator between all the entities and forces on both sides of the left/right divide.

Although Aje ("witches") also straddle the two sides of the divide, they, unlike Esu, are not neutral. They are allies of the Ajogun.... The Aje are, however, sometimes benevolent.

Human beings are also on the right hand side of the universe. Although humans are not regarded as supernatural powers, the belief is that every individual has the potential to become a divinity.

The "plus 1" referred to above does not refer to any particular divinity. Rather it is a principle of elasticity by which the Yoruba account for any newly defined Orisa.... This "plus 1" principle allows new beliefs, new thought systems, and new deities to be brought into the fold of Yoruba culture.[36]

A few prefatory comments about Ifa, also known as Yoruba, Orisa (Orisha, Orixa), and other names: This religion is monotheistic, insofar as a nongendered Supreme Being, Olodumare, created and rules the universe.[37] The Orisa, who were created by Olodumare, are simultaneously divinities and representations of particular principles, whose role and composition can be compared with the Elohim of Judaism,[38] the Buddhas and bodhisattvas of Buddhism, the Archangels, angels, and saints of Christianity, and the Neters of KMTic religion. Olodumare also created the Ajogun, showing that the Supreme Being is above good and evil yet created a predominantly good universe.

The feature of this cosmology that I have found most useful in my thinking about the invisible realm and my practice of spiritual activism is the idea that, while the universe contains both good and evil, good trumps evil in a certain lawful proportion. This understanding provides a justification for dispensing with moral relativism and also for figuring out how to mobilize forces against evil in the world, insofar as "evil" often undergirds conditions of social and ecological injustice, violence, and suffering. Furthermore, given this cosmological arrangement, good can be counted on to prevail over evil, providing inspiration and hope to continue working for "the good" when evil seems overwhelming. The Ifa cosmos also provides a ground for understanding the inner workings of good and evil within individual humans who are, in a certain kind of way, buffeted between various bids on their energy, attention, and choice presented by both good and evil influences.[39] Humans, being at the bottom or least powerful pole of the spectrum are, despite being essentially good, relatively weak (or energetically dense) in the scheme of things unless they are fortified through spiritual and ethical education, the practice of virtue (however defined), the wisdom borne of life experience, and an acknowledged connection to "Higher Beings." Thus, human good has to be cultivated to reach its full potential, which, as specified by the Ifa cosmology, is divinity. Therefore, activities that promote spiritual and ethical education, virtue, and wisdom are modalities of spiritual activism and social change. Finally, Ifa offers an elaborate discourse on sacrifice (i.e., placation,[40] or restoration of spiritual equilibrium) that highlights the interconnectivity of all beings—divinities, humans, animals, plants, and "the elements"—and all realms, namely, natural and supernatural (whether good, evil, or liminal). Through this thread of interconnectivity we can trace the evolving flow of energy within the universe and learn to "work it" on the earth plane, even in sociopolitical or ecological situations.

AN EXAMPLE FROM BUDDHISM: MEDITATION AS ENTRY POINT INTO INVISIBLE REALMS AND SPIRITUAL ACTIVISM

Meditation is not the exclusive domain of Buddhism. In fact, contemplative practices, of which meditation is just one, can be found in virtually all religions (whether orthodox or indigenous), many initiatic traditions, as well as outside the spiritual domain (such as in the health fields). However, meditation and other forms of contemplative practice are central to most types of Buddhism, and Buddhism as a whole, viewed broadly, has an extremely well-developed corpus on the subject of meditation and related practices. While I have learned meditation from a variety of sources (and, as a result, have been exposed to many different types of meditation), I have found Buddhism to have a particularly well-elaborated discourse on meditation. Meditation serves many purposes, but one that is important to this discussion is the purpose of transporting one out of ordinary consciousness into other ("higher"/nonordinary) forms of consciousness. As such, meditation is an avenue (or vehicle) into invisible realms of experience and existence.

Meditation, in its most general sense, is the practice of quieting the mind in order to achieve various forms of consciousness or strengthen the mental and psychic powers. Meditation is like exercise for the mind, if mind is understood as a multilayered apparatus with subconscious, conscious, and superconscious aspects; bodily, emotional, rational, psychic, and spiritual/cosmic dimensions; autonomic, attentive, sensory, mnemonic, astral, and causal features; and individual as well as collective expressions. Meditation allows us to explore the fact that mind is not just "thinking," and, in so doing, gain first-hand experience of the structure and dynamics of invisible reality. It provides a type of experience that cannot be achieved via typical avenues to intellectual development, such as reading books or listening to lectures.

Buddhism as a major world religion has many subtypes, including Tibetan, Zen, Mahayana, Theravada, and Pure Land as well as newer types such as Engaged Buddhism. All of these offer specific insights on, and practices of, meditation designed to cultivate and refine different faculties of mind as well as a variety of ethical orientations and feeling states. One cannot ignore the geographic and historical relationship between Hinduism and Buddhism. One of the most influential texts on meditation, Patanjali's *Yoga Sutras* of the third century, reflects a bridge between Hindu wisdom (Vedanta) and Buddhist practice.[41] The first few lines of this text (as translated by Alistair Shearer, one of many translators) establish a general disposition with regard to meditation:

1. And now the teaching on yoga begins.
2. Yoga is the settling of the mind into silence.
3. When the mind has settled, we are established in our essential nature, which is unbounded consciousness.
4. Our essential nature is usually overshadowed by the activity of the mind.[42]

As this translation of Patanjali's original text goes on to state, "Understanding is correct knowledge based on direct perception, inference, or the reliable testimony of others,"[43] while "Misunderstanding is the delusion that stems from a false impression of reality."[44] Meditation helps clarify one's perception of reality by making direct perception of reality possible through the systematic elimination of various interferences (internal or external) and the opening up of previously unknown, unused, or unpracticed channels of awareness and understanding. Inference is essentially rationality or logic, that which our current formal education system teaches and valorizes; however, direct perception is a level/avenue of knowledge above inference and accessible only through specialized forms of training or unique and rare forms of spontaneous awakening (for example, the "satori" of Zen). Similarly, the "reliable testimony of others" is basically the "information" or "content" aspects of our current educational system; it is what we study, what we call "just the facts," assuming that these facts originate from sound sources. Whether this testimony comes in the form of books or speech, it is the beginning but not the end of knowledge for humans. Indeed, Patanjali's assertions reflect the Ladder of Learning that I defined in chapter 3, that is, the movement through information, knowledge, wisdom, and ultimately enlightenment that comes through optimal education. Within this formulation, meditation becomes one method of moving up the Ladder of Learning.

As mentioned, Buddhists have offered a number of meditative methods, each with a specific purpose. Three methods that I will mention because of their ready applicability to spiritual activism work include mindfulness meditation, one-pointedness, and lovingkindness meditation. Mindfulness practice has been made popular in recent decades by Thich Nhat Hanh, a Vietnamese monk who founded the Tiep Hien Order, or Order of Interbeing in the mid-1960s, which he still heads. This order is associated with Engaged Buddhism, a religious perspective that, not unlike liberation theology, combines spiritual insights and practices with social and ecological justice goals and activism.[45] Thich Nhat Hanh has pioneered a number of methods for using meditation in the service of social change goals, particularly those associated with peace and peace-making. Doctrinally, his spiritual philosophy and praxis sits at the intersection of Zen, Theravada, and Tibetan Buddhist perspectives. These methods and perspectives were developed in the crucible of war when Thich Nhat Hanh, or Thay (as he is known to followers), was a youthful and outspoken peace activist during the French and American phases of the Vietnam War. During that period, Engaged Buddhism and the practice of mindfulness for peace was articulated and developed along with Sister Chan Khong, one of the first members of the Order of Interbeing, and others.

Mindfulness meditation teaches three things (1) being in the present moment, (2) increased awareness of the present moment, and (3) self-control through breathing. The primary activity is focusing on breath or another bodily activity, such as sitting or walking, or sensation, such as connectedness to earth or listening. Being in the present moment means letting go of past or future considerations in favor of what is going on right now. For example, if one is stressed about a past conflict (that already happened) or an upcoming presentation (that hasn't happened yet), being in the present moment allows one to realize that the conflict or the presentation isn't happening now, thus reducing stress about the event in question and allowing us to examine what is good and peaceful about the present moment. For example, we may reflect on the fact that, in the present moment, we are alive; we have eaten; we are not in pain; we are able to breathe; we are sitting inside a shelter; trees are still growing; the sun is shining. In mindfulness meditation, one observes the flow of thoughts rather than struggles with it; one pulls oneself back to focus when one's concentration strays; and one notices the calming effect on the body of breathing properly. Additionally, one learns to broaden one's awareness of the environment in which one is situated and to attune to its many elements. For example, one learns to hear birds singing or trees rustling or even airplanes overhead or the refrigerator buzzing that one didn't listen to before; one learns to feel the earth beneath one's feet and notice the constant support it provides (as in walking or sitting meditation); to enjoy the rhythm of mopping the floor or the scent of soapy water while doing the dishes (as in working meditation); or to truly hear what another person is saying when one ceases to plan one's next response before another has finished speaking (as in listening meditation)—a practice similar to what AnaLouise Keating refers to as "listening with raw openness."[46] Mindfulness practice, then, helps us to "tune in" in social, political, or ecological situations that we wish to improve by helping us to (1) assess the situation dispassionately and without preformed ideological notions or objectives, (2) stay peaceful and centered and humane (i.e., high vibrating) even when people or conditions are frustrating and exhausting, and (3) effectively notice unexpected or emergent opportunities for making positive change.

One-pointedness is a type of meditation that builds concentration, which is the ability to focus on one thing at a time and marshal one's energy toward a single goal, thus increasing the intentionality and efficacy of one's actions. One-pointedness practice also cultivates the ability to merge with an object (physical or conceptual) and embody its consciousness, thus releasing one from ego boundaries and allowing more profound experiences of interconnectedness and union. When we have acquired one-pointedness, the ability not just to achieve but also to sustain concentration, our ability to do what we say we are going to do or what we intend to do is much higher, which in turn increases our integrity and our vibrational power. Because our attention is pulled in so many different directions—by the media's constant bids for our attention, other people's constant bids for our energy, and our own constantly proliferating and competing desires—our energy and efforts, individual and collective, are often scattered and ineffectual. The practice of one-pointedness counteracts this entropic pull. Practices that build one-pointedness occur in a variety of traditions, including but not limited to Hindu and Buddhist. A variety of contemplative techniques exist to increase one-pointedness; however, what they tend to have in common is developing the ability to block out irrelevant stimuli (inner and outer), increase the length of time and intensity of focus on a single thought or object, and heighten awareness of the interconnected nature of reality.

Lovingkindness meditation, sometimes called *metta* meditation, is the cultivation and application of a particular sentiment, known variously as *metta*, *bodhicitta*, or simply lovingkindness, an affable sort of friendliness that combines compassion, goodwill, and good cheer. Alternately, it may mean the desire to relieve the suffering and promote the enlightenment of all sentient beings, which is the animating sentiment of bodhisattvas, or enlightened beings within the Buddhist cosmology who have delayed their own ascension to Nirvana for the sake of helping all other sentient beings to do the same. In one variation of the practice of lovingkindness meditation, the meditator chooses three people to contemplate—one liked, one disliked (or aggravating), and one neutral—and successively visualizes them surrounded by light. While holding them in such a vision, a phrase expressing lovingkindness is usually repeated, such as "May you be well, may you be happy, may you be at peace," along with the conscious direction of corresponding lovingkindness energy toward this person. Lovingkindness meditation operates on the principle that our connection with other beings is beyond space and time and that thought is able to reach anyone, anywhere. A variation on the lovingkindness meditation allows us to direct *metta* toward ourselves, in an act of self-love. In another version of the practice called *tonglen*, the meditator breathes in the pain of the world or a suffering subject (in order to inwardly transmute it) and breathes out peace, love, happiness, and relief in its place.[47]

In a talk titled "Suffering Too Insignificant for the Majority to See," Alice Walker addressed a gathering of African American Buddhists on the topic of using lovingkindness meditation to heal the wounds of racism, past and present. In the transcript of this talk, published in the Buddhist magazine *Shambhala Sun*, Walker provides the following mantra for a *metta* practice:

> May you be free
> May you be happy
> May you be at peace
> May you be at rest
> May you know we remember you[48]

In the talk, Walker recounts the true story of George Slaughter,

> a white farmer's son by a black woman, who came to a horrible death because he "didn't keep his place." Ambushed by white men, including his own father, he was shot while riding his horse because the saddle horse was "too fine." The story goes that when he was found, "the horse was drinking his blood."[49]

By the end of the talk, Walker leads those assembled in the recitation of the above-cited mantra for all the key actors in this racist drama: George Slaughter, his black mother who found him dead, his white father who killed him, the white men who rode with his father and participated in the murder, and George's horse who also endured the trauma and stood by his murdered companion. In this exercise, Alice Walker models the encompassing nature of *metta* and its ability, indeed, its necessity to demonstrate compassion for all living beings and engage in vibrational actions that move all in the direction of justice through personal and societal, even historical transformation. For some, this practice is unthinkable because the idea of extending lovingkindness to the perpetrators of evil and the architects of injustice is an affront to the pursuit of justice and peace. Yet, Buddhism pushes us to understand that, based on the principle of interrelatedness—"interbeing," as Thich Nhat Hanh labels it—others' evil is also our own, and our goodness is also others'. As we transform together, we move all humanity in a direction together, toward our intended ends of justice, peace, and liberation. Such work is spiritual activism.

Buddhist psychology, which undergirds Buddhist meditation as well as being informed by its insights, offers practices to aid in the transmutation of "destructive emotions" (classically identified as anger, clinging, and ignorance) and thus contributes to mental alchemy, which is the ability to transmute inner states and, ultimately one's vibrational level. This topic is extensively treated in a book by His Holiness the Dalai Lama with Daniel Goleman titled *Destructive Emotions: How Can We Overcome Them?* The question raised by this book's title has far-reaching implications for the practice of spiritual activism because many of the problems that spiritual activism (or any kind of activism, for that matter) addresses have their roots in one of the so-called destructive emotions or one or more of their variations. The corporate authors of this book (which encompasses a two-week conversation between H.H. Dalai Lama, a group of Buddhist psychologists, and a group of Western psychologists, led by Daniel Goleman) offer practical transmutation strategies.[50] For example, a strategy for transmuting jealousy, which, according to Buddhist psychologists, sits at the intersection of anger and clinging, is a mantra such as "I rejoice in your happiness." A mantra like this obviously reflects the attitude of lovingkindness, and the practice of meditation facilitates a deep engagement with the mantra's meaning and energetic vibration. These authors emphasize that the timing of an intervention on one's own psyche is important. Beginners typically intervene after the destructive emotion has arisen; intermediate practitioners intervene just as the emotion is arising; advanced practitioners preempt the destructive emotion so that it cannot arise at all or, if it does, only in diminished form.[51] This advice is reminiscent of a famous quote attributed to Milarepa, an eleventh century Tibetan murderer-turned-monk, who said, "In the beginning nothing comes, in the middle nothing stays, in the end nothing goes."

Another example of social change activism that builds upon meditation is work that I have done with youth, inside and outside academic settings, to introduce them to contemplative practice as a means of increasing self-awareness, insight, ethical reflection, and intentionality. Based on a Contemplative Practice Fellowship grant I received from the Center for Contemplative Mind in Society, I developed an academic course called "Womanist Perspectives on Spiritual Activism" in which one component was exposure to and practice of twenty-two different contemplative modalities drawn from different traditions around the world. In addition to learning about, trying, and evaluating these modalities, we also read and discussed texts by activists from around the world, most of them women, who used contemplative or faith-based practice in their social or ecological transformation work.[52] Students engaged in social, ecological, or self-change projects that incorporated the contemplative practices they were learning. In so doing, they added a reflective, ethical, and wisdom-based dimension to their education and political participation. While I held this fellowship, I also created and led a small, community-based pilot program for refugee and immigrant Liberian teens, many of whom had been impacted by Liberia's civil war. None of the teens in this group had been exposed to contemplative practice before, and while this was only one component of our group's activity, those who participated described it as helpful and enjoyable. None of this work at the community level referenced religion specifically, but it was designed in part, based on my commitment to providing support for youths' spiritual and ethical development in ways that would fortify them, to contribute to their self-actualization, and recognize their Innate Divinity in a world that often viewed them and treated them as anything but divine beings.

CONCLUSION

Spiritual activism is key to womanist praxis. Defined as social or ecological transformational activity rooted in a spiritual belief system or a set of spiritual practices—or, more simply, as putting spirituality to work for positive social and ecological change—spiritual activism is the bedrock of spiritualized politics. Spiritual activism is predicated on three principles: (1) the Innate Divinity of humans and creation; (2) the existence and lawfulness of the invisible realm; and (3) humans as energy transformers who can "perform miracles" by learning and applying metaphysical laws that are encapsulated within the world's mystical and esoteric wisdom traditions. As highlighted by the work of numerous authors cited in this chapter, spiritual activism requires both inner and outer technologies of change, informed by globally diverse spiritual practices as well as advances in scientific understanding of the universe and life. Womanism, with its historical links to women's culturally embedded practices of everyday spirituality inside and outside of recognized religious spheres, serves as a platform for democratizing these diverse spiritual tools and technologies in the interest of solving social and ecological problems, indeed, crises, for the common survival and healing of humanity and Earth.

2

WOMANIST SPIRITUAL ACTIVISM: FIVE CASE STUDIES

TRANSFORMING WAR INTO PEACE:
SISTER CHAN KHONG AND *LEARNING TRUE LOVE*

When I was a little girl, one of the things I remember most vividly was my family of seven watching nightly news of the Vietnam War on TV while we ate dinner in our modest kitchen. It was the early 1970s, and I was a young but precocious elementary school kid. There is one particular evening that stands out in my mind, when my mother, a homemaker, asked my father, then a doctoral student in social science education with an emphasis on anthropology and a background in Asian studies, "Are the people over there really green?" In my childish mind, unable to tell whether my mother was being facetious or serious, I awaited the answer to this question. I looked at the screen: the people really did look green on this particular night. However, my father's answer relieved me: "No dear, it's just the TV acting up."

Now, as an adult, when I reflect back on those times of watching man's inhumanity to man on what seemed like a perpetual, repeating loop, those nights of watching scared, bloody people running down dirt roads not unlike those not too far from where I lived in small-town Georgia at that time, those times of listening to gunfire and bombs and tanks, even if only in 30 minute (or shorter) segments on the nightly news rather than in person like the people I was watching—I think about all that I knew and all that I did not know. My family was Baha'i, my parents were an interracial couple with five "civil rights" babies (myself being the eldest), and even as a child I participated in the "Deep South Campaign," knocking door-to-door to tell people about Baha'u'llah's message of world peace, interracial amity, and equality of women and men (who were, as I was told and told others, like the wings of a bird—both necessary for humanity to fly). So I "knew" that peace was the answer, that love was the way, and that oneness was the future. I "knew" that "service to humanity" was my calling and my mission. What I did not know at that young and tender age was how complicated the world was, what people other than Baha'is were doing to make the world a better place, and how I might actually, over the course of my unfolding life, make a positive difference in things.

In *Learning True Love: Practicing Buddhism in a Time of War*, a memoir by Sister Chan Khong billed as "a nun's journey from Vietnam to France and the history of Thich Nhat Hanh's Buddhist community," I discovered a lot of what I was missing. For me, this text filled in numerous gaps in my understanding of a war that shaped my parents' generation and filled my youthful mind with images and feelings, but that the history courses of my high school and college years always stopped short of covering, as if knowledge about contemporary issues and times might overempower our minds. Sister Chan Khong's book was originally published in 1993, however, a second edition with additional chapters was produced in 2007 after Sister Chan Khong had the opportunity to return to Vietnam after many years of exile. For me, this book was a beautiful synthesis of history, politics, spirituality, everyday life, and self-reflection—and it was even a very special kind of love story—that allowed me to contemplate not only the questions and yearnings of my own youth, but the larger project of spiritualized social change. In this chapter, I read it as a womanist text for the purpose of illuminating the meanings of womanist activism and womanism as a spiritual movement, particularly as it pertains to issues of war and peace.

BASIC BIOGRAPHY

Born Cao Ngoc Phuong[1] in 1938 to a middle class family in Ben Tre, Vietnam—a small town in Central Vietnam in the Mekong Delta region—Phuong, who later in her life became Chan Khong, was the second youngest of nine children. A precocious girl who could easily be described using such womanist terms as outrageous, audacious, courageous, and willful—or by the phrase, "wanting to know more and in greater depth than is considered 'good' for one"[2]—Phuong excelled in school and, unlike most girls of her time and place, was able to attend high school, college, and even graduate school (where she received a degree in biology and ultimately became a member of the Faculty of Science at Saigon University). She states, "As long as I can remember, I struggled against authority.... I remember telling my sister Tam over and over, 'I don't care about your age or authority! I am right!'"[3] Analyzing her own childhood and youth, she wrote, "To survive in a culture that rewards seniority over truth, I had to develop a kind of toughness.... As a result, it has always been easy for me to empathize with those who appear as rude or unkind."[4]

Although Phuong was raised a Buddhist, she did not begin to take Buddhism seriously until her late teens and early twenties. Indeed, her activism and her Buddhism effectively emerged together and intertwined immediately. In 1957, when Phuong was 19, two notable Buddhist monks came to Ben Tre City and imparted the Five Precepts to her parents. Her parents encouraged her to meet with these monks and, after some resistance, she did, full of questions. When she ultimately asked to receive the Five Precepts herself, she was told by one of the monks, "I don't think so. It would be better to wait. You are a strong young woman, and when you do something, you do it completely. I suggest that you take the time to study and understand the precepts more thoroughly before receiving them."[5] Slightly taken aback, Phuong did indeed study the precepts for a year. Similar to the Judeo-Christian Ten Commandments, the Five Precepts form the cornerstone of Buddhist morality; they include not killing, not stealing, not committing adultery, not lying, and not consuming intoxicants. At this time, Phuong was given the name Dieu Khong, or "Wonderful Emptiness," because of her propensity for asking questions about the Buddhist notion of emptiness. She expressed an interest in becoming a Buddhist nun, but was told by this same monk, "I do not think becoming a nun would suit you, because nuns have to follow the traditional discipline. You might rebel against it."[6]

Clearly, Phuong had already established a reputation for free thinking and critical inquiry. Early on, she interrogated the monks about their lack of involvement in charitable activities for the poor, compared with Catholic missionaries in the area.[7] Her passion for change-oriented social work was written off by these monks as "merit work" (i.e., work that would merely lead to a "higher" incarnation in a future life, but not to enlightenment). She was advised to pursue enlightenment so that she could "save countless beings" in some indeterminate future, yet her main concern was the immediate suffering of everyday people all around her. "There was so much to do right in the present moment," she writes.[8] Some monastics even went so far as to tell her that "if [she] practiced diligently, [she] could be reborn as a man in [her] next life."[9] Offended and dismayed by this hypocritical response (based on the common teaching that anyone, presumably male or female, could become a Buddha), Phuong writes, "[T]heir description of enlightenment as a state with miraculous powers sounded irrelevant to me and also discriminatory against women. I did not want to become a man, or even a buddha. I just wanted to help the children whose suffering was so real."[10]

Because of all her questioning, she was not satisfied with the explanations of many teachers and decided to make her own kind of Buddhism by going to the slums, healing the sick, creating jobs for the poor, and helping to bring street children to school, all while continuing to attend Buddhist lectures. She was directed to another young monk, respected yet already branded a renegade for his attempts to "renew Buddhism" in Vietnam, named Thay Nhat Hanh, now known as Thich Nhat Hanh.[11] Twelve years her senior, "Thay" as he was called, captivated Phuong immediately. She began a three-month course of Dharma talks under his tutelage and, after it was over, maintained a correspondence with him for guidance in her social service work, as he had plans to go to the United States to research comparative religion. Based on their shared interest in Buddhism *and* social change, combined with his ecumenical approach to spirituality and his gentle, loving, yet resolute personality, she knew she had found her teacher at long last.

In 1966, Thay founded the Tiep Hien Order, known in the West as the Order of Interbeing, a new and unconventional Buddhist religious order for monks, nuns, laymen, and laywomen. Phuong was one of the original six—three women and three men—to be inducted. When the Order was founded, Thay gave each member the option of deciding whether to practice as a monastic or a layperson. All of the women chose to practice as monastics, while all of the men chose to practice as laypersons. This order was founded at a time when extreme gender asymmetry between Buddhist monks and nuns was the norm, and formal monastics were expected to shave their heads and wear robes. The nuns of Tiep Hien neither shaved their heads nor wore robes; indeed, Phuong was notorious for riding around Vietnam on her motorbike, beautiful black hair flowing in the wind behind her. Yet, Thich Nhat Hanh established the Tiep Hien Order on the principle of gender equality from the beginning, in intentional contradistinction to the religious culture of the time—indeed, the religious culture into which he himself had been socialized and ordained. Thus began the life of their *sangha*, or Buddhist spiritual community.

Thay became an internationally known peace activist during the Vietnam War era and Phuong became known for adding the most concrete part of this peace work, by arranging material help for war victims, orphans, and hungry children. Both Thay and Phuong were exiled from Vietnam for their activities and views. Today, both are also known as master teachers of mindfulness meditation as well as peace activists. Thich Nhat Hanh's work has been cited as profoundly influential by such womanists as Alice Walker and such feminists as bell hooks. Thay was nominated by Martin Luther King Jr. for the Nobel Peace Prize in 1967, and is better known today by the general public than Chan Khong, particularly in the West. *Learning True Love* reveals the extent to which Chan Khong's material, emotional, and political support of Thay's work, as well as her independent action, is an integral part of the story we associate with Thich Nhat Hanh's spiritually based peace activism.

WOMANIST WORK

The focus here is, of course, on Chan Khong's activist work as viewed through a womanist lens. How can her lifetime of work for peace and social change help us understand womanism—whether in terms of a womanist perspective or in terms of womanist activist praxis? The embeddedness of her work within a profound and life-spanning teacher–student relationship as well as an ever-evolving sangha is not inconsequential; we have few models for this in the West. The language I prefer to use is the language of spiritual collaboration. Spiritual collaborators are people who work, and at times live together, for the purpose of advancing one or more spiritual ideals or objectives. Often, for spiritual collaborators, their spiritual ideals and objectives are the most important dimensions of their lives, and their realization involves deep and close interactions with like-minded others, for both practical and psychological reasons. In this chapter, I examine the result of such spiritual collaboration through the lens of one individual, Sister Chan Khong, to highlight a model of spiritual activism and also to show how spiritual collaboration is one expression of the womanist idea. Sister Chan Khong has engaged in spiritually based social change work for the benefit of all humanity, with an emphasis on everyday people and those marginalized by poverty, war, hunger, lack of education, medical conditions, disability, or imprisonment, for the entirety of her adult life. In so doing, she has not only left a legacy of practices, but also a legacy of perspectives that align with and illuminate the womanist idea.

RADICAL BODHISATTVA

In Buddhism, a bodhisattva is a being—human or supernatural—who, animated by bodhicitta,[12] postpones the final step of her or his own enlightenment until all beings have likewise achieved enlightenment and can also ascend. Bodhisattvahood is a precursor stage to Buddhahood, and the Buddha was himself a bodhisattva for many lifetimes before becoming the Buddha. Many Buddhists uphold the bodhisattva figure as a kind of selfless ideal for service to humanity; thus, many monastic orders are based on the practice of bodhisattva vows. Avalokitsvara is the chief bodhisattva, or bodhisattva's bodhisattva, and is universally revered if not prayed to (particularly in times of great suffering or emergency) by Buddhists in the Mahayana tradition.[13] One incarnation of Avalokitsvara (who is sometimes portrayed as a male, other times as a female, and—rarely—as a transgender being) is the popular Kuan Yin, the female bodhisattva of compassion, who maintains a particular interest in children. Chan Khong's social change praxis is informed—if not undergirded—by the bodhisattva model, as well as her own personal reverence for Avalokitesvara (mentioned throughout *Learning True Love*), radicalized and updated to suit contemporary human problems and social conditions. Thus, as a way to capture Chan Khong's tireless, creative, and spiritually based activism, I characterize her as a "radical bodhisattva."

In *Learning True Love*, I noted nearly 50 distinct activist methods employed by Sister Chan Khong. All of these methods are underpinned by a common set of spiritual principles rooted in her "engaged" Buddhist spirituality.[14] In the sections that follow, I select highlights.

MINDFULNESS AS METHOD

Chan Khong's own personal power and agency is rooted in the daily practice of meditation, prayer, and the cultivation of serenity. Her practice—indeed, her activism—is rooted in the principle that outer peace is founded upon, or emanates from, inner peace. Thus, the responsibility of the individual is, first, to cultivate peace within the self, second, to help others cultivate peace within themselves, and, third, to cultivate peaceful social structures and peace in the natural environment. In fact, all of these peace cultivations are taking place simultaneously. Chan Khong practices a type of meditation called mindfulness, rooted in the Zen tradition, but developed into a specific format by her teacher, Thich Nhat Hanh. Mindfulness meditation involves using the breath to "stay in the present moment." Her practice involves daily mindfulness exercises as well as a weekly "Day of Mindfulness" that is part of her Tiep Hien vows. In the text, she refers many times to her spontaneous prayers to Avalokitesvara for help, usually in "emergency" situations.

Learning True Love relays several anecdotes in which Chang Kong cultivated serenity in stressful or dangerous situations in order to give herself a greater degree of power and agency to achieve a particular political or social service aim. In one story, for instance, when she was about 26 years old, she used the cultivation of serenity to calm her activist coworkers and to keep them from all getting shot during an episode when the group was caught in cross-fire:

One night, we stopped in Son Khuong, a remote village where the fighting was especially fierce. As we were about to go to sleep in our boat, we suddenly heard shooting, then screaming, then shooting again. The young people in our group were seized with panic, and a few young men jumped into the river to avoid the bullets. I sat quietly in the boat with two nuns and breathed consciously to calm myself. Seeing us so calm, everyone stopped panicking, and we quietly chanted the Heart Sutra, concentrating deeply on this powerful chant. For a while, we didn't hear any bullets. I don't know if they actually stopped or not. The day after, I shared my strong belief with my coworkers, "When we work to help people, the bullets have to avoid us, because we can never avoid the bullets. When we have good will and great love, when our only aim is to help those in distress, I believe that there is a kind of magnetism, the energy of goodness, that protects us from being hit by the bullets. We only need to be serene. Then, even if a bullet hits us, we can accept it calmly, knowing that everyone has to die one day. If we die in service, we can die with a smile, without fear."[15]

Using language that is relatively informal, Chan Khong refers in this passage to a concrete form of energy manipulation, a vibrational method—as defined previously in my discussion of David Hawkins's work on the logarithmic "Levels of Consciousness."[16] In another, much later anecdote from 1977, Chan Khong reports on cultivating serenity in order to calm herself enough to continue with a massive project she had undertaken, namely, commandeering a ship to rescue Vietnamese boat people after the end of the Vietnam War:

Many times on our rescue boat, I learned that following each breath mindfully was the best way to avoid getting seasick. One time we were caught in a storm. Everyone was vomiting, but I held tightly to one beam on the roof of the boat, sat cross-legged, followed my breathing, and I recovered my equilibrium.[17]

Thus, cultivating serenity is a spiritual method she has used to help her accomplish other political and social service ends, and it constitutes a foundational method insofar as it makes other actions possible, effective, and powerful.

"MEN ARE NOT OUR ENEMIES"

Other spiritual methods are employed specifically to connect spiritually with others for purposes of healing, community building, spiritual education, and inspiration. "Looking deeply" and "listening deeply" are two methods designed to allow one person to get "inside the skin" of another, in order to evoke empathy, compassion, forgiveness, understanding, and the realization of "interbeing."[18] The assumption is that, when interbeing is realized in situ, conflicts dissolve and healing takes place spontaneously through the energies described above. "Looking deeply" is used more commonly when one is trying to understand someone with a different point of view—such as an "enemy" or opponent—whereas "listening deeply" is generally used in a counseling-type situation when the speaker is in need of love, understanding, and healing. The purpose of both methods is to prevent people from developing or maintaining fissures and oppositionality by applying the Buddhist principle of nonduality. Because of the impact of the looker/listener's energy on the other party, these methods can also be considered vibrational—but also psychological. A good example of Chan Khong using the "looking deeply" method is relayed in this story, when, in 1967, she was asked to write the eulogy for several of her compatriots who had recently been killed by military or paramilitary grenades:

> After one Day of Mindfulness by myself, I wrote this eulogy, which was delivered by Thay Thanh Van [then head of the School of Youth for Social Service (SYSS)]: "We cannot hate you, you who have thrown grenades and killed our friends, because we know that men are not our enemies. Our only enemies are the misunderstanding, hatred, jealousy, and ignorance that lead to such acts of violence. Please allow us to remove all misunderstanding so we can work together for the happiness of the Vietnamese people. Our only aim is to help remove ignorance and illiteracy from the countryside of Vietnam. Social change must start in our hearts with the will to transform our own egotism, greed, and lust into understanding, love, commitment, and sharing responsibility for the poverty and injustice in our country."[19]

As a result of this compelling eulogy, the United Buddhist Church of Vietnam offered their previously withheld support for the SYSS, which had been founded by Thich Nhat Hanh in 1966 and largely spearheaded by Chan Khong's visionary and practical leadership. The nonaligned SYSS was the main social work outlet for both urban relief and rural development during the Vietnam War, and thus this endorsement gave a much-needed boost to their efforts.

Another eulogy again inspired by "looking deeply," written by Chan Khong for another occasion, namely, the murder of four SYSS workers by four men acting under orders, was similarly impactful and efficacious:

We set the date for the funeral, and again, Thay Thanh Van asked me to write a eulogy for him to read. Pro-communist Vietnamese told us, "You should cry out against the Americans! It was the CIA agents who killed your friends!" Pro-American Vietnamese said, "You should speak out against the communists. It was they who killed your friends." Even among the Buddhists, there was strong pressure for us to condemn the killers. But we knew that, according to the teaching of the Buddha, humans are not our enemies. Misunderstanding, hatred, jealousy, and confusion are our enemies. Still, it was hard to put that into words when confronted with the corpses of our four dear friends. For three days and nights, I could hardly sleep. I dwelled in mindfulness, reciting gathas, mindfulness verses, as I did my everyday activities: "Washing my hands, I vow to have clean hands to embrace the path of love. I pray that the thoughts and deeds of those who killed my friends will be cleansed." During the third night, the murderer's words that Dinh had told me, "I am sorry, but we have to kill you," sprang into my mind, and I began to see the message of understanding and love that Thay Thanh Van had delivered at the last funeral had reached even the killers. It was obvious that these men had been forced to kill our friends, for if they refused, they themselves could have been killed. In the speech I wrote for Thay Thanh Van, I thanked the murderers for saying that they were forced to kill. "That proved that you did not want to kill us, but for your own safety, you had to do it. We hope that one day you will help us in our work for peace." The funeral was held four days after the murders, and from then on, we received support everywhere we went. The number of workers in the SYSS increased quickly, and we had the full cooperation of monks and nuns throughout the country.[20]

The depth and pervasiveness of Chan Khong's Buddhist principles and spirituality in her politics as well as activist praxis is evident in this passage. This passage illustrates some of the ways that political activism based on Buddhist spirituality differs from typical U.S. notions of activism and, indeed, how political thought based on Buddhist sensibilities differs substantially from Western secular political thought, which tends to be dualistic and "take sides." Even our conceptions of "fighting for the oppressed" often involve taking sides, which eliminates the possibility that we can recognize and realize Chan Khong's statement that "man is not our enemy." In other words, it is impossible to realize the oneness of humanity so long as such a dualistic perspective about warring or oppositional factions is maintained.

An inkling of this perspective is conveyed in the opening pages of Ana-Louise Keating's book *Teaching for Transformation* where she quotes M. Jacqui

Alexander, who writes, "There is great danger...in living lives of segregation. Racial segregation. Segregation in politics. Segregated frameworks. Segregated, compartmentalized selves. Our oppositional politic has been necessary, but it will never sustain us; while it may give us some temporary gains,... it can never ultimately feed that deep place within us: that space of the erotic, that space of the soul, that space of the Divine."[21] Keating then writes,

> [O]ppositional politics lead to "enforced separations," segregations, and other forms of division that at best bring only partial relief. Based on binary (either/or) thinking and dualistic ("us" against "them") models of identity, these oppositional movements inhibit social change by generating nonproductive conflict, suspicion, competition, and debate. For these reasons..., I adopt a connectionist approach and posit interconnectivity as a theoretical and pedagogical framework for social change.[22]

Both Alexander and Keating come to the same conclusion as Chan Khong, namely, that it is time for a nondualistic politics of interconnectivity, interbeing, and oneness. Alexander and Keating are from completely different spiritual traditions (namely, Yoruba/Voudoun/Santeria and New Thought, respectively), so this perspective is worth considering closely, particularly among critically inclined academicians with an interest in social change.[23] This perspective, multisourced as it is, is aligned and consistent with the womanist idea.

THE IMPORTANCE OF SPIRITUAL COMMUNITY

Spiritual community is central to Chan Khong's personal and political life. From the time she met Thay Nhat Hanh, she was involved in one form of spiritual community or another, from the "thirteen cedars,"[24] the SYSS youth corps, and their "Pioneer Villages"[25] in the 1960s, to the intimate spiritual–activist community she shared with Thay and others in the Paris suburb of Sceaux in the early 1970s, to the Sweet Potato farm in the mid- to late 1970s, to its successor, the internationally known Plum Village sangha in Southern France from the 1980s to the present. Spiritual community here refers to an intentional community based on shared spiritual principles and practice. It can be a site where spiritual collaboration builds momentum and achieves validation as well as concrete expression. In Chan Khong's case, Thich Nhat Hahn was the acknowledged leader and visionary architect of these communities; however, based on his egalitarian, democratic, and communalistic beliefs, these communities were coconstructed, coconstituted, and comanaged by all their members, including Chan Khong, whose role was often second only to that of Thay. These communities revolved around Buddhist principles of nonviolence, the practice of mindfulness, and social change labor around peace, poverty alleviation, child welfare, and later, refugee concerns. Together, they constituted a contemporary reworking and reinvigoration of the traditional Buddhist sangha model.

Historically, sanghas were communities of practice for monks or nuns (not monks and nuns together), supported indirectly by communities of laypersons who supported the monastics materially and socially in exchange for spiritual education and benediction. Traditional sanghas had no particular political objectives and were not activist as such. With the introduction of "engaged" Buddhism, Thich Nhat Hanh and his followers updated the sangha model to include spiritually based and ethically grounded political and economic development activity designed to respond to contemporary human needs, at once material, social, psychological, and cultural. Today, Plum Village is considered an exemplary intentional community in both spiritual and political circles.

From a pragmatic standpoint, whether in the traditional or contemporary sense, the sangha serves the purpose of assisting its members to fulfill their intentions for living, which are often quite distinct from, or even at variance with, larger community norms. For example, traditional sanghas aided monks and nuns in their intention to live a life of celibacy by surrounding them with others of like intention. In ways that would not have been possible or even desirable in the outside world, these communities shaped the physical and social environment in ways that discouraged or curbed the expression of sexual impulses. Furthermore, they set up an environment conducive to the practice of meditation and its refinement. Contemporary sanghas perform a similar function by setting up environments that support such intentions as maintaining a vegetarian (or even vegan) diet or the deep practice of nonviolence in thought, word, and deed. Sangha members obtain support for and feedback on their intended behavior, while empowering themselves to work as a coordinated group (for example, as peace activists). For Chan Khong, the sangha served all of these functions, thus facilitating her activism.

Many sanghas also provide spiritual education for both laypersons and novice monastics. For instance, today, Plum Village is known worldwide as a place to receive education about mindfulness, particularly as it relates to peace, and this education is offered to both monastics in the Tiep Hien Order and to interested laypersons of all backgrounds from around the world. Furthermore, the Plum Village sangha serves as a center for Vietnamese cultural education for refugees and other dislocated persons, particularly children and adolescents, in the postwar/globalization era. Both spiritual and cultural education are forms of activism from a womanist perspective. Finally, one thing that has been particularly important for all Tiep Hien Order sanghas has been the promotion of gender equality within Buddhist practice and institutional life. The realization of this intention has had an impact on Buddhism, Buddhists, and Buddhist-oriented unofficial practitioners worldwide, particularly given recent concerns and debates about the dwindling number of Buddhist nuns in the global Buddhist community.[26]

A HANDFUL OF RICE

Chan Khong's earliest activism took place in the slums of Saigon, near the University of Saigon where she was a biology student. On breaks in between classes and labs, Chan Khong would visit the slums and listen to people's stories, pretending to be a relative of someone in the community. Through listening, she learned details of people's hardships and devised many ingenious ways to assist the community, particularly its children. For example, upon learning that many families, especially single-parent families, prohibited their children from going to school because children were needed to peddle on the streets and thus contribute to the family's meager daily income, Chan Khong devised a system of "rice scholarships" that not only got the children to school (a class she taught "under the shade tree") but also contributed to families' income and food security. By collecting a handful of rice each morning from well-to-do families outside the slum, she was able to create "rice scholarships" for children inside the slum who showed up for class. In turn, these children took the rice home to their families, thus appeasing their parents' anxieties about food and obtaining some education in the process.

Upon learning that the biggest impediment to children's enrollment in public school was the lack of birth certificates, Chan Khong again took action. For parents who had not filed for a birth certificate at the time their child was born, the process of obtaining one was cumbersome and expensive, involving the submission of an application and payment of a penalty at the police station, six months of waiting as the paperwork wended its way through a District Center and Central Court, followed by a court case at which the applicant must produce two corroborating witnesses to confirm the child's birth date. For slum dwellers, many of whom were illiterate and most of whom had to work all day to survive, this process was not viable. "So," wrote Chan Khong,

> I decided to intervene. A friend of mind invited a young judge to come to the
> slum and set up a court right there, and on the spot, the judge issued a birth
> certificate at no charge to anyone who came forward and had two witnesses

to confirm the day his or her child was born. My friends and I had already filled in many of their applications in advance, and eventually, hundreds of children were able to go to school.

Chan Khong then turned her attention to the adults in the community. By collecting the equivalent of a dime from each of the same well-to-do families who funded her rice scholarships, she created a revolving microloan fund for individuals living in the slum who desired to start small businesses. Running this fund in a way that foreshadows the microcredit agencies of today, Chan Khong reinvested loan paybacks in new clients. In order to facilitate working among the community's single mothers, she also organized a rotating childcare system by which five mothers would take turns watching each other's children so that each could work four days per week. Finally, using her own motorbike, Chan Khong ran a community ambulance service, delivering critically ill patients to doctor friends of hers in the outlying community who agreed to treat patients on a pro bono basis.

These years of do-it-yourself "social work" in the slums of Saigon conscientized Chan Khong with regard to the real-life impact of various forms of systemic oppression and cemented her identity as a self-motivated and resourceful agent of change. Over the course of her life, she would time and again engage in various forms of collaborative economic empowerment work, increasingly informed by and informing of her Buddhist spiritual convictions and worldview. Her early work in the slums as a young woman shows the organic, holistic nature of her approach, which I view as womanist in character.

An interesting lesson about economics came a short time later after Chan Khong met Thich Nhat Hanh and decided to make him her teacher. In order to blend in with the community she was serving, Chan Khong, who was essentially middle class, had taken to wearing shabby clothes. She writes:

> One day, I attended a public lecture by Thay Nhat Hanh at the An Quang Pagoda. I was wearing an old gray dress that was much too big for me, and afterwards Thay invited me to the reception room and asked "Don't you have a better dress?" I was startled and started to cry. I thought he would understand that I wanted to dress like the poor people I worked with in order to be close to them, but Thay seemed to have another idea. Surprised, and even a little embarrassed to see me cry, he sweetly explained, "A person's beauty must been seen from the outside as well as from the inside. You don't have to wear fancy or expensive dresses. Very simple ones are fine, but they should be decent and lovely. If you shaved your head, you would wear a beautiful nun's robe. But now your hair is long, and you should wear a simple, beautiful dress

like other young people your age. It will encourage those who might like to join you in your work. One's mind, actions, and dress should all communicate one's quality of being. This is the correct way for a bodhisattva.[27]

Chan Khong's association with Thay corresponded with a marked scaling-up of her social change work. Immediately she became swept into an emerging social change apparatus that was being built by Thay, yet her involvement proved influential to the ultimate character of it all. At first through the Buddhist Student Union, then through the Thirteen Cedars, Van Hanh University, the School of Youth for Social Service (SYSS), the Tiep Hien Order (Order of Interbeing), two pioneer villages, and later the work in France (including Sceaux, Sweet Potato Farm, and Plum Village), Chan Khong engaged in holistic social change activities that synthesized education, peace-building, and everyday activism. In 1966, Thay Nhat Hanh left for the West, leaving Chan Khong and the rest of the Tien Hiep order to carry on in Vietnam. During this period, Chan Khong exhibited exceptional leadership, courage, and ingenuity.

TRANSFORMATION DURING THE TET OFFENSIVE

Tet is the Vietnamese New Year, celebrated in January with great festivity. In January of 1968, warring parties on both sides agreed to a brief truce in honor of the holiday. Yet, this truce was never honored and the massive attack by the communists, ultimately beaten back by U.S. forces, that came to be known in the United States as the "Tet Offensive" was one of the worst episodes of the Vietnam War. The initial conflagration lasted for roughly two months, reasserting itself in the form of minioffensives in May and August of 1968. During this period, Chan Khong was both a biology professor at Saigon University and one of the volunteer social workers at the SYSS. In May, the SYSS became a refugee camp housing over 11,000 people. In *Learning True Love*, a chapter is devoted to this time of the Tet Offensive (known in Vietnam as the "General Offensive and Uprising" or, simply, "Tet, Year of the Monkey"),[28] and in it we find numerous anecdotes illustrating Chan Khong's womanist spiritual activism. The first anecdote reveals the transformational possibilities of dialogue when it is powered by mutual intergenerational respect and an appeal to people's higher natures. The second anecdote reveals a womanist approach to disaster management. The third anecdote reveals a combination of the two.

After the Tet Offensive in January, Chan Khong authored a peace petition that she persuaded one-third of the Saigon University faculty to sign. This petition was published in the newspapers and drew the attention of the Vietnamese government, which suspected that the faculty members may have had a role in planning or instigating the offensive. One day shortly thereafter, Chan Khong heard the Minister of Education reading out the names of the signatories over the radio—every half hour—and instructing them to make an appearance at the ministry without delay. "I was very afraid, but I thought that since the petition had been my idea, I had to take full responsibility and go."[29] When she showed up, only twenty of her colleagues had appeared. Collectively, they were asked to "retract [their] peace appeal and sign a new petition condemning the communists."[30] All but three—Chan Khong, Father Nguyan Ngoc Lan, and Professor Chau Tam Luan—agreed to do so, out of fear of lethal reprisal if they did not do so. These three argued that they could not sign the petition because their students had heard their names on the radio and would know that they had succumbed to government pressure. She stated, "The most important gift a teacher can give his students is dignity. We have always tried our best to be worthy of our students' trust. If we die under violence, our spirits will blossom in their hearts. But if we sign the petition offered by the government today, it means we have submitted to the government's threats. This is not what we want to teach the younger generation."[31] Everyone was released from the meeting, but she knew it was not over.

Later in the evening, she was recalled to the office of the Minister of Education, who informed her that the Chief of Police had asked him to settle the matter with Chan Khong. He informed her that her refusal in this instance would lead to her immediate arrest as well as the loss of her university position. Chan Khong responds:

> I breathed deeply and said in a very firm voice: "Sir, I came to you today because I know that you were once a professor, my elder brother in teaching. When you speak in such a threatening way, it is impossible for us to have real communication. So do what you want with me. Please send me to jail. If I allow you to coerce me as you suggest, I would be no better than Colonel Lieu, the cherished comrade of President Thieu, who, as soon as he was arrested by the communists in Ben Tre, called upon all South Vietnamese soldiers to join the side of the North."
>
> With tears in my eyes, I continued more gently. "Sir, I am like a bamboo shoot among university teachers. I am young, but my spirit may grow strong and beautiful. I spoke out frankly about the situation of the country, not for my own sake, but for the sake of the nation, even though prison may await me as a result. I appeal to your conscience as an elder brother to help me grow in this attitude, not to bow before coercion. Don't force me to go against

my conscience. If I agree to sign your petition under threat of violence, then tonight if unknown men enter my house with guns and force me to sign a petition saying, 'Long live Mao Tse Tung,' must I not also sign that? If I sign under the threat of guns against my conscience and belief, who will be at fault? Do you really want to teach me that way of coercion?"

He seemed embarrassed and his attitude changed immediately. He said that I had misunderstood him, that he only wanted to protect me. Then he let me go without signing anything, and the police never came to arrest me. Apparently he protected me from the police.[32]

While this exchange is clearly steeped in conversational conventions associated with Asian culture, its basic principles are universally applicable: Even with an opponent, enter the exchange with respect, focusing on and appealing to that person's higher nature—whether or not it is operative in the moment—and invite the person to help you in the realization of your own higher nature as well as some larger common good. Such an exchange has the power to produce genuine transformation, even if incremental, rather than merely strategic repositioning. Stated more plainly, it changes the spirit of things and creates new social and political trajectories.

When another offensive began in May, as mentioned, the SYSS campus became a camp for 11,000 refugees. With only 37 social workers on staff at the time, the situation presented a significant logistical challenge. Yet, with womanist ingenuity, the social work students, led by Chan Khong, managed it ingeniously. She reports:

At that time, there were only thirty-seven social workers at the school, organizing the care of almost 11,000 refugees. We invited a few hundred of those able to take responsibility for themselves to help us, and we divided into teams—one team to do the medical work, one for childcare, one to cook, one to distribute food, one to take care of water, one to clear the road, and one to clean the rooms and the bathrooms. In addition, we dug a number of holes outside to use as latrines.

During the eight-day period of their confinement, eight people died and were buried and 10 new babies were born. On the third day, when a rumor that the campus would be bombed began to circulate, Thay Thanh Van, the senior monk on staff, himself a young man, took it upon himself to leave the campus surreptitiously and appeal to both the South and North Vietnamese armies not to fire on the school, its refugees, or its staff, and not to allow planes to bomb the campus. Both sides agreed, but they expressed concern that if the other side heard them not firing, they would think they had surrendered. Thay Thanh Van asked them to fire into the air instead, and they did. He did not reveal the story of his negotiations to his comrades until four months later.

A final anecdote is taken from a time when the SYSS staff received reports that guerrillas had infiltrated their camp, posing as refugees. There was fear that if the infiltrators fired their guns, it would attract bombing to the campus. Without knowing who the infiltrators were, Chan Khong and associates asked the elders within the camp to help them curb any violence. She writes: "Because in Vietnam we respect our elders very much, we decided to ask the oldest persons among the refugees to go around and say to everyone, 'We pray that those who have guns will not use them. If you know anyone who has a gun, please advise him to bury it, for the safety of 11,000 people.' Finally, there was no trouble at all."[33]

This anecdote merges the wisdom of the previous two anecdotes, demonstrating the power of intergenerational respect along with the creativity of womanist ingenuity. While Chan Khong carefully writes to convey the collective character of leadership and service within SYSS, it is clear that the actions of the SYSS social workers reflect womanist attributes regardless of the gender of the people involved. A respect for the higher natures—arguably, the innate divinity—of all involved, whether combatants, refugees, or comrades, as well as a "do it yourself" mentality that "made a way out of no way" allowed Chan Khong and her associates to not only save the lives of nearly 11,000 people, but also to advance the cause of peace during a violent and terrifying episode in Vietnam's history. Summarizing the period, she writes: "Those eight days were a turning experience for me. Seeing so much death and despair, I learned that we must resist war at any price. Once a war gets started, it has a momentum and intensity that are very hard to stop."[34] Showcasing these less well-known stories from a conflict that is entrenched in the global popular imagination provides us with new avenues for thinking about peace and peacemaking, particularly in our current era characterized by new and even more complicated forms of war.

PEACEMAKING IN EXILE

In July of 1968, Chan Khong left Vietnam for Hong Kong at the request of Thay Nhat Hanh, who had left Vietnam two years previously for a stint in the West and, now unable to return to Vietnam due to his peace activity, was temporarily located there. Their reunion was quite emotional, since they had been forced to curtail their communications as a result of the war and its surveillance. She wrote, "I wished I could sob in his arms, but, at that time, Thay had not yet taught us hugging meditation."[35] That evening, the scope of her peace-building work scaled up as a result of a request that Thay Nhat Hanh made of her. She recounts: "Considering each word carefully, he said that if the monks wished him to stay in the West, he would desperately need an assistant to help him bring the message of the suffering of the Vietnamese people to the world. He asked me to join him in this work, saying that I could be more effective in bringing the war to a halt outside of the country."[36] Remarkably, Chan Khong refused, arguing that the SYSS would not be able to survive even a week without her. Nevertheless, neither she nor Thay would return to Vietnam again until January 2005.

By the end of 1968, both Chan Khong and Thay found themselves in Paris. In June of 1969, they held a peace conference that birthed the Vietnamese Buddhist Peace Delegation to the Paris Peace Accords, an organization through which they would conduct their peace work for some time. They rented a small office in a poor neighborhood and both worked as teachers to make enough money to live while they spent the bulk of their effort on peace-related activities. Over time, they attracted a group of supporters of all ages and multiple nationalities that enabled the work to expand. Chan Khong in particular was skilled at keeping their activities alive in the media, whether newspapers or television.

In 1973, shortly after the Paris Peace Accords were signed, formally ending U.S. involvement in the Vietnamese conflict, Chan Khong, Thay, and six of their collaborators acquired a residence in Sceaux, France, a suburb of Paris, where they lived and worked communally. With hostilities still raging in Vietnam despite the accords, their actions on behalf of peace were still badly needed. During this period, Chan Khong traveled extensively throughout Europe and eventually to the United States. Having taught herself English in order to speak to journalists without the risk of having her words purposely distorted, and already fluent in French in addition to her native tongue of Vietnamese, she was a very effective spokesperson.

One of the discoveries made by Chan Khong and Thay in the course of their interactions with Western peace activists was the cultural difference between understandings about the meaning of peace as well as methodological approaches to the achievement of peace. This reflective paragraph embedded within the section of her memoir that deals with their Western travels highlights her encounter with U.S. peace activists in particular:

From 1966–1968, Thay had cultivated deep friendships with a number of spiritually-based, social activists, including Martin Luther King, Jr., Thomas

Merton, Daniel Berrigan, Dorothy Day, Joan Baez, and Jim Forest. But by 1970, we discovered that the American peace movement as a whole was rather young. We could not expect all peace workers to have the spiritual maturity of these great men and women, but by the time I arrived to help Thay, we were surprised to see how many people in the peace movement, frustrated by the prolonged war, were calling for a victory by Hanoi as the only hope. They thought that a victory by North Vietnam and the NLF would end the war quickly. This was extremely painful for us to hear, because we knew how much suffering one bomb or one bullet brings. And from our own experience of the violence perpetrated by the North during the 1968 Tet Offensive, and from the book, *The Forest of Reeds*, in which Doan Quoc Sy described how much violence the Hanoi government had already perpetrated against its own people who were not communist, we knew that a victory by the North would not end the suffering. We only wanted an immediate cease-fire, and it was shocking for us to hear so-called peace activists advocating for a victory by one side.[37]

Chan Khong's frustration is traceable to the attitude that she expressed in the eulogy she delivered for her fallen compatriots in 1967, in which, based on the political interpretation of the Buddhist principle of nonduality and interconnectedness, she stated "Men are not our enemies." The only route to peace, from her perspective, was through the cessation of the perpetuation of violence, in act or in spirit; peace could not be won through the gun or attained through expediency. To quote Thay's words that would come much later, "Peace is every step." For this reason, Chan Khong's Buddhist-based peace praxis is instructive within the context of womanist spiritual activism, in which the transformation of energies, leading to the transformation of material reality, including human relationships and the human relationship with nature, is the goal as well as the method. Her presence in the West, along with Thay's, allowed this perspective to enlarge within Western pacifist discourse.

In addition to speaking out on peace in the West, Chan Khong initiated a number of projects to offer hands-on help to Vietnamese people still suffering inside Vietnam. Of particular interest to her were children whose lives had been upended by the war. In a manner reminiscent of her earlier do-it-yourself social work in the slums of Saigon during college, she created a fund for Vietnamese orphans and raised considerable support among Europeans. "By April 1975, the end of the war, we had the support of 14,000 families in Holland; 1,000 in Switzerland; 2,000 in France; 1,000 in the United States; and hundreds in other countries, nearly 20,000 sponsors in all. It was a great linking of the human family."[38] Unfortunately, the regime change (or consolidation) at the end of the Vietnam War brought setbacks to the orphan project. After a $150,000 contribution mysteriously disappeared in transit, her European supporters were no longer willing to fund projects in Vietnam, and they turned their attention to other suffering countries, including Bangladesh, India, and Ethiopia. Chan Khong was heartbroken at the loss of this pipeline, but over time she devised new ways to stay connected with and help Vietnamese children.

Between 1971 and 1975, Chan Khong, Thay, and friends developed a rural property in France that came to be known as Sweet Potato Community ("Les Patates Douces"). Purchased cheaply and barely habitable initially, years of weekend renovation trips eventually made the farm a suitable location for what was rapidly becoming a sangha. Chan Khong and Thay were both lovers of horticulture, gardening, and the mindfulness-inducing aspects of interaction with plants and Earth. Indeed, many particularly beautiful descriptions of landscapes, plants, gardens, herbs, and fruits are sprinkled throughout *Learning True Love*, establishing Chan Khong's ecological sensibilities, passions, and delights. For example, she reminisces:

> Our life in Sweet Potato Community was meditative and joyful. We did not feel strong enough to sing traditional Vietnamese songs, but we sang songs that arose from our meditations on being in touch with nature—the trees, the birds, the sunshine, the snow. We printed and bound books for refugees and planted vegetables.... We planted lettuce, carrots, mustard greens, coriander, mint, and many Vietnamese herbs, and we discovered that Thay Nhat Hanh was also an expert gardener. He taught us how to use a hoe, how to dig without bending our backs too much, and how to aerate and cultivate the soil. In that atmosphere, my mind was not disturbed by painful images of Vietnam.[39]

Her descriptions linking nature, mindfulness, and peace resonate with the womanist triadic focus on humans, nature, and spirit and convey the truly integral nature of womanist activism, further illuminating the notion that womanism is not an ideology, not a philosophy, not a theory, but, rather, a "spirit" and a "way of being in the world."

ACTIVISM ON THE HIGH SEAS

Nearly every womanist activist has at least one dramatic story of her "outrageous, audacious, courageous, or *willful*" behavior in the interest of social or ecological change. In 1976 and 1977, Chan Khong, the mindful gardener of Sweet Potato Community, doubled as a ship captain intent on securing justice, peace, and relocation for Vietnamese boat people. With the backing of the World Conference on Religion and Peace (WCRP), she and Thay initiated a project called Mau Chay Ruot Mem ("When blood is shed, we all suffer"). With funds raised by WCRP, they set up shop in Singapore, rented a cargo ship and an oil tanker, and cruised the high seas rescuing vulnerable boat people—refugees from the Southeast Asian postwar regimes. Their goal was not only to rescue people, but also to publicize the plight of the refugees and obtain more visas for them in countries such as the United States, Australia, and Guam. During this mission, they gathered 566 refugees onto a ship. When they were kicked out of Singapore on short notice due to a disagreement with the UN High Commissioner for Refugees office, they decided to sail directly to Australia. "Thay was confident that I would be able to lead the expedition to Australia, and he departed for Perth to wait for us."[40] However, the day after Thay left, the WCRP fired Chan Khong and sent her packing. Despite a frantic search for alternatives to continue the work to which she had committed herself, she ended up flying to Australia, where she immediately contacted the Australian press, publicized the plight of the boat people, and entreated the Australian government to change its policy and begin receiving refugees. It did. Nevertheless, 534 of the original 566 boat people—those who had been unable to obtain refugee visas—floundered on the ship for months, unable to immigrate anywhere.

Chan Khong and Thay returned to France, regrouped, and launched another, more independent rescue operation out of Thailand that involved a "fishing boat." By keeping a lower profile, they were able to rescue more people by directing escape boats to a hospitable province where they would be admitted to a refugee camp and providing them with needed food and fuel for the journey. However, they also risked—and skillfully averted—encounters with local pirates. "The violence on the high seas was so great that our Thai friends quit as soon as the Thai police warned us about the sea pirates. Eventually, there were only my brother Nghiep, the four Vietnamese crew members, myself, and Avalokitesvara Bodhisattva. We did this silently for almost a year."[41] As a result of this sustained and mindful labor, U.S. President Jimmy Carter increased the U.S. quota of Vietnamese refugees from 1,000 to 7,000, then again to 15,000. "Looking back," writes Chan Khong, "even though we failed to bring all of the 566 boat people to Australia and Guam, we did help in bringing the cries of the boat people to the world's ears."[42]

A LARGER COMMUNITY

In 1982, Chan Khong and Thay relocated from Sweet Potato Community to a new property that they named Village de Plumieres, or Plum Village. With them was a group of recent Vietnamese immigrants, some of whom were old Buddhist colleagues from Vietnam. Sweet Potato Community had grown too small for the crowds who were gathering to hear Thay's dharma talks and retreating to study mindfulness practices as taught under the auspices of the Order of Interbeing, as well as for Chan Khong's social work-inspired community and cultural projects. Three beautiful hamlets were purchased in a more southwestern region of the French countryside. A humble retreat center, as well as a monastic sangha, was established. Hundreds, then thousands of people, began flocking to the site for spiritual restoration and instruction. This is her initial description of the center:

> Together, we practice sitting meditation, walking meditation, tea meditation, work meditation, and Dharma discussion.... Families and friends practice joyfully together, and every day Thay gives a talk in Vietnamese, English, or French, with simultaneous translation into those languages plus German and Italian. We have many cultural activities for Vietnamese children—the older children teach the younger ones about their homeland, and there is a lot of singing. We also have beautiful programs for Western children.... The teachings of Thay Nhat Hanh during the summer retreat are for children and adults to create peace in themselves and in the world.[43]

Since 1982, Plum Village has been a center of spiritualized social change work, where emphasis on the inner foundations of peace—strengthened through mindfulness practice—has gradually been elevated to meet the world's demand for rethinking and rebuilding the outer foundations of peace. The nature, scope, and scale of programming at Plum Village has constantly expanded over time. Visitors come from all over the world, as do new monastics, both female and male.[44] In fact, Plum Village is now at the center of an international network of practice centers aligned or affiliated with the Tiep Hien Order to which Thay, Chan Khong, and other members of the sangha travel cyclically. While both Thay and Chan Khong have continued to engage in more external, public forms of peace-building and peace activism, including writing, speaking, media appearances, and peaceful appeals, Plum Village has served as an elegant milieu as they move into their vibrantly venerable years.

FROM STUDENT TO TEACHER

There is a famous saying that, "When the student is ready, the Teacher appears," and a corollary saying that, "When the Teacher is ready, the student appears." These sayings articulate the interdependent and reciprocal nature of the relationship linking two people at different stages of the spiritual path. Implied in this relationship, which can be both intense and life-altering for both parties, is the prospect that the student will one day become a teacher and the teacher will one day become a student again. Also implied is the reality that, sometimes, the student teaches the teacher and the teacher is a student of the student.

A spiritual student–teacher relationship can be a lifetime, committed relationship. Speaking in general terms, it may or may not involve libidinal energies. It may or may not be exclusive. It may or may not involve a family—whether biological or spiritual—or domestic responsibilities. At its foundation, however, is an agreement about fostering spiritual evolution, generally on both individual and collective planes of experience. What is unfortunate is that many modern societies have lost any schema for this kind of relationship, lacking language, exemplars, and appreciation for the possibilities of this unique form of relationship. However, the language of spiritual collaboration and spiritual collaborators may help us to reclaim some of these possibilities, particularly given the role of spiritual education and development in self-actualization, commonweal, the Ladder of Learning, and LUXOCRACY.

One reason that Sister Chan Khong's life narrative is captivating is that it provides a window into the experience of spiritual collaboration. As mentioned at the beginning of this chapter, Sister Chan Khong's relationship with Thich Nhat Hanh began as a spiritual student–teacher relationship, shaped by Buddhist (and earlier Hindu) traditions. Through her story, not only are we able to observe her evolve into a teacher in her own right, but we are also able to observe the very human dimensions that complicate and ultimately deepen spiritual student–teacher relationships. Because everyday human relationships are the first site of peace-making, it is important to look deeply at them. It is also important to look deeply at moments of transformation in relationship, when roles and relationships change.

The years 1987 and 1988 were turning points in Chan Khong's life as a practitioner of Buddhism and student of Thich Nhat Hanh. Although they had worked collaboratively as functional equals nearly since the inauguration of the Tiep Hien Order in 1966, Thich Nhat Hanh's subtle leadership asserted itself in a number of ways and, at the same time, Chan Khong maintained a customary sort of deference to him, despite her bold and at times irreverent personality, which he appreciated and admired. By the time Plum Village was up and running, Chan Khong had clear areas of responsibility and leadership that were her own, even though the world acknowledged Thich Nhat Hanh as the center's spiritual and administrative head. However, Chan Khong writes:

> In 1987 in Australia I began to teach the Dharma. When people have mental wounds, they want to share them only with someone they really trust, someone like Thay Nhat Hanh. But Thay cannot see everyone, so when we were in Australia to lead mindfulness retreats for Australians and Vietnamese refugees there, I offered to listen to people's difficulties, report them to Thay, and transmit Thay's advice to them. I listened to so many people that my reports became longer and longer until Thay finally said, "Please look deeply into each person's problem and help him or her yourself. I'm sure you can do it." In fact, I was able to see solutions to many of their difficulties and share them with these friends, thanks to the method of looking deeply taught by Thay. I did my best to "be in the skin" of each person and to help them understand themselves and each other. Thanks to this work, a number of families made peace among themselves for the first time in years, and since then, slowly seeing my ability to help, families have come to me at retreats in the U.S., Europe, and Plum Village for that kind of consultation.[45]

Of course, in many respects, Chan Khong had been teaching the dharma all along. But in 1987, 20 plus years after ordination, she felt ready to claim the role of teacher and embrace her unique talents as a counselor and healer of the heart and spirit. Her success—indeed, her genius—as a teacher emanates from her clear seeing of the worlds, inner and outer, through her own eyes. She writes: "The greatest reward is to see those who have been healed later become sources of joy, peace, and generosity for others. Thay Nhat Hanh emphasizes that any teachings must be born from one's own experience, not just by repeating the words of the Buddha or some other authority.... To be authentic, our own teaching must also be the fruit of our own looking deeply, not someone else's."[46]

Traditionally, in Vietnam, monastics—be they male or female—shave their heads and wear monastic robes. When the Tiep Hien Order was formed in 1966, as noted at the beginning of this chapter, Thay Nhat Hanh gave his ordinees the choice of ordaining as monastics or laypersons. The three men chose to ordain as laypersons—meaning they could marry and live as householders—whereas the three women chose to ordain as nuns. However, they made a conscious choice to serve as "formless" nuns who, among other things, did not shave their heads or wear monastic robes.[47] At the time, they were young, beautiful women and, even with their humble temperaments, they recognized certain advantages to maintaining an appearance that blended in with the general population. Yet, Chan Khong carried with her a persistent sense that, eventually, for her own reasons, she would surrender to these meaningful traditions. That day came in 1988. Inspired by the sudden passing away of one of her elder role models in Vietnam, the high nun Su Ba The Thanh, a warm and courageous advocate for children, Chan Khong decided that it was time.

"My Tiep Hien sisters helped me prepare for the ceremony by cutting my long hair and shaving most of it off. Thay Nhat Hanh symbolically cut some of my hair and said, 'Shaving the head, all attachments are cut off.'"[48] He also gave her a poem called "Open the Road Wider." From that point forward, she was known by her dharma name, Chan Khong, or "True Emptiness"—"We inter-are, and therefore we are empty of an identity that is separate from our interconnectedness."[49]

After four decades in exile, Sister Chan Khong and Thich Nhat Hanh, accompanied by members of their sangha, again set foot in Vietnam. The trip, which had been several years in the making, was a strategic effort on the part of the communist Vietnamese government, which wanted to gain admission to the World Trade Organization (WTO). Officials knew that such a feat would be impossible if they continued to exile the internationally respected Thich Nhat Hanh. At the same time, Thay had a younger generation of followers in Vietnam who longed to practice with him and hear him teach the dharma in person. Thus, an exchange was negotiated, insofar as Thay hoped that Vietnam's entry into the WTO would help democratize the country and loosen restrictions on the practice of Buddhism. The visit lasted three months, contained several control measures (specifying, for example, where Thay could and could not speak, and how many people could accompany him or attend each event), and frequently presented setbacks (issues with luggage or badges). Yet, the experience was momentous. Sister Chan Khong in particular experienced a transformative moment:

> Before his Dharma talk, Thay asked us all to offer a chant evoking the name of Avalokitesvara. Thay asked everyone to send our compassionate energy to the pains in our body and in our mind, and to those we love who were not there. Or we could send our loving energy to the sick or the needy while the monastics called out the name of Avalokitesvara. I usually try to send my energy to a particular person I know who is not very well, like a sister who is ill, for instance. But that day in Bang A Temple, silently I sent this thought: "Here among us there are possibly people who are suffering, who have no opportunity to talk to anyone who can show them how to practice with their difficulties. I wish that these people can receive the compassionate energy of

the assembled Sangha, to transform their suffering." And in front of such a big audience, in concentration and in compassion, slowly I was overwhelmed by this tremendous feeling: I am now standing on the very land which is the cradle of Vietnam with its 4,000 year history. On this sacred land, millions and millions of Vietnamese fathers and mothers have lived and died: all those fathers who aspired to do something great, beautiful, and wholesome for the young generations, all those mothers who dedicated their lives to loving and nourishing their children, raised them up and was ready to give them to the nation. I had the sense that I was touching deeply my blood ancestors and my land ancestors, as well as my spiritual ancestors.[50]

With this experience, Cao Ngoc Phuong as Sister Chan Khong had come full circle.

LEARNING TRUE LOVE: LESSONS LEARNED

Looking over the life and work of Sister Chan Khong, as presented in her memoir, *Learning True Love*, I see that the wisdom of her transformational praxis can be distilled into eight major tenets. Although Chan Khong does not refer to herself as a womanist, these tenets are consistent with the womanist idea. In the womanist spirit of "getting it done," I present the tenets in the form of a "to-do" list:

Lesson 1 *Don't take sides, because there is only one side*—the human side, the humanitarian side, the side of healing, the side of peace.

Lesson 2. *Cultivate vibrational power*—spiritual power, the power of principle. Do whatever it takes to make and keep your vibration higher than that of war and the warring parties, whether that includes mindfulness, prayer, meditation, or self-care. This is a form of protection as well as a method for transforming the situation without violence. The practice of peace, inner and outer, requires the ability to cultivate vibrational power.

Lesson 3. *Live simply*. Keep your possessions to a minimum, stay mobile, learn to live with less, eat simply, appreciate simple pleasures, share what you have, and cultivate nonattachment.

Lesson 4. *Cultivate spiritual community*. Take refuge in a sangha, surround yourself with like-minded people, help others build communities, engage in "social work," engage in community healing work—everywhere you go and everywhere you are. Such a community facilitates spiritual collaboration.

Lesson 5. *Stay close to nature.* Learn how to farm, how to garden, eat "close to the ground," garden for mindfulness, garden to appreciate interbeing, take walks in nature, live close to the elements in order to appreciate simplicity and the ways in which nature is safe.

Lesson 6. *Whenever possible, DIY—do it yourself.* Don't wait for authority; do what's needed, exercise leadership where you are, question laws and policies that don't work. Answer only to peace, love, respect, and healing. Also, don't be attached to your own sense of self.

Lesson 7. *Have a refuge.* Whether that refuge is a practice, like mindfulness, or a peaceful, sacred place, like Sweet Potato Farm, or a spiritual collaboration with one or more other human beings, having such a refuge is part of self-care, and thus a pillar of social and ecological transformation.

WORDS OF WISDOM

In 2009, I had the opportunity to visit Plum Village as part of my Contemplative Practice Fellowship sponsored by the Center for Contemplative Mind in Society. I participated in a 21-day retreat called "The Path of the Buddha: Buddhist Elements for a Global Ethic." While on this trip, I learned mindfulness practice, lived and worked with nuns and other laypersons, and attended several dharma talks by Thich Nhat Hanh. My greatest anticipation had been about, and my greatest excitement came, however, from meeting Sister Chan Khong. When the French taxi driver unceremoniously dropped me off at the New Hamlet of Plum Village, I was alone for some time before anyone came to receive me. I considered it auspicious that the first person I saw and spoke with was Chan Khong. Defying her 70+ years, she sped into the driveway in a tiny car and rushed into the monastery. "Are you OK?" she asked breathlessly, with a kind, direct gaze, even though she was clearly on her way to somewhere. "Yes," I said, "I'm wonderful." She quickly informed me about a meeting I might consider attending—the one she was on her way to—and then disappeared down a hallway.

Later in the retreat, after hearing Chan Khong speak several times in group settings, I had the opportunity to meet with her one-on-one. Although I came prepared with a list of questions, we never got past the first one: "What are your words of wisdom for teaching people spiritual activism?" Here are my notes from that meeting, based on what she said:[51]

Core theme: Buddha's moment of epiphany. We make it complex but it is really simple: How can I change myself to change the world around me, how can I end suffering in myself to end suffering in the whole world? Most of our problems are caused by thinking we see clearly when we don't really, then being attached to what we think we know and getting angry about it. Buddha taught us to look deeply to see clearly, and this is the main practice that we need to follow (to change the world and ourselves). Most of the time, even when we are "paying attention" and we think we are listening intently/carefully and seeing deeply, we are not. Only about 20% of our mind is doing this, and we are only seeing things superficially. We may be focusing on what we think we're paying attention to and at the same time our mind/attention is attending to 80% other things. Buddhist practice/mindfulness teaches us to increase the percent we are using to concentrate on one thing—the present moment—and see more clearly/deeply and/or listen more deeply and really hear. In this way, more of the truth is revealed to us and we can make wiser decisions.

Example of a story about wrong perceptions, sixteenth century Vietnam: A couple was in love and the wife got pregnant. The husband got drafted into the military and had to go to another country. The wife was unable to know where he was or how he was, but still she waited. She had the baby, and when the baby (son) was about 4 years old, he asked the mother, "Who is my father? All the other kids have a father, but I don't." When evening came and she let lit the lamp, the mother pointed to her shadow and said, "See, that is your father." So the kid thought the shadow was his father. About a year and a half passed and the father came home from the war. The wife was so glad to see him and he was so glad to see her. The wife said, Please watch the boy so I can go to the market and get some things to prepare a feast in honor of the ancestors for your safe return. When she left, the man said to the boy, "I am your father," and the boy said, "No, you're not—my father comes to my mother at night and lays down with her then leaves in the morning." When the wife returned, her husband treated her coldly, but she did not question it; she prepared the meal as planned. However, after dinner, he left the house and went to the tavern, spending the whole night drinking. After that, their marriage was never the same because he maintained the belief that his wife had betrayed him. At the same time, the wife developed a belief that she was no good, because her husband treated her so coldly. Eventually, she threw herself in the river out of grief. The community, knowing the truth, built a shrine in her honor. One night, when the father lit the lamp, the son said to him, "There's my father!" And suddenly the father knew the truth, but it was too late. Both the husband

and the wife had succumbed to wrong perceptions by not looking deeply, by lack of communication, and holding to views.

This story has a moral about wrong perceptions generally, but also about relationships in particular, and the importance of looking deeply, listening deeply, nonattachment to views, and dealing with anger in a certain kind of way. The upshot of these same principles can be seen in terrorism and the problems countries are having with mindful communication. Examples include the jealous husband, post-9/11 talks by Thay in Berkeley and New York City, and Sister Chan Khong's own work with Palestinians and Israelis, especially families of terrorists. The point is, when we are angry or jealous, we tend to engage in provocative speech that escalates conflict—thus, it is important not to speak when we are angry—not even to think, if possible—and allow ourselves to calm down—30 minutes is good, 3 hours is better, several days is even better. Then, when we go back to the other person, we say, "I know you are a good person and I was surprised/hurt when [...] happened. Can you help me to understand what happened so that I can consider what I might have done differently or what my wrong perception might have been?" The point is that this kind of speech is beautiful, loving, and compassionate, and it opens the door to the person opening up and disclosing what's really going on, as well as our hearing them deeply, unclouded by our anger or other negative emotion. We always remember the other person's buddha-nature. We know and remember that even people who we think are "evil" have buddha-nature, and we seek out that buddha-nature even when we are dealing with harms and sufferings. Also, through these kinds of conversations, we become able to see when wrong perceptions (others' or our own) are in play and we can avoid reacting to them. This leads to peaceful, effective conflict resolution.

When we speak out of anger, jealousy, or agitation, we become ugly and provocative. In the case of couples, both partners contribute to the conflict and its escalation, as well as the breakdown of communication—and mindful communication is the way out (deep listening, looking deeply, nonattachment to views, acknowledging but not expressing anger, jealousy, etc., and loving speech). Also needed are our own mindfulness practices to keep ourselves in a mindful, peaceful state in general. We have to take care of ourselves when we are tired so that our tiredness doesn't cloud our perceptions or interfere with our ability to communicate mindfully. Thus, being peaceful yet effective entails taking care of ourselves and the world simultaneously and being like the Buddha.

CONCLUSION

I chose to focus on Sister Chan Khong as the first of five womanist spiritual activist profiles, or case studies, for several reasons. First, as documented in her memoir, *Learning True Love*, she exemplifies spiritual activism. The parallels between her spiritual beliefs and practices and her social justice and healing work are undeniable. As the eldermost of the women profiled in this section, we are able to observe a lifetime of committed transformational work, allowing us to be secure in our assessment that her activism is truly part of who she is, part of a life mission, and not just a flash in the pan. Second, launching the section with a Vietnamese woman who maintained strong connections to her Vietnamese culture and heritage, despite a lifetime of international relocations that included exile and forced migration in addition to voluntary travel, enabled me to drive home the point that womanism is global and the womanist idea knows no racial, national, cultural, or religious boundaries. Third, the fact that she self-identified as neither feminist nor womanist—indeed, making no reference to either in her memoir—allowed me to emphasize that the womanist idea often functions "under the radar," unnamed yet vigorous in its passionate engagement with things about life on Earth that need to be changed. Where there is social (or ecological) change work fueled by love, where there is a connection with and commitment to "everyday women" and "grassroots people," where there is inexhaustible creativity that continually "makes a way out of no way" relying on "do-it-yourself" methods, where there is the spirit of collaboration that is also not afraid of the authority of leadership, where there is the certainty of the sacredness of all human beings and indeed all life, *there is womanism*.

Fourth, Sister Chan Khong's emphasis on peace as her issue of choice, which encompasses both its inner (psychological/spiritual) and outer (political) dimensions, allowed me to move the discourse about womanism beyond "the mantra" of race/class/gender/sexuality and racism/classism/sexism/heterosexism *and* to highlight the fact that all forms of outer political change are predicated upon inner personal change.

A big part of womanist social change work involves changing the landscape of the psychospiritual interior. This is done through everyday methods—such as producing, preparing, and serving food to people, taking care of children, partners, elders, or neighbors, or gardening—as well as through large-scale political mobilizations and mass media interventions, all of which we see in Chan Khong's work. It also requires conscious self-care, an essential component of any social transformation regime. Taking time out, knowing when to rest, knowing when to exult or grieve, knowing when to just let loose and have fun are all part of the womanist walk. Finally, and not unimportantly, Sister Chan Khong's story allows us to examine the role of spiritual collaboration, in the larger social change scheme. Her evolving relationship with Thich Nhat Hanh and the Tiep Hien Order was essential—not only to everyone involved, but also to the larger publics whom they served, individually, jointly, or as a sangha. Womanists value relationship and interconnection in its manifold forms. Indeed, livingkind's exquisite diversity and variety is a source of fascination and delight as well as a cause for celebration.

In sum, Sister Chan Khong exemplifies both spiritual activism and womanism as I understand it. Her case study displays the metaphysical architecture of the womanist idea and epitomizes womanist methodology in action. In so doing, it begins to intimate how womanism relates to LUXOCRACY and how womanist spiritual activism is a vehicle to its realization. In succeeding chapters, I examine through their memoirs the lives of other women who also illuminate the womanist "way" or "spirit," including Immaculée Ilibagiza of Rwanda, Kiran Bedi of India, Pregs Govender of South Africa, and Wangari Maathai of Kenya.

THE ALCHEMY OF FORGIVENESS: IMMACULÉE ILIBAGIZA AND *LEFT TO TELL*

Between April and July 1994, in a time span of 100 days, somewhere between 500,000 and 1.1 million people were killed in the Rwandan genocide.[1] This event stands as one of the horrors of the twentieth century. The Rwandan genocide was the culmination of a civil war that had raged since 1990, which itself was the upshot of decades of postcolonial ethnic tension between Tutsi and Hutu peoples in the small, formerly Belgian-ruled (and earlier German-ruled) country. As a result of the genocide, Rwanda lost between 10 and 20% of its population, and at least 2 million people were displaced as refugees. Many died in refugee camps, but over 1 million of the refugees returned to Rwanda after the end of hostilities. As with many conflict-ravaged countries of the contemporary era, people who were victims of hostilities were forced by circumstance to live side by side with people who were perpetrators of hostilities—and a significant subset of these individuals were both victims and perpetrators, carrying the trauma of victimization along with the guilt of perpetration into the psyche of the postconflict societal rebuilding process. Thus, social reintegration has emerged as one of the most compelling yet complex challenges of the postconflict period.

Immaculée Ilibagiza's memoir of her experience in and immediately after the genocide, *Left to Tell: Discovering God Amidst the Rwandan Holocaust* (2006), offers not only a first-hand account of this episode in history but also an intimate reflection on psychospiritual survival of horror. Ilibagiza's story does not end with survival, however; rather, it delivers us all the way to redemption and what Marianne Williamson, in another context, calls "a return to love."[2] Crucial to Ilibagiza's survival, healing, and subsequent social transformation work, is the development of what might best be called "radical forgiveness."[3] Ilibagiza's journey through terror, rage, grief, bitterness, and forgiveness is rooted in her Christian faith (specifically Catholicism)—including practices of prayer, scriptural reading, spiritual visions and dreams, and meditation and contemplation. Her story also reveals faith in, and deployment of the transformational power of the Bible and other spiritual objects and a belief in, and reading of divine signs. Thus, in *Left to Tell*, we are gifted with a detailed document of the inner workings of Christian miracle-making.

THE SIDELINED GENOCIDE

In 2004, one full decade after the fateful "100 days of killing," the film *Hotel Rwanda* was released in the United States to considerable critical acclaim and moderate box-office success.[4] For many Americans, this film—a fictionalized account of a true story about Paul Rusesabagina, who saved over 1,200 lives—served as their eye-opening introduction to the Rwandan genocide. While most Americans knew that "something had happened in Rwanda," for many, myself included, general awareness of the details was sketchy. In part, this is likely attributable to the fact that so many other historically significant and sensational events were occurring at the time. It is telling, for instance, that the film's opening soundscape, which plays before any images of Rwanda have even appeared, is a radio news broadcast where a female announcer can be heard stating, "Today, President Clinton voiced concerns at the deteriorating situation in Sarajevo." Those who can remember know that, in terms of international conflicts, the situation in the former Yugoslavia dominated the U.S. airwaves that year. Characterized strategically as an "ethnic cleansing" (genocide lite, perhaps?), this conflict was situated on the continent of Europe, the relationship of whose leaders with the United States has always been one of greater political friendship and readier military assistance when compared with the countries of the African continent. The ongoing conflict in Somalia, the Zapatista uprising in Mexico, and the Iraq–Kuwait showdown were also making news in the spring of 1994. Yet, other kinds of events were simultaneously captivating the world's attention. South Africa's first postapartheid democratic elections, for instance, which made Nelson Mandela president on April 27, 1994, inspired many and defined that year's focus on Africa. Domestically, the O. J. Simpson murder story, which broke on the evening of June 19, 1994, provided a sensationalistic counterpoint. The Rwanda story trailed far behind attention-grabbers such as these.

British political scientist David Patrick argues that Western audiences (specifically, U.S. and UK audiences) had become desensitized to the topic of genocide by 1994, but also that racism and anti-African prejudice affected the downplaying of the Rwandan genocide in leading international news outlets.[5] When stories did appear, the focus was often on outsiders (e.g., the evacuation of foreign nationals, the arrival of the French, the impact of refugees on Zaire or Congo, the environmental impact of a river clogged with corpses); the precipitating conflict was typically characterized as a tribal one, rather than a residue of colonialism; and the Rwandan combatants were often characterized as savage and barbarian, in keeping with prevailing and age-old stereotypes about Africans as primitive and violent.[6] It is ironic that, in 1994, the film *Schindler's List*, a blockbuster that presents a dramatized account of an episode of the Jewish Holocaust during the World War II era, swept the Oscars, meaning that the theme of genocide had been recently resurrected in the U.S. popular imagination, not to mention the U.S. mainstream media, by the time the Rwandan genocide began.[7] Yet, the U.S. State Department is on record as having carefully modulated its use of the word *genocide* to refer to events in Rwanda, preferring instead the watered down term *acts of genocide*. Four years after the fact, President Bill Clinton addressed U.S. inattention to the Rwandan genocide. To quote journalist Samantha Power: "In March of 1998, on a visit to Rwanda, President Clinton issued what would later be known as the 'Clinton apology,' which was actually a carefully hedged acknowledgment. He spoke to the crowd assembled on the tarmac at Kigali Airport: 'We come here today partly in recognition of the fact that we in the United States and the world community did not do as much as we could have and should have done to try to limit what occurred' in Rwanda."[8]

Today, Rwanda's success at recovery from its national nightmare has made the small nation something of a celebrity on the global stage, most recently for becoming the first nation in the world to have a female majority in its national legislature. After the genocide, women and girls made up approximately 70% of Rwanda's population. Paul Kagame, who had emerged as a hero by leading the RPF forces that effectively ended the genocide and who ultimately was elected president, made a point of advocating for a type of social engineering designed to benefit women and reverse many discriminatory policies and laws. One result was that, by 2008, women had risen to fill one-third of the presidential cabinet positions and had taken a majority (56%) in the Rwandan national parliament, including the speaker's chair.[9] In the wake of Ellen Johnson Sirleaf's 2006 inauguration in Liberia as Africa's first democratically elected woman head of state, Rwanda's successes in the legislature only increased the world's attention on Africa as a laboratory for women's transformative leadership. Societies such as these, where grassroots women's social change leadership, environmental destruction born of war, and spiritual crisis born of trauma converge, are particularly appropriate sites to examine womanist praxis in action. One thing that we find is that this activist praxis takes many forms—political, spiritual, environmental, and everyday. In the most horrific of situations, it may even begin with the inner dynamics of survival and self-care, which in turn yield uncommon depths of empathy and compassion for others as well as survival wisdom and inspirational leadership ability. We see these qualities in the story of Immaculée Ilibagiza. Her story enables us to consider the question, "How does one person or nation move past genocide?"

BASIC BIOGRAPHY

Immaculée Ilibagiza was born circa 1970 in Mataba village of Kibuye province in western Rwanda to a middle class Catholic family of Tutsi ethnicity. Both of her parents were highly respected schoolteachers and her father Leonard, in particular, was a community leader who ultimately became a Catholic school principal and district administrator. He was known for being one of the few individuals in the community with two vehicles—a motorbike and a car—as well as for being a generous-spirited community problem-solver. Her mother Rose was also sought out as an advisor, especially by women in the community who were having relationship problems. Two elder brothers, Aimable and Damascene, preceded Immaculée, and a younger brother, Vianney, was born three years after her. All of them were lively and well-respected boys, and she was particularly close with Damascene. Despite belonging to the dominant ethnic group of the time, her parents had many prominent Hutu friends and the respect of both Tutsi and Hutu community members. As Immaculée writes, "Everyone was welcome in our home, regardless of race, religion, or tribe."[10] In fact, Immaculée was not even aware of her ethnic heritage until a watershed moment in fourth grade when a militant Hutu teacher demanded that she reveal it. Unsure of when to stand as the Tutsis, Hutus, and Twa were called, she was shamed by her teacher and asked to leave the classroom. As the story goes, Immaculée went home to ask her parents, and thus began not only her education about ethnic dynamics in Rwanda, but also her descent into the horror that would become a turning point in her life story.

Immaculée was an intellectually precocious girl who had the privilege of growing up in a family that valued education for both women and men. At the conclusion of eighth grade, Immaculée, who was then 15 years old, graduated as class salutatorian. Although her grades should have merited a scholarship at one of the region's top public schools, she and her school's male valedictorian were both passed over due to their Tutsi ethnicity. Not willing for Immaculée to forego an opportunity for the elite education for which she had worked so hard, her father sold two of the family cows and searched the district for a private school that would admit her. As Immaculée characterized the situation, "Cows are status symbols in Rwandan culture and extremely valuable—selling one was extravagant; selling two was an invitation to financial ruin."[11] She studied math and physics at the school her father found for her, again finished as a top student, and this time obtained a scholarship to attend one of Rwanda's top high schools, the Lycée de Notre Dame d'Afrique. She remarks: "Lycée was an excellent girls' school where many of the daughters of the country's highest-ranking politicians had attended. Not only would I get the best education available to any young Rwandan, but my parents wouldn't have to struggle with the private-school fees anymore."[12] It was during Immaculée's third and final year at this school that Rwanda's escalating ethnic tensions ultimately erupted into civil war. No longer could she—or her family—blend in as the ethnically unbiased "good Samaritans," because the stakes of ethnicity were now life and death.

Despite the war, Immaculée received a scholarship to attend the coeducational National University in Butare, where she studied electronic and mechanical engineering. While there, she dated a young man who was both Hutu and the son of a Protestant minister.[13] "Don't forget that you're a Catholic," her dad reminded her, more concerned about religion than ethnicity.[14] Her first two years went by smoothly, as the conflict picked up steam in the north, leaving Butare, which was a long way off in the south end of the country, virtually untouched. Yet, arrests and other signs of intensifying hostilities accelerated around the country. Immaculée's father was arrested, although later released, portending disturbances to come. The notorious Interahamwe became active and visible, even crossing paths with Immaculée on one of her visits to the capital city, Kigali. Using religious faith and visible self-confidence to get through the incident—which involved a menacing group of young men with machetes—Immaculée launched her career and trademarked her methodology as a spiritual activist.

INTO THE BATHROOM

Immaculée Ilibagiza is best known for the 91 days she spent in a three by four foot bathroom with first five, then seven, other women and girls during the fateful spring and summer months of 1994. These 91 days were embedded within the 100 days of the genocide. The bathroom belonged to a Hutu minister, Pastor Murinzi, a friend of her father's who risked life and limb to protect her and her compatriots. Over the course of her confinement, Immaculée would observe the minister descend into a morass of ethnic hatred fueled by the Hutu propaganda surrounding him and the pressures on and from his other Hutu family members, who were living in the house at the time, to the point where his protection of her and the other women was a true paradox. Moderate Hutus were in nearly as much danger as Tutsis during the genocide, and Hutu loyalty was constantly tested by people with the power to kill. Ultimately, the pastor released Immaculée and the other women out of fear for his own life—and theirs—not knowing whether any of them would live. In the end, both Immaculée and the pastor survived. During the course of the strife, Immaculée lost all members of her immediate family except for her eldest brother Aimable, who was away at medical school in Senegal, as well as many members of her extended family, including an infant, most to violent deaths.

A womanist reading of Immaculée's narrative hones in on those moments when spirituality translated into self-change or social change, and *Left to Tell* reveals many. Through her lens, we are able to observe how terror, rage, grief, and bitterness are transformed into an unqualified love and forgiveness—even for those directly responsible for killing her family members. We are then allowed to witness the effects of that transformative power of forgiveness and love on others, particularly those who perpetrated the atrocities. We then observe the beginnings of Immaculée's career as a motivational speaker and erstwhile spiritual teacher whose mission is to inspire and assist others to find forgiveness and exercise love even when they think it is impossible. Through this work, Immaculée herself finds peace and enlarges peace in the world.

SELF-CHANGE: BUILDING SPIRITUAL POWER

Immaculée Ilibagiza was already a religious woman—a confirmed Catholic with a prayerful and pious disposition and genuine reverence for the Bible, Jesus Christ, and Mary, Mother of Jesus—by the time she entered confinement in the tiny bathroom. She habitually carried a rosary and prayed in times of both stress and gratitude. Yet, in the bathroom, her faith underwent a transformation and new avenues of spirituality, spiritual power, and consciousness were opened up to her through a series of extraordinary experiences. I argue that these experiences served to elevate and concentrate her spiritual (vibrational) power in ways that made "miraculous" feats possible at crucial moments in her own and others' survival. One uncanny ability, for example, that emerged at multiple points in the story was Immaculée's ability to "blind the killers," making them seemingly unable to see what was right in front of them and would have allowed them to realize their lethal intentions toward her or her companions. Another element that grows over the course of the narrative is Immaculée's ability to exercise what I call "energetic leadership," or the ability to elevate and fortify the spirit and resolve of others through a process of vibrational entrainment.[15] At all points, she relied on prayer, the power of the Bible, and her personal relationship with God or Christ, to fuel her and provide her with the spiritual or material resources needed to accomplish what was needed. However, her ability to marshal these resources grew out of her increasing spiritual power. A few anecdotes from the text illustrate these claims.

The initial wave of fear that Immaculée felt during the earliest days of her confinement in the bathroom produced a voice of doubt and violence within her that she identified as the voice of Satan, whispering to her and taking advantage of her vulnerability. She responded to this voice with prayer:

> I grasped the red and white rosary my father had given me, and silently prayed with all my might: *God, in the Bible You said that You can do anything for anybody. Well, I am one of those anybodies, and I need You to do something for me now. Please, God, blind the killers when they reach the pastor's bedroom—don't let them find the bathroom door, and don't let them see us! You saved Daniel in the lion's den, God, You stopped the lions from ripping him apart ... stop these killers from ripping us apart, God! Save us like you saved Daniel!*[16]

Very shortly thereafter, she says,

> I struggled to form an image of God in my mind, envisioning two pillars of brilliant white light burning brightly in front of me, like two giant legs. I wrapped my arms around the legs, like a frightened child clinging to its mother. I begged God to fill me with His light and strength, to cast out the dark energy from my heart: *I'm holding on to Your legs, God, and I do not doubt that You can save me. I will not let go of You until You have sent the killers away.*[17]

At the time, Interahamwe had surrounded the house and searched it. They had walked up to the pastor's bedroom (to which the small bathroom was annexed), but left it alone because it was neat, vowing to search it on their next visit. After this scary encounter, Pastor Murinzi opened the bathroom door to warn the women.

When I saw that pastor standing in the doorway, a crystal clear image flashed through my mind. "I have an idea," I told him in a hushed but insistent voice. "Can you push your wardrobe in front of the bathroom door? It's tall and wide enough to completely cover it, so if the killers can't see the door, they'll never find us. It will be as though they're blind!"

Pastor Murinzi thought for a moment and then shook his head. "No, it wouldn't change anything; in fact, it would probably make matters worse. If they look behind the wardrobe and find the door, they will be even more vicious with you."

"Oh, no! Pastor, please, you must ..." I was certain that God had sent me a sign. In my soul, I knew that if the wardrobe were in front of the door, we'd be saved. But the pastor was immovable, so I did something I'd never done in my life: I got on my knees and bowed down to him. "Please I'm begging you," I said. "I know in my heart that if you don't put the wardrobe in front of the door, they're going to find us the next time they search. Don't worry about making them angry—they can only kill us once. Please do this for us ... God will reward you if you do."[18]

With that, the pastor slid the wardrobe in front of the bathroom door and, despite several more intensive searches, the Interahamwe never looked behind it.

This anecdote illustrates a link—perhaps causal, perhaps correlative, perhaps showing the synchronicity[19] between prayer and inspiration, prayer and insight—those flashes of "direct knowing" when we are provided with ideas and answers that we did not arrive at in a logical fashion. There are many ways to pray, and anecdotal literature such as this highlights prayer as a causative process that can affect material as well as psychological realities. This theme is explored in depth by Gregg Braden, a former scientist who now researches and writes on spirituality, in such books as *The Isaiah Effect: Decoding the Lost Science of Prayer and Prophecy* and *Secrets of the Lost Mode of Prayer*, in which he argues that prayer is a transformative activity with lawful characteristics that have been codified within sources as diverse as the Nag Hammadi (Dead Sea Scrolls), the Bible, Tibetan Buddhist archives, and Native American ritual.[20] According to Braden's research, it is the strength and quality of feeling that determines prayer's measurable effectiveness, not the words recited. Thus, prayer is human energetic communication with a responsive, energy-filled universe.

While trapped in the bathroom, Immaculée prayed for several hours a day. When she was not praying, she was typically reading the Bible. However, she engaged in a few other activities as well, such as teaching herself English with the aid of a French-English dictionary and two English-language books provided by Pastor Murinzi at her request. The idea to teach herself English (which she accomplished in three weeks' time by studying morning to night) had also come in a flash of insight in which she saw her future self as a translator. Due to the colonial influence of Belgium, French was the official colonial language of Rwanda, yet many of the Tutsi rebels who had spent years in Uganda were English-speakers. Similarly, English was an official language of the UN and she foresaw the need to communicate with UN peacekeepers and other personnel. One of her first acts upon learning English was to pen a detailed letter of gratitude to her imagined future rescuer—an act of creative visualization. As Immaculée wrote of her experience:

> God had planted a seed in my mind. He'd told me to learn English, and that practice was showing me that a rich and exciting life was waiting for me on the other side of the genocide. I knew that whatever I envisioned would come to pass if I had faith and visualized it with a pure heart and good intentions, and if it were something God thought was right for me. It was then that I realized I could dream and visualize my destiny. I vowed that I'd always dare to dream for what I wanted. And I would only dream for beautiful things like love, health, and peace, because that is the kind of beauty God wants for all His children.[21]

The Interahamwe killers returned to Pastor Murinzi's house looking for Immaculée specifically because it was the last place she had been seen. In the pastor's bedroom, they tormented him while repeatedly announcing their intention to find her, kill her, and possibly rape her. Immaculée, on the other side of the wall, could hear all of this and became so terrified that she fainted. Beginning with her period of unconsciousness, she recounts the following events:

> I felt faint—consciousness slipped away from me until the killers' thundering voices were only a soft, distant rumble. Then I was sleeping ... and dreaming a sweet dream of Jesus. I floated like a feather above the other women. I saw them trembling below me on the floor, holding their Bibles on their heads, begging God for mercy. I looked up and saw Jesus hovering above me in a pool of golden light, and his arms were reaching toward me. I smiled, and the constant aches and pains that had become part of my body after weeks of crouching disappeared. There was no hunger, no thirst, and no fear—I was so peaceful ... so happy.

Then Jesus spoke: "Mountains are moved with faith,[22] Immaculée, but if faith were easy, all the mountains would be gone. Trust in me, and know that I will never leave you. Trust in me, and have no more fear. Trust in me, and I will save you. I shall put my cross upon this door, and they will not reach you. Trust in me, and you shall live."

Suddenly I was back on the floor again with the others. Their eyes were still closed, but mine were wide open, staring at a giant cross of brilliant white light stretching from wall to wall in front of the bathroom door. As I looked, radiant energy brushed my face, warming my skin like the sun. I knew instinctively that a kind of Divine force was emanating from the cross, which would repel the killers. I knew that we were protected and safe, so I jumped to my feet, feeling like I had the strength of a lioness. I thanked God for touching me with His love once again, and then I looked down at the others.

For the first and last time while I was in the bathroom, I shouted at my companions: "We're safe! Trust me ... everything is going to be okay!"[23]

Days later, Immaculée and her companions were released into the night to make their way to the French soldiers who had established a rescue compound at a Protestant nunnery within walking distance from Pastor Murinzi's house. The pastor had persuaded his children and other visitors to form a circle of killer lookalikes who carried guns, spears, and machetes to walk the women and girls halfway. Along the way, they were passed by over 60 assembled Interahamwe patrolling the late-night walkways. Many of them greeted and encouraged the entourage, assuming that they, too, were on the prowl. Gripped by a fear of their own, the pastor and his group eventually bid farewell to the women and turned to flee back home. Weighing only 65 pounds of her original weight of 115, Immaculée sprinted with her companions and made it the last 500 yards. But their journey of survival was not yet complete.

ENERGETIC LEADERSHIP: EXERCISING SPIRITUAL POWER

Hours of prayer in the bathroom, intense episodes of meditation and contemplation on the meaning of Christ's love, God's will, and human nature, the choice to remain optimistic by studying English and visualizing her rescue(r), plus the experience of multiple spiritual visions and dreams had made Immaculée Ilibagiza into a different person spiritually from the one who had entered the bathroom three months before. She had learned mental alchemy, or the art of transmuting inner states and thus vibrational levels, by transforming her own fear into calm, rage into compassion, and bitterness into forgiveness. One constant throughout this alchemical process was her sense of being "plugged in" with God, Christ, or a Higher Power, and allowing this Power to work through her or to fill her. In general, Immaculée did not claim the power she evidenced as her own, but rather attributed it to God or faith, with herself as the channel or vehicle for its expression. This feeling of being a channel for divine power was quite palpable for Immaculée, who often referred to it in terms of gaining or regaining strength.

Immaculée had begun to show energetic leadership in the bathroom, such as the ability to elevate and galvanize the spirits, feelings, or attitudes of others; however, her real moment to shine came after she and her companions were released back into the wide-open world. The genocide was not yet over, the streets were not yet safe, and Tutsis and "Hutu traitors" were still hunted. The streets and fields were filled with rotting corpses, familiar places had been abandoned or destroyed, and none of her loved ones were anywhere to be found. Shortly after she and her companions made it to the French field camp, they were transferred to the larger base camp, whereupon they largely dispersed and never spoke again. However, Immaculée rose to prominence as a translator, medical aide, and all-around counselor and comforter for the steady stream of Tutsi refugees coming to the camp. Along the way, she learned the chilling fates of all her slain family members. Despite intense grief, she managed to serve and lead other survivors, many of whose experiences were even worse than her own.

One particularly long anecdote crystallizes Immaculée Ilibagiza's energetic leadership, reflecting the spiritual power of which she had now gained command. This anecdote occurs near the end of the refugee phase of her journey, at a moment when she and a group of other refugees were abandoned by the French soldiers who were supposed to escort them to their final destination, an RPF (Tutsi rebel) camp amidst a huge field of Interahamwe killers. The French soldiers were being pulled out of Rwanda without warning:

> I was the last one to climb into the back of the truck. The tailgate slammed shut, the canvas tarp was rolled down to conceal us, and the truck rolled forward. I took out the rosary my father had given me—the one possession I would never surrender—and said a prayer. I asked God for His blessing on our new beginning, and to shepherd us safely to the Tutsi soldiers.
>
> The truck pulled past the semicircle of armored vehicles, down a service road, and into a sea of killers! Through a crack in the tarp, I saw thousands of Hutus were trudging along the main road toward Lake Kivu [an escape route to Zaire, now Democratic Republic of Congo]—and hundreds of them wore the uniform of the Interahamwe and carried machetes.

"Oh, God," I said, falling back in the truck. "Not again!"

We inched along the crowded road, honking at Hutus to give way and let us by. I knew that if we were stopped, or if the truck broke down, the Interahamwe would fall upon us within minutes. I hadn't felt this frightened since I left the bathroom.

"Please, God," I prayed, "You have brought us this far—now take us the rest of the way! Blind these killers ... don't let them look in the back of this truck. Merciful God, shield us from their hateful eyes!"[24]

At this point in the story, the French captain who was driving the truck stopped abruptly and ordered all of the passengers, including Immaculée, out of the truck. They were halfway between the two camps. On behalf of all of her companions, Immaculée, pleaded with the captain—with whom she had been friendly—not to leave them alone amidst the throng of armed Interhamwe. Claiming to have his orders, the captain was immovable. Failing to express any sympathy whatsoever, the captain then ordered Immaculée to get the rest of her people out of the back of the truck, leaving her and her companions in utter disbelief and dismay. Yet, despite her own fear, drawing on her spiritual resources, Immaculée rose to the occasion. The story continues:

> The cries of disbelief and fear coming from the back of the truck drew even more attention from the killers, who were now moving toward us. I looked one Interahamwe straight in the eye and held his gaze. My heart told me that he was a person just like me, and that he really didn't want to kill. I held my rosary and summoned all my will to send a message of love to him.[25] I prayed that God would use me to touch the killer with the power of His love.
>
> I didn't blink ... and we stared into each other's eyes for what seemed like a lifetime. Finally, the killer broke my gaze and looked away. He turned his back to me and dropped his machete, as if the devil had left his body. But there were plenty of other devils to take his place. At least 15 Interahamwe were now standing a few yards from the truck, with machetes in their hands and smirks on their faces. They were figuring out what was happening, waiting to see if any of my companions would dare leave the truck.
>
> We had no choice but to come out. One by one, my friends hopped out, until all 30 of us were standing there facing the killers. When everyone was out, two French soldiers lifted Aloise [a disabled woman in a wheelchair] down onto the road and deposited young Kenza and Sami [Aloise's children] beside her. Then the soldiers climbed into the cab, and the truck pulled away at high speed, leaving us in a cloud of dust and uncertainty.[26]

At this point, the Interhamwe gathered in close around Immaculée and her companions, taunting them with epithets and maligning the French soldiers who had been their escorts and protectors. Terror swelled within the group, and everyone looked to Immaculée for guidance. Within herself, she decided that she would not die nor would she let her companions die. This decision constituted a pivotal act of energetic leadership:

> "Let's go," I said. "We'll walk to the RPF camp—their soldiers are close by."
>
> The killers heard mention of the RPF and got nervous.
>
> We began moving but didn't get too far. The road was so strewn with rocks and bodies that it was practically impossible to push Aloise's wheelchair—so when a wheel became stuck in a rut, we all stopped. Aloise's children were also crying and clutching their mother's arms.
>
> I pulled my friends Jean Paul and Karega away from the group. "You two come with me—the rest of you stay with Aloise ... and pray. I'll find the Tutsi soldiers and come back with help. Don't move from this spot or I won't be able to find you in the middle of all these Hutu refugees."
>
> Aloise looked at me doubtfully. "Are you sure you want to go? They'll kill you for sure! Let the men go instead," she implored.
>
> "No, I'm going ... you just concentrate on praying."
>
> With that, I struck out in the direction that the French had been taking us before they abandoned us. As we walked, I prayed my rosary, talking to God with all my heart and soul:[27] "God, I really am walking through the valley of death—please stay with me. Shield me with the power of Your love. You created this ground that we're walking on, so please don't let these killers spill Your daughter's blood on it."
>
> Three Interahamwe followed us as we broke away from the larger group, and one of them recognized me. "I know this cockroach," he said. "This is Leonard's daughter—we've been looking for her for months! I can't believe she's still alive ... we killed the rest of them, but this little cockroach gave us the slip!"
>
> "Dear God," I prayed, walking as fast as I could and holding my father's rosary tightly in my hand. "Only You can save me. You promised to take care of me, God—well, I really need taking care of right now. There are devils and vultures at my back, Lord ... please protect me. Take the evil from the hearts of these men, and blind their hatred with Your holy love."
>
> I walked without looking at my feet, not knowing if I was about to stumble over rocks or bodies, putting all my trust in God to guide me to safety. We were moving very briskly, but the killers were all around us now, circling

us, slicing the air with their machetes. We were defenseless, so why were they waiting to strike?

"If they kill me, God, I ask You to forgive them. Their hearts have been corrupted by hatred, and they don't know why they want to hurt me."

After walking a half mile like that, I heard Jean Paul say, "Hey, they're gone ... they're gone!"

I looked around, and it was true—the killers had left us. Jean Paul said later that it was probably because they knew the RPF soldiers were close by, but I knew the real reason, and I never stopped thanking God for saving us on that road![28]

Although Immaculée, Jean Paul, and Karega made it to the RPF camp, the drama did not end there. They were greeted with a gunpoint welcome until a rebel commander—a former Hutu neighbor who had gone to fight with the Tutsis—recognized Immaculée and ordered his men to lower their guns. The soldiers had failed to believe that any Tutsis could have survived and made it this far; they assumed that Immaculée and her companions were Hutu spies. Nevertheless, in short order, RPF soldiers returned to where Immaculée had left Aloise and the others, and everyone was brought safely to the RPF camp. Another passage reveals the long reach of Immaculée's profound spiritual power that afternoon:

"Whatever prayers you've been saying, keep saying them, Immaculée," Aloise [known for her lively and jocular temperament] chuckled. "Those killers were looking at us like they wanted to cut us to pieces, but they couldn't move. It was as though they were frozen to the spot! We were like Daniel in the lions' den ... just like Daniel in the lions' den!

Aloise pulled her children to her, hugged them tightly, and laughed and laughed until tears ran down her cheeks. My heart lifted, and I said, "I didn't know if I'd ever live to say this, but we'll never have to face the killers again. The genocide is over—God has spared us and given us a new life. Praise the Lord! Thank You, God! Thank You, God!"

Aloise smiled at me and said, "Amen, Immaculée ... Amen!"

Presumably, the same power that made the first Interahamwe drop his machete and the later Interahamwe throng disappear also made the killers surrounding Aloise and the others "freeze," taking no action.[29] Immaculée had created a circle of protection around herself and those for whom she had assumed responsibility in the moment. The ability to mobilize people like this and to "work the energy" of a situation—producing palpable, positive results by causing actions in the invisible realm to manifest in the visible realm—is the product of energetic leadership and one form of spiritual activism.

MWAMI SHIMIRWA: THE LOVE THAT IS BEYOND OUR UNDERSTANDING

Immaculée Ilibagiza's odyssey did not end at the camp, but rather continued all the way to an unexpected encounter with one of the individuals who killed members of her family. Once the genocide ended, Immaculée got the job with the UN that she had visualized, and through some connections there was taken on a helicopter tour of the area where she and her family had lived before the displacement. On this trip, she was able to properly bury her mother and brother Damascene, although not her father or her brother Vianney. This experience provided some closure for her. After a period of time, she had a dream that she recounts here:

> I was in a helicopter flying over my family's house, but I was trapped in a dark cloud. I could see Mom, Dad, Damascene, and Vianney high above me, standing in the sky and bathed in a warm, white light that radiated tranquility. The light intensified and spread across the sky until it engulfed the dark cloud hiding me. And suddenly, I was with my family again. The dream was so real that I reached out and felt the warmth of their skin, the gentleness of their touch. I was so happy that I danced in the air.
>
> Damascene was wearing a crisp white shirt and blue trousers. He looked at me with a joyful glow and gave me his brilliant smile. My mother, father, and Vianney stood behind him, holding hands and beaming at me. "Hey, Immaculée, it's good to see that we can still make you happy," my beautiful brother said. "You've been gloomy far too long and must stop all this crying. Look at the wonderful place we're in ... can you see how happy we are? If you continue to believe that we're suffering, you'll force us to return to the pain we've left behind. I know how much you miss us, but do you really want us to come back and suffer?"
>
> "No, no, Damascene!" I cried out, as tears of joy poured from my eyes. "Don't come back here! Wait for me there and I will come join you all. When God is done with me in this life, I will come to you."
>
> "We'll be here waiting, dear sister. Now heal your heart. You must love, and you must forgive those who have trespassed against us."

My family slowly receded into the sky until they disappeared into the heavens. I was still hovering over my house, but I was no longer in a dark cloud ... and no longer in a helicopter. I was flying like a bird above my village, above the pastor's house and the French camp, above all the forests and rivers and waterfalls of my beautiful country—I was soaring above Rwanda.

I felt so liberated from grief and gravity that I began to sing for joy. I sang from my heart, the words tumbling happily from my mouth. The song was "Mwami Shimirwa," which in Kinyarwanda means "Thank You, God, for love that is beyond our understanding."[30]

Immaculée had a chance to prove her "love that is beyond all understanding" on a second trip back to Kibuye province:

"Do you want to meet the leader of the gang that killed your mother and Damascene?"

"Yes, sir, I do."

I watched through Semana's office window as he crossed a courtyard to the prison cell and then returned, shoving a disheveled, limping old man in front of him. I jumped up with a start as they approached, recognizing the man instantly. His name was Felicien, and he was a successful Hutu businessman whose children I'd played with in primary school. He'd been a tall, handsome man who always wore expensive suits and had impeccable manners. I shivered, remembering that it had been his voice I'd heard calling out my name when the killers searched for me at the pastor's. Felicien had hunted me.

Semana [the burgomaster, head of the facility] pushed Felicien into the office, and he stumbled onto his knees. When he looked up from the floor and saw that I was the one who was waiting for him, the color drained from his face. He quickly shifted his gaze and stared at the floor.

"Stand up, killer!" Semana shouted. "Stand up and explain to this girl why her family is dead. Explain to her why you murdered her mother and butchered her brother. Get up, I said! Get up and tell her!" Semana screamed even louder, but the battered man remained hunched and kneeling, too embarrassed to stand and face me.

His dirty clothing hung from his emaciated frame in tatters. His skin was sallow, bruised, and broken; and his eyes were filmed and crusted. His once handsome face was hidden beneath a filthy, matted beard; and his bare feet were covered in open, running sores.

I wept at the sight of his suffering. Felicien had let the devil enter his heart, and the evil had ruined his life like a cancer in his soul. He was now the victim of his victims, destined to live in torment and regret. I was overwhelmed with pity for the man.

"He looted your parents' home and robbed your family's plantation, Immaculée. We found your dad's farm machinery at his house, didn't we?" Semana yelled at Felicien. "After he killed Rose and Damascene, he kept looking for you ... he wanted you dead so he could take over your property. Didn't you, pig?" Semana shouted again.

I flinched, letting out an involuntary gasp. Semana looked at me, stunned by my reaction and confused by the tears streaming down my face. He grabbed Felicien by the shirt collar and hauled him to his feet. "What do you have to say to her? What do you have to say to Immaculée?"

Felicien was sobbing. I could feel his shame. He looked up at me for only a moment, but our eyes met. I reached out, touched his hands lightly, and quietly said what I'd come to say.

"I forgive you."

My heart eased immediately, and I saw the tension release in Felicien's shoulders before Semana pushed him out the door and into the courtyard. Two soldiers yanked Felicien up by his armpits and dragged him back toward his cell. When Semana returned, he was furious.

"What was that all about, Immaculée? That was the man who murdered your family. I brought him to you to question ... to spit on if you wanted to. But you forgave him! How could you do that? Why did you forgive him?"

I answered him with the truth: "Forgiveness is all I have to offer."[31]

"THE GENOCIDE IS HAPPENING IN PEOPLE'S HEARTS"

There's a place in the narrative where Immaculée is having a conversation with an old friend, Jean Paul, who also happened to survive, about how such extremes of good and evil can coexist within the hearts of individual participants in genocide. The conversation revolves around a young Hutu man named Laurent, who hid, housed, fed, and protected Jean Paul—a Tutsi with whom he had been friends—yet, by day, roamed the streets with the Interahamwe killing people. According to Jean Paul, Laurent would come home in the evenings spattered with blood and clean his knife in front of him, just like they were "old friends" as usual and nothing had changed. Jean Paul was horrified, but at the same time he recognized that Laurent was saving his life. The paradox mystified Jean Paul. At this juncture in the conversation, Immaculée waxed philosophical and remarked, "The genocide is happening in people's hearts."[32]

This observation by Immaculée captures the essence of a womanist perspective on violence. All violent action begins with a violent thoughtform fueled by a violent emotion, brought into material expression through an identifiable set of contextually facilitative factors. Under other circumstances, Laurent might never have been a killer. It is clear, as suggested by Ifa cosmology, that Laurent had the possibility of going in either direction—good or evil—and that he "sat at the crossroads." Many of the circumstances that predisposed Laurent to becoming a killer are circumstances that we can collectively or individually control or influence. If we choose not to control (or influence) those circumstances, then we produce the killer. Thus, the genocide is also in our hearts and minds, not just in the hearts and minds of those holding the machete. We may be thousands of miles away, but the condition of our hearts and minds influences the condition of the hearts and minds of other people who are interconnected with us, as well as the material causal chains that produce the very events and actions we abhor. To invoke Thich Nhat Hanh again, "We inter-are." Thus, womanist solutions revolve around changing hearts and minds anywhere and everywhere to "shift the center" of humanity's vibrational energy (and thus the manifest effects of its collective energy) through love-based technologies of social transformation.

During and after the Rwandan holocaust, Immaculée Ilibagiza carefully cultivated and ultimately embodied this verse translated from Patanjali's *Yoga Sutras* (2.35), whether or not she ever read it:

When we are firmly established in nonviolence,
All beings around us cease to feel hostility.[33]

This verse reflects the well-known nonviolent social change principle of *ahimsa*, popularized by Mahatma Gandhi and adopted by Bayard Rustin and Martin Luther King Jr. in the United States in the 1950s and 60s, and embeds this principle within an alchemical syllogism: *If* one becomes firmly established in nonviolence—meaning, if one attains/masters the ability to transmute inner states that generate conflict, such as anger, hostility, and bitterness into love, tranquility, peace, and so on—*then* (implied: through vibrational entrainment) other beings (who are presumed to be vibrating at a lower, weaker level associated with hostility) will cease to feel hostility. From a vibrational perspective, this is how peace is built; this is how one moves past and prevents future episodes of genocide. So, a womanist social change praxis looks closely at such alchemy, regardless of the religious, spiritual, or even scientific tradition from which it stems.

Today, genocide and other forms of mass killing are still happening. Darfur, Sudan and the Democratic Republic of Congo (DRC) are two prominent examples. Historically, there have been many others, including the decimation of North and South American First Peoples (Native Americans) and Australian Aborigines. The transatlantic slave trade is considered by many to have been a form of genocide. Already mentioned in this chapter were the Jewish Holocaust, "ethnic cleansing" in the former Yugoslavia, and, of course the Rwandan genocide itself. The genocides in Cambodia and East Timor in the 1970s still shape recent memory. These are but a few examples from a list that could be very long.[34]

I raise these many and diverse examples to show that "genocide" is a persistent thoughtform that we have collectively failed to eradicate from our common psychic structure, despite some efforts and some desire to eradicate it. Consequently, this thoughtform has reasserted itself repeatedly across time and place. We "Earthlings"[35] are not "so advanced," as we like to think; rather, we are still parties to brutality. It is ironic that, despite the banner of "Never Again" that was raised after the Jewish Holocaust, here we are again—grappling with genocide and indifference.[36] How did this happen? How did we get here? A womanist argument would be that we did not change hearts and minds enough—that despite the valiant efforts of many political and spiritual activists, we have not yet reached the threshold of collective mental alchemy that would remove the genocide thoughtform from our species. Yet, womanists would also argue that we can—and must—always begin in the present moment, starting with ourselves, as suggested by Sister Chan Khong in the previous chapter.

LEFT TO TELL: LESSONS LEARNED

In her gripping narrative, *Left to Tell*, Immaculée Ilibagiza offers us an inside view on self-change that paves the way for social change. She shows us the "inner work" that must precede the "outer work"—a demonstration made all the more compelling by its unfolding within an extremely high-stakes situation, the Rwandan genocide. Although Immaculée's praxis emerges out of her Christian faith, its tenets are not limited to Christians. Furthermore, even though she does not name herself a womanist, her praxis is consistent with womanist ideas about social transformation, mental alchemy as a foundation for social change, and the ability of everyday people to "perform miracles."

Immaculée Ilibagiza's story—her social change praxis—has implications anywhere in the world that individuals and communities are faced with the challenge of recovering from devastating hostilities and reintegrating the parties to those hostilities. Nations such as Liberia and Sierra Leone, for example, whose hostilities have ended in recent memory, as well as nations such as the Democratic Republic of the Congo, which will be faced with such challenges once their hostilities end, stand to gain from Immaculée Ilibagiza's perspective. It shows a particular way, exemplified by an African woman, that people of any background can approach overcoming the potentially debilitating residues of anger, fear, or grief that result from conflict-based trauma and witnessing the unspeakable. Her praxis adds a new dimension to such policy innovations as UN Security Council Resolution 1325,[37] known as "Women, Peace, and Security," as well as to the important and difficult work of Truth and Reconciliation Commissions (TRCs—such as those in South Africa, Liberia, and elsewhere); international tribunals, such as the UN's International Court of Justice and the International Criminal Court, and relief and recovery-oriented nongovernmental organizations or community based organizations, whether faith-based or secular.

Below I distil Immaculée's praxis into a set of tenets for moving beyond genocide and, perhaps more importantly, eliminating the forms of consciousness that produce genocide—including the ability to stand by while it is occurring:

Lesson 1. *Cultivate a relationship with Divine Power.* Divine Power is like water—we're made of it, and we need lots of it to function optimally. We know we're "plugged in" when we feel inspired, powerful, altruistic, and energized.[38] Once we plug in to Divine Power, our ability to mobilize others becomes stronger and more effective.

Lesson 2. *Pray.* Prayer is communication with Divine Power. That communication requires both heart and mind, feelings and words. Ardent desire fuels intentions and creates the energetic environment for their material manifestation. To quote Immaculée: "I was living proof of the power of prayer and positive thinking, which really are almost the same thing. God is the source of all positive energy, and prayer is the best way to tap into His power."[39] Prayer also cultivates an attitude of reverence, inclining us to treat all creation as sacred. Reverence and a sense of the sacred are energetically antithetical to violence.

Lesson 3. *Engage the tough questions until the answers feel like Truth.* While in confinement, Immaculée wrestled with such questions as "If God exhorts us to love everyone, how do you love a killer?", "Is revenge ever justified?", "How do we decide who deserves to live and who deserves to die?", and "What do I do with my rage/hatred/bitterness so that it does not re-create violence?" She pondered these questions until she got answers she was satisfied with that transformed her internally, making her able to engage the outside world differently.[40]

Lesson 4. *Learn to see and trust Divine signs.* At many points in the story, Immaculée experienced a sudden flash of insight that suggested that she should do (or say) one thing or another. Alternately, she found directional meaning in certain events (e.g., a thunderstorm, a randomly opened Bible verse). She learned that these signs were guidance and that things went better when she followed them. Sign-reading, then, becomes a method for "making a way out of no way." Sign-reading requires that we trust our intuition, which is an internal sign and a manifestation of supra-intelligence.[41] Sign-reading is a womanist value that makes its first appearance in Alice Walker's 1981 review of *Gifts of Power: The Writings of Rebecca Jackson* and is extensively discussed in Chela Sandoval's culturally, theoretically, and spiritually synthetic text *Methodology of the Oppressed* (2000).[42]

Lesson 5. *Active self-reflection is the foundation of effective social transformation work.* Therefore, perpetually scour the self for vestiges of hate, prejudice, vengeance, and actively transmute them into love, amity, and forgiveness. As stated by 'Abdu'l-Bahá within the Baha'i tradition,

"[T]he breeding ground of all these tragedies is prejudice: prejudice of race and nation, of religion, of political opinion; and the root cause of prejudice is blind imitation of the past—imitation in religion, in racial attitudes, in national bias, in politics. So long as this aping of the past persisteth, just so long will the foundations of the social order be blown to the four winds, just so long will humanity be continually exposed to direst peril."[43]

Lesson 6. *Recognize the power of creative visualization.* The creation of the futures we desire, whether personal or political, begins with visualization. Although Immaculée made no mention of the Kabbalistic Four Worlds (see chapter 6), her implicit awareness of their implications is evident in her tendency to make concrete change (in Assiyah, or the "world of action") by first visualizing that change (in Beri'ah, or the "world of creation," and Yetzirah, or the "world of formation"). As the Bible states in Proverbs 23:7, "As a man thinketh in his heart, so is he."[44] After Immaculée, we might here paraphrase, "As a woman thinketh in her heart, so is she."

Lesson 7. *Cultivate "radical forgiveness."* Radical forgiveness is a way of finding or restoring peace by cultivating a shift in perception that allows one to see the larger spiritual meaning of events.[45] Radical forgiveness ultimately eliminates the victim/perpetrator duality by focusing on the divine nature of all actors in a seemingly unjust or violent situation and the ways in which the situation generated essential spiritual lessons for all concerned.[46,47] Radical forgiveness is predicated on a notion of an invisible world (however defined) that overlays or interpenetrates the visible, material world, in which events may have implications different from what seems obvious by customary social standards, and thus is consistent with spiritual and religious perspectives that endorse some kind of meaningful invisible or supernal realm. Although it might seem as though radical forgiveness implicitly endorses an "anything goes" morality, it does not. Rather, it provides tools for reinterpreting events in ways that shift the energetic patterns created by those events from lower (e.g., rage, vengeance, depression) to higher vibrating states (e.g., love, forgiveness, peace). As such, it is useful for individual and group healing as well as peacebuilding[48] more broadly.

WHAT WOULD JESUS DO?

In the 1990s, the phrase "What Would Jesus Do?" became popular among U.S. Christians, particularly youth. The idea behind this phrase was the examination of Jesus as moral exemplar and not simply Savior—an idea dating back to the late nineteenth century when Christian Socialist Charles Sheldon published the novel *In His Steps: What Would Jesus Do?* (1896), and even farther back to the Christian doctrine known as *imitatio Dei*, or "imitation of God."[49] Although the phrase "What Would Jesus Do?" (abbreviated to WWJD) became the subject of mockery and reinterpretation[50]—not to mention a commercial phenomenon (in the form of bracelets and other WWJD paraphernalia)—it also created a kind of popular discourse and erstwhile social movement for Christians young and old who were concerned about the variety of troubling conditions in the world yet felt little resonance with aspiritual or patently antireligious Marxist- and New Left-inspired activist modalities. While a full discussion of this movement is beyond the scope of this chapter, I raise it because we can observe the spirit of "What Would Jesus Do?" in the social change praxis of Immaculée Ilibagiza. When Immaculée prayed *"please God, give me Your forgiveness"* (78) or challenged herself with the question *"How can you love God but hate so many of His creatures?"* (92) or meditated on single words such as *"forgiveness, faith,* or *hope ... [and] surrender"* (95), she embodied a genuine and authentic WWJD stance. Not unlike Sister Chan Khong modeling her own praxis after bodhisattvas such as Avalokitesvara and Kuan Yin, Immaculée Ilibagiza found transformational resources in a sacred Figure whom she perceived to be of greater power and wisdom than herself. Ultimately, by modeling herself after this sacred Figure (variously characterized as God or Jesus), she discovered the ability to "perform miracles" just like her cherished sacred Figure had done, thus manifesting her own innate Divinity. *This* is womanist social change praxis—womanist spiritual activism—in action.

CONCLUSION

I selected Immaculée Ilibagiza as the second profile, or case study, of womanist spiritual activism for a variety of reasons. First, she is a Black, African, Christian woman, returning our discourse to a familiar place, given that womanist thought was initially articulated by women of African descent who were of Christian heritage, especially in the theological arena. Yet, this surface level familiarity is disrupted by the fact that her politics were not forged within the familiar contours of the U.S. civil rights movement and its sequelae, Black nationalism as reflected in Black Power, Pan-Africanism, of Afrocentricity, or even the postintegrationist crucible of "conscious" Hip Hop—arguably the political imprimatur of her generation. Rather, her politics were forged within the converging contexts of evangelical African Catholicism and the enveloping Rwandan holocaust. These politics could be summed up in four words: *save people, transform people*. Thus, her case allows us to look at womanist praxis with fresh eyes.

In contrast to Sister Chan Khong, who is the eldest exemplar, Immaculée Ilibagiza is the youngest. Rather than capturing a lifetime of service, her memoir captures a few memorable and transformative years in the life of a woman who still has the proverbial lifetime ahead of her. Like Sister Chan Khong, Immaculée Ilibigiza neither names herself as womanist or feminist nor invokes either terminology within her text. Rather, she names herself as a Christian— a conservative one at that—and her activist role model is Jesus Christ. Thus, my second reason for including her story here is that her narrative presents us with the opportunity to reexamine, through a womanist lens, the socially transformational possibilities of evangelical perspectives in ways that defy the usual wholesale dismissal of evangelicalism by progressives. From my perspective and in my experience, charismatic[51] Christianity maintains understandings about the energy dynamics of the invisible world and their relation to manifest (visible) reality that more intellectual denominations of Christianity have foregone. It is in these fundamentalist branches of Christianity that miracles are real and not just metaphorical. Thus, there is something to learn here, even if we must reconfigure certain aspects of the social ideology that sometimes accompanies these branches of Christianity to meet womanist standards of loving universality. *In Left to Tell*, Immaculée Ilibagiza shows us what *womanist* evangelical, charismatic, fundamentalist Christian spiritual activism might look like, particularly from an African perspective—and, interestingly, it ends up looking a lot like certain forms of New Age spirituality and even African traditional religion. I suggest that this is because all of these are tapping into a common cosmological source: Divinity.

My third reason for selecting Immaculée Ilibagiza as a model womanist spiritual activist is similar to another of my reasons for choosing Sister Chan Khong: her activist issue of choice stretches our understandings of what womanist activism is about; that is, what a womanist has the authority to address. Immaculée Ilibagiza's issue is genocide. This is not an issue that womanists have taken up previously, references to the transatlantic slave trade and historical decimation of Native American Indians or other indigenous populations notwithstanding. Stated differently, contemporaneous episodes of genocide have not been addressed by self-proclaimed womanists. Yet, as I argued at the end of the previous chapter as well as in the introduction to *The Womanist Reader*, womanism frequently goes about its business unannounced, more concerned with problem solving than labels or identity. Is Immaculée Ilibagiza a womanist? It doesn't matter, because her transformational activity—inner and outer—reflects, embodies, and enlarges the womanist idea. Therefore, it moves us further along the road to LUXOCRACY.

CHAPTER

9

TURNING A PRISON INTO AN ASHRAM:
KIRAN BEDI AND *IT'S ALWAYS POSSIBLE*

What did we want the prison as an institution to be?[1]

—*Kiran Bedi*

Between 1993 and 1995, Kiran Bedi engineered a radical transformation of
Tihar Central Jail, the Asia-Pacific region's largest prison and one of its worst.
Situated in Delhi, India, and bursting at the seams with over 9,000 inmates in
an aging facility built for 2,500, Tihar Jail had become a cesspool of corruption,
violence, misery, and disease, with subhuman living conditions and indifferent
management. Only about 1,000 of Tihar's diverse occupants had actually been
convicted of a crime; the remainder were people awaiting trial, many of whom
had been confined to Tihar for years. At times, the lines between inmates and
corrections staff were blurred by shared participation in a variety of illegal
activities, from drug use and drug peddling to other forms of smuggling, theft,
extortion, and assault. Although the majority of the inmates of Tihar Jail were
men, 250 to 300 women also resided within the prison, along with approximately 60 preschool children, most of whom had been born inside Tihar. The
jail also housed roughly 1,000 adolescents who had been arrested or convicted
for alleged crimes of their own; the vast majority were boys, but a few were
girls. The largely Indian population of Tihar Jail, comprised of Hindus, Muslims, Sikhs, Jains, Parsis, Buddhists, and Christians, was interspersed with men
and women from other parts of the world, including Afghanistan, Australia,
Canada, France, Germany, Ghana, Italy, Nigeria, Senegal, Somalia, Sri Lanka,
Tanzania, the United Kingdom, and 25 other nationalities, bringing not only
cultural and racial diversity but also linguistic diversity. And, of course, it goes

without saying that a number of inmates were drug-addicted, sufferers from mental illness, or people with chronic health conditions. It was into this world that Kiran Bedi stepped in early May of 1993. By her own account, her first question was, "Am I going to be part of this rotten system or am I going to change it?"[2]

Over the course of the next two years, the answer became evident as Kiran Bedi transformed Tihar Central Jail into Tihar Ashram. To accomplish this, Bedi devised an eclectic, synthetic, and holistic approach that involved honing in on and cultivating the innate yet undernourished spirituality of the prisoners and staff under her charge, encouraging their self-actualization, and building community within the walls of the prison. This method involved addressing the physical, emotional, mental, social, spiritual, and environmental needs of prisoners as well as correctional staff, promoting self-sufficiency and self-governance, and beautifying the prison grounds. Ultimately, it also involved strategic use of the media to transform public opinion about what prisons and prisoners are capable of. In sum, I argue that Kiran Bedi's method for transforming Tihar Jail—its inmates, its staff, the grounds, and the surrounding community—was womanist in nature and exemplifies a womanist approach to reconfiguring how societies deal with crime, criminals, and the notion of criminal justice, with implications for the global prison-industrial complex.

BASIC BIOGRAPHY

In 1972, Kiran Bedi (née Peshawaria) became the first woman to join the Indian Police Service (IPS). She had already gained a considerable reputation and public presence as a tennis champion, having won five national or international tournaments in India and throughout Asia.[3] She was a star student who had graduated with honors in English and completed a master's degree in political science at the top of her class. She had recently wed a man named Brij Bedi, nine years her senior, in an unconventional, nonarranged marriage in which both parties had agreed to live independently as "soul companions" in order to pursue their considerable professional goals. In sum, by 1972, Kiran Bedi had established herself as a woman predisposed toward "functioning as an equal, speaking the truth as she saw it, having and implementing original ideas, working hard, and garnering success."[4]

Kiran was born in Amritsar, Punjab, India in 1949, the second of four daughters in a well-to-do landed family.[5] Her father, Parkesh Lal Peshawaria, a talented tennis player of mixed Hindu-Sikh parentage who worked for his wealthy father, a hotelier and industrialist, was described as a sensitive man who was "disturbed by the way women played a subservient role in society." Eventually, this resulted in a clean break with his own family over an arranged marriage disaster involving his eldest daughter—a situation that left a deep impression on young Kiran. Parkesh Lal strove to provide the best educational and athletic opportunities for all four of his daughters, who ultimately became an artist, a high-ranking civil servant, a clinical psychologist, and a lawyer, respectively.[6] He seemed unusually unconcerned about the lack of a son. A voracious reader with a preference for positive psychology books, such as those by U.S. authors Dale Carnegie and Norman Vincent Peale, he was known to wake his daughters up in the middle of the night to share exciting passages. Demonstrating concern for the welfare of the less fortunate, Parkash Lal's family owned several pilgrim houses for poor travelers which they ran as charities rather than for profit.

Kiran's mother, Prem Lata Peshawaria, was the only child of a wealthy and charitable Hindu family of cross-border traders and has been described as "a brilliant student whose schooling had been curtailed by early marriage." Her own "unfulfilled desire to pursue higher education" fueled her parenting of her four daughters, whom she refused to teach to cook so that they might study in preparation for more fulfilling and public pursuits. Prem's father was famous for refusing to take his own breakfast before he had fed fifty needy people each morning, setting an example for charitable community service, indeed social work, for his extended family. Due to her own family's wealth, she was able to garner resources for her household when her husband's money ran thin. In the afternoons, she would bring food to her daughters on the tennis court. At dinner, she and Prakash would talk their daughters through day-to-day challenges, while after dinner she and her husband would retreat to the exclusive Amritsar Service Club, of which they were third-generation members.

Kiran attended Sacred Heart Convent School where she had the opportunity to refine her English. She recalls that the nuns made no attempt to convert the majority non-Christian student population or to make them attend church. Yet, one of her favorite and most memorable classes was moral science, "the study of being a good human being."[7] It was during this period, at age 9, that she began playing tennis. At 14, she began amateur competition and continued throughout her undergraduate and graduate studies at Government College for Women and Punjab University, respectively.[8] As mentioned, by age 22, she had already won five national or international tournaments. Even after joining the IPS, she went on to win six more. It was on the tennis court that she met her husband-to-be. For two years (1970–72) prior to joining the IPS, she lectured in political science at Khalsa College for Women in Amritsar.

As a new police officer, she distinguished herself through a string of tough assignments, from traffic postings to narcotics control to VIP security. In 1982, she became notorious for towing Prime Minister Indira Gandhi's car for a parking violation while the latter was on tour in the United States.[9] Afterwards, she suffered years of backlash in the form of retributive job assignments and denied requests for family medical leave when her daughter Saina, born in 1975, faced a lengthy and serious illness.[10] As she characterizes this period, "'I had placed myself in a very vulnerable situation'" because "the only people who could help [me] were exactly those 'who had been offended by my 'equal enforcement of law.' I found them attempting to teach me my first lesson—favor your seniors blindly, if you want favors.'"[11] From that point forward, Kiran Bedi's career oscillated between the stunning successes and bitter setbacks of a strong-willed woman trailblazer.

Over time, she obtained two additional degrees—a bachelor of law (LLB) in 1988 and a PhD in social science in 1993. She focused her dissertation on drug abuse and domestic violence—all the while continuing her police work. At one point, she represented India as a Civilian Police Advisor for UN peacekeeping operations and was awarded a UN medal for her service in this capacity. In 1993, she was appointed Delhi, India's Inspector General of Prisons, the first woman to hold this high post, which inaugurated her involvement with Tihar Central Jail, to which she was assigned. This work, which is the focus of this chapter, brought her international recognition and acclaim, most notably the Ramon Magsaysay Award (known as the Asian Nobel Prize) in 1994, as well as an honorary Doctor of Law degree in 1995 for her "humanitarian approach to prison reforms and policing."[12] Over the course of her career—both before and after her stint at Tihar Jail—Kiran Bedi received numerous awards and accolades as well as a great deal of media exposure.[13]

In 2007, while holding a post as Director General of India's Bureau of Police Research and Development (BPRD), Kiran Bedi submitted for and received voluntary retirement from the IPS in order to spend more time on her academic and social work, including "protection against crime, social reforms and protection of women."[14] This includes ongoing work with her two legacy organizations, Navjyoti[15] (which means "new enlightenment"), founded in 1987, an organization devoted to drug abuse prevention, which is now run under the auspices of the IPS; and the India Vision Foundation (IVF),[16] founded in 1994, an organization devoted to police and prison reform, women's empowerment, rural and community development, disability and addiction management, and sports promotion. IVF also focuses on the welfare of vulnerable children and HIV/AIDS education and prevention and manages the website

SaferIndia.com to assist Indian citizens whose complaints have been ignored by the police. Since 2000, Kiran Bedi has authored or coauthored several books and hosted a court-style TV program called *Aap Ki Kachehri: Kiran Ke Saath* on the Indian Star-Plus network. She has also maintained a blog, "Crane Bedi" since 2006.[17] Two English-language documentary films focus on Kiran Bedi's life and work—*Doing Time, Doing Vipassana* (1997), directed by Eilona Ariel and Ayelet Menahemi, and *Yes, Madam, Sir* (2008), directed by Megan Doneman.

In the remainder of this chapter, I focus on Kiran Bedi's spiritual activist praxis, making a case for its womanist character. I draw heavily but not exclusively from her memoir, *It's Always Possible*, a text which, in its very form, reflects the eclectic, synthetic, and collaborative nature of womanist social change work.

ENTERING TIHAR PRISON

There is a beautiful and well-known anecdote about Kiran Bedi's first visit to Tihar Jail as Inspector General (IG) in May of 1993, which she recounts in her memoir. I present it here at length because it sets the tone for her work inside Tihar and also provides considerable insight into her spiritual activist praxis:

> Inside the ward, I saw a sprawling mud compound and a few tall trees. No doubt it had been a long time since an Inspector General had visited the place. The inmates in the courtyard began to walk slowly toward me, but the staff abruptly signaled them with their *lathis* (sticks) to sit down at a distance. The word had apparently gone around that there was a visitor in the prison and it was none other than the Inspector General. I was taken aback by the blank stares all around me. I stood facing them, not knowing what expression would be most suitable for the moment. The prisoners seemed to be wondering why I have come right to their den. By being out of uniform, I hoped to signal my desire for informal communication, not authoritative distance. I had already begun to empathize with them, wondering if our criminal justice system was designed to help offenders and forgive those who were willing to mend.
>
> Perhaps it was that thought that prompted me to break the silence by asking, "Do you pray?"
>
> No one answered.
>
> I repeated: "I am asking you, do you pray? Please tell me." I spoke in Hindi.

The men looked toward the warders [guards] as if to ask if they were permitted to speak. The warders seemed confused, and I could sense their nervousness. I had obviously put them in a bewildering and perhaps unprecedented situation. In the past, an inspection by the Inspector General meant a headcount of all the inmates by loud roll calls, and locking the inmates back in their barracks well before the Inspector General's expected arrival to insure that the visit went without a hitch. The warders would stand outside the locked barracks to show their own presence. A prisoner had bitten off a former Inspector General's finger during a round many years ago. And here I was asking them, "Do you pray?"

I moved closer to the bunch and directed the question to one randomly chosen inmate.

He answered, "Yes, sometimes," nodding his head.

"Very good. Who else does? You?" I pointed at another prisoner, again at random, getting even closer to the crouching men.

And then one after another, voices joined in saying, "Yes, I also do. I recite the *Path* (holy prayers). Most of us pray on our own...."

With some relief I thought that perhaps the first human contact had been made.

I probed on: "Would it be better if we say a prayer together? Would you like that?" I realized that I was becoming part of that "we."

They fell silent again, and I wondered if they had a collective voice. They had never prayed together.

Then one of them, with one eye on the staff and the other on me, said hesitantly, "Yes...." Others nodded their heads in agreement, wanting to be part of the prayer.

I said, "All right, which prayer should we sing together? Can you suggest one?"

Silence. I volunteered one from a popular film I knew they would all know.

This time there was an enthusiastic and instant positive response. I said, "Get up and sing together." They began to rise to their feet, but the omnipresent staff with their sticks stopped them. Raising my voice, I asserted, "I told you to stand up and sing."

The staff got the message and withdrew their batons. I told the inmates, "Close your eyes and sing with me."

And we sang. When we opened our eyes, all my fingers were still intact. I felt that we had together succeeded in creating the first sign of mutual trust, and the foundation of our work together. The words of prayer reflected the message of closing our eyes: "I am willing to trust you, you may try trusting me, and we could work together for the benefit of all."[18]

What are we to make of this episode? Did Kiran Bedi walk into a secular setting and impose a religious ritual? Or did she use her power to command as a means through which to invite others toward a more liberated existence? While both readings are possible, I prefer the latter and I argue that we can observe five important dimensions of womanist spiritual activism within this scene. First, we see the assertion of female power and authority. As the first woman to join the IPS and now the first woman to be appointed Inspector General of Prisons, Kiran Bedi embodied female power. To be more specific, she embodied the intersection of female personhood and traditional male power, insofar as the "law and order" domain has historically been a bastion of male social power and an arena for unbridled expressions of masculinity. Thus, by this very embodiment, it became inevitable that Kiran Bedi would somehow define this new social location of authority: female corrections officer. She could either define the job in the way it had always been defined and "act like a man," thus reinforcing the status quo, or she could do something different. She chose the latter—not by walking away from power and the authority that comes with the job, but by asserting it in a new way: a commingling of "power over" with "power with."[19] Whether this difference was a gendered difference or a difference made possible by gender is debatable, but its most notable feature is the fact that she infused her expression of power and authority with spirituality, thus opening up new ways for corrections officers of any gender to approach their job.

Second, we see the disruption of an alienating and dehumanizing environment and social structure. While it is thinkable that Kiran Bedi could have become a prison abolitionist, thus rejecting the notion that prisons have redeeming social value or ethical currency, this was not her calling. Rather, she felt attracted to "the khaki" (as her biography reports) and she felt it her vocation to involve herself in police work to "do good [and] undo wrongs." She viewed police work as a way to promote morality within the larger society and to improve the common welfare. Sentiments such as these are not surprising given that Kiran was born right after India's partition and grew up in a nationalist household inspired by the political philosophies and social change methodologies of Mahatma Gandhi and Jawaharlal Nehru. Thus, from her perspective, she entered her nation's police force not only to make it better but also to make India better. Thus, when she came upon the corrupt and dehumanizing situation in Tihar Jail, she immediately intervened. By not wearing a uniform, meeting the prisoners face-to-face, and appealing immediately to their spiritual natures through an invitation to prayer, she broke with past protocols and broke through structures of (masculinist and colonial) power that had only served to demoralize and demean before. In so doing, she created a punctum, an aporia, a critical rupture in which a new, more humanizing and liberatory process could be inserted.[20] Without the power with which she had been invested as a high-ranking member of the IPS, or as a police officer more generally, she might not have been able to command this change.

Third, we see energetic leadership. As mentioned in previous chapters, energetic leadership is the ability to elevate and fortify the spirit and resolve of others through a process of vibrational entrainment, thus mobilizing and motivating them to think, feel, or do something specific. When Kiran Bedi arrived inside Tihar Jail, both inmates and guards were operating at a low level of functionality, which was presumably based on a carefully manufactured sense of learned helplessness.[21] Prisoners had been conditioned by violence and deprivation so that they were powerless and worthless within that system, and guards had been conditioned to feel that the exertion of any amount of effort beyond the bare minimum within the system would go unrecognized and unrewarded. Within such a framework, popular notions of prisoners as social detritus and guards as ineffectual yet necessary civil servants that circulated both inside and outside the prison could continue undisturbed. Kiran Bedi's first job upon encountering this low-vibrating field of energy was to "shake it up" and stimulate it out of entropy. By showing up as a woman, thus eliciting surprise, she created the opportunity; by appealing to spirituality, she raised the metaphorical "energetic bar" within the situation. By cultivating herself as a person of principle and passion prior to her entry into this stultified environment, she had already done the necessary work of preparation, whether consciously or unconsciously, to achieve results. The fact that she was direct, authoritative, compassionate, and creative, and that she exhibited her "magical" blend of "gentleness and firmness," drew the prisoners and the guards out of their habitual state of mind and into a new, as yet unexplored and unarticulated, yet stronger and higher-vibrating one.

Fourth, we see spiritual awakening. Arguably, Kiran Bedi's energetic leadership facilitated the inmates' and guards' own sense of innate divinity, and thus the seeds of self-actualization. At the moment when the inmates realized that they *could* stand and speak and pray—the same moment that the guards realized that they could no longer issue dehumanizing commands or resort to unprovoked acts of violence—a type of spiritual awakening occurred. It was an internal "Aha!" moment for all concerned—even for Kiran Bedi herself. This spiritual awakening was not religious in nature, it did not derive from a particular faith-based protocol but rather from faith in humanity and in the divine on its own terms. Clearly, Kiran Bedi was able to capitalize on certain cultural understandings and practices embedded within a majority Hindu culture (such as collective prayer singing or a generalized acknowledgment of the existence of divinity[ies]); however, these understandings and practices merely served as a platform for, not as a constraint or even a guide to, how she chose to invoke inmates' and corrections officers' sense of their own sacredness. It might be tempting to try and figure out whether Kiran Bedi herself was operating from a particular religious affiliation, given that she was raised in a mixed Hindu–Sikh household and later introduced a methodology—Vipassana meditation—loosely associated with Buddhism. She clarified the matter in a later interview in which she declared: "My temple has all religions in it. It is the power of *spirituality* that I worship, not the form. I don't have any religion as such."[22]

Fifth, we see the liberating power of the everyday. When Kiran Bedi was put in the position to choose a prayer for the inmates to recite with her, it was not to the canons of any religion that she resorted, but rather to popular film. While the unnamed film in question may very well have had religious overtones or content, the fact that she used a popular film as a unifying mechanism conveys that she was looking to be ecumenical, to meet the needs of all, and to bring everyone under a common umbrella. This employment of "the everyday" was a method of breaking down barriers, releasing tensions, and creating levity during a profound and potentially confusing moment. Such use of "the everyday" for sacred and transformative purposes is fundamentally womanist.

ON TO THE WOMEN'S WARD

Kiran Bedi's next stop on her first tour of Tihar Jail was the women's ward, home to between 250 and 300 women and 40 to 60 preschool aged children, including some newborns, as mentioned earlier. Although only 60 of these women had actually been convicted, not surprisingly, most were in for prostitution, drug trafficking, or petty economic crimes such as theft or swindling. In keeping with the rest of the prison population, a few were in for murder or terrorist activities. The female population of Tihar included a number of foreigners who were segregated from the Indian women. Children stayed with their mothers.

Kiran Bedi's approach upon first meeting the women prisoners was slightly different. She writes:

> Next I moved to the women's ward. I knew that the women would be waiting for me. As I entered, all the women in the courtyard rushed toward me, uninhibited and happy, cheering my visit, a total contrast to the men. Was this homecoming? The women promptly sat around me, wanting to hear what I had to say. They had taken it for granted that I would visit them. Looking at their faces, I felt they were my children and I had indeed come home for them. I sensed that each one needed a comforting hand on her shoulder. Yet,

in spite of their grief and agony, all of them put on a cheerful appearance for my sake.

I asked them, "Do you read and write here?"

"No."

"Would you like to?"

"Yes."

"Very good. We will study here, and before you leave, you will be literate." They applauded in excitement.

My prayer with the men gave me the joy of seeing hope and acceptance; but with the women, something deep within pulled at me. I was "imprisoned." Tihar was my destiny.

Understandably, the women of Tihar Jail welcomed Kiran Bedi as a heroine and met her with great anticipation. This reception fortified Kiran, elicited her motherly feelings, and brought out the visionary pragmatist. Again an expression of the womanist value placed on "everydayness"—everyday settings, dispositions, and activities—Kiran Bedi's focus on the cultivation of basic literacy as a method of liberation for the imprisoned women of Tihar foreshadowed what she would later prove: That the road to utopia is often built upon small, practical steps.

From this point forward, Kiran Bedi's sweeping reforms inside Tihar Jail revolved around practical and spiritual adjustments that shifted the mood of inmates and staff, improved physical and mental health, increased the beauty and functionality of the grounds, created a sense of community, promoted initiative and self-governance, increased trust and transparency, and reduced recidivism. Public relations improved as a result of her efforts, bringing new levels of community support and involvement. Over time, she even established a level of economic sustainability for the prison, generating income for inmates and funds for prison programming. Last but not least, some of the more innovative projects ultimately enabled Tihar Jail to "run green" and contribute substantially to its own energy self-sufficiency. Such achievements were made possible by a confluence of vision with an ecological approach, a collaborative spirit, and a pervasive sense of the sacred, even in the most unholy of environments.

THE MAKING OF TIHAR ASHRAM

Although the dates are not clear, soon after her investiture as Inspector General of Prisons, Kiran Bedi had the word *Ashram* painted over the word *Jail* everywhere it appeared at Tihar.[23] This straightforward visual reminder set the stage for a new thoughtform to emerge within the Tihar community. Within the Indian tradition, an ashram is a place of spiritual community where people come to focus on spiritual education and practice, typically under the leadership of a spiritual teacher. It is a kind of retreat from the everyday life of a householder, a place where one can contemplate life's deeper meaning and focus on the nuances of self-refinement and self-mastery. To rename Tihar Jail as Tihar Ashram was to reframe a place of confinement as a place of potential liberation—to remove the connotations of it being a place to which one might be banished and substitute instead the connotations of a place in which one might be thankful to reside.

In conjunction with this renaming, Bedi turned her attention to the most quotidian aspects of life at Tihar: food, water, sanitation, health, education, and landscaping. Upon discovering, for instance, that, due to administrative apathy, the large iron pots used to cook food were also used for washing clothes, storing water, bathing, and carrying dry garbage, she immediately ordered new pots for the exclusive use of cooking and serving food. Upon realizing that the first meal of the day was not served until 11:00 a.m., causing those prisoners who left in the morning for court to spend the day without food, she immediately regularized the daily meal schedule and instituted an early morning breakfast. Upon learning that lunch and dinner rarely varied from cold chapatti and watered down dal, she set the prison cooks to preparing more nutritious and appealing meals. Taking things one step farther, she devised a separate menu for the prison's children comprised of foods designed to foster their physical and cognitive growth, with extra milk and vegetables. Not only did she remove kitchen staff who had communicable diseases like tuberculosis, but she also involved members of the prison population who had food preparation training or expertise to plan menus and cook for the prison. With such basic changes as these, prisoners began to feel cared for, which renewed their optimism and increased their investment in other prison reforms.

Water, sanitation, and health were all connected within Tihar. To quote Bedi, "Water was the most precious item inside the prison."[24] There was never enough to go around—for drinking, cooking, or cleaning—and it was rarely sterilized. This meant that prisoners rarely bathed, often wore dirty clothes for days, and frequently consumed food or beverages that could make them sick. Furthermore, basic sanitation was compromised, creating a facility-wide health hazard and medical risk. No flushing toilets existed in Tihar, and nonpotable water from a few unreliable hand-pumps was used to wash out sanitation pots. Frequently, illiterate prisoners would drink water from these pumps. Due to inadequate water supply, a stench frequently engulfed the atmosphere. As a result of water issues such as these, morale was low and anxiety was high within Tihar. When IG Bedi arrived, the prison was forced to rely on Delhi's Public Works Department (PWD), whose motto, she wrote only half-jokingly, was "Never put off until tomorrow what you can put off indefinitely."[25] PWD had a monopoly on service to Tihar, and the facility, not surprisingly, was among its lowest priorities. Eventually, Kiran learned that the only way to solve these problems was to bypass the PWD, employing instead the ingenuity and resourcefulness of prisoners and guards who had technical and mechanical expertise and the helpful collaboration of outsiders, such as academics and NGOs. In the crucible of such indifference, the "DIY"[26] character of many of Kiran Bedi's reforms was born, and she unwittingly and in womanist fashion aligned herself with the long line of women of color who "make a way out of no way."

IG Bedi's emphasis on the sacredness of all human beings translated on the mundane front into encouragement to prisoners to maintain standards of grooming. With better access to water, inmates were able to bathe more frequently, wear clean clothes, and, for the men, engage in daily barbering. Not only did Kiran Bedi order more soap for prisoners, but she also set up barber shops on each ward and made sure that they were regularly staffed by sartorially skilled inmates. These small acts seemed to improve prisoners' morale and cause them to present themselves with more dignity. This, in turn, influenced prisoners' interactions with each other and the prison staff, leading to fewer conflicts, less insubordination, and a more congenial cooperation. It also had a notable impact on disease reduction among the population of Tihar. Cleaner bodies meant cleaner food and a cleaner physical plant. Once inmates began to take care of themselves, they also began to take care of the space around them, keeping their barracks clean and taking care of common areas.

IG Bedi instituted a weekly *shram daan* (voluntary labor and service) time, after a Gandhian practice, and emphasized beautification of the premises. Beautification included landscaping, and in one project, 3,000 fruit trees (mango, guava, pomegranate, jamun, and lemon) were planted that produced not only beauty and shade, but also healthy food.[27] Another project that simultaneously impacted beautification, sanitation, vocational training, energy generation, and income generation involved turning Tihar's garbage into compost.[28] This compost was used for internal landscaping and biogas generation and also sold outside the compound's walls to generate income for Tihar. Inmates who participated in the project gained vocational skills that would be applicable once they were released. This innovative project was executed in collaboration with an industrial scientist, K. C. Shroff, who generated the idea and volunteered to work with Tihar's personnel on implementation. A jail superintendant by the name of D. P. Diwedi designed sacks printed with the words *Green Tihar*, which was the brand used to sell compost to the community on behalf of the facility, thus creating an element of institutional sustainability.

Kiran Bedi characterized the healthcare within Tihar Jail at the time of her arrival as "medical disservice."[29] Apathetic prison doctors rarely saw patients, rarely conducted the required inspections of incoming or outgoing inmates, and rarely prescribed appropriate medication, whether for minor ailments, chronic conditions, life-threatening illnesses, or major drug addictions. Geriatric patients and children were particularly vulnerable. Doctors were prone to arrive late, leave early, and, on the night shift, not show up at all. On site, doctors rarely wore uniforms and presented with a rude or indifferent attitude toward their captive patients. Given that many of Tihar's inmates had already arrived with the compromised health profiles characteristic of slum dwellers and other individuals from underprivileged backgrounds, IG Bedi had a crisis on her hands. In fact, she stated that this situation made her feel helpless for the first time in her career.[30] Not one to shrink from a challenge, however, and stimulated by profound compassion, she set to overhauling Tihar's health care system. Her first action was to replace all of the old, ineffectual doctors, with young, vibrant doctors.[31] This change alone shifted the tone of medical care within the facility. Over time, allopathic, homeopathic, and ayurvedic medicine all had a place within Tihar. Dentists were also hired and, eventually, a monthly "Health Care Day" invited scores of local Delhi doctors into Tihar to perform pro bono medical examinations. Another innovation included the creation of mobile dispensaries that could travel from ward to ward, simplifying patients' access to medicine and creating more opportunities for doctors to monitor health care situations on each of the wards. A system of health care education that empowered inmates to engage in prevention, manage minor first aid emergencies, and guard public health through proper hygiene was created. These courses also explained and encouraged healthy nutrition. One program was focused on HIV/AIDS education and testing. Interspersed with these programs were health-related exhibitions and films. In sum, IG Bedi promoted, protected, and preserved the health of Tihar's inmates and by extension its staff, by promoting both health care and health empowerment.[32]

Drug addicted inmates were a special concern of IG Bedi. She had developed the holistic Navjyoti program during an earlier assignment in the Northern (border) provinces where drug trafficking rates and hence drug abuse and addiction rates were high, and she had just completed a doctoral thesis on drug addiction and domestic violence, so Bedi came to Tihar equipped with a mindset and a skill set to address and reduce drug-related problems. Her strategy involved isolating drug addicted inmates in a ward of their own and turning this ward into what came to be known as the "Therapeutic Community," or TC. Prior to the creation of TC, habitual substance users were randomly interspersed with other prisoners, often leading to crises within the wards. For example, newly imprisoned addicts deprived of their regular fixes frequently screamed throughout the night, keeping other prisoners awake and anxious. Alternately, drug users were implicated in much of the crime and corruption within Tihar. While the jail did contain a single drug treatment center, Ashiana, it was largely nonfunctional due to years of professional neglect. Inside TC, addicts were immediately provided with medical care (including daily visits by homeopathic doctors) and physical detoxification (including a special diet). Throughout the prison, daily searches for contraband were conducted to cut off supplies. Several outside voluntary organizations and NGOs, including the local branch of Navjyoti, began to cooperate with Tihar to bolster programming and professional support. Local media took an interest, and their interviews of drug-addicted inmates who told their life stories brought additional community support. Inside TC, with the help of Dr. Harinder Sethi, a respected psychiatrist and addiction researcher, a therapeutic psychosocial program called Aasra Parivar (meaning "a joint system of families") was developed. Participants met three times a week to share life stories, experiences in court, and other details of their lives. Yoga classes were introduced on the ward, and a special landscaping project for this population was undertaken, resulting in the addition of a pond with a bridge, a waterfall, an aviary, a fountain, and a garden within the walls of Tihar. The result of all this: A reduction in the number of drug-addicted inmates, increased enthusiasm for drug-free lifestyles,[33] and better health and morale within Tihar.

SPIRITUALIZING TIHAR

Kiran Bedi is perhaps most famous for the introduction of vipassana meditation into Tihar Jail and, in particular, the organization of a mass meditation involving over 1,000 inmates—one of the largest in modern vipassana history. Many assume that she entered the prison herself a vipassana practitioner, a Buddhist even. However, as her memoir reveals, the idea was not originally her own. Rather, it was the good idea of one of her subordinates, which she immediately investigated and adopted, all the while crediting the idea's originator. As Kiran recounts:

> On the rounds one day, Rajinder Kumar, a young Assistant Superintendant, overheard me saying that I wished I possessed a magical therapy to help the inmates rid themselves of corrosive emotions. He promptly came to me and

said that he knew of such a therapy—vipassana meditation. I was naturally curious to know more about it. He said that if I wanted additional information, I should talk to his wife. So I did. His wife revealed that Rajinder had been an ill-tempered, easily provoked man before taking a vipassana meditation course. I verified the authenticity of her claim from other sources as well. Ram Singh, the former Home Secretary of the Rajasthan State Government, had introduced vipassana meditation programs into Jaipur and Baroda prisons. Rajinder was sure he would more than welcome our invitation to bring vipassana to Tihar.[34]

What is vipassana? To quote Kiran Bedi again: "Vipassana is an ancient meditation technique. Its basic objective is purification of the mind. Vipassana meditation is secular in all respects, non-sectarian, and an effective tool."[35] More recently, vipassana meditation has been popularized and globalized through the teaching of S. N. Goenka, who was trained by a Burmese master and teaches in the Sayagyi U Ba Khin tradition.[36] Vipassana means "to see things as they really are" and in fact derives from Buddhist tradition. Its purpose, succinctly stated, is "self-purification through self-observation."[37] Its goals include the promotion of peace and harmony through the eradication of negativity and reactivity, as well as increased balance, nonattachment, equanimity, compassion, sensitivity, and clarity. The basic technique involves 10 days or more of not less than 10 hours of silent meditation (with some talking on the last day), plus nightly instructional lectures, and vegetarian meals in a single-sex environment. Practitioners spend time purifying themselves physically and morally, developing concentration, and cultivating insight. Purification revolves around attention to the traditional Five Precepts: not killing, not stealing, not engaging in sexual misconduct, not lying, and not consuming intoxicants. Concentration is developed through focused attention on breath and bodily sensations that relate to emotion. Insight emerges once the capacity for self-observation has been attained through preparation by way of the previous two steps. Ideally, vipassana meditation produces liberation from suffering by teaching the individual to prevent negative emotions that occur when a nondesired event occurs or a desired event fails to occur. According to S. N. Goenka, the vipassana technique is universal: "Everyone faces the problem of suffering. It is a universal malady which requires a universal remedy, not a sectarian one. When one suffers from anger, it's not Buddhist anger, Hindu anger, or Christian anger. Anger is anger. When one becomes agitated as a result of this anger, this agitation is not Christian, or Jewish, or Muslim. The malady is universal. The remedy must also be universal."[38]

It is easy to see why vipassana meditation has been adopted in prisons around the world[39] and why, as a method, it appealed to Kiran Bedi in the context of reforming Tihar Jail. Perhaps more than any other action on her part, the development of the highly visible and transformative vipassana meditation program within Tihar Jail contributed to the popular understanding of how Tihar Jail became Tihar Ashram. However, as I am suggesting in this chapter, the introduction of the meditation program was only one element of Kiran Bedi's spiritualization of Tihar Jail, which ultimately illustrates womanist spiritual activist praxis. Spirituality is one element of the womanist triad that also includes the natural environment and human relations, and Kiran Bedi as Inspector General of Prisons addressed all three in a holistic and ecological fashion. What her introduction of vipassana meditation into the Tihar did uniquely was to bring coherence to all her other more "mundane" actions, demonstrating to the prisoners, the guards, and the world that all elements of life are ultimately spiritualized and that to recognize this is to liberate the power of life through recognition of its divine underpinnings.

Vipassana meditation is one method for practicing mental alchemy. As mentioned in the previous chapter, mental alchemy is the art of transmuting one's inner states and thus one's vibrational level. Through mental alchemy, negative, draining, or destructive mental or emotional states are transmuted into positive, energizing, and constructive mental or emotional states. The power to transform oneself internally in this fashion is key to changing the world because people's thoughts and feelings are the energetic foundation for all aspects of the material world, including its social processes and many of its natural environmental conditions. Furthermore, all human beings are "energy transforming machines" and are constantly affecting the energy of the people and things around them, whether consciously or unconsciously. One aspect of mental alchemy—and of vipassana meditation—is the cultivation of increased consciousness of the impact of one's energy. One grows from being aware of one's energetic impact to being intentional about one's energetic impact to being a complete master of one's energetic impact. In so doing, one increases one's capacity for making positive change in the world, whether social or environmental. Hence, spiritual technologies (such as vipassana meditation, as well as other techniques mentioned in this book) are of great importance to social change and, from a womanist perspective, constitute a unique and underrecognized[40] foundation for social change praxis that differs qualitatively from materialist social change methodology.

As Kiran Bedi's memoir recounts and the documentary film *Doing Time, Doing Vipassana* illustrates, the introduction of vipassana meditation into Tihar

Jail transformed prisoners' lives. Prisoners who had gone through the vipassana training, spontaneously reported instances when they had experienced insight, inner transformation, and mental alchemy. These two self-reports from inmates are typical of what was documented:

> Prior to coming to Tihar, I thought the stick was all powerful. After undergoing this meditation course, the helpful and cooperative attitude of the senior officers who were instrumental in reforming and rehabilitating the prisoners, my view has been transformed by love and affection. Now I think love and affection have greater powers for curbing negativity. I now believe that a man has to pay for his misdeeds sooner or later. I promise before all that I will not again harm anybody. (Satbir Singh, former constable, sentenced to 10 years for offenses committed in the 1984 Delhi riots)[41]
>
> Before undergoing this meditation course, I was polluting my mind with feelings of revenge. I wanted to either kill the judge who delivered the wrong judgment, or kidnap his children, or stage an accident of the judge's vehicle. My mind was flooded with negative feelings. Consequently, I spent many restless nights. But now, after undergoing the meditation course, all my negative feelings have disappeared. Now I have become a firm believer in God. I shall not take revenge on anyone. My mind is now full of *karuna* (compassion) and *maitri* (benevolence). (Om Prakash Bairwa, serving a sentence for kidnapping, after reportedly being falsely accused by political rivals)[42]

The introduction of the practice into the prison community also positively impacted the lives of prison guards and other staff, as they too were invited, indeed encouraged, to practice.

S. N. Goenka himself visited Tihar on New Year's Day 1994 to provide an inspirational lecture on a day that had been designated as a prison-wide day of meditation. During his lecture, the full text of which is reproduced in Kiran Bedi's memoir, he exhorts prisoners to consider liberating themselves from the prisons of the mind, including "anger, hatred, ill will, and animosity" as well as "craving, greed, passion, attachment, and ego."[43] This classic message took on particular relevance for this audience for whom the physical prison of Tihar Jail was also very much a reality. However, the speech quite possibly caused them to think about the connection between the two, as well as the ways in which their unique experiences in prison (such as with vipassana meditation or other of Kiran Bedi's reforms) might lessen their mental imprisonment in the world beyond release, even in ways that exceeded the forms of liberation enjoyed by their putatively free peers. In April of 1994, S. N. Goenka returned to Tihar to lead a mass meditation retreat involving 1,003 men and 49 women, thus fulfilling a prediction delivered by his Burmese guru years before that he would ultimately lead a vipassana meditation of over 1,000 persons. Logistically, preparation for this retreat was a large and complex undertaking that involved scores of inmates and staffers in the labor of construction, food preparation, and the like; however, the event was successful and, at its conclusion, S. N. Goenka dedicated a permanent vipassana meditation center within Tihar. From that point forward, two 10-day retreats per month were run for members of the Tihar community.

The introduction of vipassana meditation was not the only spiritually oriented reform (or spiritual technology) introduced by Kiran Bedi during her tenure at Tihar. Mornings began with *prabhat pheri*, when "a team of 10 to 12 prisoners circled the entire inner periphery of the jail ... with soft musical instruments, singing devotional songs at the crack of dawn to wake up sleeping prisoners."[44] Some Swiss journalists reported, "thousands of inmates gather in clean, shaded courtyards every morning for prayer and meditation."[45] Yogis were invited into Tihar to teach yoga and breathwork to inmates. Various kinds of spiritual lectures were offered regularly, and at 5:00 p.m., inmates were required to attend *sarva dharma sabhas*—"ethical therapy congregations"— where "eminent visitors addressed the inmates on topics such as morality, peace, harmony, and good conduct"[46] for one hour. These eminent visitors included "Christian and Muslim priests, Sikh *granthis* (preachers), Hindu pandits, and others from the OSHO Mission, the Chinmaya Mission, Brahma Kumaris, Ramakrishna Mission, International Society for Krishna Consciousness (ISKCON), and innumerable others."[47] When no outsider was available, inmates were invited to share their own personal stories during these congregations. Each session, regardless of speaker, was followed by a question-and-answer session. Kiran wrote: "Perhaps never before in their life had they received such sustained value-based education. These discourses led them to question who they were and why and what they could be."[48] The Swiss journalists offered this assessment: "[IG Bedi] transformed the prison ... into a monastic place of self-examination, learning, and work ... meditations courses meant to show that being imprisoned is not only a physical state but also a psychical attitude."[49]

It is clear from these illustrations that Kiran Bedi intended to provide Tihar inmates with spiritual inspiration "by any means necessary," and that her ecumenical approach was meant to maximize the chance that inmates would find something they could relate to within the cornucopia of offerings. Furthermore, it is clear that she went out of her way to expose students to multiple paths—an indication that her approach cannot be equated with proselytizing. Rather, it can more properly be called spiritual education—arguably womanist because it connects to all stages of the Ladder of Learning (see chapter 3). IG

Bedi's spiritual programs provided her incarcerated "students" with information and knowledge, thus stimulating the cultivation of wisdom and creating opportunities to experience enlightenment.

There is also a great deal of evidence in her memoir and elsewhere (for example, in subsequent interviews) that Kiran Bedi was enamored of the idea of "moral education."[50] Perhaps this can be traced back to her own fondness for the moral education class at the Sacred Heart Convent School or her early socialization in the philosophies of Gandhi and Nehru. Either way, we see evidence that education *via* religion was not offered simply for the sake of education *about* religion, but rather as a means toward the cultivation of moral behavior and the emotional sentiments and mental attitudes or beliefs that support it, on the understanding that moral behavior is essential to a well-functioning, peaceful society. In the United States (and other parts of the world), where moral education has fallen out of favor because of its putative (and at times historically verifiable) associations with particular religions and their hegemonic tendencies, Kiran Bedi's eclectic and polyvocal moral education praxis quite possibly provides us with an avenue by which we might reopen consideration of the value of moral education in a diverse world with complex moral challenges. How, for example, might something akin to universal moral education be achieved in a nondominating or nonoppressive way? Are there any insights we can gain from *womanist* practices of moral education? I offer these detailed examples of womanist spiritual activism precisely to stimulate deeper reflection on questions such as these.

FROM DEMOCRACY TO LUXOCRACY

Perhaps no more hierarchical social institution exists than the criminal justice system. When Kiran Bedi entered the IPS as the first woman, despite her gender she was immediately invested with a type of social power and authority that few people of any gender enjoy. As discussed previously, she could have easily chosen to exert that power in ways that reinforced the oppressive, dehumanizing nature of power-assertive hierarchies, or, less easily but based on democratic convictions, chosen to work for the abolition of prisons from within the system. Instead, she chose a third way.[51]

We see the earliest intimations of this "third way" in the "Do you pray?" anecdote that appears near the beginning of this chapter. When Kiran Bedi asked the prisoners to stand, and the prison guards used their batons to keep the prisoners seated, and Kiran Bedi then reasserted her command/invitation for the prisoners to stand—and they did—we observe the subversion of authority by authority, the dissolution of an oppressive hierarchy, the temporary substitution of a benevolent hierarchy as a democratizing move, and what I ultimately argue is an invitation to LUXOCRACY and an example of "luminous leadership" (see chapter 1). This multiple-simultaneous embodiment and articulation of hierarchical, democratic, and Luxocratic stances within a single moment *and* the orchestration and reconfiguration of multiple mindsets and positionalities at once, employing a love-based vibrational technology in the interest of liberatory aims, *is* womanist. When Alice Walker presented the mother–daughter conversation in paragraph 2 of her womanist definition, we observed benevolent democratizing hierarchy *and* its inversion, as well as a love-based technology in action. This *is* "womanish" behavior. As Chela Sandoval writes, this is a type of differential moral, intellectual, activist, and spiritual positioning that "permits its practitioner to act both from within and from outside ideology" and to "[break] with ideology while also speaking in and from within ideology." This mode of action is "metatransitive"[52] because it allows a change agent to "act upon social reality while at the same time transforming [her or his own] relationship to it." During her "Do you pray?" moment, Kiran Bedi was simultaneously transforming the prisoners, the prison guards, the prison, the larger societal thoughtform that undergirds "the prison" as concept and institution, and herself. In so doing, she was instigating, engineering, and experiencing a kind of spiritual awakening or moment of liberation—punctum—that was energetically shared with and coconstituted by everyone present. This moment anticipated LUXOCRACY.

Further reforms ostensibly launched by Bedi as Tihar's (self-)appointed social engineer demonstrate this same kind of chiasmic intensification of a self-governing, participatory atmosphere in which self-actualization and spiritual/energetic evolution become the raison d'être. One good example is the establishment of the Prisoner's Panchayat (Cooperative) System—a type of internal self-governance system—in June 1993. To quote Kiran:

> I am of the view that there is no substitute for community participation to forge reformation in a substantial way. Reformation and correction require integration and acceptance. A community creates the best environment for transformation, and in the case of Tihar, helped a prison become an ashram.[53]
>
> With the prison staff shouldering increasing responsibilities, and the outside community eagerly contributing to reform in Tihar, how could the prisoners not respond? In fact, the jail itself housed the greatest strength—human resources. The men and women confined to Tihar had time, energy,

and professional skills—the foundation of any vibrant society. Here was a waiting mass of human potential. It was only necessary to identify their talent and then give direction and guidance.[54]

In response to this set of conditions, IG Bedi along with her staff assisted the prisoners in forming the Teachers/Education Panchayat (charged with achieving total literacy within the prison, with educated and more literate inmates teaching less literate or illiterate inmates); the Medical Panchayat (to assist prisoners needing urgent medical attention by escorting them to doctors, also responsible for administering basic first aid and prevention education); the Legal Panchayat (which functioned like an internal, prisoner-governed legal aid society that collaborated with external legal aid entities); the Ward Panchayat (for maintaining cleanliness and discipline on the wards); the Mess Panchayat (responsible for food); the Sports Panchayat (organized games, teams, and tournaments for a variety of sports); the Cultural Panchayat (responsible for songs, theater, and artistic activity); the Yoga Panchayat (oversaw yoga classes); and the Nai Punja (Barber) Panchayat. Later, as the need arose, the following panchayats were established: the Mulhaiza Panchayat (orientation for new inmates); the Public Works Panchayat (comprised of inmates with mechanical, technical, or engineering skills); the Cable Panchayat (to oversee the internal cable TV system and programming); the Canteen and Provision Shops Panchayat (which ran Tihar's small shops); the Patrolling Panchayat (to prevent abuses of the panchayat system); the Insaaf (Justice) Panchayat (comprised of elders, who settled internal community and relationship disputes); and the Vipassana Panchayat (oversaw the vipassana programming). Finally, there was the Mahapanchayat, which was a periodic congress of the leadership (over 400 persons) of all the above-named panchayats, which interfaced with IG Bedi and other top members of the "official" prison administration. To quote Kiran:

> This mahapanchayat marked a turning point in the internal administration of Tihar Jail. It signaled the advent of a meaningful, collective, corrective community system. It did not matter that these men and women were in jail. They displayed enthusiasm, energy, and willingness to participate in a self-governance program of what was effectively a township of over 8,000.[55]

Additionally,

> All of these activities were the result of sincere, heartfelt, and invigorating enthusiasm and diligence on the part of the inmates and productive, coop-

erative coordination between the staff and the inmates. The earlier environment of mutual suspicion and even hostility was replaced by trust and an attitude of community service ... Tihar Jail had been transformed into an ashram.[56]

In 1994, Kiran Bedi was awarded a medal of honor for her work in the field of prison reform, and she agreed to accept the award only on the condition that medals would also be awarded to those prisoners who had also had a major role in the prison's transformation. Back at Tihar, four separate ceremonies were required to hand out all of the medals and certificates provided to participating inmates. This anecdote shows the degree to which Kiran Bedi was serious about the democratization of both Tihar as a site and corrections as an activity/field. It also shows the extent to which she was conscious of the vibration-raising value of the medals and certificates to the inmates, whose vibrational level she was constantly cultivating upward. Forms of recognition such as these generated happiness, pride, and the desire to continue with good works among people who were under confinement for and by the opposite of these conditions. Thus, they were small, practical steps toward the creation of LUXOCRACY.

Key in the translation of democracy into LUXOCRACY was Kiran Bedi's emphasis on the self-actualization of all members of the Tihar community. Her vision for prison reformation included ideas about how to create the conditions that would predispose and precipitate processes of self-actualization among the inmates and prison staff, and the activity of bringing this vision to realization was also part and parcel of her own self-actualization. This emphasis on creating the conditions that facilitate self-actualization is actually very similar to the notion of creating the social conditions that facilitate optimal human development that falls conceptually within the domain of liberation psychology, particularly that of thinkers such as Ignacio Martín-Baró.[57] The notion here is that humans and social institutions (as well as social processes and the natural or material environment) operate in an inseparable and mutually constitutive hand-in-glove fashion that requires simultaneous coordination of all sectors to achieve lasting transformation in any of them. Therefore, for example, raising inmates' and guards' vibration (improving mood, optimism, values, spiritual awareness, etc.) at the same time as the prison itself was being beautified and repaired *and* at the same time as inmates' and guards' bodies were being given attention through improved food, cleanliness and grooming, sports, and yoga was a recipe for real, integral transformation (social and ecological change) in a Luxocratic direction.

MANAGEMENT AS METHOD TOWARD METAMORPHOSIS

Management gets a bad rap in progressive circles because of its associations with corporate culture, bureaucratization, and governmentality. The exclusive focus on these pernicious dimensions of management as an activity, however, obscures the ways in which management can serve humanistic, liberatory, and even spiritualizing ends, particularly in our complex global society in which highly impersonal yet seemingly necessary (or, at the very least, intransigent) social institutions have permeated the fabric of everyday life. In other words, while we can imagine a retreat to village life, for those of us living in the global metropolises, it is unlikely to happen any time soon on any kind of mass scale, barring natural or man-made disaster. Even so long as we persist in the belief that we need some form of external government—that is, before we achieve LUXOCRACY, or completely internalized "rule by Light"—then we must give some thought to how best to manage and be managed. Thus, the consideration of managerial "best practices"—particularly those that are clearly aimed at people's "full humanization"[58]—are worth examining.

Throughout *It's Always Possible*, Kiran Bedi discusses her management philosophy. Here are a few highlights:

> In my view, the role of management is that of a facilitator. In other words, it is management's duty to solve problems and not create new ones. It is my firm conviction that if we do not solve problems, we become part of the problem ourselves. In many cases, in government service, we can become part of the problem by the way we choose to function, exercise our authority, and utilize our discretion.[59]
>
> Apparently, it [her appearance as IG] was the first time in the history of Tihar that the mission, goals, and objectives of the institution were stated, and steps to achieve goals were defined. We [she and her staff] also discussed strategies. "The use of force," I explained," will only increase hostility and anger. The collection of a few currency notes by illegal means will continue to demean Tihar as an institution. We need to conduct ourselves in a manner that increases honor and respect for the work we do. Each one of us shall have to work hard as a team. From merely keeping security we must create security. From watchmen, we must become educators,...[60,61]
>
> We shall prove that this infamous jail is the best model jail of India.[62]
>
> I am of the view that there is no substitute for community participation....[63]
>
> [D]irect intervention is absolutely necessary to make an institution serve as a reservoir of hope and reassurance. In my close observations of jail systems

in different parts of the world, I have found that wherever management is interactive, the institutions produced better results.[64]

Each one of us, irrespective of who we are or what we are, is a product of our own time management. How an individual spends his or her waking hours determines the value he attaches to himself and shapes the present as well as the future. This was a lesson I learned early in life.... This philosophy has been a basic motivation in all my actions, both personal and professional.[65]

Whenever determination is combined with innate goodness, anything is possible.[66]

Beyond her own commentary, other aspects of her management methodology are observable. Her praxis involves setting a vision and mobilizing others around that vision in a highly participatory way that relies on the perpetual cultivation of positive physical, emotional, and mental energy. As previously mentioned, a "magical" combination of gentleness and toughness is her trademark.[67] She is thus able to exercise authority in ways that people find palatable, if not inviting. The purpose of her exercise of authority seems to be to get others, particularly marginalized others, to discover and exercise their own authority and its inherent power—an authority rooted in their own innate goodness, sacredness, or divinity. This methodology could be considered a "spiritualized" version of Paulo Freire's "pedagogy of the oppressed."[68] Kiran Bedi encourages a do-it-yourself mentality to make life better, rather than one that relies on bureaucracy. Her day-to-day modus operandi include lots of face-to-face interaction: "management by walking around,"[69] the exercise of hospitality (particularly the meetings with superiors or staff that she held over lunch or tea,[70] as well as the encouragement of festive religious and national holiday celebrations with the inmates), and the spatial integration of people working at different levels of the system (for example, the joint participation of inmates and guards in the vipassana retreats and the fact that the vipassana instructors resided in the wards with the inmates during the retreats).

At many points in her memoir, Kiran Bedi refers to herself in motherly terms. "I really feel like a mother to them," she told reporters, for example.[71] While this statement could be read as either p(m)atronizing or empowering, I read it as the expression of a womanist leadership modality that is at once loving and authoritative, nurturing and disciplining. This modality was ably described by womanist education scholar Tamara Beauboeuf-Lafontant, who argued that motherly modes of leadership entail both offering care to and demanding accountability from one's charges,[72] be they children, students, or inmates. Because motherly modes of leadership are inherently embedded within family-based metaphors of human interrelationship—indexing indissoluble bonds as well as love and a certain kind of friendly informality—they overwrite override certain negative aspects of more bureaucratic or patriarchal forms of leadership. Even though they inherently reference a form of hierarchical relationship, ostensibly and ideally it is what I earlier referred to as benevolent (and mutually transformative) hierarchy. This form of hierarchy reflects the fact that, while people are existentially equal on the basis of innate goodness, innate divinity, or what Chogyam Trungpa calls "basic goodness,"[73] in virtually all other respects, they are not the same—and some forms of difference, such as age, experience, or wisdom, can serve as routes to people's growth, empowerment, and liberation.

Kiran Bedi's use of motherly terminology is further reminiscent of womanist literary critic Chikwenye Okonjo Ogunyemi's discussion of the *Iyalode*, or community mother, which she draws from West African (Yoruba/Igbo) culture.[74] Ogunyemi writes that the *Iyalode* is "an illustrious, older woman who is politically recognized by being formally installed to minister as mother in the public domain."[75] Furthermore, "Part of her authority derives from people's fear of her alleged occult power."[76] We could read this as spiritual power, or power within the invisible realm that governs people's everyday lives in inscrutable ways, as Kiran Bedi invoked through her continual recourse to spiritual activities involving spiritual experts. "The *Iyalode* is often called on to deal with intractable situations"[77]—think Tihar Jail, India's most notorious prison—thus, she must be someone with exceptional, creative, and innovative problem-solving ability. The point here is not to conflate Yoruba tropes of motherhood with those available to Indian women, but rather to articulate the characteristics of the *Iyalode* figure, however they may manifest in different cultural contexts, as exemplary of a highly effective mode of uniquely womanist leadership.

What is it about Kiran Bedi's management style that proved to be so wildly transformative inside Tihar Jail? My argument is that a single quality caused all of the aforementioned actions and attributes to hang together, and that quality is *love*. The energy of love pervaded Kiran Bedi's gentleness as well as her toughness; it motivated her hospitality and her walking around; it fueled the ingenuity that found solutions inside the prison when there were no resources to speak of, and cultivated resources where none had existed before; it inspired prison beautification as well as prisoners (and guards) to be their most beautiful selves. While this love was not without its costs in Kiran Bedi's personal and professional life (see, for instance, the documentary film *Yes, Madam, Sir*, which presents a nuanced and very human portrait of Kiran Bedi), it was still quite palpable and powerful. Theorist Chela Sandoval provides some of the best commentary on the nature of love as a political force: "It is love that can access and guide our theoretical and political *'movidas'*—revolutionary maneuvers toward decolonized being."[78] Also, "[L]ove is reinvented as a political technology, as a body of knowledges, arts, practices, and procedures for re-forming the self and the world." Other names for this kind of love include *revolutionary love* and *prophetic love.*[79] Like romantic or sexual love, this kind of love resonates at a frequency that transcends the mundane, but unlike romantic or sexual love, its object is not singular, but, rather, plural, collective, universal, or cosmic. It seeks not just to merge two people, but to merge communities, to merge humanity, creating the kind of "oneness" (i.e., dissolution of binaries, dissolution of the self/other distinction or the appearance/reality distinction) to which mystics from many traditions refer. What Kiran Bedi shows in her metamorphic management style, or luminous leadership, is that this very kind of love is embedded in and channeled through a million small, practical actions that bring love to life and transfer it from one being to another, creating an unending chain reaction and generating critical mass for transformative social and environmental change. Thus, as I wrote earlier, her story shoes how the road to utopia is paved with small, practical actions.

IT'S ALWAYS POSSIBLE: LESSONS LEARNED

When I distil the "lessons learned" from Kiran Bedi's spiritual activist praxis, I come up with the following list:

Lesson 1. *Begin with vision.* Proverbs 29:18, which opens chapter 1, is apropos here: "Where there is no vision, the people perish." Vision is a concrete manifestion of Beria'h, the "World of Creation," or Yetzirah, the "World of Formation." That is, it is the invisible mental and energetic foundation of that which manifests on the material plane. To define a vision with intentionality and detail is to lay the groundwork for its realization, and that is what Kiran Bedi did when she entered Tihar Jail as Inspector General.

Lesson 2. *Promote self-actualization—others' and your own.* Kiran Bedi was able to see the best in people in whom the rest of society saw the worst. By promoting self-actualization within a prison population, she demonstrated that radical internal and external transformation is "always possible." Furthermore, in the process of transforming others and a place, she herself was transformed.

Lesson 3. *The most ordinary things make a big difference.* Food, water, sanitation, health, literacy, beautification, exercise: These everyday elements of life in Tihar were improved by Kiran Bedi upon her arrival, causing inmates and guards to become more relaxed, healthier, more focused, more cooperative, and more invested in changing their environment for the better. Womanists know that when people are well-fed, rested, appreciated, and treated to life's small delights, positive political change becomes that much easier to accomplish and maintain.

Lesson 4. *An ecological approach to change produces comprehensive change.* Kiran Bedi was not a single-issue activist. Rather, her goal was to overhaul the quality of life—inner and outer—for a defined group of people. She refigured the motto, "It takes a village." She addressed her village's physical, social, mental, emotional, environmental, and spiritual challenges all at once—and not singlehandedly. Her holistic, collaborative approach produced remarkable results for a defined community.

Lesson 5. *Introduce contemplative practice to help people discover their own power.* At the suggestion of her subordinate, Kiran Bedi brought vipassana meditation to Tihar Jail, which revolutionized the spiritual life of the inmates and guards by helping them to "see reality clearly." The integration of this contemplative practice into everyday life at Tihar reinforced and illuminated other activities that were designed to help inmates and staff-persons discover their own power and develop a do-it-yourself (ourselves) attitude. Side benefits of this practice included the cultivation of inner peace, self-forgiveness, compassion and altruism, an ethical orientation, and community cooperativeness.

Lesson 6. *Community mothering can make a difference where other social change methods fall short.* Mothers are masters of doing whatever it takes to get the job done when the well-being of their loved ones is at stake. IG Bedi combined care and nurturance with standards and tough love. When one group of guards proved to be recalcitrant with regard to the new standards of treatment and accountability that she had established at Tihar, she ultimately paid them not to come to work in order to preserve the integrity of the environment she was stewarding into existence within the prison. The level of chaos they brought was not worth following customary employment protocols. She creatively used her authority to benefit the larger community. Community mothering as a social change modality teaches us one way that certain forms of hierarchy can be put to good use.

Lesson 7. *Love is a powerful social change technology.* Love is an invisible form of energy—a level of vibration—with the following attributes: It attracts people, it makes people feel good, it gives people energy, it inspires optimism and confidence, and it aligns people with positive ideals and principles. To be embody love, to physically carry it into a social or natural environment and emanate it from your person, is a powerful yet simple form of transformational activism. To cultivate a loving spirit within oneself with great intentionality "supersizes" other activist efforts. Kiran Bedi entered Tihar Jail with this kind of love and, with this energy, made it possible for others to become bearers of this kind of love as well. Love leads to LUXOCRACY.

AFTERMATH

An obvious question is, what happened after Kiran Bedi was transferred from Tihar Jail? Did Tihar Ashram continue to exist? A number of reports seem to indicate that, in many respects, Tihar Ashram fell apart.[80] Prison administrators who succeeded her were less than fond of her unconventional programs. Tihar inmates informally renamed Tihar Ashram as Tihar Anaath Ashram and called it "an orphanage,"[81] implying that they had lost their mother figure and hence their source of nurturance and safety. Interestingly, inmates went to great lengths to keep these programs alive. For example, when subsequent administrators threatened to shut down the Tihar branch of Indira Gandhi National Open University (IGNOU) at a time when about 200 inmates were about to take final exams, stating that the University would need 600 students before they would approve its continuation, leaders of internal prison gangs "forced" 400 students on their ward to sign up for IGNOU, thus compelling prison officials to keep the program alive.[82] Of course, the irony of this "means to an end" cannot be overlooked; however, it demonstrates that IG Bedi's programs had given prisoners a new sense of possibility about themselves and influenced their value systems, however unevenly. There is, however, another important lesson within this anecdote: It is the reminder that, to be effective, social supports for social change must be sustained. That is, the proverbial hand-in-glove must remain together. Changed people make changed environments, and changed environments make changed people—if the environment that creates and sustains people's goodness deteriorates, then people's goodness will deteriorate; likewise, if people's goodness deteriorates, the environments those people create will deteriorate or they will become unable to sustain the good environments that they created previously. Activists must take this twofold relationship into consideration at all times, and devise ways to sustain people and environments simultaneously. As I argue throughout this book, one way to do this is to establish universally the idea of the innate divinity (and hence the sacredness) of people, all livingkind, and, ultimately, all that exists. This thoughtform shift would do more to effectuate activism than perhaps any other kind of changed practice or belief. This is the essence of the womanist idea.

CONCLUSION

I had never heard of Kiran Bedi until the spring of 2008 when my cherished colleague Laurie Patton, a religious studies scholar, and I cotaught a community education course called "World Religions and Women's Economic Justice: Womanist, Feminist, Secular, and Sacred Perspectives" organized by the Atlanta Women's Foundation as part of their "Faith, Feminism, and Philanthropy" initiative. Once each month over the course of 10 months, Laurie and I would come together with a local faith-based activist from one of the world's major religions (we covered Native American religion, African traditional religion, Christianity, Islam, Judaism, Hinduism, Buddhism, and New Age religions) to provide an overview of the tradition and its economic content (Laurie), a womanist take on the tradition and its possibilities for women's economic empowerment (me), and an activist example of the faith in action (guest). It was during this course that someone mentioned Kiran Bedi as an example of an activist who had used meditation in her social change work by turning a prison into an ashram. I was fascinated! Having just finished Sister Chan Khong's *Learning True Love* and still reeling in the afterglow of that inspiring read, I found it hard to believe that I would so easily come across another text that would captivate me so completely. Yet, *It's Always Possible* did.

When I thought about how Kiran Bedi's social change praxis embodied the womanist idea and why it informs our understanding of womanist spiritual activism, I was struck by many things. First, like Sister Chan Khong and Immaculée Ilibagiza, Kiran Bedi doesn't name "it," she just does "it." This nonnaming seemingly does not emerge from a lack of language or a lack of awareness of things like "womanism" or "feminism" or even "Buddhism" or "Hinduism," but rather a deliberate choice to take concerted action outside the confines of a label. Such a choice severs, indeed frees, one from the strictures of ideology and generates a space of cognitive and practical flexibility and fluidity in which each new situation or challenge can demand its right response and be built from the resources and tools at hand. This flexibility and fluidity allowed Kiran Bedi to do what is almost beyond imagination: turn a prison into an ashram.

Second, Kiran Bedi's choice of issue—prison reform—stretches our sense of what womanist activism can "be about." Within U.S. social change and social justice discourses, notions like the "prison-industrial complex" and "prison abolition" dominate the discussion. These are reasonable responses to the very real proliferation of both for-profit prisons and increasingly invasive surveillance systems; however, they fail to account for the transformative power of the spiritual dimension. Kiran Bedi's spiritualized prison reform praxis presents a welcome "third way" or "middle path" that opens new possibilities affecting both what goes on inside prisons and how to rid society of them altogether. What distinguishes her method and makes it womanist is its insistent emphasis on sacredness—the sacredness of the prisoners, the sacredness of the corrections officers, and the sacredness of the prison itself, not *as* prison but rather as *place of epiphany* and *ground of liberation*. Kiran Bedi showed prisoners and guards how to spiritualize themselves and their environment, as well as how to liberate themselves from mental prisons, which are the root cause of all other prisons. Like the spiritual activists in the previous two chapters, she demonstrated the inseparability and ultimate necessity of both inner and outer transformation. She also showed—indirectly, through what happened after her departure—the importance of establishing structures and processes that sustain spiritualization in fragile environments.

Third and finally, she demonstrated the importance of self-actualization. Her eclectic, synthetic, holistic method of transforming Tihar Jail encouraged and evoked the "highest and best" in nearly all members of the Tihar "township." She created an object lesson for the world by taking what some would consider the worst possible environment—a place of confinement, a virtual living hell—and transforming it into something much closer to "heaven on Earth" by providing inspiration, support, and material conditions for people's self-actualization. I say this not to make light of incarceration, but, rather, to drive home the point that the potentials latent in any abominable situation are frequently much greater than we acknowledge or believe. It takes "outrageous, audacious, courageous, [and] *willful*" people like Kiran Bedi to show us that LUXOCRACY is "always possible."

SPEAKING TRUTH *INSIDE* POWER: PREGS GOVENDER'S *LOVE AND COURAGE*

And as we let our own light shine, we unconsciously give other people permission to do the same.

—Nelson Mandela, quoting Marianne Williamson

In September 2007, I traveled to Kleinmond, South Africa, to attend a two-week pedagogy workshop organized by the International Feminist University Network (IFUN), a continent-spanning collaboration of feminist activists, academics, artists, and government actors who had been meeting biannually since 1999. This go-round, the gathering was being funded by a large foundation, which offered the suggestion that IFUN invite an African American feminist to represent the United States. Other than South Africa, the host country, no country had more than one or two representatives, and, in the case of the United States, I was it. It was only my second trip to the African continent—the first being a solo trip to Uganda to attend an African social science conference in 2000 (which was, in fact, my first international trip ever) where I was one of only two U.S. citizens present—and, thus, it was my second experience of being the "American minority." As an African American feminist representing not only the United States but also womanism along with Black (U.S.) feminism, a minority amidst a sea of women of color from all over the world as well as white women representing their countries and cultures, I was immersed in the kind of challenging yet thrilling global conclave of feminists that many U.S. feminists of any race or color dream about, as we write and think about difference in a global context.

As one of the new invitees to this gathering, I was informed upon arrival that this meeting would be different from past gatherings in a very significant way—it would be the first year that IFUN had made an attempt to include spirituality in the discussions and activities of the group. To aid and assist with this big and uncertain undertaking, the leadership of IFUN had invited one Pregs Govender to lead the group in a series of regular meditation and self-reflection exercises that would be interspersed between the other sessions that were focused on "Globalisation and Feminism," the "real" topic of the seminar. As proof positive, however embarrassing, that I embodied the proverbial culturally self-absorbed American, I had never heard of Pregs Govender and had no idea who she was. I had been told that she was South African, but beyond this I knew nothing. However, as we awaited her arrival, most of the other people at the gathering spoke of her in the kind of hushed and awestruck tones that one uses when speaking about celebrities or legends. I thought, Wow, I can't wait to meet her.

The first morning after breakfast, I was sitting quietly in the main meeting hall amidst the bustle and chatter of people who already knew each other well, waiting for something structured to happen. Guests were arriving minute-by-minute and, being new, I was studying faces and gestures, listening to accents, and getting a feel for the group. At one point, a handsome, statuesque woman with close-cropped hair who appeared to be of East Indian heritage walked into the room without fanfare. Immediately, I was bowled over by her aura. The words that came to me were "Tsunami of Light." Her energy field was large, luminous, peaceful, and powerful. Without having any idea who she was, and before any words had been spoken, I felt drawn into her spirit. As it took me only a few moments to figure out, *this* was Pregs Govender. Soon, the energy of the whole room shifted.

Over the course of the next 10 days, I had the opportunity to listen to and learn from Pregs and over 20 other women from around the world. As one of the leaders of the workshop, Pregs not only led us in daily meditation exercises, but also spoke with us from her own experience about the uses of silence and meditation in political work. Just the week before, her memoir, *Love and Courage: A Story of Insubordination*, had been published; at the end of the workshop, all of us were given copies as take-home gifts. On the 19-hour nonstop flight from Johannesburg to Atlanta, I managed to read it cover-to-cover, unable to put it down. So much did I wish to prolong the euphoria that the seminar, and particularly the spiritual aspects, had generated in me, that I absorbed every word raptly. Adding to this inspiration were ongoing reflections about a couple of one-on-one conversations I had enjoyed with Pregs during the trip, both of which left a momentous impression on me, particularly in terms of how I think about spirituality, activism, and humanity's distant future.

At the heart of Pregs Govender's spiritual activist praxis is meditation, or the practice of "going into the silence." For her, it has been not just a personal practice, but also a political practice—one used in overtly political group situations as diverse as labor education meetings and the hallowed halls of parliament. In addition, her praxis emphasizes love as a politically transformative mindset. I use the word *mindset* because, as explored in the previous chapter, love, in this sense, is much more than just a feeling or an emotion; it is a vibrational state and a way of being in the world. As she herself has stated, "Developing a human rights culture requires a transformation of institutions and mindsets."[1] A third, and perhaps the most revolutionary dimension of Pregs Govender's spiritual activist praxis is the refusal of religion, "God-talk," the notion of divinity, or even the term *spirituality* in her approach. It was the unraveling of this paradox that caused me one of the greatest epiphanies of my spiritual and political life. In this chapter, I use Pregs Govender's narrative of her own life and work as presented in *Love and Courage*, as well as other published and unpublished accounts of her work and speeches, including my own notes from the IFUN workshop, to explore these themes in greater depth and to further illustrate womanist spiritual activism in its living embodiment.

BASIC BIOGRAPHY

Pregs Govender is an "activist's activist." Born Pregaluxmi Govender in Durban, South Africa, in 1961, her name is a composite of the traditionally male name *Prega*, which means "one who overcomes all obstacles," and the traditionally female name, *Luxmi*, which means "love," and was created by her father, noted South African playwright Sathieseelan Gurulingam "Ronnie" Govender. Her mother, Kamalam Govender, a generous schoolteacher whose own mother had died only five days before Pregaluxmi's birth, described her as "a miracle." A fourth generation South African with South Indian roots (her forbears had come over as indentured laborers), Pregs grew up in a largely working class household and experienced the painful relocations associated with South Africa's apartheid system created by the Group Areas Act of 1950. Despite frequent moves and hazardous living conditions, she grew up surrounded by family, and was particularly influenced by the practical spirituality of her paternal grandmother, called Aya, who protected Pregs from the constant threat of gender subordination and occasionally liberated herself from subordinated womanhood through dancing the wild Shiv Shakti trance dance. Aya helped found a temple in Cape Town as well as the Rylands Hindu Women's Association, which inspired Pregs's orientation toward women's solidarity. Her grandmother's observant Hinduism provided a contrast to her father's creative mixture of youthful atheism and informal Hinduism. Alluding to her father's unconventional brand of Hinduism, and perhaps also to that of Mohandas K. Gandhi during his formative South African period, she wrote,

> Growing up, I had also known Hindus who may or may not have used the term "Hindu" as a description of parentage or place of origin. They placed emphasis on the practice of good in action and refused to be complacent in the face of injustice and suffering. Detachment for them was the ability to transform negative emotions so as to act more resolutely and effectively with love. I saw in them a deep respect for every other human being as well as a tolerance that every path to truth has validity and no one can claim that theirs is the only path.[2]

Her paternal grandfather, Dorasamy (known as Thatha), was a trade unionist with a reputation for standing up to white bosses and "not tolerat[ing] bullies or thugs of any colour." A man who had been harsh with his own children, he was gentle with his grandchildren, leaving young Pregs with an impression of male tenderness. Two brothers deepened this impression, namely, Daya, her "older brother and hero," a playful, generous-spirited figure who taught her both yoga and karate, and Pat, the charming and adorable baby of the family.

From 1994 to 2002, Pregs Govender served as a Member of Parliament (MP) in South Africa's National Assembly. While in that post, she left a string of legacies that had national and global impact. As a member of the Finance Committee, she initiated and helped develop the first Women's Budget and made gender budgeting a regular part of South Africa's 1998–1999 National Budget. South Africa's example inspired women in over 70 other countries to push for gender budgeting.[3] She also influenced how statistics about women's participation—paid and unpaid—in the national economy were gathered and analyzed. As chairperson of the Joint Monitoring Committee on the Improvement of the Quality of Life and Status of Women, she oversaw South Africa's compliance with the Committee on the Elimination of Discrimination against Women (CEDAW) and the Beijing Platform, influencing South Africa's law and policy with regard to marriage, women's inheritance and succession rights, child custody, child maintenance (support), domestic violence, sexual offenses, sexual harassment, maternity rights, child care, and women's economic equality in the workforce. Famously, she was the only MP to register her opposition to South Africa's arms deal in the Defence Budget itself—a veritable Rubicon with regard to the establishment of the new government's priorities—an act that won her respect externally but cost her power and influence internally.[4] Ultimately, she resigned from the South African National Assembly over the arms deal in addition to the government's treatment of the HIV/AIDS issue and child rape victims. By this point, Pregs was both exhausted by "putting up the good fight" in a government whose idealism had morphed into realpolitik pragmatism, even within her own party, and by the growing ineffectualness of South Africa's governmental machine to realize the ideals for which she had spent the major part of her life struggling. It was time to apply her talents elsewhere.

After leaving the National Assembly in 2002, Pregs Govender became an internationally sought-after expert on both women's empowerment and alternative politics. In 2002, she began "writing, researching and educating for policy leadership and institutional transformation" through her organization WOMENS-LIP ("Leadership in Politics").[5] This led to a variety of positions at academic institutions, including the African Gender Institute at the University of Cape Town, where she served as Senior Associate researching "spirituality, sexuality, politics, and power," the Center for Women's Global Leadership at Rutgers University, where she researched gender, neoliberal globalization, and governance as a Fulbright New Century Scholar, and the Journalism School of the University of Witwatersrand, which awarded her the first Ruth First Fellowship. Beyond these academic posts, she has "worked with governments, parliaments, and civil society globally"[6] to monitor adherence to principles of democracy, human rights, and gender equality. In 2007-2008, for example, she chaired the Independent Panel of Experts charged with reviewing the South African National Assembly. She has worked with the Inter-Parliamentary Union (IPU) in building the skills of women parliamentarians globally and wrote the IPU position paper for its First Global Conference on HIV/AIDS. For the Club of Madrid (the organization of former heads of state), she worked as the gender equality expert on their Women's Leadership Project in Africa. In 2008, she was appointed to an international Panel of Eminent Persons, selected by the Swiss government and chaired by former Irish President Mary Robinson, which developed a twenty-first century human rights agenda for the 60th anniversary of the Universal Declaration of Human Rights.[7] She currently serves as Deputy Chair and Commissioner of the South African Human Rights Commission. Throughout this illustrious life-to-date of achievement, she has consistently avoided being publicly profiled, placed on a media pedestal, or succumbing to celebrity status—uncharacteristic for a person of her stature and level of accomplishment.[8] This active avoidance of the limelight reflects her belief in the collaborative nature of social movement, her desire to share recognition with less socially powerful actors, and the subtle yet powerful long-term impact of ego-minimizing spiritual practices.[9]

THE SPIRIT OF A REVOLUTIONARY, OR
THE SPIRITUALIZED REVOLUTIONARY

An imaginative and idealistic child, Pregs once wrote a school essay addressing the topic "What will I be when I grow up?" in which she claimed that, "After solving India's poverty,... I was going to solve the poverty of South Africa and then the rest of the world. Not content with all this, which would be complete by the time I was 40, I would adopt two children. After raising them, I would do yoga and reach nirvana at 60."[10] By Standard 7, the formerly shy Pregs, now a young teenager, had emerged as a student activist. Beginning with the refusal to sing "Die Stem," the national anthem of apartheid South Africa, by Standard 9 she had progressed to such activities as attending political protests with her brother Daya and raising money for an illegal fund to aid political detainees. Inspired by the recent decolonization of Mozambique as well as by escalating antiapartheid activity in South Africa, she became a part of South Africa's antiapartheid youth movement. She was greatly impressed by Mozambican revolutionary Samora Machel's assertion that "The liberation of women is a fundamental necessity for our revolution, a guarantee of its continuity and a precondition for victory."[11]

During this same period, an irreverent spiritual inquisitiveness emerged as she asked, looking at the troubled nation all around her, "Where was this God when good people suffered?"[12] Why were women "referred to as sources of the 'temptation of lust'" in Hindu scriptures?[13] Why did Gandhi test his "commitment to sexual abstinence by sleeping next to young virgin girls" in his "'experiments with truth'"?[14] Karl Marx's claim that "'Religion is the opiate of the masses'" resonated with her.[15] She also began questioning the curious racial logic of South Africa—not only the racial segregation and displacement caused by white (European) supremacy, but also "Indian teachers who seemed more European than the white nuns"[16] and the paradoxical, on-again-off-again antagonisms between Indians and Blacks.[17]

While a student at Durban Indian Girls' High School, she met the young man who would, in the early 1980s, become her first husband and the father of her older two children, Parusha and Yashodan. At that time, he was a boy from the rival Gandhi Desai High School who debated her and a team of "serious young feminists who may or may not have heard the term 'feminist'"[18] on the topic "Women are the weaker sex." This husband-to-be, who became her first

serious boyfriend after they reconnected in college, represented the "pro" position, yet her opposing team won, which perhaps explains why, after years of both
political comradeship and marital travail, he became her ex-husband. Later, she
would meet Paul Benjamin, a labor lawyer for South Africa's National Union of
Mineworkers, who became her life partner and "soulmate."[19] In 2000, they had
a son, Saien, whose name means both "blessing" and "blessed."

Of her youth, she writes:

> I was a rebellious teenager in apartheid South Africa. On a warm summer
> evening that year [1976—a turning point for student organizing in the anti-
> apartheid struggle], as my mother and I walked along the beach to buy ice
> creams, some white youths whistled and catcalled at me. I ignored them and
> they shouted out, "Go back to India, coolie bitch" and other obscenities. My
> mother was anxious as I turned round and challenged them: "You bastards,
> who do you think you're talking to?" "Just walk on," my mother whispered
> under her breath. "You never know what they could do to you." She was
> angry with me; she knew what they did to you. But I refused to accept that I
> belonged elsewhere, not in my country or on my continent.[20]

These anecdotes give a flavor of Pregs Govender's evolving activist
temperament, giving life to the subtitle of her memoir, *A Story of Insubordination*.
As her radicalism increased, she identified more and more with Black South
Africans. As she writes, "Biko's Black Consciousness appealed to me and I
readily accepted and identified myself as Black,"[21] despite believing, as she also
notes, "that we are a single human race."[22] Her brother Daya, who attended
the University of Natal's Medical School, also Steve Biko's school, was
instrumental in raising her racial consciousness. A lover of physics who linked
physics concepts with concepts from the Bhagavad-Gita, he also stimulated
her thinking about "the fluidity of energy that is life"[23] and the implications of
the theory of relativity (and similar physics ideas) for the future of humanity.
Around the same time, she enrolled in the University of Durban-Westville,
initially intent on an engineering degree. Disabused of this fantasy, she yearned
to become a journalist, inspired by an uncle who had written a biography of
Patrice Lumumba, Congo's first democratically elected prime minister—an
idea to which her mother was adamantly opposed. The conflict caused her to
drop out of university for a while, but once she returned, she took up English
and History, focusing on the "political struggles in the rest of Africa, in South
America, Russia, Cuba, China, India, and Europe."[24] During her senior year
of college, "students across South Africa joined a boycott," and she became a
party to the boycott and a woman student leader in Durban.[25] This boycott

culminated in a high-intensity confrontation with the South African army on her campus, complete with guns, dogs, and batons. Undeterred, Pregs and a group of valiant young students picked up sticks and pipes and miraculously scared away the men with guns. As exhilarating as this initial victory was, Pregs learned valuable lessons—about organizing, and about the internal politics that can undermine political solidarity—that she would carry with her moving forward.

After university, Pregs worked as a teacher to support her husband's work as a trade unionist. It was during this period that she birthed Parusha, a girl whose name means "the flowing waters," and Yashodan, a boy whose name means "one who helps others."[26] While her children brought her delight, these years were difficult for Pregs and she wrote, "As a young mother, I could not sustain my activism as before and came to be harshly judgmental of myself."[27] Yet, her meditation and yoga practice also deepened during this period. She writes, "I knew that my yoga practice helped me, most times, to shut out workday worries and listen to [my children]."[28] For a variety of reasons, her marriage began to unravel and she did not have the support at home that could have helped to mitigate the situation. Even many women's organizations she found were not child-friendly. Nevertheless, one of the founding meetings of South Africa's first feminist magazine, *Speak*, was held her home in 1982, "with children playing around us."[29]

Her interest in women's issues and women's solidarity deepened. She became involved with the regional Natal Organization of Women (NOW) and lost friends and comrades to assassination and other forms of state violence. Women's organizations such as NOW attempted to relaunch the decades-dormant national Federation of South African Women and were crushed when this effort was blocked, not once but twice. Throughout her ongoing involvement with the political movement, she endured sexist insults and frequently brushed against levels of intrigue that went against her principled and humanitarian nature, including some that came close to being life-threatening.[30] Time and again she was reminded of how easily idealistic political movements and organizations could be torn apart from within on the basis of ego struggles and the temptation for leaders to sink into the very forms of exploitation that they had started out to eradicate. Eventually she landed a job with the Garment Workers Industrial Union as a media specialist, which allowed her to both organize and politicize women. With the women, she helped land a victory against intrusive strip searches of women garment workers by posing this question to a manager: "Would you allow your mother, your daughter or your wife to be subjected to one of your searches?"[31]

News of this win spread to other unions, leading to an expansion of women's power within the labor movement nationally. Pregs was elected national educator for the newly consolidated Garment and Allied Workers Union. The goal of this position was to influence union membership to endorse becoming part of the powerful Congress of South African Trade Unions (COSATU). This effort caused African-Indian tensions to resurface and threaten the effort. Pregs used cleverly designed role-playing games to get people to realize the folly of their prejudices and the need to remain vigilant about being divided by the apartheid state. Later, in 1991, she would found South Africa's first Worker's College at the University of the Western Cape.[32] All along, one of the most difficult struggles was male sexism within the ranks of supposedly progressive organizations. The risk of insubordination within these organizations, as Pregs was to learn, was ostracism or worse.[33] In 1990, exhausted from it all and with few remaining political options in the area, she packed up and left Durban with her two children for Cape Town. This was just after Nelson Mandela's release from 27 years in prison at Robben Island, an event that, over time, would place Pregs and her activism on a different footing.

Within a few years of Mandela's release, as planning for South Africa's new democracy, organized by the Convention for a Democratic South Africa (CODESA) was well underway, it became clear that women's voices were still being excluded. A large national coalition of women's organizations from across the political spectrum, called the Women's National Coalition (WNC), formed to address the problem, and Pregs was asked to apply for the headship. She accepted the challenge, relocated with her children to Johannesburg, and began the work of "co-ordinat[ing] and plan[ning] all aspects of the campaign."[34] As a result of her orchestration of this effort, the voices of over two million South African women from all political persuasions and all walks of life were consolidated in what became known as the Women's Charter. This document formed the basis of the gender content in the new, groundbreaking South African Constitution and catapulted Pregs to a national level of recognition for her advocacy of women's issues. During the historic elections of April 27, 1994, this translated into Pregs becoming "part of the establishment" as a member of the winning ANC slate. She was now *inside* power.[35]

INTO THE SILENCE: MEDITATION AS SOCIAL CHANGE MODALITY

From the opening pages of her book *Love and Courage*, Pregs Govender establishes that a regular meditation practice has been central to her life, political work, and personal survival over the years. A notable feature of her memoir is the recounting of several significant instances where the practice of meditation—whether individual or collective—made a difference in political outcomes. Yet, she writes, "In my activism, I did not discuss meditation."[36] As she explained later, "This enabled me to share the practice with others whose prejudice or preconceived notions may have otherwise prevented them from experiencing the benefits."[37] In these statements, I detect a sentiment that I have witnessed before among political activists who engage seriously in "unauthorized"[38] spiritual activities, namely, what I call "being in the closet about spirituality."[39] For a multiplicity of reasons—from fear of ridicule at one extreme to sworn secrecy under initiatic oaths at the other—activists often keep their spiritual practices to themselves. This approach of keeping spiritual practice out of public view has both pros and cons. On one hand, it protects the integrity of the practices by confining them within an informed community of avowed practitioners and keeps the practices, which must be learned and studied in order to be used properly, from being misused and misapplied. On the other hand, it deprives the wider mainstream of learning about an entire class of social (and environmental) change modalities that could be of good use, particularly as humanity and Earth accelerate toward crisis points. What more and more spiritually oriented activists are discovering and reporting, however, is that, after a point, it becomes impossible to keep spirituality and activism separate. One purpose of the present volume is to open the door to this discussion of the spirituality–activism interface and to contribute to the democratization of information about useful spiritual practices.

What one must glean from Pregs Govender's memoir is the tremendous social change power with which her meditation practice infused her political work and the dynamics by which this translation of spiritual power into political power took place. A few anecdotes from the text itself are illustrative. The following story takes place in the context of her leadership of the massive national coalition of women's organizations that produced the Women's Charter for the new South African Constitution by gathering input from over two million women:

> Another major hurdle was our funding. Our main donor had suspended its funding to the coalition as a result of the impasse signaled by Debbie Budlender's resignation as research coordinator. Rosina Wiltshire, a Caribbean feminist, was sent by the donor to evaluate the coalition and recommend whether its suspension should be lifted. Rosina needed to see that the coalition was capable of achieving its objective of empowering women through its participatory research campaign. I worked with our research committee on plans to hold a workshop to develop research skills in women from the

regions. Our treasurer, however, refused to fund it, insisting that it was too great a risk to take. In my view the workshop was the only way we could break the logjam. I finally told the treasurer that I would pay the costs myself if the workshop failed to convince the donor, but she needed to release the funds immediately. It was a risk—I had very little money in the bank and had taken out a mortgage for my home—but there didn't seem to be any other way.

At the workshop, Rosina sat quietly, observing. I had never met her before. At tea she asked, "So, what *did* you do there this morning?" I was nervous and explained about the ice-breaker and the team-building exercises. "No," she responded impatiently. "What did you really do there? I have never seen energy being released like that before." I was silent, not knowing how to answer her question. She scrutinised me and a broad smile broke through, like the proverbial cat who has found the cream. "You meditate, don't you?" I relaxed. This was someone who was familiar with meditation. In my activism, I did not discuss meditation. Yet I knew there was nothing complicated about it. Meditation was that silent time, after I dropped Parusha and Yashodan at school and before heading into the office, when I focused on experiencing the inner power of peace, joy, and love. In such silence, I saw the deeply engraved patterns of self-negation, yet was able to trust the clarity that emerged. Meditation also enabled me to listen with deep recognition and respect for the gifts others had to share. I did not know how to explain this in the coalition's workshop, but with Rosina's intuitive intelligence words were unnecessary. "If you can release that kind of energy in even ten women, the coalition will certainly receive our funding," she said happily.[40]

In this anecdote, even with the sketchy details, we can tease out two major streams where Pregs Govender's meditation practice impacted on political outcomes: its impact on women workshop participants and its impact on securing major funding for the coalition. With regard to the former, we can discern from Rosina Wiltshire's question—"What *did* you do there?"—and her comment—"I have never seen energy being released like that before"—that something beyond mere "ice-breaking" and "team-building" took place. Or, rather, that the ice-breaking and team-building exercises that Pregs Govender led were transformative and not just perfunctory. Most of us have attended workshops or seminars or other types of gatherings that were either hopelessly ineffective or miraculously transformative. People who actively "work the energy"—meditators being just one example—are able to recognize and name "energy work" when it is taking place. This is what Rosina saw and named in Pregs's work. We could simply attribute it to Pregs's "skill" or "charisma";[41] however, to name it as energy work made possible by her meditation practice is probably not only more accurate but also a truer reflection of her own attribution regarding what happened. This fact precipitated the second outcome of interest, namely, the awarding of the grant. Although it is possible to argue that the grant was awarded simply because of shared group membership—as might happen with two individuals who belong to the same church, social club, or even social demographic—I argue that Rosina Wilshire's awareness, as a meditator, of the transformative benefits of meditation on group process and their alignment with the very social change possibilities that her putative donor organization existed to facilitate was the more likely reason for awarding the grant. Without the grant at this crucial point in its work, the women's coalition may have fallen apart.

Once inside parliament, Pregs found it necessary to go "into the silence" with increasing frequency to stay centered about her social change priorities and to withstand the energetic assaults of oppositional colleagues. Many who had struggled side by side with her as members of the ANC or other revolutionary antiapartheid organizations now resented her unrelenting commitment to society's most marginalized—women and girls, the poor, rural communities, and people with HIV/AIDS[42]—which they read as idealism, folly, or worse now that multiracial South Africa was poised to join the world stage of nations. Her narrative skillfully captures that rare and delicate moment when revolutionary organizations "win" and, becoming the establishment, must figure out how or even whether to translate their revolutionary platforms into "new, creative"[43] uses of power or just some slightly revised version of "business as usual." What makes her text particularly valuable is that she narrates from the inside of this process.[44]

That Pregs would be a different kind of MP in more ways than one was signaled by her organization, with a 70-year-old yoga teacher, Ivan Agherdien, of a yoga class in the parliamentary gym.[45] Like-minded colleagues would spend their lunch hours here instead of in the more traditional dining rooms, pubs, and cafeterias where much of the informal business of parliament was conducted. She comments extensively on the ongoing struggle of women MPs, particularly those not from economically elite backgrounds, to achieve work–life balance, including questions about whether and at what rate to hire domestic help.

As a representative of the National Assembly at the Association for Women's Rights in Development (AWID) conference in 1996, speaking on the newly created Women's Budget that she had instigated as a member of the parliamentary finance committee, she "began with an exercise on power that illustrated the need to work with deep respect for ourselves and others: the power of love and courage."[46] This use of hands-on exercises that included contemplative components was a controversial signature strategy of Pregs's, loved within activist circles and rued by politicians. At the AWID conference, she reports,

"After my speech there was silence before the room erupted."[47] Later, when she was asked to present on the South African Women's Budget at a Commonwealth ministers meeting in Trinidad and Tobago, one of her colleagues "harangued me, asking me not to 'play your games, as these are ministers, not trade unionists.'"[48] She did it anyway, reasoning that "[c]onducting such exercises was premised on respecting participants, whether ministers or unionists."[49] Some months later, a delegate from the Trinidad and Tobago meeting reported that "he had never understood power as well as he did after 'that game,'"[50] thus vindicating Pregs's use of her unconventional strategies.

One of the turning points in Pregs's political career was her decision to go against her party and vote against South Africa's first postapartheid arms deal. Her reasoning was that South Africa was not under military threat and that the monies used to fund the arms deal should be reallocated toward social programs that would fulfill the promises of the ANC's original social change agenda. As she writes,

> Redressing apartheid's legacy of poverty and violence as well as the impact of HIV/AIDS were critical needs that desperately needed funding. Instead it was the 2001 defence budget vote which was increased, to provide for payments for the arms deal. Even within the defence department there were many other priorities. The racist mind-set that had normalised state-sponsored violence had to be transformed; we had to teach male soldiers to respect women and girls instead of seeing them as objects they could rape at will; soldiers taught to kill had to learn how to create a peaceful society; retrenched soldiers had to be equipped with the skills to ensure that they wouldn't be discarded into unemployment and poverty. Instead of tacking these vital issues we were borrowing money from countries like Britain, Germany and Sweden to buy arms that they themselves found redundant.[51]

In mounting her opposition to the arms deal, Pregs raised the disapprobation of her party leader, President Thabo Mbeki, who addressed her directly when he stated in a public meeting, "[W]e were elected by the ANC. We gained and lost our positions as chairs of committees through the ANC."[52] As chairperson of the Joint Monitoring Committee on the Improvement of the Quality of Life and Status of Women, Pregs felt her party's official censure of her dissent. She writes:

> As Mbeki's voice droned on, I slowly made my way back to a quiet place in my heart. I remembered that the ANC was not just the party hierarchy; the ANC was also the poor and the powerless who had voted us into power, who

might not even afford membership cards. Their interests could not be ignored in favour of those who made large donations to the party. I meditated on the power of love and, despite my initial trepidation, began to feel a calm power fill me. When Mbeki delivered his famous 'I am an African' poem-speech to parliament years earlier, this power had shone in his obvious self-respect and respect for us all. In his talks on the arms deal and on HIV/AIDS, I listened and longed to hear this power resonate in our president's voice once again.[53]

Pregs's inner monologue in this passage resonates with the level of forgiveness and goodwill in Sister Chan Khong's public speech on the occasion of her assassinated comrades' funeral, in which she said "Men are not our enemies." In that speech, she was able to resuscitate the humanity of the killers by pointing out that they were just following orders and doing the best they could within the framework of their current level of understanding. In Pregs Govender's monologue above, she exhibits a forgiving gentleness when she intentionally calls to mind Thabo Mbeki's earlier inspiring poem-speech, "I Am an African," reminding herself of his humanity despite the current impasse. In so doing, she exhibited not only mental alchemy but also the social transformational power of meditation.

At the previously mentioned IFUN meeting, Pregs discussed this episode of her political career in the following words, taken from my notes at the meeting: "How do you disagree with your party and get your party's support?... It's a matter of how you present what you're saying—reconnecting people to what brought them there, where they came from, and who they were accountable to, speaking from a place of truth and deep respect not only for yourself, but also those you are speaking to." "Debate tends to be very pugnacious," she said on this same occasion, yet she was intentionally holding to a different way of communicating. "How you hold your space is very important."[54]

To continue her story, ultimately,

I told them I'd decided to vote against the arms deal. Then I was going to resign from parliament as soon as I had wrapped up my work and made a recommendation as to who could replace me as chair of the women's committee—it would take about six more months. I had thoroughly enjoyed my work as an MP since 1994, despite the difficulties. But with the arms deal I had begun to feel worn down by the way cabinet seemed to ignore the needs of the majority of people who had voted us into power. I had grappled with the question of who ANC MPs, including myself, should be loyal to.... [M]y mind was made up.... We had been voted into power by millions who were still waiting patiently for the changes they were promised; they trusted that once in government we would not trash their hopes and dreams. In the National Assembly, breathing into the fear that was rumbling through me, I pressed the yellow button, registering my opposition to the arms deal.[55]

Not long afterwards, Pregs as Joint Committee Chair addressed a national gender summit with the visibly disgruntled Minister of the Status of Women, Youth, and the Disabled by her side. She describes the event:

> Before I began my speech I asked all the participants to close their eyes and focus on the power of love and courage within their hearts. I heard the minister breathe out his exasperation. At the end of the short exercise, I asked participants to hold the hand of the person next to them and consciously send that power to them, so that "we may work with this power rather than the power of hate and fear that drove apartheid, slavery, Nazism and all the other wars that have plagued humanity." As I reached out my hand to the minister at my side, he clicked his tongue angrily.[56]

Later in the meeting, when the minister spoke out against Pregs, the audience booed him and a group of women stood up to challenge him. Although this challenge did not relate to the meditation exercise but rather to the minister's attack on Pregs's positions on women and poverty, it suggests that Pregs's peace-building group meditation exercise—expressive of her loyalty to everyday people and her desire to build bridges at once social, political, and energetic—had had an impact that outweighed that of the minister, whose only argument rested on an appeal to party loyalty that, by this point in time, had lost a semblance of connection to loyalty to the party's grassroots constituency. Would this event have gone the same way if Pregs had not done the meditation exercise? Maybe, but it is hard to detach that question from the fact that Pregs, through years of meditation, had built up and concentrated a kind of love-based field of energy around herself that could no longer be detached from her political persona.

THE MECHANICS OF MEDITATION

When we consider the process by which Pregs Govender's meditation practice translated into spiritual power, which, in turn, translated into political (social change) power, we must consider the mechanics of meditation itself because meditation works in a multiplicity of ways. Different types of meditation develop different faculties of mind, some of which can only be called psychic faculties. At the most basic level, there is "stress relief" meditation that works by simply quieting the mind and relaxing the body; it has no particular spiritual orientation and it could be considered "entry level" meditation—however, it does directly impact one's ability to achieve mental alchemy through the use of biofeedback to influence neurochemicals. Furthermore, it heightens body awareness and sensory acuity, making the body a partner in the pursuit of knowledge, wisdom, and enlightenment, and increasing the facility for self-healing.[57]

Bodily forms of meditation, of which yoga could be considered one, are a pathway to these physical effects and their psychic correlates. Yoga in particular teaches people to identify and press through their limits to discover deeper levels of flexibility and previously unknown levels of strength.[58] Pregs Govender was introduced to yoga by her brother Daya as a child and continued the practice into adulthood, as confirmed by several anecdotes in *Love and Courage*. Not only did she practice it herself, but she shared the practice with others, including fellow Members of Parliament.

Numerous types of meditation have been developed in various spiritual, religious, and mystical traditions. Mindfulness meditation, for example, helps people to "be in the present moment" by focusing on the breath, observing the mind's thoughts without judgment, letting go of past and future concerns, and increasing awareness of the environment and its details in any given moment. This type of meditation has implications for equanimity in tense social situations (such as Pregs Govender encountered in parliamentary debates and party politics) as well as deep listening (such as she engaged in when collecting input from rural South African women for the Women's Charter). One-pointedness concerns the ability to concentrate and focus attention on one thing to the exclusion of other things and ultimately, to merge one's consciousness with that thing in order to know its essence in an immediate, nonrational way; this method of meditation requires one to focus on a single object (e.g., candle flame), activity (e.g., breathing), or mantra (e.g., "Om") in order to focus the attention and enter higher states of awareness. Social change implications of one-pointedness include the ability to tune out opposition when one is focused on embodying a particular principle and to resist temptation when one's principles risk being compromised by expediency or personal gain. It is noteworthy that mindfulness and one-pointedness as specific practices develop different faculties—one the faculty of broad awareness, the other the faculty of very specific awareness—each with complementary functions.

Contemplation is a type of meditation that allows a person to concentrate on a specific topic or question, to consider it from a variety of angles while allowing spontaneous insight to also take place, which may come in the form of "divine inspiration" or a "burst of insight" or an "epiphany" or simply a "small, still voice." With contemplation, one may pose a question—any kind of question— and receive an answer "from within." Pregs Govender frequently engaged in insight-based contemplation when faced with a dilemma of one sort or another, and reports many epiphanies within her memoir. The processes of insight medi- tation, whether conscious or unconscious, are often behind the proverbial abil- ity to "make a way out of no way." Finally, some forms of meditation, such as those practiced within Kabbalistic, Sufic, Ifa, or Native American traditions, are more active and may involve chanting, dancing, or ritualistic movements; that is, "energy moving" activities designed to impact one's power, conscious- ness, or relationships with various dimensions of the Cosmos or Higher Beings. While these were less evident within the text, they are worth noting.

Just as consistent physical exercise influences the strength and shape of a person's corporeal physique, any of these forms of meditation, when practiced consistently and earnestly, can improve a person's "energy body."[59] With such an improved "energy body," a person becomes a stronger "attractor site" with greater capability for attracting others and entraining their energy. Stated dif- ferently, this is a form of concentrating one's spiritual power, creating a store that can be used for political or ecological activist work. It becomes a method for transforming a low-vibrating situation into a high-vibrating situation.

In sum, by using various kinds of meditation practice, Pregs Govender was able to increase the efficacy of her activism by concentrating her spiritual power and thus performing as a more efficacious social change agent. As she has remarked, "Meditation is the experience of my inherent dignity. The quality of that experi- ence is infused with love, peace, joy, bliss.... It is the practice of maintaining that awareness in my relationships with myself and others and enables me to respect my own and others' dignity."[60] This was reflected in the "Tsunami of Light" that I felt upon encountering her for the first time, as well as her numerous successes in mobilizing large groups of people and diverse constituencies around princi- pled social change actions, such as the Women's Charter (before 1994) and the Women's Budget (after 1994). We also see evidence in the numerous reports of her transformative quality offered by people whose lives she touched, particu- larly throughout her advocacy of and work with ordinary South Africans during the transition out of apartheid and into a democratic state. Finally, it is reflected in her unwavering commitment to principles of participatory democracy, social equality, economic justice, and peace-through-love, despite strenuous opposition from many of her former revolutionary comrades and numerous invitations to political expediency and compromise for personal gain. As her memoir reveals over and over, even those who were frustrated by her unrelenting commitment to principle respected her for her dedication to high ideals and her courage in speaking the truth *inside* power, whether the power of the ANC or the power of parliament. Thus, Pregs Govender's activist praxis is a testament to the power of spiritual practice to influence social change.

SPIRITUALITY BEYOND RELIGION

Around midnight on September 20, 2007, I wrote in my journal: "I just met this woman named Pregs Govender and already I have learned something very important from her.... We were having a conversation about spirituality the other night, and she told me what it meant to her without even using the word 'God.' I thought to myself, this is the future. This is what it will be like when all humanity has collectively merged with the reality of the innate divinity of the entire Universe: There will no longer be any need to speak of it, because it will 'just be.'"

In my reflection on this conversation, my intent was not to deny God's existence but rather to imagine a world in which we no longer separated ourselves from God or Divinity; that is, a world in which we were simply suffused by it. In this world, we no longer viewed God as "over there" and us as "over here." Virtually every religion that maintains a concept of God separates people from God and posits some trajectory by which people may rejoin with God. Thus, in my conversation with Pregs Govender, I had a flash, a premonition, of a future in which humanity no longer needed or professed religion because the joining, the merger, the reconnection, had been accomplished on a mass scale; that is, universally. In this world, humans functioned in the fullness of their divinity "without fanfare," which expressed itself both in terms of new forms of collectivity and in new forms of individuality. This flash was not just an intellectual exercise, but, rather, it was a brief moment of "being there." It was the first time I had ever actually envisioned a world in which religion or "God-talk" played absolutely no role—and not because of atheism, but rather, because of LUXOCRACY. Even though I had been reflecting on the concept of LUXOCRACY (i.e., "rule by light") for some time before meeting Pregs Govender, I had not actually pushed those reflections to the point where I imagined what a global postreligion society might look like, much less imagined in detail what divinity-infused, postreligion individuals might think, act, or feel like. In my encounter with Pregs that evening, all of these thoughts and images came flooding into me and revolutionized my understanding of humanity's potential and humanity's future.

When I asked Pregs whether she believed God existed, she said, "I don't know. But I don't really need to know to believe in the power of love or the power of humanity." In *Love and Courage*, she writes: "I do not like the language of God, entrapped within its very specific historical and cultural context. But I do appreciate the call—whoever makes it—to respect the love that resides within every human being when we ourselves may have completely lost sight of it."[61] When I asked her about spirituality, she spoke about it in terms of "the best in the human spirit." In fact, quite independently, she addressed the topic of spirituality in one of her IFUN sessions, stating, "The word 'spirituality' is so loaded—it is important to define it from our own experience and share that."[62] She characterized her own perspective as a "deep belief in the Power of Love, rather than 'religion' or 'God' or 'spirituality.'" She stated that she hasn't used the label "spirituality" to describe herself, but that others have used it to describe her and she has tried to understand why. She asked the group, "What is it in our own conditioning that allows us to uphold patriarchy, religion, and other authoritarian systems?" and then asserted that, "In different moments, each of us has the power to uphold life or destroy life." She affirmed that she has chosen to oppose those policies that destroy life.

These sentiments reflect a statement she made about feminists in her May 2002 farewell address to parliament: "[T]he strongest feminists I have met have been in the rural parts of South Africa,... Women who have never heard the words 'feminist' or 'socialist' or 'democracy,' but whose lives celebrate the power of the self, of each other, of the earth, of the sun, the stars and the moon. Whose celebration triumphs over the poverty, violence and HIV/AIDS that is tragically part of daily existence."[63] These references to "women who have never heard the words 'feminist' or 'socialist' or 'democracy'" evoke Alice Walker's 1979 definition of a womanist as "a feminist, only more common";[64] the references to women who "celebrate the power of the self, of each other, of the earth, of the sun, the stars and the moon" are reminiscent of the third part of Alice Walker's 1983 "womanist" definition, in which she wrote "[a womanist] Loves the moon. Loves the Spirit.... Loves the Folk. Loves herself. *Regardless*."[65] They also invoke traditional African notions of women's inherent metaphysical power related to their life-giving and life-preserving qualities, inclinations, and roles, such as those detailed in Mercy Amba Oduyoye's excellent text, *Daughters of Anowa: African Women and Patriarchy*, where she writes, "If there is anything that characterizes the continent [of Africa] it is love and respect for life, of people and of nature,"[66] and also "while there is a contradiction between being a woman and destroying life, there is *no* contradiction between being a woman and being powerful."[67]

Further cementing the notion that innate divinity, innate goodness, or "the best of the human spirit" is at the heart of our power to both make change and "be the change," Pregs Govender referenced Marianne Williamson's well-known passage, made famous by being misattributed to Nelson Mandela, from Williamson's book *A Return to Love*, in her remarks at the IFUN workshop:

> Our greatest fear is not that we are inadequate. Our deepest fear is that we are powerful beyond measure. It is our light not our darkness that most frightens us. We ask ourselves, who am I to be brilliant, gorgeous, talented and fabulous? Actually, who are you not to be? You are a child of God. Your playing small does not serve the world. There's nothing enlightened about shrinking so that other people won't feel insecure around you. We were born to manifest the glory of God that is within us. It's not just in some of us, it's in everyone. And as we let our own light shine, we unconsciously give other people permission to do the same. As we are liberated from our own fear, our presence automatically liberates others.[68]

These words express a similar sentiment—the notion of everyone's innate divinity, the possibility of its universal recognition, and the transformative power that such a universal recognition would have. They also reflect Pregs Govender's political/activist modus operandi.

In *Love and Courage*, she credits Nelson Mandela's principled leadership with supporting—indirectly as well as directly—this contemplation-based, visionary, and love-oriented praxis. For example, in one place, she writes:

> One of my last duties [as leader of the women's coalition that authored the Women's Charter] was handing over the coalition campaign report to Madiba [Nelson Mandela], as part of the coalition's delegation. It was the first time I would meet Madiba, a real privilege. I do not deify Mandela, who, aware of his fallibility, often pokes fun at himself. But my experience in India made me realise how much I had benefited from his leadership. In attempting to live by spiritual values, I was sometimes deeply hurt by the actions of people grasping for personal or political power. Madiba's humanity in the face of personal and political pain was re-assuring. When he was released from Robben Island, he insisted on speaking only the best of De Klerk, despite the fact that De Klerk had presided over terrible state-driven violence in apartheid's last years. Madiba's hurt and anger at De Klerk's betrayal of trust with the Boipatong massacre was palpable. Madiba had battled with the spiritual imperative of love that looks for the highest potential in every

human being. He had elevated De Klerk to a Nobel Prize-winner and had been met in Boipatong by cynical real politik. Yet Mandela himself did not become a cynic.[69]

In another place, she quotes Mandela directly as saying, "If 27 years in prison have done anything to us, it is to use the silence of solitude to make us understand how precious words are and how real speech is in its impact upon the way people live and die...the poor on our continent would, if anyone cared to ask their opinions, wish that the dispute about the primacy of politics or science be put on the backburner and that we proceed to address the needs and concerns of those suffering and dying."[70] More recently, she wrote, "We forget the 27 years of daily transformative practice in which Mandela reclaimed his own heart in silence and solitude, not as a saint 'but as a sinner that keeps trying'; the discipline that enabled him to mirror the best of our humanity (beyond the limitations of learnt masculinity)."[71] By practice, she is referring to contemplative practice, thus drawing a parallel and a connection between her social change praxis and Mandela's.

During the IFUN workshop, Pregs stated, "The idea of silence is very threatening to us as feminists because it is what we have fought to break. But there is another kind of silence in which we can find our true voices."[72] This "other kind of silence," which refers to meditative silence, that "going within" that leads to insight, inspiration, and illumination, the ability to hear the proverbial "still small voice," and, perhaps more importantly, connect directly with our own truth—is what I see as womanist. This kind of silence then precedes transformative speech, that is, speech with the vibrational power to change things in the direction of our highest intentions and visions. At another point in the workshop, she said, "Silence is a way into our way of being. Silence is a space to transform patriarchal emotions by empowering something else within ourselves: Love. It changes things completely. It is a space in which to develop incredible clarity and work with integrity. It's shifting what controls us within ourselves and allows us to discern between things. It's a way of bringing the mind and the heart together." She urged us to "Use the silence in a very nurturing way for ourselves [because] it is such protection to go within ourselves and know ourselves. It is a deep protection, a way of being not just for ourselves, but for others, because it has a ripple and gives others confidence for their way of being." It is this portion of Pregs Govender's activist praxis in which I most strongly see the womanist idea reflected; that is, the notion that, by acknowledging and accessing our innate divinity, we can power up our ability to make positive change in the world and lead others both by example and through attraction. It need not be called "spiritual" to work; as I have written elsewhere in this volume, we can just as easily invoke the more neutral language of "the transcendental" or the "invisible world" or, simply, "energy," to the same effect. The point is that there is something beyond, and more powerful than pure reason and pure materiality that we can tap into to aid our activist efforts. This, by any name, is spiritual activism.

LOVE AND COURAGE: LESSONS LEARNED

Lesson 1. *Discover the power of silence.* The first step is to discover silence. The second step is to become comfortable with silence. The third step is to go deeper into silence.

Lesson 2. *Show up—and stand in—with a different kind of politics.* Sometimes it's not just about showing up with a particular kind of view or ideology, but a particular kind of energy and a particular kind of being—a being whose energy alone is transformative.

Lesson 3. *Speaking truth* to *power and speaking truth* inside *power are both valuable transformational strategies.* Change agents need to be everywhere!

Lesson 4. *Find your way back to love, no matter what.* With deep enough reflection, it always returns. This is particularly important in times of conflict, political or personal.

Lesson 5. *Peace must reside in the body* and *the heart/mind/soul.* If your body is not at peace, engage in practices that bring peace to the body, such as yoga, dancing, mindful eating, and other joyous physical practices.

Lesson 6. *Make peace with sexuality.* As long as it emanates from the respectfulness of love and does not oppress, exploit, or harm someone else, sexuality too is an expression of the divine as well as a source of socially transformative power. This topic, while not explored in depth here, is a subtle and important theme within *Love and Courage.* "The year 1987 marked the time when I reclaimed myself ... and left all marital convention behind."[73]

Lesson 7. *Bring meditation "out of the closet."* Meditation is a powerful tool for self- and social transformation. It deserves a more prominent and unapologetic place in our social change repertoire. As Pregs Govender recommends, we must find ways to "communicat[e] the practice *in being* so people learn without being hindered by their socialisation."[74]

A NEW KIND OF POWER

It is time to claim an alternative kind of power and treat it as real.

—*Pregs Govender*[75]

In February 1994, Pregs Govender attended an international leadership conference in India. It was her first trip to the land of her ancestors, and upon arrival she was immediately struck by some of India's most profound paradoxes: street children serving as unpaid household laborers for wealthy, upper caste people who called them "God's children" and wrote the exploitation off as karma; "white" Aryan Indians from the North openly discriminating against "black" Dravidian Indians from the South; prestigious international gatherings of invited guests containing no Black Africans; and highly respected, "supposedly spiritual" people, engaging in and justifying all of these behaviors. As an African woman of Indian descent who had personally struggled to help end apartheid in Africa's most segregated nation, these scenes deeply disappointed Pregs:

> This is a country in which "untouchable" Hindus have been killed because their shadows crossed those of upper caste Brahmins, who claim to respect life so much that they refuse to eat meat. Against these criticisms, I encountered a powerful woman yogi, Dadi Janki, who has become an inspiring friend. The 78 year old woman looked deeply into my eyes as she handed me the rose and I felt the vision, the vibrations of good and the breadth of her spirituality. I do not like the language of God, entrapped within its very specific historical and cultural context. But I do appreciate the call, whoever makes it—to respect the love that resides within every human being when we ourselves may have completely lost sight of it. It is this recognition that characterises encounters with people like Madiba or Dadi.[76]

As one of the scheduled presenters at the conference, she wondered how she might use the opportunity to further advance the cause of liberation for all human beings, not only those of South Africa. Across several days of meditations, she reflected on the matter until the answer came to her. On the day of her presentation, she addressed those gathered with a series of challenging questions: "How would we combine love and power, both essential to change the world and address the suffering of people? How would we develop leaders of vision and inspiration, of humility and dignity? How would we ensure creative, responsive and effective systems, not dull and deadened bureaucracies?" She continues: "I shared my belief that there was hope in the power of good and in the human spirit." Although she dared to name and challenge the status quo—not just in India, but in the world—in her speech, she received a standing ovation. The message of love and courage was heard; an alternative kind of power was claimed and made real. Letting her own light shine, through her luminous leadership, she had given others the permission to do the same, thus bringing the world that much closer to LUXOCRACY.

CONCLUSION

As with the other activists whose spiritually grounded transformational work I have profiled in this book, Pregs Govender has not labeled herself a womanist. My choice to include her as an example of womanist spiritual activism emerged from two primary impetuses: First and foremost, the fact that she is a confirmed and committed meditator whose meditation praxis has shaped her political work is illuminating because it sets an example and establishes spiritual activist strategies. Her emergence from, solidarity with, and commitment to "grassroots people," especially women, particularly African women, with whom she has engaged this practice resonates with the womanist idea. Secondarily, her "activist credentials" are untouchable by customary radical–revolutionary standards. As an active member of the ANC from the time of her youth until the end of apartheid in South Africa in 1994 as well as a long-time labor organizer and women's organizer, her work covers "race, class, and gender." Thus, those who might argue that womanists are not radical enough or that they do not participate in revolutionary forms of activism would have to reconsider based on the case of Pregs Govender. Focusing on her work demonstrates the diversity of womanist activist strategies and the range of modalities through which womanists make liberatory change in the world. Yet, like Sister Chan Khong, Immaculée Ilibagiza, and Kiran Bedi, Pregs Govender's activism addresses the importance of both inner and outer change. Finally, her inclusion reminds us that both identity and spirituality are changing. While culture remains important, planetary and cosmic identities are also forming. This African woman of Indian ancestry who refuses spiritual labels but embraces and emanates Love causes us to confront a central tenet of LUXOCRACY, namely, that the identity of the future is the Inner Light.

CHAPTER

11

SPIRITUALIZED SUSTAINABILITY: WANGARI MAATHAI, *UNBOWED*, AND *THE GREEN BELT MOVEMENT*

In December of 2009, a few weeks before my marriage to a Liberian in Liberia, I visited Kpelekpalah village, the place of my now husband's birth and childhood. It was a multipurpose occasion: his mother had transitioned two months before, necessitating a commemorative feast; his brother was returning after 30 years away, necessitating a welcome ceremony; and the community wanted to meet the new American bride, providing one more reason for festivity. Although I had traveled in Africa before, I had never spent any substantial time in a rural African village. My husband-to-be, quite concerned about my ability to withstand the visit despite my great and enthusiastic anticipation, arranged for the village to build its first outhouse on my behalf several months before my arrival and asked his sister to make me a special meal, even though I didn't ask for it. This visit to Kpelekpalah with its all-day celebrations was among the most memorable experiences of my life, but what struck me more than anything, other than the excitement of meeting my new relatives, was the different relationship with nature I felt while I was there.

Three things contributed to this feeling. First, the village had no running water and no electricity, which meant a tranquilizing quiet behind and between the sounds of human activity and the motions of plants and animals. At night, it meant an experience of darkness such as I had never had before. The stars in the sky came alive, and those villagers who had not turned in early to bed stayed up around fires—a bonfire and dying cooking fires—to talk, tell stories, laugh, and doze. Quiet nighttime by starlight and firelight is a qualitatively different experience of night than night by artificial light, filled with the on-again, off-again buzzing of refrigerators and air-conditioners and all manner of electrical gadgets that hum, not to mention strains of passing automobiles and airplanes. It is almost a meditative experience; it feels easier to attend to, and sense the invisible world.

Second, the land around the village was the source of water and food. Most of the villagers were rice farmers, and many grew vegetables on the side; palm nuts produced palm oil, and pineapple plants cropped up like shrubs all over the village. These were the foods we ate while I was there. A chicken, a goat, and a small hog were slaughtered in my presence. There was no avoiding the connection between life and death or the way it is mediated by humans; there was no pretending that the meat in the food had not recently been walking around or, in one case, flying: Neighbors from an adjacent village sent me a freshly killed hawk as a gift, which my niece presented to me upside-down by the foot, and my husband's relatives gave us a goat as a take-home Christmas gift. Likewise, much of the community's water use revolved around a small, spring-fed pond at the edge of the village. Surrounded by forest, it was the site of bathing, washing, and, until a hand-pump had been installed two years before, drinking and cooking. Even city folk, like my husband, brother-in-law, and niece enjoyed a ritual bath in the pond (women and men bathed separately, usually in groups) to remind them of their youth and reestablish their connection with the village and its long traditions. A showering area had been created in the outhouse just for me, but no one else would use it. The pond's water was considered vivifying.

Third, the community's knowledge of the local flora and fauna, particularly their medicinal properties, was mind-boggling. Even my husband, who had more or less left the village for the city as a young teenager, was able to give me a walking tour of medicinal plants in and around the village, as well as detailed explanations of all farming and harvesting procedures. "If you take this leaf when it is young and boil it, you can give a handful of the water to a baby and it will cure..." ; "If you boil this leaf and rub it over a broken bone and add some chalk made out of this leaf, it will heal in less than a month, sometimes even two or three weeks..."; "If you chew this leaf and swallow the juice but not the leaf, it instantly cures... ; we use it in the hospital when we run out of medicine for..."; "If you run out of water in the bush, cut this vine open and you will get one or two glasses full to drink..."; "If you cut this vine and soak it, it can cure sore stomach and restore a man's vitality..."; "This pepper must grow under the eaves of the roof because the rain dripping down will make it bear fruit all year...." The people of Kpelekpalah had a qualitatively different relationship with nature than any people I had met in the West—even my relatives who farm. Being there changed me; as genuinely ecologically oriented and fascinated by nature as I had been since childhood, in Kpelekpalah, my ecological sensibilities relocated from my intellect to my gut and my spirit, and my ecological politics became more fluid and flexible. It changed the way I read and interpret, feel and embody ecological texts and discourses, particularly as they tend to crop up in Western academic and progressive settings.

This experience prepared me to reread and rethink Wangari Maathai's environmental activism in Kenya in light of both womanism and spirituality. My experience in Kpelekpalah village and my (translated) conversations with my sisters-in-law and other women (and men) who live there offered me a window into the lives, perspectives, and aspirations of women who reside and work in rural farming villages—women like the ones who founded and tended the Green Belt Movement's tree nurseries in Kenya. Additionally, my own immersion in Kpelekpalah's natural environment imprinted on me a new level of environmental reverence, one that enabled me to imagine what might have initially instigated and later fueled the Green Belt Movement. About six months before visiting Kpelekpalah, I had heard Wangari Maathai speak at a conference, which cemented my feeling that I wanted to include her books in a course that was then only in the planning stages: Womanist Perspectives on Spiritual Activism. That course spurred many of the reflections that form the substance of this chapter. In this chapter, I rely on two texts by Wangari Maathai to make the case that Wangari Maathai and the Green Belt Movement exemplify womanist spiritual activism: *Unbowed*, her 2006 memoir, and *The Green Belt Movement: Sharing the Approach and the Experience*, a "how-to" manual that she originally published in 1985 and revised several times thereafter as the Green Belt Movement evolved. I also draw from Lisa Merton and Alan Dater's 2008 documentary, *Taking Root: The Vision of Wangari Maathai*.[1]

BASIC BIOGRAPHY

Wangari Maathai was born Wangari Muta on April 1, 1940, in Ihithe Village of Nyeri District, Kenya, a region of the central highlands near the foothills of the Aberdare Mountain Range, where, "to the north, jutting into the sky, is Mount Kenya." It was in this region, shared by Kenya's settled Kikuyu and nomadic Maasai tribes, that her parents and grandparents were also born. Her mother, Wanjiru "Lydia" Kibicho, of mixed Kikuyu and Maasai heritage, gave birth to her at home with the aid of a local midwife and surrounded by women friends, who brought green bananas, sweet potatoes, and blue-purple sugarcane for mother and baby alike. Her father, Muta Njugi, also of mixed heritage, ritually slaughtered and roasted a fatted lamb to welcome the arrival of this newest baby, his first daughter after two sons. Her parents were a part of the first generation to adopt the Christianity brought by missionaries to Kenya during the early twentieth century, and her father, in particular, was among the first to leave subsistence farming for paid wage labor, thus enabling the family to join the monetary economy and gain a modicum of power within the British colonial administration that dominated Kenya from 1888 until 1963. From 1952 to 1960, the nationalist Kikuyu-led Mau Mau uprising, an anticolonial campaign that destabilized the colonial administration of the British in Kenya created an internal state of emergency that impacted Wangari's family deeply, particularly due to limitations placed on the movement of native people. Her parents remained physically separated while her father was in hiding and Wangari, at that time an adolescent boarding school student, was even detained briefly.

Although it was not customary in Kenya for girls of Wangari's generation to go to school, her parents enrolled her after her older brothers innocently asked why she was not attending with them. She proved to be an outstanding student who earned admission to a series of Catholic boarding schools, beginning with St. Cecilia's Intermediate Primary School, where she voluntarily converted to Catholicism. Although she had already been baptized Miriam as an infant, she took the name Mary Josephine at confirmation and used it for some time, being known at Mary Josephine Wangari. She attended Loreto Girls' High School, where she graduated at the top of her class, and was subsequently selected for the 1960 Kennedy Airlift, which landed her at St. Scholastica College in Atchison, Kansas. The airlift had been arranged by Kenyan nationalist leaders Tom Mboya and Gikanyo Kiano, who ingeniously approached a number of U.S. political and civil rights leaders, including Sidney Poitier, Jackie Robinson, Harry Belafonte, Martin Luther King Jr., Thurgood Marshall, Ralph Bunche, Andrew Young, and, ultimately, then-U.S. Senator John F. Kennedy, about providing transportation and scholarships to train a generation of promising Kenyans for leadership because of the country's impending political independence.[2] In fact, Wangari was on holiday break from St. Scholastica in December 1963 when Kenya's independence from British rule was formally declared, and she celebrated with the small group of transplanted Kenyans in Atchison. By this time, she had changed her name back to Wangari Muta, reflecting both her Kenyan heritage and her traditional family name. After completing a bachelor's degree with a major in biology (and a minor in German), she proceeded to the University of Pittsburgh for a master's degree in biological sciences, where she specialized in veterinary histology and conducted research on the pineal gland. This landed her a job in zoology back home at the University College of

Nairobi, then nearing its end as a subunit of the University of East Africa (now Makerere University in Uganda). By this time it was 1966.

Unfortunately, when Wangari arrived back in Kenya, the job that had been promised to her had been given to someone else: a man, from a different tribe. For several months, she floundered until a position opened up "across the courtyard" in the University College of Nairobi's Department of Veterinary Anatomy in its School of Veterinary Medicine. While an instructor in this department, she was simultaneously able to obtain her PhD from the University College of Nairobi (one of the last graduates before it became the independent University of Nairobi in the early 1970s), after spending 20 months studying electron microscopy at the Universities of Geissen and Munich in Germany under the tutelage of one Professor Hofmann, the professor who had hired her at the University College of Nairobi.[3] She was the first woman in East and Central Africa to earn a PhD.[4]

Wangari married Mwangi Mathai in 1969, after returning from Germany. She had met him in 1966 through friends. Five years her senior, "[h]e was a good man, very handsome and quite religious."[5] Mwangi was a businessman with political aspirations who, like Wangari, had studied in the United States. Despite this and despite her level of education and independent professional accomplishments and status, once they were married, he expected her to be a "traditional African woman" and "good wife," with implications of subservience and domesticity. Mwangi ultimately became a Member of Parliament in Kenya, serving from 1974 to 1979, and his two campaigns for office (the first unsuccessful, the second successful) intensified these expectations. Even though she loved her husband, Wangari's designs for herself and her life were different, causing tension in the marriage, which ultimately led to its very public and painful dissolution in 1977. From that point forward, Wangari, who had given birth to three children with Mwangi—a son Waweru, a daughter Wanjira, and another son Muta—became marked in Kenyan society as a divorcée, which would exacerbate her political troubles during the 1970s, 80s, and 90s. Fortunately, the children were able to move back and forth between the two households, allowing them to maintain good relations with both parents and allowing Wangari's career and activism to continue to advance. She writes that her children were "the reason I got up in the morning and continued working."[6] Nevertheless, once they divorced, Mwangi Mathai demanded that Wangari stop using "his" last name. She writes: "I got the idea of adding another 'a' to 'Mathai' and to write it as it is pronounced in Kikuyu. And so I became 'Maathai.' The extra syllable also signified that although a part of me would always be connected to Mwangi and his surname, I had a new identity. Henceforth, only I would define who I was: Wangari Muta Maathai."[7]

A series of political and professional troubles followed Wangari for the next decade. The year 1982 was particularly challenging. During this year, she attempted to run for parliament, which required her to first resign from her university post. When she showed up to register as a candidate, she was disallowed on a technicality. When she returned that same afternoon to the university to request her job back, she was rebuffed with the information not only that her job had already been given to someone else, but also that she would have to vacate her office and university housing immediately. Of this weekend of reversals, she wrote: "On Monday, I woke up and was confronted with the question of what to do with my life. I had no job and no salary. I had no pension and very few savings. I was about to be evicted from my house. Everything that I had hoped for and relied on was gone—in the space of three days. I was forty-one years old and for the first time in decades I had nothing to do. I was down to zero."[8] However, it was this removal of other "superfluous" responsibilities that ultimately made it possible for her to focus all of her energies on the Green Belt Movement, allowing what had once seemed like a side venture to manifest as her life's mission.

The Green Belt Movement (GBM) had begun with a landscaping and tree-planting business called Envirocare Ltd that she had started to help fulfill her husband's campaign promise of more jobs for the community. For a variety of reasons, this business failed; however, the idea of involving the community in tree-planting survived. Under the auspices of the National Council of Women of Kenya (NCWK), she initiated a volunteer project called Save the Land Harambee, designed "to inspire Kenyans, both wealthy and poor, to plant trees to protect our country from desertification."[9] Eventually, Save the Land Harambee morphed into the Green Belt Movement proper, separating from NCWK. Over time, the Green Belt Movement became a platform for a number of issues beyond tree-planting, including women's rights, multi-party democracy and government transparency, sustainable development, and the release of political prisoners. As international acclaim for the Green Belt Movement grew, troubles at home increased, leading to multiple arrests for Wangari Maathai as well as near constant surveillance and frequent harassment. Nevertheless, through the Green Belt Movement, she managed to avert the building of a skyscraper in Uhuru Park, Nairobi's most expansive green space; to prevent public lands in Karuru Forest from being distributed as political favors to governmental cronies; to run a symbolic campaign for president in order to unite opposition political parties; to obtain the release of 49 political prisoners; and to smooth ethnic tensions in the Kenyan countryside—all while continuing with the tree-planting and reforestation of Kenya. In 2002, she ran for office a third time and was elected to parliament. In 2004, Wangari

Maathai was awarded the Nobel Peace Prize, the first African woman to be so recognized.

In the remainder of this chapter, I look at Wangari Maathai's environmental activism as exhibited in the Green Belt Movement through the lenses of spiritual activism and womanism. What makes her spiritual activism so illuminating from a womanist perspective is the way in which it braids and blends three spiritual strands, Kikuyu traditional/cultural spirituality, Christianity, and ecospirituality, with conscientization and justice work grounded in the sensibilities and methods of grassroots women. Like Pregs Govender, Wangari Maathai exhibits the womanist characteristic of "belligerent pacifism," named by Chikwenye Okonjo Ogunyemi to connote a spirited and insistent—if not unrelenting—approach to making peace in a world overrun with violence, injustice, and other destructive forms of chaos.[10] More than any other womanist spiritual activist examined in this book, Wangari Maathai demonstrates that human life and its improvement are inextricable from deep ecological and environmental considerations; indeed, she demonstrates that we must come to see the natural environment and all its species and elements, livingkind, as our peer and collaborator in social transformation. From a womanist perspective, such a move requires recognition of the environment's inherent sacredness.

THE SPIRIT OF KIRINYAGA, PLACE OF BRIGHTNESS

How does ecospirituality develop? What experiences are necessary to cultivate an awareness of nature's sacredness? "When I was a child, my surroundings were alive, dynamic, and inspiring,"[11] writes Wangari Maathai. Growing up in sight of Mount Kenya—known among the Kikuyu as Kirinyaga, the "Place of Brightness," Africa's second highest peak—meant growing up immersed in reverence for all things associated with the mountain. "Everything good came from it: abundant rains, rivers, streams, clean drinking water. Whether they were praying, burying their dead, or performing sacrifices, Kikuyus faced Mount Kenya, and when they built their houses, they made sure the doors looked toward it. As long as the mountain stood, people believed that God was with them and that they would want for nothing."[12] This belief was substantiated by the providence all around: "We lived in a land abundant with shrubs, creepers, ferns, and trees, like the *mitundu*, *mikeu*, and *migumo*, some of which produced berries and nuts. Because rain fell regularly and reliably, clean drinking water was everywhere. There were large well-watered fields of maize, beans, wheat, and vegetables. Hunger was virtually unknown. The soil was rich, dark red-brown, and moist."[13] Kikuyu people lived simply and sustainably. "As long as the rains fell, people had more than enough food for themselves, plentiful livestock, and peace."[14] Such was the reverence for water—rivers and rain—that "'May you sleep where there is rain and dew' was the final blessing given when someone was laid to rest."[15] The entire human life cycle was intertwined, physically and spiritually, with longer and shorter cycles of nature—mineral, animal, vegetable, ancestral. Awe arose from everyday encounters with natural beauty as well as the social construction of sacred meaning associated with those encounters.[16] These experiences imprinted Wangari early.

I define ecospirituality as a spiritual mindframe comprised of the following five elements, at minimum: (1) a sense of nature's sacredness and associated feelings of awe and reverence; (2) a feeling of human interconnectedness with nature; (3) a sense of responsibility for or stewardship of ecological balance; (4) an awareness that the spiritual, transcendental, energetic, or invisible realm also relates to nature as it does to humans, and (5) an awareness that the optimization of human life (including the achievement of social justice) *requires* optimization of the relationship between humans and the natural environment, including the ecological restoration and healing and the rediscovery of living in a balanced way with nature.[17] Because of the womanist triad, which encompasses human–human relationships, human–nature relationships, and human–spiritual relationships, ecospirituality is an inherent dimension of the womanist idea. Wangari Maathai's spiritual activism vis-à-vis the Green Belt Movement helps us to see ecospirituality in action and aids us in visualizing how to participate in rehabilitating both nature and our relationship with it. In her work, we see a sustained and spiritualized effort to reverse ecological damage already done by humans and to reacquaint people with eco-harmonious worldviews and practices vis-à-vis the everyday actions of grassroots women.

THE WISDOM OF FIG TREES

At the center of this sacred web of life for Kenyan women, whose responsibility it was (and sometimes still is) to collect both water and firewood, is the African fig tree. Wangari explains:

> When my mother told me to go and fetch firewood, she would warn me, "Don't pick any dry wood out of the fig tree, or even around it." "Why?" I would ask. "Because that's a tree of God," she'd reply. "We don't use it. We don't cut it. We don't burn it." As a child, of course, I had no idea what my mother was talking about, but I obeyed her.[18]

As a scientist, she explained:

> I later learned that there was a connection between the fig tree's root system
> and the underground water reservoirs. The roots burrowed deep into the
> ground, breaking through the rocks beneath the surface soil and diving
> into the underground water table. The water traveled up along the roots
> until it hit a depression or weak place in the ground and gushed out as a
> spring. Indeed, wherever these trees stood, there were likely to be streams.
> The reverence the community had for the fig tree helped preserve the stream
> and the tadpoles that so captivated me. The trees also held the soil together,
> reducing erosion and landslides. In such ways, without conscious or deliberate
> effort, these cultural and spiritual practices contributed to the preservation
> of biodiversity.[19]

This anecdote about the fig tree moved me deeply and produced an "Aha!"
moment for me. Years ago, I lived in a small college town on a piece of property
to which an old house had been moved from one location to another and renovated. It was the largest piece of property on the street. Adjacent to my property, just beyond the fence, stood a vacant wooded lot on which a small stream
bubbled up from a spring. Behind my yard and down a slope sat an apartment
complex. When it rained, a riverlike gully would form between my yard and
the parking lot of the apartment complex. Growing there were two tall, old wil-
lows. Inside my fence, about equidistant from the spring and the gulley, grew
a short, stout fig tree. A lover of trees but not a lover of figs, I often observed
the tree (and its attendant bees) affectionately, but never consumed the copious
fruit that hung from the branches and fertilized the ground below. I always
assumed that the fig tree had been planted ornamentally by someone in the distant past, plus, being more or less an urbanite by birth I was at that time rather
afraid to just eat fruit from a tree in my yard. After reading Wangari Maathai's
scientific explanation about the role of fig trees in the ecosystem, a light bulb
went off and I realized that my own former yard was the very sort of riparian
ecosystem of which she spoke.

An additional detail will help explain why: In a conversation with the man
from whom the house was purchased—a contractor who had himself relocated,
renovated, and lived in the house with his family—I learned that the low-lying
lot containing the apartments had once been a lake, and that the land my property occupied had once been unoccupied lakeside property. His brother, also a
contractor who builds apartments, had wanted to build apartments on the land
where my house—a very old, historic house built in the 1920s by the founders
of a local grocery store chain—originally sat, across town. He told his brother,

if you move this house, I will sell it to you for $1. So, his brother moved the house to the location where it was when I bought it. It just so happens that this "new" property was parceled off land also owned by his brother, where another apartment complex had been built—atop the drained lakebed! Therefore, I was living with the legacy of a disrupted ecosystem—a lake, fed by a spring, feeding a forest, including two elegant willows and a humble fig tree, which, whenever it rained heavily, would attempt to reassert itself through flooding. Without knowing all this, I had always felt so happy to have a spring on the land, stating once to my partner at the time that, should disaster ever strike, we would be so lucky to have natural access to water. The neighbors across the street, a lovely older couple, had purchased the lot adjacent to our yard in order to avert further development and preserve the watershed, because they were able to remember when their house faced the lake. In a town with a teeming, ever-expanding, and relatively prosperous college student population, every parcel of land was vulnerable to "quick and easy" exploitation for profit. Although a century past and a half a world away from colonial expansion in Kenya, in my land-grant university town where new apartments and housing subdivisions often debuted with "Colonial" or "Plantation" in the name, the parallels—including the wisdom of the fig tree—did not escape me.

Colonial activity in Kenya brought plantation agriculture with its ecologically disruptive practices of clear-cutting and monoculture. Forests were cleared in order to plant a single type of cash crop, primarily for export, a practice which, over a period of decades, led to soil erosion and landslides, as well as the decimation of soil quality, food shortages, and cultural disruptions of farming practices and foodways. These crops included tea and coffee and even nonnative tree species produced as a commodity for ornamental landscaping. Wangari's generation was a transitional generation—one that had learned the "old ways" during childhood but, through the process of Western education, experienced a qualitatively different adulthood from that of their parents. To quote her: "People who are colonized lose a lot of knowledge accumulated through the ages—in the food they eat, the way they prepare it, in the way they pass the art of agriculture to the next generation—because we lose the values that we associated with that natural world."[20] Wangari's gift as an activist was the ability to bridge the old and new worlds, to draw connections between them through memory and intergenerational interweaving, and to bring a critical lens to ecological and social change. What was essentially a spiritual quest to restore the environment—for the sake of the people as well as the environment's own sake—was aided by her research skills and credentials as a biologist. This passage from her memoir, set in the early 1970s, highlights a turning point in her own understanding of the connections between culture, spirituality, economics, environmental sustainability. I present it here in all its detail for impact:

> While I was in the rural areas outside Nairobi collecting the ticks [for her postdoctoral research on a tick-borne bovine disease affecting imported cattle], I noticed that the rivers would rush down the hillsides and along paths and roads when it rained, and that they were muddy with silt. This was very different from when I was growing up. "That is soil erosion," I remember thinking to myself. "We must do something about that." I also observed that the cows were so skinny that I could count their ribs. There was little grass or other fodder for them to eat where they grazed, and during the dry season much of the grass lacked nutrients.
>
> The people, too, looked undernourished and poor and the vegetation in their fields was scanty. The soils in the fields weren't performing as they should because their nutrient value had been depleted. It became clear to me through these observations that Kenya's and the whole region's livestock industry was threatened more by environmental degradation than by either the ticks in the cows' ears or the parasites in the ticks' salivary glands.
>
> When I went home to visit my family in Nyeri, I had another indication of the changes under way around us. I saw rivers silted with topsoil, much of which was coming from the forest where plantations of commercial trees had replaced indigenous forest. I noticed that much of the land that had been covered by trees, bushes, and grasses when I was growing up had been replaced by tea and coffee.
>
> I also learned that someone had acquired the piece of land where the fig tree I was in awe of as a child had stood. The new owner perceived the tree to be a nuisance because it took up too much space and he felled it to make room to grow tea. By then I understood the connection between the tree and water, so it did not surprise me that when the fig tree was cut down, the stream where I had played with the tadpoles dried up. My children would never be able to play with the frogs' eggs as I had or simply to enjoy the cool, clear water of that stream. I mourned the loss of that tree. I profoundly appreciated the wisdom of my people, and how generations of women had passed on to their daughters the cultural tradition of leaving the fig trees in place. I was expected to pass it on to my children, too.
>
> Whatever the original inspiration for not cutting these trees, people in that region had been spared landslides because the strong roots of the fig trees held the soil together in the steep mountains. They also had abundant, clean water. But by the early 1970s, landslides were becoming common and sources of clean water for drinking were becoming scarce. Ironically, the area

where the fig tree of my childhood once stood always remained a patch of bare ground where nothing grew. It was as if the land rejected anything but the fig tree itself.[21]

We can be thankful that Wangari's trained scientific eye enhanced her ability to read the landscape for the meaning of the ecological changes she observed, because many people living in the modern world have lost the ability to note and interpret such changes in the natural environment. Even I notice a major generational shift when I compare my parents' horticultural knowledge with my own—my father, who grew up a farmer but became a professor, could name virtually every species of tree, shrub, flower, or weed, and my mother, who grew up in the inner city and became an artist, used to feed our family from her own backyard garden when I was a child; while I enjoy nature, the countryside, and freshly grown food probably more than most urbanites, my first-hand knowledge of flora and fauna comes nowhere near that of my parents. At the heart of the trouble conveyed within this passage from Wangari Maathai's memoir, however, is the loss of a sacred object—the fig tree—and, more broadly, a loss of the sense of the sacredness of nature in general. Her insights highlight the way in which "traditional" or "cultural" notions of the sacred are often rooted in a scientific reality, as well as the ways in which scientific reality is suffused with sacred energy. Why did Kikuyu women call the fig tree "the tree of God" and forbid its felling or exploitation by humans? Why did nothing grow on the spot where the fig tree had once stood after the plantation owner felled it?

The Kikuyu worldview was predicated upon the material and spiritual interconnectedness of all elements in the ecosystem: human, animal, plant, mineral, and ancestral, and divine; the colonists' worldview—the Western scientific/ commercial worldview—was predicated upon the material separability and exploitability of all elements of the ecosystem, with no reverence toward it, no sense of its sacred nature, to put human behavior in check.[22] Any reference to the spiritual was largely limited to church on Sunday, where even "spirituality" rationalized human control over nature—and other humans. The Kikuyu knew ever-renewing abundance, yet their worldview required them to live simply—in a way that many inhabitants of "modern" or "developed" societies would view as an anathema. The colonists knew ever-accumulating abundance, yet their worldview ultimately depleted and disrupted first the world around them (i.e., those whom they colonized) and later their own world (which is what we are observing today). In this distinction,[23] we see the seeds of spiritual sustainability and the reason why the recovery and reinstantiation of African cosmological systems (and others with similar metaphysical attributes) is central to the womanist idea and womanist methodology. It is not cultural bias, but, rather, human psychological and ecological necessity. Stated more bluntly, it is a way to avert pending extinction—of humans and other species.

AFRICAN COSMOLOGY, CHRISTIANITY, AND SPIRITUALIZED POLITICS

While it is a gross oversimplification to encapsulate anyone's spiritual life in a nutshell, in Wangari Maathai's life story, we see some distinct elements and key shifts. First, as already established, her early childhood was characterized by immersion in Kikuyu traditional/cultural ecospirituality that generated a deep reverence for and enjoyment of nature. Second, her memoir details how formal schooling produced a strict and pious Catholicism combined with a religiously rooted humanitarian service orientation. Third, international travels to the United States and Europe, associated with the pursuit of tertiary education, caused questioning, coincident with Vatican II, which took place while she was in college and liberalized Catholicism.[24] This questioning was intensified by the global African independence movement, which expressed itself through such diverse forms as the U.S. civil rights movement, Black nationalism, the Nation of Islam, and, of course, Kenya's own independence, along with other African countries, during the 1960s.[25] By her own report, all of these events and ideational strands influenced her spiritual and political sensibilities. Ultimately, what resulted was an eclectic and synthetic form of spirituality that respected both religion and culture, but was bound by neither. In *The Green Belt Movement: Sharing the Approach and the Experience*, she summarizes, "The foreign experience deepened my spirituality rather than my religion and encouraged me to seek God in myself and in others, rather than in the heavens."[26] In *Unbowed*, she explains the process by which she came to understand that African traditional culture and spirituality were in no wise incompatible with Christianity, thus allowing both to inform, inspire, and sustain her praxis:

> My exposure to Europe, which had brought Christianity to Kenya, helped me see that there should be no conflict between the positive aspects of our traditional culture and Christianity. After all, Europeans themselves were very close to their culture: How could it be bad when Africans held on to their culture even as they embraced Christianity? This was important to me because my culture was ruthlessly destroyed under the pretense that its values and those of Christianity were in conflict. I watched in awe and admiration as Westerners embraced their culture and found no contradiction between it and their Christian heritage.[27]

It is perhaps obvious how Kikuyu traditional/cultural spirituality generated an ecospiritual disposition in Wangari Maathai, but what may be less obvious is how her ecospirituality was also shaped by Christianity. The opening epigraph to *Unbowed*, which stands alone on a page of its own, lends some insight:

> The trees of the field will yield their fruit and the ground will yield its crops; the people will be secure in the land. They will know that I am the LORD, when I break the bars of their yoke and rescue them from the hands of those that enslaved them. (Ezekiel 34:27, NIV)

In the Bible, there are abundant references to the natural environment, beginning with the Days of Creation in the book of Genesis, many of which encourage reverence for the ecosystem and an ecospiritual disposition. A closer look at the Days of Creation (Genesis 1:1-31, 2:1-4), particularly when they are read in Hebrew rather than in their various English translations, reveals the creation of a divinely inspired Universe and Earth, including its plant and animal life, in which human "dominion" is more benevolent stewardship than domination and exploitation.[28]

This interpretation is supported by ecologically oriented Biblical scholars, such as Mark I. Wallace, who writes, "Christianity often acts like a 'disincarnate' religion—that is, a religion that sees no relationship between the spiritual and physical orders of being.... In fact, however, Christianity is *not* a disincarnate religion ... Christians also believe that since the dawn of creation, throughout world history and into the present, God *in and through the Spirit* has been persistently infusing the natural world with divine presence."[29] This viewpoint is remarkably similar to the immanent ecospirituality expressed in many African traditional/cultural religions, including the Kikuyu, and it digresses significantly from colonial interpretations of the Bible's commentary on human–nature relations. Such an ecologically inspired Christian viewpoint precipitates concern about the relations between human life, questions of justice or human well-being, and activism. To quote Mark I. Wallace again, "A deep-green recovery of Christianity's central teaching about the unity of God and nature is essential to awakening both a sense of kinship between our kind and otherkind and the concomitant desire for the well-being of the land that is our common home and destiny. Unless we can experience again a spiritually charged sense of kinship with the more-than-human world, I fear that the prospects of saving our planet, and thereby saving ourselves, are dim and fleeting at best."[30] This sentiment resonates with that expressed by Wangari Maathai, who addressed it by taking vigorous restorative action in the form of the Green Belt Movement.

KWIMENYA: SELF-KNOWLEDGE AND CONSCIOUSNESS

At a certain point in time, Wangari Maathai began to use the language of *kwimenya*—which is an indigenous Kenyan word for "self-knowledge"—and consciousness. This language found its way into her public work and writings and represents a highly holistic moment of spiritual self-authorship in which all of the previously mentioned threads—Kikuyu traditional/cultural spirituality, Christianity, and ecospirituality—become seamlessly integrated. "You cannot enslave a mind that knows itself, that values itself, that understands itself," she pronounced in an interview documented in the previously mentioned film, *Taking Root: The Vision of Wangari Maathai.*[31] This self-knowledge, or kwimenya, references both self-knowledge as an individual and communal self-knowledge based on one's culture and heritage. Elsewhere, she has written,

> Cultural revival might be the only thing that stands between the conservation or destruction of the environment, the only way to perpetuate the knowledge and wisdom inherited from the past, necessary for the survival of future generations. A new attitude towards nature provides space for a new attitude toward culture and the role it plays in sustainable development: an attitude based on a new understanding—that self-identity, self-respect, morality, and spirituality play a major role in the life of a community and its capacity to take steps that benefit it and ensure its survival.[32]

In *Unbowed*, she writes: "Each person needs to raise their consciousness to a certain level so that they will not give up or succumb. If your consciousness is at such a level, you are willing to do what you believe is the right thing—popular opinion notwithstanding."[33] This recourse to the language of consciousness and consciousness-raising subtly alludes to the energetic dynamics of vibration, as alluded to in chapter 6 of this volume. Wangari again invokes this language in her Nobel Prize acceptance speech: "In the course of history, there comes a time when humanity is called to shift to a new level of consciousness, to reach a higher moral ground."[34] I highlight this emphasis on the language of self-knowledge and consciousness because both terms serve as a point of linkage between exoteric and esoteric aspects of spirituality and both serve to more deeply contextualize the spiritual activism of Wangari Maathai by illuminating one aspect of its source of power.

THE EVOLUTION OF THE GREEN BELT MOVEMENT

The Green Belt Movement (GBM) began as a single, local idea—"plant trees"—and blossomed into a full-fledged, multi-issue, multi-method social movement with global reach that conscientized millions not only about the benefits of tree planting but also about the relationship between environmental stewardship, human rights, and peace. It was perhaps seeded in the fertile soil of Wangari's indigenous Kikuyu-based ecospirituality, but it was watered by the scientific acumen gained through the years of her formal education, culminating as a PhD-level biologist, and pruned by the humanitarian sensibilities cultivated through her staunch Catholicism that ultimately softened into a more ecumenical spiritual orientation. As Wangari's spirituality evolved, so did the Green Belt Movement.

As stated previously, the Green Belt Movement (GBM) had begun with a landscaping and tree-planting business called Envirocare Ltd that she had started to help fulfill her husband's campaign promise of more jobs for the community. She reasoned that wealthy Kenyans would enjoy speedy, on-demand landscaping services, allowing her to employ poor Kenyans and, at the same time, to run a sapling nursery that would involve ordinary Kenyans in ecological restoration and rehabilitation through tree-planting. Unfortunately, she was wrong in her first assumption and the business failed, leaving her with a house full of saplings and little revenue. Through her leadership role in the National Council of Women of Kenya (NCWK), an umbrella organization led primarily by elites but bringing together Kenya's wide diversity of women's groups, she initiated Save the Land Harambee, designed "to inspire Kenyans, both wealthy and poor, to plant trees to protect our country from desertification."[35] Through this initiative, she planted her very first green belt in Nairobi's Kamunkunji Park. As I will detail below, this action established the GBM imprimatur as well as Wangari Maathai's unique model of ecological spiritual activism, as it combined an environmental act—tree planting—with culturally inspired spiritual actions designed to impact people's sensibilities about the sacredness of nature. I reproduce here the full description of Wangari Maathai's first tree-planting from her "how-to manual," *The Green Belt Movement: Sharing the Approach and the Experience*, first published in 1985:

> I did not persuade the members of the committee [within NCWK] to adopt the name Envirocare but instead came up with another name that better explained the objective of the project: to carry out a tree-planting campaign through the *Harambee* spirit.

Harambee means "Let us all pull together!" in Kiswahili. Many communities used and still use the word "harambee" to boost the morale of participants during communal work. The word was popularized and made into a national slogan by the late Mzee Jomo Kenyatta, the first president of Kenya. In his early political rallies, he galvanized Kenyans around this slogan and called upon them to unite for the advancement of their new nation. I suggested that we call the NCWK campaign "Save the Land Harambee." Rather than collect funds for community projects, Kenyans would be encouraged to collectively re-dedicate themselves to save their country from the threat of desertification through their active participation in forestation and reforestation. At every tree-planting ceremony, the participants re-affirmed their dedication to this cause by reciting the following committal:

Being aware that Kenya is being threatened by the expansion of desert-like conditions; that desertification comes as a result of misuse of the land and by consequent soil erosion by the elements; and that these actions result in drought, malnutrition, famine and death; we resolve to save our land by averting this same desertification through the planting of trees wherever possible. In pronouncing these words, we each make a personal commitment to save our country from actions and elements which would deprive present and future generations from reaping the bounty [of resources] which is the birthright and property of all.

The first Save the Land Harambee tree-planting ceremony took place in Nairobi on World Environment Day, June 5, 1977. Participants walked from the Kenyatta International Conference Centre, where the newly created offices of the National Environment Secretariat were located, to the grounds popularized as Kamunkunji, a park on the outskirts of the city.

Present at the ceremony were, among others, the then Mayor of the City of Nairobi Margaret Kenyatta, the then Minister for Water Development Julius Gikonyo Kiano and George Muhoho, who was then the Director of National Environment Secretariat. To make tree planting more meaningful, all Save the Land Harambee tree-planting ceremonies had a theme. This first ceremony focused on honoring deceased Kenyans who had made outstanding contributions to the community or national level. The idea was inspired by my observation of the contrasting ways with which my grandparents', parents' and my generation perceived these outstanding members of society. Unlike the former two, many in my generation marginalized them and disregarded their great achievements. This was partly as a result of colonialism, which condemned our heroes and role models and instead praised those who collaborated with them.

I felt deeply that the leaders who had sacrificed so much on our behalf were part of our history, and that they deserved our respect and honor for their extremely significant and selfless contributions. Seven trees were therefore planted in honor of Wangu wa Makeri from Murang'a, Madam Ketilili from Kilifi, Waiyaki wa Hinga from Kiambu, Nabongo Mumia from Luwero (now known as Mumias), Ole Lenana from Maasailand, Gor Mahia wuod Ogalo from Nyanza and Masaku Ngei from Machakos.... It was the first green belt.[36]

If we look at the elements of this first ceremony, we see a latent method for womanist environmental activism: First, by invoking the call "Harambee," Wangari Maathai was invoking the spirit associated with the global African independence and decolonization movement.[37] During the 1960s and 1970s, Kiswahili (also known as Swahili), as a pan-African language, was used as a vehicle for uniting and conscientizing people of African descent around the world, that is, the global African diaspora and making them conscious of their unity of purpose. Although it was something of an imposed language within Kenya, its symbolic meaning globally had inspirational value. Its use invoked indigenous African traditional/cultural spirituality and was deployed in such uses as the creation of the holiday known as Kwanzaa (a word drawn from a Swahili phrase meaning "first fruits of the harvest") and the associated Nguzo Saba ("seven principles of Blackness").[38] In voicing "Harambee," therefore, Wangari Maathai *spiritualized* the act of political consciousness-raising.

Second, the collectively recited "committal" by all tree-planting participants served as both a form of collective prayer and an informal type of initiatic oath or vow. The act of saying the words together energetically bound the group, creating a kind of vibrational entrainment around the ideals contained within the committal and creating a shared memory among participants. These ideals included nature's bounty and the notion of shared/communal property, also known as the commons. Furthermore, it tethered reciters to a set of agreements—"We resolve to save our land...," "We each make a personal commitment..."—that reminded them of their responsibility to the yet unborn (i.e., "future generations"). Finally, the committal evoked a "call-and-response" format that is familiar to and respected by people of African descent, whether on or off the African continent.

Third, Wangari Maathai solemnized the event by the purposeful inclusion of leaders with formal responsibility for the domains in question—Kenya's natural habitat, its water, and its major metropolis. This created symbolic and perhaps actual buy-in by these offices and their leadership, increasing the stakes of state-level involvement in the issues at hand. In *Unbowed*, where she also presents an account of this event, she mentions that officials from UNEP (the UN Environment Programme) as well as members of the Kenyan parliament and press were also in attendance. Even President Jomo Kenyatta sent a statement to be read.[39]

Fourth, she included honoring of the ancestors. By dedicating the *first* tree-planting to "deceased Kenyans who had made outstanding contributions to the community or national level," she was resurrecting a time-honored African tradition of asking the ancestors and elders for permission to proceed with an enterprise and offering the first fruits of an enterprise to the ancestors and elders. To proceed without doing so could have been read as impudent, thus undermining future tree-plantings and making it easier for opportunistic opponents to discredit the whole Green Belt Movement. I am not suggesting that Wangari Maathai's action here was primarily strategic—my sense is that it was a genuine expression of respect for those who came before—however, its strategic dimensions cannot be overlooked. In honoring the ancestors that she did—each of whom originated from or was associated with a different tribe or geographic region—she made an implicit appeal for tribal unity, making this the fifth element of her signature methodology. It is worth noting—sixth—that her choice of honorees included women and men, reaffirming Kenya's history and tradition of male *and* female leadership and power. In this ceremony, women were the leaders and the principal tree planters; however, Wangari Maathai acknowledged Men of the Trees, whose pioneering tree-planting work during the early and mid-twentieth century had given her both inspiration and ideas.[40] Seventh and finally, she situated participants as generational bridge-builders (like herself) by highlighting their privileged intermediary status between the ancestors and the unborn and by investing this status with a level of responsibility. Her reasoning appears in the section where she compares her generation's thinking about these ancestors with that of her parents' and grandparents' generations, and notes the disruptive influence of colonialism on cultural memory and cultural orientation.

As a result of political pressure, the Green Belt Movement eventually separated from NCWK. Not only was the GBM attracting considerable attention from international environmental organizations, but its social critique focusing on the connections between environmental destruction and other issues (cronyism and corruption in government, neocolonial dimensions of modernization and development, women's rights or the lack thereof, etc.) was expanding every day and challenging the status quo, particularly through the conscientization and mobilization of grassroots women. To quote her, "As the Green Belt Movement developed, I became convinced that we needed to identify the roots of the disempowerment that plagued the Kenyan people.... Gradually the Green Belt Movement grew from a tree-planting program into one that planted ideas as well."[41] A big part of the GBM's modus operandi was to conduct in-depth "civic education" courses on topics as diverse as governance, culture and spirituality (including *kwimenya*), Africa's development crisis, and human and environmental rights.[42] State officials began to recognize that the GBM was not just a tree-planting organization and not just a women's organization, and they positioned themselves to block or delegitimize her activity.

One important aspect of the Green Belt Movement was its emphasis on sidestepping government to get things done. This emphasis resonates with womanism's do-it-yourself character, wherein community women decide what is important and develop autonomous community structures to "take care of business." This passage from *Unbowed* reflects these sentiments clearly:

> As long as the Green Belt Movement was perceived as a few women raising seedlings, we didn't matter to the government. But as soon as we began to explain how trees disappear and why it is important for citizens to stand up for their rights—whether environmental, women's, or human—senior officials in the government and members of Parliament began to take notice. They soon realized that unlike some other women's organizations in Kenya, the Green Belt Movement was not organizing women for the purposes of advancing the government's agenda, whatever that might be. We were organizing women (and men) to do things for themselves that, in most cases, the government had no interest in doing.[43]

In another, longer anecdote, she describes some of the early civic education classes in which she would ask attendees about their understanding of the source of their problems. "Almost to a person they put all the blame on the government,"[44] she wrote. "However, I felt strongly that people needed to understand that the government was not the only culprit. Citizens, too, played a part in the problems the communities identified."[45] In this sense, "personal responsibility" rhetoric also played a role in her DIY discourse, reminiscent of early twentieth century "uplift" discourse employed within the U.S. Black women's club movement and other African American mutual aid enterprises.[46]

By her own account, these were "difficult years."[47] Not only was she frequently harassed or placed under surveillance, but she was also arrested and imprisoned a number of times. Since she took great pains to live as a law-abiding citizen, her arrests often took on a ludicrous quality. One particularly problematic law that plagued her time and again was an old colonial-era statute prohibiting more than nine individuals from gathering without governmental permission. This law was widely disregarded, but in a manner similar to vice laws in the United States, it remained on the books as a means to squash insurgent political activity or "unruly" individuals. One particularly funny anecdote involves her inviting police officers to come inside and join an environmental consciousness-raising meeting in progress in her home when they showed up intending to arrest people; another involves her inviting the police surrounding her house to join her in coffee and sending one of them to the store with her money to purchase the needed cream. These anecdotes reveal Wangari's indefatigably irreverent yet hospitable womanist spirit, always looking for opportunities to bring diverse— and sometimes opposed—people together at the same time as she was trying to subvert an unacceptable and sometimes absurd status quo.

Another method employed by the government to interfere with her activity involved preventing her freedom of movement, typically by refusing to issue her travel documents. By the late 1980s, Wangari Maathai was receiving numerous international awards and being invited to numerous international speaking engagements. In 1984, for example, she won the "Right Livelihood Award," often referred to as the "alternative Nobel prize."[48] In 1986, she won a medal from the Better World Society, a foundation created by U.S. media mogul Ted Turner; in 1987, she made UNEP's Global 500 honor roll for environmental achievement. In 1989, she, along with Mother Teresa and Mildred Robbins Leet, received an award from UK-based WomenAid, which was presented to her by Princess Diana. To state that she received one or more international awards every year from 1984 onward would not be an overstatement.

At home, however, these awards generated a cost. She writes, for instance, that in June 1992, "I was due to address the UN Conference on Environment and Development (UNCED) in Rio de Janeiro, better known as the Earth Summit. But I was also due in court again because of my arrest for the coup rumors, so my lawyer had to appeal to Nairobi's chief magistrate for permission for me to miss a court date to attend the summit. This time, the magistrate agreed. So President Moi and I both went to Rio"[49]—where she not only spoke but participated in a press conference with both then-U.S. senator Al Gore and His Holiness the Dalai Lama. As a second example, in early 1993, Wangari Maathai's political work to quell politically instigated ethnic clashes in the Kenyan countryside forced her underground for her own safety. During this period, Mikhail Gorbachev's Green Cross invited her to a meeting in Tokyo. When she informed the organizers that she was in hiding and would be unable to obtain the necessary travel documents to make the trip, Mikhail Gorbachev himself contacted President Moi to ensure her freedom of movement. She writes, "The Kenyan president expressed shock. He claimed that he knew nothing about my inability to travel and sent a message through the press saying he could not understand why I thought I couldn't go to Tokyo."[50] Although she was unable to make it to Tokyo in time, from this point forward, her travel difficulties were diminished significantly, allowing the Green Belt Movement to accrue tremendous international support and allowing Wangari Maathai to publicize Africa's environmental issues along with women's inventive solutions and responses everywhere she went.

FROM "BELLIGERENT PACIFISM" TO NOBEL PEACE PRIZE

Once you have self-knowledge, move wisely like the serpent, always staying calm like the dove.

—*Wangari Maathai paraphrasing the Bible (Matthew 10:16)*[51]

Three additional episodes in Wangari Maathai's activist life deserve reflection. The first involves her efforts to forestall the erection of a skyscraper within Nairobi's Uhuru Park, a green space comparable to Central Park in New York City or Hyde Park in London; the second involves the GBM's involvement in a motherist[52] movement to free Kenyan political prisoners; and the third involves a GBM campaign to prevent the "gazetting" (distribution to private individuals as a political favor) of public lands within Kenya's Karuru National Forest. In each of these cases, Wangari Maathai embodied what Chikwenye Okonjo Ogunyemi has labeled "belligerent pacifism" and led others to do the same. This "belligerent pacifism" bears a striking resemblance to, as well as marked differences from, nonviolent resistance methods associated with the principle of ahimsa ("nonviolence") derived from Eastern thought, particularly the Gandhian interpretation, known as satyagraha (meaning "Soul force," "truth force," or "holding on to truth"). These Eastern methods were adapted for the U.S. civil rights movement, particularly by visionary strategists like Bayard Rustin, a Black Quaker who taught Martin Luther King Jr., thus becoming part of the "Black" social change toolkit. Yet, in the African context, where Marxist- and Negritude-inspired liberation struggles often took on a distinctly different flavor from U.S. civil rights struggles, we find "belligerent pacifism" as an African women's inflection on the nonviolent revolutionary social change tradition of the mid-twentieth century.

In fact, "belligerent pacifism" could almost be described as an African womanist version of ahimsa. Its roots, like the roots of ahimsa, run much deeper than the generations of current memory. We find, for instance, Ogunyemi's discussion of the powerful nineteenth century *Iyalode* and trader Madame Tinubu, who maintained peace in Yorubaland (modern-day Nigeria) by maintaining her own private army, keeping the colonial army in check, and engineering uprisings of market women when colonial power exceeded its bounds. Her power and authority to do so rested in even older diarchic traditions that reserved the all-powerful market as women's domain and linked women of all social strata through the bonds of women's initiatic societies. Market women's uprisings obtained such a currency that, in 1929, Igbo women (also in Nigeria) masterminded *Ogu Umunwanyi*, translated as the both the Women's Struggle and the (Aba) Women's War—"it was organized by market women who were feeling the pinch of global depression through their British tax/taskmasters and their Nigerian underlings."[53] This incident reminds us of U.S. liberationist Harriet Tubman's 1863 "guerrilla action" at the Combahee River near the end of the U.S. Civil War: "This action freed more than 750 slaves and is the only[54] military campaign in American history planned and led by a woman."[55]

Of satyagraha, Gandhi wrote, "The Satyagrahi's object is to convert, not to coerce, the wrong-doer."[56] It relies on moral power rather than physical force or aggression (the objective of which is to gain ascendancy over the wrong-doer). Like womanism, satyagraha relies upon understandings of fundamental and indissoluble human connectedness and notions of energetic transformation (or transformations of consciousness) *within* relationship rather than purely political victories characterized by a shift in visible form but not underlying substance (i.e., energetic vibration). Belligerent pacifism occurs when love-based technologies of transformation are applied in "outrageous, audacious, courageous or *willful*"[57] ways, which may also be animated, loud, or colorful. The bottom line is *insistence*. Wangari Maathai exhibited this when she and a group of mothers whose sons were political prisoners showed up at the office of the Kenyan attorney general in 1992 to demand the sons' release: "'When we see him [the attorney general], we'll tell him, 'We will wait in Uhuru Park for three days for all the sons to be released. During that time we'll go on a hunger strike and pray.' I also recommended that we take our bedding with us to the meeting. Then the attorney general would know, I said, that the mothers wouldn't leave Nairobi for their villages without their sons and that we were prepared to sleep in Uhuru Park while they waited." Needless to say, this campaign went on for a year before the sons were released, but they *were* released.

Returning to our thread, Madame Tinubu and the *Ogu Umunwanyi* in turn inspired early twentieth century Nigerian activist Funmilayo Ransome-Kuti, whose commitments to Nigerian decolonization and independence, women's equality, and international peace during the World War I and II eras are ably detailed in *For Women and the Nation*, a biography by Cheryl Johnson-Odim and Nina Emma Mba. Of Ransome-Kuti and her belligerent pacifism, Ogunyemi writes: "[S]he fomented a large-scale civil disobedience with her market women's army, paralyzing the Egba kingdom in 1947. Her action influenced the colonial government's indirect rule policies, as women reiterated the point that their southeastern [Igbo] predecessors had made and that women continue to make: there should be no taxation without adequate governmental representation. Democracy is not democratic without women's full participation: we need two houses to represent us—one made up of men, the other of women from all walks of life."[58] Parallel with Wangari Maathai's early start in the relatively nonpoliticized NCKW, Funmilayo Ransome-Kuti began her activist career with the Abeokuta Ladies' Club, whose focus was etiquette and handicrafts, but which later transformed itself into, first, the Abeokuta Women's Union (focused on uniting Christian, Muslim, and Yoruba women in Nigeria) and later, the National Women's Union (which advocated for universal suffrage, equal political representation for women, and Nigerian independence). Wole Soyinka's assessment of Funmilayo Ransome-Kuti's activist evolution has been encapsulated thus: "The movement...begun over cups of tea and sandwiches to resolve the problem of newlyweds who lacked the necessary social graces... became all tangled up in the move to end the role of white men in the country."[59] Ultimately, Funmilayo Ransome-Kuti, like Wangari Maathai, ran for public office; however, because she (FRK) ran at a time when women were still unable to vote in Nigeria (although they could stand for public office if nominated by men), she never won—despite being Nigeria's most popular woman leader. Such were the times.

When Wangari Maathai ran, for the second time, in 2002, she won a seat representing her district with 98% of the vote, and ultimately became not only a Member of Parliament, but also Kenya's Assistant Minister for Environment and Natural Resources. To quote her:

My [campaign] slogan was "Rise Up and Walk," which was inspired by the story from the Bible (Acts 3:1-10) when the disciples Peter and John come across a beggar, who has all the characteristics of a disempowered person: He is poor, self-effacing, dejected, and has no sense of pride in himself. On seeing him in such a dehumanized and humiliated state, Peter says to him, "Silver and gold we do not have, but what we have we give to you." And, taking him by the right hand, Peter helps the lame man stand up. "In the name of Jesus Christ of Nazareth, rise up and walk!" Peter says.

What I wanted the voters to understand was that I could not give them alms or even miracles, but together we could lift ourselves up and address the conditions of our poverty and disempowerment and regain our sense of self-respect. Together, we could establish governance that was responsible and accountable to the people. The slogan was the essence of what the Green Belt Movement had been trying to do all those years: "Rise up and walk!"[60]

Fueled by both spiritual inspiration and political resolve, what had begun as a movement "outside power" and, at times, "against power," had found its way "inside power" with an intent to transform "power over" into "power with." "Eventually," Wangari Maathai writes, "the Green Belt Movement would help establish more than six thousand nurseries, managed by six hundred community-based networks; involve several hundred thousand women, and many men, in its activities; and, by the early years of the twenty-first century, have planted more than thirty million trees in Kenya alone."[61] In 2004, as a result of this work, belligerent pacifism and all, Wangari Maathai was awarded the Nobel Peace Prize in recognition of the way the Green Belt Movement highlighted the interconnections among "peace, sustainable management of resources, and good governance."[62] She became the first African woman to receive this high honor.

ECOWOMANISM AND ECOSPIRITUALITY

This intersection of spirituality, ecology, and activism that represents Wangari Maathai's social change signature is addressed, directly or indirectly, in the work of several womanist scholars, including Shamara Shantu Riley, Pamela A. Smith, Melanie L. Harris, and Xiumei Pu. Their work creates additional context for thinking about Wangari Maathai's environmentally focused activity in terms of both ecowomanism and womanist spiritual activism. Ecowomanism is a womanist approach to ecological and environmental issues, predicated upon the womanist triadic concern with human beings, nature, and the spirit world simultaneously. As Shamara Shantu Riley asserts, "Womanism and ecology have a common theoretical approach in that both see all parts of a matrix as having equal value."[63] Ecowomanism is almost a redundant term, since womanism itself places a high priority on the natural environment and sees the environment, just like human life, as spiritualized. Furthermore, womanist concerns with healing, justice, and other modalities of transformation apply just as much to the natural environment as they do to people and society (not to mention self). Nevertheless, the term *ecowomanism* allows us to highlight the environmental "leg of the stool" when it is the most prominent feature of an activist's work or concern. Womanism—and, in turn, ecowomanism—banks and builds itself upon everyday women's historical relationship of intimacy with the natural environment—one reason we refer to everyday women and everyday community activity as *grassroots*: The term *grassroots* is inherently ecological in spirit.

Race-ing ecofeminist perspectives, Shamara Shantu Riley argues that modern ecological destruction has resulted from a dualistic worldview in which humans and the environment, men and women, and whites and Blacks, have not been afforded equal value. She views a return to African cosmology as one route away from this philosophical dualism that has produced the human and environmental hierarchies that have supported ecological decimation and destruction as well as social injustice. She writes, "In utilizing spiritual concepts to move beyond dualism, precolonial African cultures, with their both/and perspectives, are useful forms of knowledge for Afrocentric ecowomanists to envision patterns toward interdependence of human and nonhuman nature."[64] Riley lists a host of cosmological constructs from various African languages, including: *Nyam* (a root word found in many West African languages), which connotes "an enduring power and energy possessed by all life"[65]; *Da* (a Fon word), defined by Luisah Teish as "the energy that carries creation, the force field in which creation takes place";[66] *Nommo* (a word that appears in both Bantu and Dogon contexts), meaning "the physical-spiritual life force which awakens all 'sleeping' forces and gives physical and spiritual life"[67] as well as "the magical power of words to cause change"[68] (Clenora Hudson-Weems has interpreted *Nommo* as simply "self-naming");[69] *Ache* (also *Ase*, *Asé* or *Ashé*, from the Yoruba language), meaning the "power to effect a change or make things happen"[70] and also "human power,"[71] more specifically "power *with* other forms of creation,"[72] with implications of "regulated kinship among human, animal, mineral, and vegetable life."[73] She concludes: "These concepts can be useful for Afrocentric womanists not only in educating our peoples about environmental issues, but also in reclaiming the cultural traditions of our ancestors."[74] (As I have already suggested, these concepts are useful not just for womanists or people of a certain ancestry, but, rather, at this point, for everybody—their relevance is now universal.) In sum, Riley argues that African cosmology, via womanist recovery, can be applied to subvert colonial forms of spirituality and, ostensibly, undo or heal their harms: "Because every entity is viewed as embodying spirituality under immanence, culture wouldn't be viewed as separate from, and superior to, nature, as it is seen in mainstream Western religions."[75]

Pamela A. Smith examines ecospirituality in the writing and activism of Alice Walker, focusing primarily on her pantheistic and neopagan beliefs. Smith notes, "Walker affirmed her animism and pantheism as early as 1973, in an interview with John O'Brien, when she spoke of animism as part of the African American heritage."[76] Walker, who was raised Christian but later explored Transcendental Meditation, Buddhism, and Earth-based religion (including entheogenically mediated experiences), often refers to Earth's sacredness and her own reverence for Earth in her writings. Additionally, she has engaged in very public acts of activism around such environmental issues as nuclear disarmament and environmental degradation in general. In keeping with other womanist thinkers, her writings reflect the perspective that Earth healing and social justice must go hand-in-hand. For instance, she writes that, "While the Earth is poisoned, everything it supports is poisoned. While the Earth is enslaved, none of us is free."[77] She (Walker) also states, "I believe the Earth is good. That people, untortured by circumstance or fate, are also good. I do not believe the people of the world are naturally my enemies, or that animals, including snakes, are, or that Nature is."[78] Since the inception of womanism in the late 1970s, and since its mainstreaming in the mid-1980s, Alice Walker has infused womanist thought and praxis with ecospiritual ideas drawn from multiple sources, reflecting the diverse spiritual archaeology of the womanist idea. Her own polyvocal ecospirituality, which incorporates the Christianity of the Southern Black Church, Buddhist, and pagan/pantheistic elements, parallels that of Wangari Maathai, which incorporates Kikuyu traditional/cultural spirituality, Catholic (originally missionary) Christianity, and ecospirituality, even though each woman integrates different source material into her spiritual standpoint.

Melanie L. Harris also uses Alice Walker's ecospirituality as a jumping off point for analysis.[79] "The history of owning and having that land taken away from the Walker family because of their race is important in uncovering Walker's spiritual value of the Earth,"[80] she writes. "It also serves as an opening through which to explore Walker's sense of environmental justice or ecowomanist perspective that places emphasis on the sense of belonging and home."[81] This focus on home and homelands resonates with Wangari Maathai's description of her early life in the shadow of Kirinyaga, as well as her later focus on restoring the ecology of Kenya as a nation. Harris identifies a thread in Walker's thought that she identifies as Earth justice—"including the Earth and nature as parts of the universal whole"—which further dimensionalizes the now canonized womanist focus on the intersectionality of race, class, gender, and sexuality, by expanding past species and embracing all livingkind.[82] "Often," Harris writes, "in keeping with an African cosmological perspective wherein the spiritual presence of ancestors, God, nature, and humanity are linked, womanist virtues exemplify basic values held by the person and the community as a way of promoting interdependence between the realms of spirit, history, and nature, and in turn, justice, wholeness, and good community for women and all Creation living with the Earth."[83]

Harris points out that Walker's womanist ecospirituality further emphasizes and authorizes the inclusion of boys and men in environmental justice work, even if that inclusion remains women-centered[84]—a transformational style of social organization also demonstrated by other womanist activists, such as Maggie Lena Walker and Callie House in the United States and Funmilayo Ransome-Kuti of Nigeria.[85] We see it clearly in Wangari Maathai's construction of the Green Belt Movement:

> When I asked the women who they wanted to take on these tasks [assistance with tree nursery duties], they almost always chose one of their husbands or sons. These became what we called "nursery attendants." Hiring them created employment for many men, who would otherwise have had few options to earn additional income.... The sight of these men was always a surprise to those who came to evaluate the Green Belt Movement's work. "We thought this was a women's organization," they would say, "but there are men here!"[86]

What we observe is that powerful, audacious, womanist women lead men and women alike, lovingly and authoritatively, with attention to political and cosmological considerations of both balance and inclusion. Furthermore, these womanist leaders—of movements, of organizations—recognize that women's inclusive leadership of men alongside women, *not* women's exclusion of men when they (women) are in positions of power, authority, or leadership is the necessary and appropriate counterbalance for decades, if not centuries or millennia, of patriarchal exclusion of and hierarchy over women. This is the womanist way. The coming Aquarian Age, mentioned at various points in this volume, is a diarchic, if not hermaphroditic, age in which the equal representation of female and male (and quite possibly transgender) energies is the sine qua non for releasing and realizing humanity's "next-level" potential.

Xiumei Pu, in her recovery of indigenous ecospirituality in China associated with the ancient goddess Di Mu and the women healers who revere her speaks directly to Wangari Maathai's exhortation to kwimenya (i.e., culturally based self-knowledge), as well as to womanist constructions of the sacredness, divinity, and power of nature.[87] As Xiumei Pu writes, "A womanist community is an ecospiritual-cultural community."[88] Her article shows brilliantly that this (eco) womanist idea springs not only from women of African descent, but also from women of other regions of the world who also find love, meaning, and healing in communion with nature. Like the Kikuyu women of Kenya, the women healers of Western China with whom Xiumei Pu shares heritage have discovered the "magical" or energy-shifting properties of plants, animals, and minerals that exist within their treasured and closely studied ecosystems. Such ecowomanist, ecospiritual recovery of knowledge bases like these is part of the womanist contribution to humanity's survival of and recovery from human-made ecological crises.

The bottom line is that ecospirituality and ecowomanism are supporting pillars of the womanist idea, weight-bearing walls of the metaphysical architecture of womanism. Thus, Wangari Maathai's spiritually infused environmental activism expressed through the ever-evolving Green Belt Movement exemplifies both womanism and womanist spiritual activism. From her example, we can learn key lessons about womanism—what it is—and spiritual activism—how to do it. These lessons will be outlined at the end of this chapter.

NATURE AND LUXOCRACY

If the argument is being made that womanism is important because it is a pathway toward LUXOCRACY as a future social organizational form for humanity, then we must consider the relationship between the natural environment and LUXOCRACY. How does nature contribute to LUXOCRACY? There are several answers to this question. One is that the Light that resides in humans also resides in nature: to quote Thich Nhat Hanh again, "We inter-are." This applies to human–human as well as human–nature relations. It also applies to human–spirit and nature–spirit relations. This Light animates humanity and nature alike; it even animates all spectra of Higher Beings that populate the invisible realm or realms. There is one Life Force and it is uniform and unified, at the same time as it is infinitely prolific and endlessly dynamic. Within this spiritual worldview, even those things ordinarily referred to as nonliving, such as minerals, celestial bodies (planets, stars, etc.), and weather elements (wind, rain, earthquakes, etc.), are actually alive. The Universe, the Cosmos, is whole and living. Consciousness is localizable—which is why we experience ourselves and imagine that we are individuals—however, it is also nonlocal.[89] Thus, LUXOCRACY, on one level, is recognition not only of one's own and other humans' innate divinity, but the innate divinity of "nature" and, ultimately, all creation.

Second, on a more concrete level, the life force inherent in elements of nature—particularly trees, rivers and streams, the ocean, and mountains—refreshes human beings, contributing to physical health and raising the human energetic vibration. Spending time in nature—with or without exertion—is a type of spiritual encounter that can have dramatic and long-lasting effects, particularly when it is approached with reverence. Even when it is not, reverence sometimes arises spontaneously. Wangari Maathai's description of what it was like to grow up immersed in the sacred beauty of Mount Kenya—Kirinyaga—and all to which it gave life is illustrative. We might speculate that Kirinyaga was named the "Place of Brightness" in part because of the spiritual light that it engendered in the humans who, for generations, encountered it daily. Beyond spending time in nature, direct interaction with natural elements, for example, through gardening, farming, animal husbandry, the preparation of natural medicines, various kinds of nature based religious practices, building homes and other structures by hand from mineral, plant, or animal materials—even cooking and serving food or fetching water or firewood—provides a deep sense of engagement with and relationship to "nature."[90] Together, these experiences provide another nature-based pathway to LUXOCRACY.

Fast-paced urban lives replete with prepackaged and prefabricated items (such as food, clothing, and buildings) and technologically mediated experiences and relationships are unable to provide the spiritual or physical benefits of sustained, direct encounter with nature, and thus do not provide the same pathway to either ecospirituality or physical/psychological/spiritual well-being as lives that exist in closer relationship to nature. This is not to say that urbanites cannot experience ecospirituality—they can and do—but rather to point out the very real risks of urbanization and urban sprawl to human spiritual and physical well-being, as well as the well-being of the natural environment (which, to some extent, is linked to human activity that is, in turn, fueled by human attitudes and human consciousness). Even with its many unquestionable benefits, urbanity fails to provide a platform for mass socialization into (or awakening into) ecospiritual sentiments. Unchecked, it also threatens human survival in the very ways that Wangari Maathai observed when she refocused her attention on Kenya after nearly a decade away studying in the United States and Germany. To quote her: "Sadly, these beliefs and traditions have now virtually died away. They were dying even as I was born.... Hallowed landscapes lost their sacredness and were exploited as the local people became insensitive to the destruction [created by missionaries, traders, and administrators], accepting it as a sign of progress."[91] Her 10-year absence allowed her to notice drastic and dramatic changes in the landscape as well as people's relationship with the land and their attitudes about the land and human activities involving land. What she observed was that colonialism had so Westernized the mindsets of indigenous Kenyans that they no longer thought in terms of the ecologically (and socially) sustainable practices that were their cultural heritage. Rather, their minds had turned to money and jobs and survival and status as though there were no other alternative, forgetting that natural abundance, working in partnership with the Earth, relaxed enjoyment of the Earth and people, and a sacred orientation had been the way of life just a generation before.

Without rejecting "development" outright, as some more radical environmentalists might have, Wangari Maathai worked as a "bridge person" to recover and reconfigure the most important elements of that previous mode of life and integrate them with what was genuinely valuable (or simply inevitable) about "modernization." Women and men who grew seedlings, for instance, were paid for sprouting, planting, and protecting the seedlings if the trees survived for six months. This provided a kind of wage for rehabilitating the environment and an alternative to participating in less salutary sectors of the economy. Later, after the Green Belt Movement had achieved international renown, she established a kind of "Green Belt Safari" ecotourism enterprise for people to come and learn about both ecological preservation and the unique work of the women and men of the Green Belt Movement. This enterprise raised revenue for the Green Belt Movement; however, it also allowed her to demonstrate—in a growing field of ecotourism enterprises around the world—how to "do ecotourism" while leaving a minimal footprint and empowering local people.[92] Finally, by protecting Nairobi's considerable green space (e.g., Uhuru Park) as well as its substantial forest belt (e.g., Karura Forest), she provided an African anchor point within the global "green cities" movement. Over time, this advocacy extended to goodwill ambassadorship on behalf of the Congo basin forest that, along with the Amazon rainforest, is one of Earth's two most important "lungs."[93] By preserving these important natural areas—both literally, as a "belligerent pacifist" and figuratively by raising people's consciousness about the natural environment, whether in terms of its importance or its sublime pleasures—Wangari Maathai has contributed to the evolution of LUXOCRACY as a new form of social organization on Earth, since LUXOCRACY requires a spiritualized sense of the environment as well as a spiritualized relationship with the environment. That is why I refer to her approach as *spiritualized sustainability*.

UNBOWED AND *THE GREEN BELT MOVEMENT*: LESSONS LEARNED

Looking over the life and work of Wangari Maathai, as exemplified in the Green Belt Movement and presented in her memoir, *Unbowed*, as well as her "how-to" manual, *The Green Belt Movement: Sharing the Approach and the Experience*, I see that the wisdom of her transformational praxis can be distilled into seven major tenets. Although, like the other women who have been profiled in this book, Wangari Maathai does not refer to herself as a womanist, these elements of her praxis are consistent with the womanist idea:

Lesson 1. *When you "recognize the connections," make sure that the environment is part of that equation.*[94] Earth justice is just as important as addressing race, class, gender, sexuality, or other vectors of difference.

Lesson 2. *Study science to understand nature better.* Knowledge is power and helps us to appreciate the splendor of creation in detail. Detailed knowledge of natural phenomena also makes us better visualizers. Even nonscientists benefit from studying science. As life-long learners, we can always return to new information.

Lesson 3: *Respect and support language diversity.* Different languages contain different vocabularies and different perspectives—on nature, spirituality, and human relations. Early on, the GBM made a decision to conduct local meetings in local languages, even if Wangari Maathai's own words had to be translated.

Lesson 4. *Learn to "have tea" with your opponents and detractors.* It's disarming, it humanizes relations, and at times it causes breakthroughs in dialogue. Food and hospitality can both "change the vibration" of a situation and create openings for amity and reconciliation.

Lesson 5. *Sometimes song and dance are the most effective way to make a statement.* This is what the women of the Green Belt Movement did when confronted with authorities in Karura Forest. Artistic media have a vibrational impact all their own.

Lesson 6. *Always remember past and future generations.* We are in the middle, creating both past and future.

Lesson 7. *When in doubt, reverence is the emotion—the vibrational energy— that will transform things.* Reverence is remembering the "Three Recognitions": Recognize your own sacredness, recognize the sacredness of everyone around you, and recognize the sacredness of all created things.

REVERENCE: THE NATURE OF LOVE

When I visited Plum Village in France the summer before I got married, I managed to procure a hand-calligraphed painting by Thich Nhat Hanh as a wedding gift for my husband. Enclosed within a circle are the words, "Reverence is the nature of my love." These words moved me the first time that I encountered them, and I realized that love at its best, for me, is reverence: a recognition of sacredness and an associated feeling of awe. Love as reverence can be evoked by and directed toward human beings, but it can also be evoked by and directed toward nature, as in the case of Wangari Maathai's spiritually empowered environmental activism. Whether that reverence manifests as quiet sitting or loud standing, it is the quality of the animating heart, the spirit of the thing that defines the action—and the outcome.

Wangari Maathai stood up and stood in for ecological wholeness—a wholeness supported by ecological diversity. She also embodied spiritual wholeness—a wholeness supported by spiritual diversity. I end with this quote by Margot Adler that, some two decades ago, I cut out from one of my yearly calendars and have saved ever since: "The spiritual world is just like the natural world—only diversity will save it. Just as the health of a forest or fragrant meadow can be measured by the number of different insects and plants and creatures that successfully make it their home, so only by an extraordinary abundance of disparate spiritual and philosophic paths will human beings navigate a pathway through the dark and swirling storms that mark our current era. 'Not by one avenue alone,' wrote Symmachus sixteen centuries ago, 'can we arrive at so tremendous a secret.'"[95]

CONCLUSION

I chose to conclude this examination of womanist spiritual activism through memoir with a look at Wangari Maathai and the Green Belt Movement for several reasons. First and most obviously, hers is the only case study that places the natural environment at the center of its activism. Because the environment is a supporting pillar of the womanist idea, the inclusion of an environmental activist was crucial. Second, the way Wangari Maathai combines Kikuyu traditional–cultural spirituality, Christianity, and ecospirituality brings womanist spiritual hybridity, as explored in chapter 5, to life. Her spiritual holism models North-South-East-West harmony and synthesis and shows how a womanist defines her own spirituality. Third, I intended to make the case that ecospirituality, as amorphous and elusive as it can seem at times, is as important as forms of spirituality that we normally associate with religion. Tracing Wangari Maathai's ecospirituality to her childhood immersion in the beautiful Kenyan countryside was part of making that case, as was demonstrating the link between ecospirituality and African cosmology. Fourth, I desired to lift up the fact that Wangari Maathai wrote a "how-to manual" about the Green Belt Movement to help others advance the cause of environmentalism. In my opinion, "how-to manuals" are very womanist, even if they are a woefully underappreciated genre of writing. Her extensive and collaborative work with illiterate women surely made her sensitive to the importance of simple, direct communication in whatever form. I would like to reclaim the dignity and worth of this genre and uphold *The Green Belt Movement: Sharing the Approach and the Experience* as an exemplary model. Finally, I wanted to begin and end with an elder. Like Sister Chan Khong, Wangari Maathai has built a lifetime legacy of spiritual activism that illuminates the womanist idea with new and exciting dimension-ality. Womanists embody and enact a spirit of respect that recognizes and honors those trailblazers, caretakers, and everyday authorities who have created the path on which we walk, sustained our work by their inspiration, and given us guidance along the way.

POSTSCRIPT

On September 25th, 2011, just weeks before this book went to press, Wangari Maathai succumbed to a quiet struggle with cancer in a Nairobi hospital, compelling the entire world to take a deep look at her astounding legacy of activism that linked the environment, women, democracy, and peace. The government of Kenya honored her with a state funeral, placing her remains in a special coffin crafted of bamboo, water hyacinths, and papyrus, draped with the Kenyan flag. Her funeral was held in Uhuru National Park, one of the many green spaces preserved by her valiant activism, after which time she was cremated. As if to pass the torch, two weeks later, the Nobel Peace Prize was awared jointly to three women—President Ellen Johnson Sirleaf of Liberia, peace activist Leymah Gbowee of Liberia and Ghana, and journalist/women's rights advocate Tawakkul Karman of Yemen. Like Maathai, these women were honored for their contributions linking women, democracy, and peace. All symbolism aside, we can celebrate not only these named women, but also the millions of grassroots women who have worked alongside them or in their own right, tirelessly advancing a diversity of issues that promote "the survial and wholeness of entire people, male and female." This *is* womanism.

3

BEYOND WOMANISM

Aliyah Karmil Phillips at high tea in London, 2009. Photo Credit: Elizabeth Ely-Kelso, used by permission.

CHAPTER

12

WITNESS TO A TESTIMONY: WOMANIST REFLECTIONS ON THE LIFE AND LOSS OF A DAUGHTER

Being of Tao, one endures forever;
though the body perishes, one suffers not.

—*Tao Te Ching*[1]

On Tuesday, November 10, 2009, at approximately 4:30 p.m., my daughter Aliyah Phillips jumped from the roof of a 14-story building in downtown Los Angeles and landed on the asphalt below, at the far edge of a small parking lot. At the time, she was 10 days shy of her 23rd birthday and nearing the completion of her degree at an Ivy League college. At 1:00 a.m. on Wednesday, November 11, 2009, which was 10:00 p.m. on Tuesday in Los Angeles, I received a phone call from my son telling me what had happened. I had just climbed into bed to go to sleep and had been roused from early slumber by the ringing of my cell phone. My son Thaddeus, 23 months Aliyah's senior, had just returned from work to find an LAPD detective at his apartment and the county coroner on the phone, both of whom were contacting him as next-of-kin based on information received from the security guards in his apartment building, who then contacted his roommate, who was the leaseholder, to confirm her place of residence. Aliyah had been staying with her brother and his roommate on a temporary basis since July while finishing up some outstanding coursework and completing her thesis. Indeed, that morning, as a receipt we later found revealed, she had checked out books at the Los Angeles public library. There had been no warning with regard to the events of Tuesday afternoon.

When I received the phone call from my son, I sat up in my bed. "I have some news and I'm afraid it's not good," he said calmly. Immediately my heart began to pound. As he told me the details, I dissolved into a sensation of spinning that made it hard for me to listen. I kept asking him to repeat what he was saying—"Wait, wait ... are you telling me that ..., because I'm having a hard time understanding what you are telling me"—and, before long, I had a pen in my hand and was writing everything down, because writing is how I deal with things. "You are telling me that my daughter, Aliyah Phillips, jumped from a rooftop at approximately 4:30 p.m. today and now she is dead." "Yes, Mom, it seems that that is the case. I know it's hard to believe. It seems strange to me, too." My son, young tender beautiful being that he is, was a rock, and I was his first phone call. That irony was not lost on me, even in the moment.

Here was the most unexpected thing that had ever happened to me and the most tragic and traumatic thing I could imagine, staring me in the face at 1 o'clock in the morning. I was alone in my apartment and that did not help matters. I was consumed by a feeling of not knowing what to do, what to do next, how to proceed. I said to my son, "I have to call my Mother, because she will know what to do." But first I called Seboe—my fiancé, my anchor, now husband—5,000 miles away in Liberia, not to talk long, but just to tell him what was going on and to ask him to hold me in his spirit. I needed his remote steadying influence—like my son after him and my father before him, he is also a love-filled rock—to help me organize my scattered energy and do what a mother needs to do in a situation like this. When I called, he was in a crowded taxi on a bumpy road—it was 6:00 a.m. there in Liberia—and he asked me to wait until he could get out of the cab and call me back. I did. We spoke briefly—like me, he shared the disbelief, the broken heart, and the utter sense of mystery about all that was happening—and then I excused myself to call Momma. My head was still spinning—I was now alternating between pacing the kitchen of my studio apartment and sitting on the countertop frozen.

I could not reach Mom immediately, so I called my sister Mary for assistance. Even though she has five phones, my mother is notoriously hard to reach. My sister, who must rise early for work, was sound asleep, but she agreed to help me get in touch with Mom. Shortly thereafter, Mom called me. We discussed the news, both dumbfounded and astounded and heartbroken and stunned. I had not yet cried because I was still too shocked and too concerned with taking all the right action steps in a timely fashion. With me in Atlanta, Mom in Jacksonville, Aliyah and Thad in LA, and the rest of our family scattered all around the country and the world, the task felt daunting. I am known for being calm and productive in a crisis, but from a purely emotional standpoint, this crisis far exceeded any with which I had been called to deal with previously. My son and I had divided the task of making phone calls—he would call his father and try to reach my former partner with whom Aliyah had maintained a close relationship, and I would call my mother and the relevant authorities in LA to begin the wrenching process of gaining access to Aliyah's body and making funeral arrangements.

My next phone call was to one of my best friends, Jonelle, the kind of friend I knew would get up in the middle of the night, come over to my house immediately, and help me get organized logistically, not to mention, stay sane at the same time as I permitted myself a complete breakdown. Those few minutes between the time I called her and the time she arrived were among the longest of my life. Alone in my apartment, it was like a hole had been ripped open in my spirit and all the demons in the world had showed up seeking admittance. From that day forward, I had night terrors for a full three and a half months. Needless to say, Jonelle arrived and gathered all of our other friends around—my sister circle—so that I didn't have to do anything but just be. Pooling their Sky miles, my frequent flyer friends arranged a plane ticket for me and in a day's time I was on an airplane. Meanwhile, I had meetings to cancel: my department's biggest faculty meeting of the semester was scheduled for that morning. The annual National Women's Studies Association conference was about to commence, finally, in my own city, presided over by one of my own mentors, the newly and historically elected president Beverly Guy-Sheftall, and another of my dear friends, Yi-chun Tricia Lin as vice president. At this conference, I was slated to cofacilitate a breakthrough workshop on spiritual activism with AnaLouise Keating—which would have been our first (and long-anticipated) presentation together—not to mention facilitate a showcase panel of emerging womanist scholars, many of whom were my own former students or protégés. Everything had to be canceled. It was a morning of phone calls and e-mails and tears.

When I think back to that day, Gloria Anzaldúa's words from the "1. el arrebato ... rupture, fragmentation ... an ending, a beginning" section of her essay "now let us shift" ring true: "Your relationship to the world is irrevocably changed; you're aware of your vulnerability ... and no longer trust the universe."[2] "[Y]ou feel like an orphan, abandoned by all that's familiar. Exposed, naked, disoriented, wounded, uncertain, confused, and conflicted, you're forced to live en la orilla—a razor-sharp edge that fragments you."[3] "It leads to re-interpreting the story you imagined yourself living, bringing it to a dramatic end and initiating one of turmoil, being swallowed by your fears, and passing through a threshold."[4]

The story I imagined myself living was one of a lifelong mother–daughter relationship unfolding, evolving, ripening, as two spirited womanists, one older, one younger, explored, savored, and shared the richness of life together.

Aliyah was a womanist's dream of a daughter—bold, brilliant, sassy, savvy, defiant yet respectful, loving yet independent, "interested in grown up doings" and "desiring to know more and in greater depth than is considered good for one." As a matter of fact, detecting these traits in her as an infant, I had nicknamed her "my little womaness." To top things off, she was beautiful but with a healthy sense of humor about herself and everyone else.[5]

By the time she was a tween, her universally acknowledged nickname was "Lil Diva" (thrown about both affectionately and, periodically, as a corrective, to "put her in check"). By the time she hit college, that nickname, now tongue-in-cheek, had become "the Queen of New York": Raised in a small college town, she had made her way to the big city and, as we often joked, taken over. In middle school and high school, Aliyah was a star student, "best all around," involved in sports, student government, clubs and events, consistently selected for leadership conclaves and talented youth retreats. She even participated in 4-H, an anomaly for her time. She was an integral member of the second most popular crowd of girls at her school (the most popular crowd being an all-white group known as "the blonde crowd")—a powerful, lively, internationally multicultural gang of high-achieving girls with sparkling personalities who had all been best friends since second grade. Our home had often been the hangout, because I was considered the most liberal of the parents, given my willingness to talk with the girls "about anything" and my own academically shaped propensity for social critique and unorthodox analyses of life—whether around the dinner table, in front of the TV, or during a car ride. I was raising my girl to be a thinker, a critic, *conscious*, and, in the spirit of the village, I extended this parenting orientation to my daughter's friends. My "radical politics" gave Aliyah a thinking-woman's latitude that few of her peers enjoyed. At the same time, I was quite strict about certain things. All the effort paid off—not only because Aliyah made it into an Ivy League school with scholarships, but also because she became an amazing human being, full of "lust for life," curious and driven, yet grounded in spirit and family and concern for the future of humanity. She seemed to embody the affirmation I had always claimed for myself: "Happiness is the substrate of my existence."

When Aliyah was in eighth grade, she went on her first international trip—a school-sponsored excursion to England and France. So imprinted was she by that experience that, from that point forward, she decided hers would be a life of global travel and global citizenship. She learned Spanish, gaining both reading and speaking fluency, spent a summer in Venezuela, and made many more trips to Europe, touring it with both family (her father, an Air Force dentist, was stationed in Germany for a time) and friends (mainly members of the international crowd she grew up with). She even made a few solo trips, much to the chagrin of her anxious parents, including an adventurous New Year's Eve jaunt to Paris. As the conclusion of her studies drew near, she announced that she intended to live in Paris for a while, and to that end, began taking French classes in summer school. Her goal was to figure out what kind of international subject to study in grad school and to begin writing a novel.

During her last two years of college, she spontaneously began to explore spirituality on a deeper level. As a young child, she had been raised as a Baha'i, my family religion, but as I moved through periods of agnosticism and spiritual–religious exploration, ultimately landing me at the feet of mysticism, she (and her brother) went along for the ride. Sometimes we attended church, sometimes we read tarot cards, sometimes we participated in Hindu religious festivals, sometimes we celebrated Chinese New Year. My children's lives were not unlike the years of my own childhood—filled with religious books, religious discussions, and visits to various religious communities. The conscious and intentional nurturance of my children's spirituality was a big part of my parenting from day one. It permeated everything—but in a way that encouraged freedom, exploration, and spiritual self-authorship. It also lent a certain strictness to our family's ethical code. Both of my children always joked about the time I put them through "moral development weekend" as a punishment for an episode of lying, requiring them to read books and conduct online research about a number of religions and their ethical codes before they could be released from "penance." Despite their aggravation at the time, they say it stuck with them.

Early in her college spiritual quest, Aliyah began asking me for reading suggestions. I recommended Thich Nhat Hanh and she found her way to *The Miracle of Mindfulness*—a book I had not read, but one she said changed her life. She also loved *The Alchemist*, Paulo Coehlo's metaphysical tale. Her reading branched out from there. Once, while visiting me, she came across a set of "Creative Visualization Cards" designed by New Age author Shakhti Gawain and became entranced with them. I gave them to her and, as I later discovered, she always kept a few on her desk. She loved "Daughters of the Moon" tarot, a womon-centered deck, and often asked me to read for her. She loved the Bible, and would frequently phone me with quotes. In fact, on one of my visits, she insisted that I bring her an identical copy of the study Bible I was using for my Kabbalah class. On that same visit, we attended a seminar at New York's Kabbalah Centre—I remember it vividly because it was the eve of Valentine's Day, the one year we had decided to spend Valentine's Day together, and it was also our last Valentine's Day together. At the time of her transition, she was reading the book of Jeremiah—

Now the word of the Lord came to me saying,
"Before I formed you in the womb I knew you,
and before you were born I consecrated you;
I appointed you a prophet to the nations."[6]

as well as *Autobiography of a Yogi*, which she had checked out from the New York Public Library (despite being half a world away with it in LA). It did not escape me that, on the fateful day I arrived in LA, one of her last personal effects was a receipt from the Los Angeles Public Library from that morning, returning some books and checking out others. She had also spent some time in a local coffee shop.

A curious aspect of Aliyah's spiritual journey is that, in June of 2009, she decided to participate in a week-long vision quest experience with a group that runs "council circles" for youth in the Inyo Mountains of eastern California. This coincided with my scheduled trip to a 21-day retreat at Plum Village in France to study with Thich Nhat Hanh and Sister Chan Khong. In a twist of fate, I missed my flight to France by just a few minutes, necessitating the purchase of a second ticket and ultimately making me 10 days late to the retreat. I was so sad, mad, and embarrassed that I refused to see or speak to anyone—other than Aliyah or Seboe—for days. Ironically, Aliyah was headed to my apartment as a pit stop between Germany and LA (where she intended to complete her last bit of outstanding coursework at UCLA while staying with her brother), so missing my flight enabled me to pick her up from hers and spend a few days with her before we each headed to our respective destinations. It just so happens that those few days were the last time I ever saw her in person. But we didn't know then what was coming. Those few days were precious and thrilling, as she was bubbling over with tales from her European travels, and I was bubbling over with tales from my recent journey to Liberia as well as the joy of the new romantic relationship I had entered into there. She seemed happier than I had ever seen her, and I was refreshed by her spirit.

Just after Labor Day of 2009, Aliyah completed her coursework at UCLA, thus filling in all the missing requirements for her diploma at Barnard. Her journey at Barnard had been an uneven one academically, although she loved the school, the quality of the education there, and the many friends she had met, particularly through Barnard Organization of Soul Sisters (BOSS), the Black women's student alliance, an organization in whose leadership she participated from the day of her arrival. A personal trauma that she experienced during her freshman year had left her uncertain of her abilities, despite her amazing gift with the pen and her uncommon intellect. She developed a kind of writer's block that haunted her throughout college. Teachers would remark that she was obviously gifted, and thus, they couldn't understand why she couldn't get her papers in on time. This dynamic, for which she had received some help, but which she never fully overcame, had led to the incompletes that necessitated her taking her last four courses at UCLA. She was so proud of herself for the As and Bs that she got that final term, so thankful that she had been able to complete all of her assignments by the deadline, so relieved that coursework was finally all over. There was still, however, a half-written thesis to complete.

After the courses ended at UCLA, Aliyah started phoning me more. Previously, we had not been people to talk every day, but she began calling me once, twice, three or four times a day, even at odd hours, which was strange. However, I was not initially alarmed—I wrote it off to the nervousness that can sometimes accompany a major life transition—like completing college and contemplating what to do with the rest of your life, or moving to a new city. Aliyah loved LA (although not as much as New York or Paris), loved UCLA (and was glad to have experienced a second college, to give her a point of comparison), and was really enjoying spending time with her brother, who had lived on the opposite coast for the duration of her college experience. Though quite different in terms of personality, they had always been close. In our phone conversations, she used me as a sounding board not only for thinking through future career possibilities, but also for discussing her ideas for a novel, some short stories, and possibly publishable travelogues. She felt her own genius, but at the same time, wasn't sure what to do with herself and how to translate her Ivy League education into the kind of opportunities it can command. I did my best to provide her with motherly counsel. Although she was anxious to some extent, her mood was generally optimistic and buoyant. Both of us felt relieved the day she announced: "I've spent the last two weekends writing and I think I have finally gotten over my writer's block!"

It wasn't until about three days before "the event" that my red flag went up in one of our conversations and I said to myself, "Something's happening here, something's wrong." It wasn't just what she was saying, but how she was saying it. After running through a list of "major epiphanies" (which had been becoming increasingly frequent), Aliyah began dictating to me about my life and speaking with a kind of forceful authority that was off-putting and, to a mother's ear, disrespectful. I was offended by her "reading me" without provocation and frustrated when my every response to her accusations was translated into the refrain "That's your resistance! You're just being resistant!" followed by "If you would just give up your resistance, you could have everything you want, everything you desire." Her insistent message to me was that I was my own worst enemy, and that she could see that clearly now. All this seemingly came out of nowhere. Her demeanor was not angry, but rather like the patronizing arrogance of a person who "gets it" when nobody else does. After two such conversations, I tried to make sense of things. It was my "red flag" that led me to a memory of a dream I had while still carrying her in my womb.

In my dream, a young woman in her early twenties was surrounded by flashing red and blue lights against the dark black backdrop of outer space. Her name was Aliyah and her hair was flowing and, in the dream, somehow I knew she was schizophrenic. At the time, I thought the dream strange, but I made no connection to my actual daughter and did not consider it prescient. Yet, when my red flag went up, I thought to myself, the moment foretold in that dream has arrived. This was Sunday night.

Monday morning, I had an e-mail message from Aliyah. It was one line, and there was no subject header. It said, "Mommy, all this channeling/trance stuff is hard. I'm ecstatic, but I'm also terrified. Any seasoned words of advice?" I received this e-mail 10 minutes before I was due in class across campus. I hurriedly typed her as detailed a response as I could muster. As fate would have it, as soon as I hit send, the e-mail disappeared into cyberspace, leaving no record of its existence. It would be my last e-mail from Aliyah.

I have spent many a day reflecting on that exchange, running it through the ringer of many possible interpretations and understandings. Was I a bad mother for not recognizing immediately the urgency of my daughter's state of mind? What was wrong with me—how could I as a PhD psychologist, not see the warning signs of a condition requiring attention? Why didn't I get on a plane that day and go see about my daughter? Why didn't I retype my e-mail after class? Is there something about the way I raised her—too much spiritual information, too much social critique, too much freedom or too much strictness—that brought this on? *Is there something I could have done to prevent this??* These are the questions of a heart that grieves.

The intrepid womanist in me, and the mystic, ask different questions. Reflecting deeply on the nature of life and death, considering the possibilities of both reincarnation and timeless, nonlocal interbeing, believing somewhat in destiny and fate at the same time as I maintain that we are radically agentive beings who choose *everything*, at the soul level *and* on earth, I have found myself asking what might be considered forbidden questions. I call them the "What ifs?" and I will return to them momentarily.

THE OFFICIAL STORY

Aliyah's death certificate lists her official cause of death as "suicide." Gathered together in Los Angeles on the day we came to reclaim her body, our extended family decided collectively that this explanation was inaccurate. When a person commits suicide, we reasoned, it is their intention to kill themselves; they take an action that they believe will end their life. After putting many puzzle pieces together, we figured out that, even when she jumped off the roof, Aliyah's intention was not to die. First of all, she had just phoned her paternal grandmother a few days before to say, cheerily, "See you at Christmas!"—Aliyah's favorite holiday. Second, she had just phoned her aunt, who lived in LA, the day before, saying "See you this weekend!" for an auntie–niece weekend they had planned. The third and fourth reasons require a bit more explanation.

When I received the phone call from my son about Aliyah's death and asked him whether she had "left a note," he said no, but, "something a little strange— she seemingly left a DVD in the DVD player and it was on pause." I asked him what movie and he said, "*Kid's Story*." I had never heard of it, but, as it turns out, it is a short film by the Wachowski Brothers (of *The Matrix* series fame) about a young man who begins getting strange messages through his computer and starts questioning the appearance–reality distinction. In the film, one of the messages that pops up on the boy's computer screen is: "If you want to know the truth, you have to risk everything." After this, the boy jumps off the top of a tall building and flies/floats down toward the ground, which we never see him hit. When he wakes up, he has crossed the boundary into another existence, not unlike this one, except "somewhere else." Later in the movie, he repeats the action and ends up back in the first reality. From that day forward, he knows things that the other kids don't know, yet he continues to walk through the halls of the school, quiet and to himself as before. Although Thad did not tell me which scene the movie had been paused on, the thematic content of this 13-minute short was enough to tip me off about what Aliyah was thinking: "Let me try it."

When we, the family, with Thad's roommate, Aliyah's best friend from high school, Lyz Jaeger, my "oldest, bestest" friend who had flown in from Philadelphia to be by my side, and Deborah Richardson, a dear senior sisterfriend who just happened to be in LA on business and angelically extended her stay to steward me through the practical logistics of dealing with that trauma, stood on that rooftop, mentally walking and talking through what could have happened after viewing the security photo that captured Aliyah on her final steps (although not the jump itself), an interesting clue presented itself. Aliyah's father reported that her paternal great grandmother had committed suicide by walking out into the snow and freezing to death. The family recorded her as being "a little touched," suffering from an unnamed and probably undiagnosed mental illness. But hearing this story at this time—as story I either did not know or had not remembered given the long time of separation between

Aliyah's father and myself—enabled us the momentary relief of knowing that maybe something about this situation was "in the genes," and thus, beyond our control. When we began to put bits and pieces of the story of Aliyah's final days together—bits and pieces that we each held separately and hadn't before now shared with each other—it became clear that Aliyah had developed a fast-acting and somewhat concealable mental illness over the last month or two. It took my grad school buddy Lyz, an even more astute student of psychology than myself, to point out that all signs pointed to mania. This, too, then became part of the "official story."

Mania is a condition that causes people to develop a superhuman sense about themselves. When under the influence of mania, people think they can do anything and they feel invulnerable. Often, they assume an attitude of grandiosity because they perceive themselves as having uncommon insights that give them Godlike consciousness. Alternately (or, sometimes, in addition), people who are manic feel wildly creative; in fact, history tells us that many of the most revered artists in all fields—music, literature, dance—even scientists, have "suffered" from mania or manic episodes. The thing about mania is that is feels good to the people who are having it. They experience the sensation of "seeing through everyday reality to *the Truth*." Typically, they share their insights with others and get offended when others don't "get it" or, worse, accuse them of being "out of their mind." Their mind races so much that they begin to stop sleeping, which has its own set of physiological and psychological risks. From a purely physical standpoint, people under the influence of mania can be "a danger to themselves" because they often attempt risky physical feats—like jumping off of rooftops. After conversing with each other and comparing notes, all of us came to the conclusion that Aliyah jumped during a manic episode—perhaps her first. Thus, she thought she could fly[7]—or, more probably, break through to another reality and then find her way back.

People who didn't know Aliyah well naturally came to the conclusion that she jumped—that is, committed suicide—because she was troubled or depressed. Most people commit suicide because they are depressed or they are trying to escape a life that seems unbearable. As a family, we ruled this explanation out with regard to Aliyah. Various forms of possibly hidden explanations were ruled out—she was not pregnant (so the coroner informed us), she was not gay (and even if she had been, the family would have accepted it), and she had not received a recent diagnosis of HIV (a safer sex conversation we had periodically engaged in since she was a teenager). Although she was a little stressed about finishing her thesis, we all agreed that this stress had not caused her to jump. Rather, we determined, she simply was doing what she had always done well—perhaps too well—and that is, responding to her curiosity.

Later that night, as I was going to bed, my son came to me with two additional pieces of information that provided additional clues. First, she had gone to bed on the last night of her life quietly "praying or singing"—he couldn't tell—in a particularly obsessive–compulsive sort of way. Second, she had been having a *Matrix* moviethon during the sleepless nights that had preceded that one. *The Matrix* is a movie that we originally saw together as a family when it first came out, during Aliyah's adolescence, and Thad in particular had become a big fan of this science-fiction-meets-philosophy series of films. As Aliyah's spiritual curiosity deepened, she had used the movie as a springboard for conversations with him about "nature of existence" type topics once she began living with him. A coincidence that did not escape my synchronicity-attuned notice was that Sophia Stewart, the African American woman who wrote the original screenplay for *The Matrix* under the original title of "The Third Eye," but who had not been given credit and subsequently sued, won her lawsuit of many years on the very day of Aliyah's departure.[8]

That night, sleeping next to my friend Lyz in my son's cramped apartment, I had a strange experience. Just as I was falling asleep, something came through me and I screamed at the top of my lungs. It woke up me and Lyz, and Thad rushed in to ask me if I was all right. "I don't know what made me scream," I said. "It was strange," he replied, "because it sounded like the scream of someone falling." The next day, he informed me somewhat sheepishly that the blanket he had given me when I told him I was cold was the blanket Aliyah had kept herself wrapped in almost all the time she was at home, particularly during her sleepless nights of movie watching. Energy, I thought, energy transfer.

In the days that followed, we made the necessary trips to the Los Angeles County Coroner's Department and the funeral home that would transport her body back to Atlanta to be buried near her maternal great- and great-great grandmothers. The mortician, who hesitated to let us see Aliyah's body because it had been so badly mangled by the impact, said, "There is one miraculous thing—her face was not damaged at all."[9] We saw her, packed in ice, with only her face showing, her soft African hair flowing out in all directions. Remarkably, there was a smile on her face.

We buried her on November 20, 2009—her 23rd birthday—in a simple ceremony attended by an unbelievable array of people from all over the country. Not only were all three parental branches of her family represented extensively, but a caravan of her college friends came down from New York, a large contingent of her high school comrades appeared, many with their parents, an unexpected number of my university colleagues attended, and even some Facebook friends. In addition, services were attended by many members of the Atlanta Liberian community, given my Liberian involvements and my then-engagement to a

Liberian man. It was a full house, with standing room only. After the funeral and burial, one of the local Liberian churches, International Christian Fellowship, opened its doors for Aliyah's "Celebration of Life," a big party organized by my friend the Honorary Consul General of the Republic of Liberia, Cynthia Blandford Nash, in collaboration with Pastor William B. G. K. Harris and Rev. Ralph Phillips, both of whom had also lost young adult children tragically. At the "Celebration of Life," we watched a slideshow documentary of Aliyah's life through photos, enjoyed a sumptuous Liberian meal prepared by church members, and ate birthday cake to the tune of "Love Train" by the O'Jays, Aliyah's theme song. Five thousand miles across the sea in Liberia, my fiancé Seboe held a simultaneous memorial service for our Liberian friends. This is the story of what happened.

There are so many more details I could give to flesh out this story. For example, the way that the lights in my kitchen dimmed three times mysteriously at 7:35 p.m. (4:35 p.m. Pacific Time) on November 10, or the way I lay in the bathtub that evening watching the movie *Death at a Funeral*—even though I normally go out of my way to avoid films that focus on death. For example, the way that Aliyah's Facebook posts in her last few weeks left clues about her transmuting mindstate, including the last two songs she sent me—Curtis Mayfield's "Move on Up" and an old blues number that sang of a good fight lost. It was as though her soul knew—and, as reluctant as I am to admit it, mine did, too. Even since that time, there have been so many signs and synchronicities to guide me along the path of discovery and healing that I know beyond a shadow of a doubt that there is "more to the story."

> O Son of the Supreme!
> I have made death a messenger of joy to thee.
> Wherefore dost thou grieve?
> I made the light to shed on thee in its splendor.
> Wherefore dost though veil thyself therefrom?
> –Baháʼuʼlláh[10]

The night I lost my daughter opened up a path of mystery deeper and more challenging than any I had ever experienced previously. Now a year has passed and a year of reflections, a year of twisting and retwisting the Rubik's cube, looking for *the solution* to *this* mystery, has also passed. I'm not sure whether I have gained *the solution*, but the quality of the *questions* has deepened and so have various forms of *understanding*. My process of reflection has taken me into territories marked "do not enter" by the norms of polite and even not-so-polite society. However, my womanist curiosity and my faith in Source have dared me to cross the line.

THE WHAT IFS

Overwhelmed, you shield yourself with ignorance, blanking out what you don't want to see. Yet you feel you're incubating some knowledge that could spring into life like a childhood monster if you paid it the slightest attention.

—*Gloria Anzaldúa*[11]

No mother wants to believe that her child is flawed, much less fatally. A mother's heart much prefers to maintain an understanding that her child is perfect, if not immortal. My mother's heart compelled me to seek understandings of Aliyah's life and death that preserved and satisfied these desires. At the same time, the mystic in me could not help but bring my evolving understandings about life's mysteries to bear upon this very concrete, personal case. What follows are some of my reflections, the kinds of questions I asked, the kinds of sources I went to for guidance, and the ways in which I linked these cogitations back to my evolving understanding of the womanist idea.

The Question of Prophets

What if Jesus came back in the body of a middle-class Black girl from urban America? Would we recognize and embrace her? In a world that suppresses young Black girls through the cooperating crucibles of racism, sexism, and often classism, could she even recognize herself? What were Jesus, Moses, Abraham, Muhammad, Buddha, and Baha'u'llah like at the age of 22? What were they like when revelation started coming to them, when they started channeling God's voice? Did their "condition" resemble mania? Was their Godlike consciousness real, or were they "out of their mind"? When they saw things that others didn't see, were the people who believed in them "crazy" or "chosen"? What is the difference between my daughter and the prophets of old?

Toward the end of her life (which, I repeat, none of us saw coming), Aliyah began to say things like, "We are all One," "Love *is* the answer—*really*," and "What it all really boils down to is 'Does this *serve*?'" During our last two phone conversations, she said things like, "I'm going to be the prophet of my generation" and "I feel like I have finally come into my name." Her name, Aliyah, is the female form of the name Ali, and, in the Baha'i writings, the first

Imam Alí is referred to as the "Commander of the Faithful." Her middle name, Karmil, refers to Mount Carmel in Israel, which is, for Baha'is, the "point of adoration," similar to the Qiblih/Ka'aba for Muslims, Jerusalem for Christians, or the Bodhi Tree for Buddhists. Just after noon on November 9, 2009—not long after she sent me that last e-mail—she wrote in her diary, "I am choosing Life and stepping into the light. I have nothing to prove. God's will on earth is and will always be done. I am the one; and I am none. My first word was the name of a prophet: 'Abdu'l-Bahá. I step now into the light of this vast prophetic tradition to take my seat as a woman at the table of the Holy Trinity."

What am I to make of this? I could write it off as "crazy," or I could consider it as a possible statement of truth. As close as I was to my daughter, how can I know her deepest spiritual secrets? As one who is mystically inclined, I know firsthand that often one's most nonordinary experiences of the higher realms cannot easily be shared with others. Perhaps my daughter was having one. How can I, in good conscience, discount this possibility? At the same time, as a mother, how can I not have rescued my daughter from the peril of such thinking in a society so unlikely to receive her as who she saw herself to be? This is the wrestling in my soul. In February of 2010, midflight to California for a conference, I wrote a poem about it.

> "Don't Read This If You Can't Handle It"
> If your daughter jumped
> from the roof of a 14-story building
> and died instantly,
> how would you feel?
> If your daughter told you
> that Jesus was waiting for her
> and that she was going to be
> the female member of the Holy Trinity,
> what would you do?
> Would you take her to the doctor,
> or would you marvel at her self-confidence
> and sense of importance
> that defies every message
> that a typical girl ever gets
> about her value or her power?
> If you had raised her to be
> smart and strong and she
> turned out to be brilliant and indomitable,
> how would you react to that?

If she thought she could fly,
where would you draw the line:
Would you put your foot down
and medicate her,
or would you just try to keep an eye on her
while she wrote her prize-winning novels
born from the insufferably deep meaning
she found in every mundane thing?
How would you live with yourself
if the one day you failed to return her phone call,
she hit pause on the DVD player
and decided to try what she had just seen,
namely, a breakthrough to another reality?
Tell me,
do you think these are easy answers,
obvious situations with clear-cut protocols
that any good mother
would know what to do??
Was there something lacking somewhere??
Am I at fault for encouraging her
on her spiritual path
or allowing her to travel the world
or make her own sexual choices at an early age
or move to New York
or move to LA
or teaching her to love herself unconditionally
and to believe that her powers were infinite??
I could not let her be consumed
by the forces arrayed to destroy her—
little black girl, little smart black girl,
little adventurous black girl, little brilliant black girl,
little ambitious black girl, little audacious black girl,
little beautiful black girl, little talented black girl,
little womaness.
No, I could not allow those forces
to destroy her.
I, the developmental psychologist,
I, the feminist antiracist liberationist activist,
I, the student on the Path, the mystic in training,
I, the teenage mother, the single parent,

I, the self-actualization consultant, tarot reader, and astrologer,
I, the womanist.
No, I could not allow those forces
arrayed against her
to destroy her.
So what happens
when a little black girl
becomes so powerful and so conscious
that she herself can no longer withstand embodiment??
Is that what happened??
What happens
when a young black girl
becomes the prophet of her generation
because she has seen The Light
and decided to follow it?
What happens
when a young black girl
does that thing
that only some unstable
young white man
on drugs
is supposed to do—
is allowed to do—
only she's not on drugs??
No, there wasn't a secret
and no she wasn't pregnant
and no she wasn't gay
and no she wasn't in debt—
she wasn't even unhappy, people!
Au contraire, she was, by her own admission,
ecstatic,
but also terrified.
What prophet isn't first terrified
by the power and visions and voices
that come with consciousness and anointment??
Think about Moses and Daniel and Elijah.
Was my little black girl anointed??
She seemed to think so,
and how could I disagree??

If your daughter had come to you and said,
Mom, I'm the prophet of my generation
because I have seen the truth
and I know what to do,
what would you say?
If your kid had been Jesus
or Moses or Muhammad
or Buddha or Bahá'u'lláh,
what would you have said??
If your daughter had said to you,
Mom, I have seen The Truth
and it is all so incredibly simple,
and it has to do with LOVE and
how does it serve community?,
what would you have done??
Would you have dismissed her
like the rest of the world had already done?
Little black girl.
Would you have said,
Well, you've got some really great ideas—
why don't you channel all that energy into
a career in advertising
where you can really make a difference
and still make money at the same time,
or some other bourgeois capitalist b.s. like that?
Or would you have said,
Write that novel, write that novel, do it
while your ideas are fresh and flowing
because I've learned the hard way
that if you don't you lose it?
Or might you have said,
You know, I'm really too busy to take your call right now—
can we schedule some time to talk over the weekend??
Or would you have said,
Wow, you know, it's so good to hear you so happy,
and I'm so glad you feel like you're over
your writer's block??
I mean, what would you have said??
It doesn't really matter,

Because she reached the point
where she was the authority
because she was downloading
directly from God.
"Mommy, listen to me—
I'm telling you—
just listen to your own resistance—
if you would stop putting up so much resistance
everything you aim for and everything you're all about
would come true instantly.
You don't see how you're standing in your own way,
but I see it."
And so it is.
What happens when
young, gifted, and black
becomes the unsustainable SUPER-SIZED version of itself
and self-destructs?
Or did it??
Did she not find,
I mean, did she not fast-track herself,
to that place people sit for decades in the Himalayas for,
that place we reserve only for yogis and let's face it
mostly men from the East?
Did she jump off a roof,
or was it just a little black girl's
Maha-samadhi??
I mean, are you qualified to tell me?
I myself was still trying to figure a whole lot out
without passing judgment.
Was that wrong?
Some would say so.
But I have to stand in my own Truth.
Is it wrong
that I taught my daughter to do the same thing?
Sure, it hurts.
Do you think I ever thought
that this experiment in truth
would lead to my precious daughter,
Aliyah K for Karmil that is Mt. Carmel of the Holy Land Phillips
named after the original Imám Alí, Commander of the Faithful,

at age 22
to jump off the 14th story of a former bank building
turned apartment
at 4:30 in the afternoon
after spending the morning at the public library
and lunchtime at the coffee shop?
Do you think I thought that???
No, I did not think that,
but that is what happened.
Everything in this poem is factual.
The world isn't ready
for little black girls who have showed up
to save the world.
Such a possibility strains the credulity
of the current self-deconstituting civilization.
Doesn't anybody ever ask—
isn't that exactly why she left??
Who wants to wait around for a self-deconstituting humanity
evolving towards its own collective Christhood
to catch up with a little black girl
who's already there?
Maybe that's what happened.
Can you dig it?
Or can you not?
That is the question,
And yes I am invoking Hamlet
Because that is what she,
little AP, Ivy League educated
thing that she was.
If everything we have always been waiting for
for forever for everybody
suddenly showed up in the form of
a little black girl could we handle it?
I'm sure she did the math,
though that had nothing to do with it.
It was just a smirky footnote in her mind,
a thought in passing on the way out.
"I'm outta here."
She saw through the eye of the needle
and that was enough.

Little black girl, little black girl
precious precious little black girl
I just want to hold you in my arms
and rock you close to my breast
you are my baby you are my fruit
you are my progeny and mine to protect
you chose me out of all the mothers in the universe
and I am still your mother, our mother–daughter bond is not lost
our mother–daughter bond has now broken the barrier
of time, space, embodiment, and identity
here we are in the Mommy–Liyah world
knowing things we know that nobody else knows
and those are our womanist secrets
I can light candles on the altar now
you are one of the ancestors now
you are one of the angels now
and I am left on earth to pray
we are tag-teaming
across the life and "death" barrier
knowing full well the thread is unbroken

The Question of Satori

There is a concept in Zen called *satori* that means "instant awakening" or "instant enlightenment." Without going into details, there are two schools of thought—one that suggests that satori is a watershed moment that occurs only once, completing one cycle of reincarnation, and another that maintains that satori can happen anew every second and therefore is essentially ongoing. I learned about this concept many years ago—from a Wayne Dyer book, if I recall correctly—and was so captivated by it that I gave it as a nickname to a young friend who struck me as particularly enlightened for her age.

After Aliyah transitioned and everyone who knew her began comparing notes and sharing stories about things she had said and done in the months leading up to her passing, I began to wonder whether Aliyah had experienced satori. I had noticed certain things about her that seemed like they could be indicators—her indefatigable happiness that only seemed to grow stronger and more profound every time I saw her, her increasing nonattachment to material things as well as other people's opinions, her increasing reports of meditation practice, and, of course, her increasing spiritual curiosity. All of these things seemed uncharacteristic for a person of her age, even though I took subtle parental pride in them. It was her final diary entry, as well as the anecdotal report of one friend of hers, that really made me consider this possibility. On November 10, 2009, she wrote: "God is good. Jesus saves. Amen/Ashé. Namaste. Agape. Joyful living." She then signed it "♥, Aliyah" under which she wrote "presented by Marvel Comix + Crazy Perfect Storm Collabz."[12] The friend, who was part of her girlhood crowd now living in LA, reported that, on Halloween, when they were out cavorting, Aliyah had pointed to an illumined church sign that says "Jesus Saves" and turned to her friend and said "Jesus really does save." Her friend, less enthusiastic about the sentiment, gave her a look, to which Aliyah responded with complete seriousness, "I mean it." The friend said that Aliyah's energy was strange in that moment, and she felt like something was different about her. But then they partied the night away. This story, combined with her final diary entry and a few others that refer to "the Light," made reason that, quite possibly, Aliyah had experienced satori.

What is unusual is that satori is often associated with long years of spiritual preparation through life as a monastic, a contemplative, a yogi, or the like. So, in fairness, I had to ask myself, how likely is it that this young woman—who certainly exhibited spiritual curiosity and openness, but who had in no wise built up years of experience with traditional forms of spiritual discipline—had actually experienced satori? I left the question open, although the examples of Jesus and Buddha, who both attained enlightenment at young ages, were in the back of my mind.

As a concept or as a state, satori is not that different from Samadhi, Nirvana, or Heaven. Within the yogic perspective, people who have attained such high states of consciousness are capable of deciding and voluntarily undertaking the moment of their departure from the Earth plane, otherwise known as death or transition. This action is called Maha-Samadhi, or "Great Samadhi." Maha-Samadhi is discussed extensively in *Autobiography of a Yogi* as well as another wonderful book called *Graceful Exits: How Great Beings Die—Death Stories of Hindu, Tibetan, Buddhist, and Zen Masters* by Sushila Blackman. The latter text contains many such accounts of publicly witnessed Maha-Samadhi events. Oftentimes, masters preparing to depart in this way will let people know in advance and even prepare "closing remarks." Typically, these masters are sitting, standing, or lying down when they depart—rarely is the separation of the spiritual essence from the body violent in any way. However, I still found myself thinking about Aliyah in terms of Maha-Samadhi. There is a passage in *Graceful Exits* by Ramakrishna that resonated with my thought process:

The body and the soul!
The body was born and it will die.
But for the soul there is no death.
It is like the betel nut.
When the nut is ripe it does not stick to the shell.
But when it is green it is difficult to separate from the shell.
After realizing God, one does not identify anymore with the body.
Then one knows the body and the soul are two different things.

—Ramakrishna[13]

My thought process was this: If she had experienced satori, then she surely knew that "the body and the soul are two different things" and she experienced that palpably. She was like a betel nut—mature in her consciousness, but physically still green. Thus, she, if she desired to hasten her journey "into the Light," would need to forcibly separate the nut from the shell. Hence the impulse to jump, which she knew would do the trick. Maybe that's why she had a smile on her face even though her body was broken—it is reported that many masters who enter into Maha-Samadhi do.[14]

The fact that, serendipitously, the saying on my "Wisdom of the East" quote-of-the-day calendar for November 11 read, as I quoted epigraphically at the beginning of this chapter, "Being of Tao, one endures forever; though the body perishes, one suffers not" seemed like a sign. *La facultad* told me that it was no coincidence. It was almost as though Aliyah had prepared that message for me.

The Question of Ancestors

Aliyah seemed like a changed person after her vision quest in the Inyo Mountains. Her sense of peace had seemed much deeper and her sense of purpose had seemed much stronger than before. Her stories of what she saw and experienced have continued to provide fodder for reflection and provide clues regarding what was to come some five months later. While on this trip, she wrote a magnificent poem that I reproduce here for the first time. It seems to presage her departure but also to reveal her deepening spiritual insights as a result of the journey. I never saw it until I received her journal in the days immediately following our loss of her. This poem lends additional weight to the hypothesis that Aliyah had experienced a special kind of awakening. It is also noteworthy because of its references to the ancestors, which I will discuss at greater length after the poem.

"Life into Death" by Aliyah Phillips[15]
To a land who has seen
  a million deaths,
felt all of them her own,
the lone, low whisper
  of the wind
calls on each and every bone.

But in this slow desolation,
  a small gray bird sings from craigy perch,
  and the evergreen jumpers penetrate
  roots fast to stony lurch.

Skyward leaning hills pulsate
  to a primordial drum;
filled by primordial intensity;
mountains peak toward the sun.

In this silent rhythm,
my searching soul burns under the undying sun.

Gazing once more on the twilit horizon
  before this cord is cut,
a robust joy for the dying loss
opens the oldest secret until
now to me shut.

Hollowed out on hallowed ground,
this body offers up its shell
prostrate across this earthen
altar, ancestors summon me close to tell

"Join us tonight in the ancient star-bound
procession from whence you came."[16]

Now lavender sky darts behind
shining crescent moon,
and robust joy meets
for the dying that would arrive
soon.

I arrange my sacred compass
to align me with the path;

the howling wind begins
its chant longing for
the aftermath.

As the final magenta curtain drops
behind a mountainous stage,
the eastern landscape becomes
an underworld, shadowy under
the blessed smoke and says

Three prayers—gratitude,
love, and faith—
assure my footsteps
toward the portal from
which no return I could make.

I step inside to start the
dance and the wheel begins
to turn.

Timeless travel across
The astral web obviates mortal senses—
no self to discern.

I see my grim cloaked shadow cast
in moonlight for the first time,
    spin around to the
    west, and know I must
    leave it behind.

Before me now a dulcet moonbeam
    signals the way
and this life death in the Inyos
transmutes my dying day

My soul vigils while my body
    shivers, sweats and fears
I sit with dual terror and
    peace, alternating silence and
    tears

What follows next is best
    kept as my own cosmic amulet.

Though within every stirring
and everything still
lies the same quiet secret:
Live in your death,
Die in your life,
You open with either one.

In this poem, Aliyah talks about joining the ancestors, who are calling her to join their "star-bound procession from whence you came." She seems intrigued and motivated. There are two ancestors in particular that seem to have had a strong pull on Aliyah—her maternal great-grandmother, Jannie Mary Glass Murphy, who died two months after Aliyah was born (Aliyah never met her in person), and her maternal grandfather, my father—Duane Dean Dumbleton, who died in early 2006. She frequently reported, from the time of childhood on (in the case of Grandmother Jannie) and during her college years (in the case of Grandpa Duane), that these figures would appear to her in dreams, often in "heavenly" scenes, and give her guidance.[17] She felt especially close to them and was not beyond talking with them in her daily life, particularly when she was having problems. One of her prized possessions was a teardrop shaped rainbow crystal pendant encasing a pair of praying hands that had belonged to Grandmother Jannie. It would not be surprising to me if these two individuals—these two spirits—were among Aliyah's guardian angels. Little did we know she would join them, becoming a "Baby Ancestor."

What happens when "the order of things" is shaken up by a child preceding a parent in death? It happens all the time, but there is something about it that is unsettling.[18] For one who engages in ancestor reverence, imagining the ancestors as "ones who came before," it is hard to wrap one's mind around the idea of one's child as part of this group. It becomes like a metaphysical knot to untie, forcing the examination of both timelessness/eternity and the agelessness of souls. It also causes reflections on reincarnation and soul groups—the possibility that we have "traveled together" before and will do so again, always for some common purpose. Possibilities such as these are explored in books such as those by psychiatrist Brian Weiss, who, although not initially a believer, began to see patients who reported memories of reincarnation.[19] Although it sits on the fringes of science, reincarnation has been extensively studied by a small group of academics,[20] and this research has influenced my thinking about spirituality and social change. I am neither a believer nor a nonbeliever, but rather one who can sustain both perspectives simultaneously and use them as a foundation for considering some of life's most perplexing questions.

The Question of Ascension

Ascension is a phenomenon discussed most widely within New Age circles; however, it bears some similarity to satori. I separate it out for discussion here because, beyond that initial conceptual similarity, it has its own genealogy and attributes. Ascension is the idea that people can experience a "shift" in consciousness that places them at a "higher" level of "vibration." Once one has experienced "the shift," one views the world and life differently, with a greater sense of interconnectedness, more bliss, and the ability to know things directly. There is a discourse about Ascended Masters, who are formerly embodied teachers who now exist only on the nonphysical plane, yet who communicate with people on Earth (for example, people who channel or people who are at high levels of a spiritual discipline, such as yogis/yoginis or initiatic adepts that are capable of receiving this kind of communication).[21] There is also a discourse about individual ascension; in one version, humanity is undergoing a period of rapid evolution in which certain individuals, like the first person to run the 4-minute mile, are ahead of the rest, or certain groups of individuals, (like the so-called Indigo, Rainbow, and Crystal children) are in the vanguard. Finally, there is discourse about group ascension, most notably, a collective shift in the consciousness of humanity associated with the emergence of the Age of Aquarius or the return of Christ through universal ascension to Christ consciousness. Group ascension can also related to smaller groups or communities who, for whatever reason, have achieved a higher vibrational level together (whether historically, as in the case of the ancient Mayans and Kemites, or contemporaneously, in the case of certain New Age communities).

In his model of "Levels of Consciousness" presented in *Power vs. Force*, David R. Hawkins argues that, after the level called 700, people have a type of super-ordinary consciousness that is characteristic of the types of individuals humanity has historically upheld as masters, prophets, avatars, manifestations of God, and the like, where participation in ordinary life is severely curtailed and they must fulfill some kind of mission for humanity as a collective. The Lamed-Vov of Jewish Mysticism and Babaji, described in *Autobiography of a Yogi*, might represent this type of being.[22] Once individuals reach the level called 1,000, their consciousness can no longer withstand physical embodiment and they depart the Earth plane.[23] While there are levels of consciousness beyond 1,000, they are possessed by beings whom ordinary humans would refer to as part of the invisible or spiritual realm, such as angels and Archangels, bodhisattvas, dakinis, and the like. Satori, then, or ascension, catapults a person into the upper reaches of the scale, and a person capable of performing Maha-Samadhi is at or near the 1,000 level.

When Aliyah and Thad were small children, the discourse about Indigo, Rainbow, and Crystal children was just picking up steam. Because I had precocious children, these discussions fascinated me and I often wondered whether my children "fit the bill" and had "come to Earth" to help humanity evolve. A sense that humanity is evolving was part of my Baha'i upbringing: I was taught that we are collectively on the verge of discovering the "oneness of [hu]mankind," "unity within diversity," the equality of men and women, and the end of racism and all other forms of prejudice, and that I should help the process along however I could. This early imprint shaped my future spiritual quests, however far-ranging, as well as my strong beliefs about service. When Aliyah died, I found myself wondering whether "ascension" had been part of the cause of death, insofar as the ascended state sounded a lot like the state that was being labeled as "mania," a mental illness. I could not escape the question of whether "mania" is simply a high-vibrating soul trying to express itself inside a low-vibrating social and material reality, and when Aliyah jumped—ostensibly to crack the betel nut—whether she had reached the point where she could not longer withstand material embodiment or life on this plane. Her desire to know the truth was just that strong.

WITNESS TO A TESTIMONY

Aliyah Phillips's life and death was a particular kind of testimony. Our challenge is to read and receive that testimony. Was it the testimony of a "young, gifted, and Black" woman on the precipice of a promising adulthood who found the world and its density—its racism, sexism, classism, xenophobia, homophobia, ageism, ableism, speciesism and every other "-ism"—a waste of her Soul's time, who discovered, once she discovered *herSelf*, that she could not flower here in line with her considerable gifts and talents and insights? Alternately, was she a human being who discovered her Higher Being and suddenly felt trapped and paralyzed by the density of Earth-bound existence in general and, like Kafka's prisoner, simply walked away from the prison? If she did walk away, can we respect that decision? Can we trust the truth of her discovery that maybe there *is* some spiritual/invisible/transcendent/energetic realm that is vaster, richer, and inconceivably more attractive than this one—a place of power and light and bliss and consciousness and freedom and LOVE, not unlike the Heaven/Nirvana/Samadhi spoken of in diverse faiths, not unlike the Divine intoxication described in the poems of Rumi or Hafiz, not unlike the domain of Angels and Bodhisattvas and Orisha and Elohim? There is a saying in the Baha'i Faith that conveys, in effect, that if we could see through to the next Higher Realm in only the amount visible through the eye of a needle, we would not hesitate to depart for that realm immediately, with all that implies. I cannot help but wonder if my daughter, Aliyah Phillips, saw through the eye of that needle.

BEYOND WOMANISM

> Out beyond ideas of wrongdoing
> and rightdoing there is a field.
> I'll meet you there.
> When the soul lies down in that grass
> the world is too full to talk about.—Rumi[24]

The womanist idea forces us to look at what happens when we bring the spiritual dimension—the invisible world—to bear upon our negotiations with and transformations of our lived reality, our daily existence. Aliyah's story, as personal as it is to me—one womanist author—has larger dimensions that inform this discussion. Aliyah, confirmed and joyous in her Black womanness, was ready to experience planetary identity, cosmic citizenship, and union with the Divine. Where was the world that was ready to receive her and nurture her as *this* being? Better yet, how—and when—are we going to create that world for all the other Aliyahs who are surely rising up in our midst? Black, brown, yellow, tan, white, or multicolored, female, male, or transgender, straight, queer, or questioning, rich or poor or middle class, urban or rural, able bodied or differently bodied, from any religion or none, from any nation or many, they will arise; they *are* here. The womanist idea exists to make a place for them, to make the world safe for them, to create an embrace for them, and to nurture them. They are our future, the growth edge of the highest and best of humanity, the babies of LUXOCRACY.

There is a story my father once gave me to read for my high school English honors paper, the subject of which was "Who's Really Insane: The Individual or Society?" The title of the story was "The River of Madness," and it originated in Iran. In the story, a king had been told that all the people in his domain had been growing mad from drinking from a particular river, which supplied water to the kingdom. Fearful of growing mad, yet fearful also of losing his ability to govern the people because, as mad people, they were living in a different reality than he was, he summoned his vizier for advice. The vizier said, "If you don't drink from the river, you will not go mad, and thus you will save your sanity. If, on the other hand, you do drink from the river, you will go mad, but you will join the people and continue to be able to rule." Considering these options, the king and the vizier both drank from the river, only to discover that it causes bliss, that the madness wasn't really madness, and that they no longer desired to rule. This Sufi inspired tale is an allegory about the human search for the intoxication of the Divine and for the power of that divine inspiration to uplift society and human affairs, even rehabilitate our strained relationship with nature and Earth. Submission to our higher energies and the higher energies available in the universe is our true liberation, even from the earthly constraint of the dehumanizing "-isms." What looks like madness in a world that is itself insane may in fact be sanity, and the proverbial madman—or madwoman—may be just the one to lead the whole tribe away from the precipice of self-destruction. If love and peace and interconnectedness and reverence are madness, then let us be mad together; let us collectively ascend into that. If on the other hand, racism, sexism, classism, heterosexism and homophobia, xenophobia, able-ism, ageism, and all of other forms of hatred and diminishment are madness, then let us leave this madness behind and build a new village someplace else. Let us build the village of Luxocracy.

A final word: The womanist idea does not exist to persist, but rather to deliver us to somewhere that it is no longer needed. Today, at this juncture in human history, when our future is uncertain and our past fills us with troubles, the womanist idea is a point of attraction to gather people together who wish to travel together in a common direction. Come who will; those who won't, peace be with you; our oneness is indissoluble, *regardless*. The powers shaping the future are both as great as us and greater than us, and whatever outcome we choose to produce, whether it is to flourish or to perish, will be okay with the Universe. It is this very impartiality that should compel us to choose what *we* want and make *that* future a reality. I close with this quote attributed to the Buddha: "There is only one moment when it is essential to awaken, and that moment is now."

EPILOGUE

....

BEYOND WOMANISM:
THE SOUL OF THE WOMANIST IDEA

....

What is the animating impulse of womanism? What is its organizing principle? What is the metaphysical architecture of the womanist idea, and how does the womanist idea manifest in the world of action? In *The Womanist Idea*, I have attempted to address these foundational dimensions of womanism systematically, allowing scholarly rigor, spiritual inspiration, and personal experience to inform my approach. Diverse bodies of literature—academic as well as nonacademic, exoteric as well as esoteric, as well as personal narrative and memoir—have been brought to bear upon the question of womanism and its place in the history of consciousness.

As I see it, humanity is headed toward a form of social organization based on universal acceptance and expression of innate divinity, the inner light. I name this horizon of human social organization "Luxocracy"—rule by Light. Spiritual activism is a form of social and ecological transformational activity that liberates us toward this end—Luxocratic social organization—by conducting interventions at the point of human consciousness formation, namely, thought and feeling. The logic of womanism is this: when hearts and minds change, the world changes. Stated differently, consciousness change is the sine qua non of social and ecological change. Womanism exists to guide humankind along this path toward Luxocracy through the permeation of the everyday sphere with love, harmony, care, interconnectedness, cosmic inspiration, and Spirit. These are the attributes, the energies that cause human beings to abandon violence, conflict, exploitation, objectification, dehumanization, and materialism in favor of altruism, peace, healing, sustainability, collective self-actualization, and reverence. These are the thoughtforms, mindframes, and inspired states that enable us to become the next, higher version of ourselves—not just individually, but as a human race together.

From my perspective, womanism is a distinct social and ecological change perspective and praxis for three main reasons: First, it takes the "invisible world" as a given, thus enlarging the context in which social, political, economic, and ecological life plays out and redefining the array of actors and agents involved. Second, it rests upon notions of the inviolable sacredness of self, all humanity, and all creation. This notion of sacredness provides a sufficient foundation for existential equality not only among humans but also between human beings and other elements of creation. It conveys the "aliveness" of all that is and invites reverence to undergird the relations of interconnection and even questions of justice. Third, it creatively applies spiritual, mystical, and metaphysical methodologies to the problems or challenges of social and ecological change. Womanists are not afraid of magic, miracles, or "medicine." Indeed, a hallmark of womanist praxis, womanist activism, is the ability to "create a way out of no way" using eclectic, synthetic, and holistic do-it-yourself methods drawn from diverse sources, both "authorized" and "unauthorized." Womanists recognize the fact that inner and outer change must go hand in hand, and they begin by working on themselves and those closest to them. Not to get stuck in solipsism, however, womanists then proceed to apply everything they know and all the energies at their command to global- and cosmic-scale matters.

Womanists think big—bigger than they have historically been given credit for being able to think. Womanism, then, is a space of redemption for the genius of everyday folk, beginning but not ending with women, especially women of color. I have shown womanist genius in action using the published memoirs of five spiritual activist women: Sister Chan Khong of Vietnam/France, Immaculée Ilibagiza of Rwanda, Kiran Bedi of India, Pregs Govender of South Africa, and Wangari Maathai of Kenya. By and large, the women profiled in these case studies self-identify as neither womanist nor feminist, yet the distinctive character of their transformational work informs our understandings of both, particularly womanism. For all of these women, spiritual practice is at the heart of what they do in their social and ecological change work; thus, they model a way of being in the world that many of us can learn from.

Throughout this book, I have alluded to the Shifting of the Ages—a cosmological phenomenon, hotly debated between those who view it as just an fanciful fad created by "out there" astrologers and "those 60s weirdos" and those who view it in all seriousness as a celestial energy pattern identified by the ancients that is far beyond the control of humans and has inevitable consequences of great magnitude for humans and life on Earth. In English, we usually call this Shift the coming of the Age of Aquarius, although it goes by other names in other languages. I'll admit it—I'm a true believer: I feel a phase shift coming, I detect a new pattern of human life in formation, and I see convergence from so many different points—religious, spiritual, astrological, technological, cultural, historical, ecological, celestial, and geophysical. I think we are privileged not only to be alive at this moment of great change but also to be participants in the formation of its character. As inevitable as this shift may be, it is not immune to our influence.

Hence, I think at this moment it is especially critical that we make some decisions about what kind of future we are going to create—not just the future we would like to create, but the one we are actually going to create. The reality is, these are the kinds of decisions we make with our actions more so than our words alone. To what extent are we going to take control of ourselves and liberate ourselves from ourselves, and to what extent are we going to succumb to ourselves by imprisoning ourselves within ourselves? To make sense of these conundrums, to transcend these paradoxes, we must identify and own that there is something within ourselves, within our very composition that can liberate us, at the same time as there is something about us that can and will cause our demise if we don't intervene. We are at that moment of decision. The Universe loves us, but it is also incredibly impartial and impassive.

How does womanism help with this? What contributions does the womanist idea make? It has been my goal in this book to illuminate womanism in a new way, so as to expose womanism's gifts to the world. I would define these gifts as:

1. The identification of a return to sacredness as a way out of current social/ political and ecological change impasses.
2. Recognition of the idea that social and ecological change interventions must incorporate both inner and outer dimensions to actually produce the desired results. Self-change and social–ecological change go hand-in-hand.
3. A family-oriented type of communalism that works through a kind of loving informality and spontaneous cooperation rather than warlike ideological formations and "progressive" resistance per se. The womanist "family" form easily harmonizes and coordinates difference while at the same time nurturing and protecting it, and it enlarges itself through attracting people with the energy of love and care rather than through the force of ideological commitment.
4. Womanists don't wait for things to change, they just change them. The do-it-yourself spirit, the sense of initiative and self-authority, a trust in one's own social–ecological change ingenuity, are conveyed upon the womanist idea. There is no need to "fight authority" when we can just be our own authority and get started on whatever plan we envision.
5. Womanist politics of invitation mean actively creating the world we wish to live in and inviting others to join. It is a kind of "build it and they will

come" paradigm that works by the force of attraction, creating new structures of life that express love, human dignity, self-actualization, liberation, peace, and vitality, and that ultimately supplant the violent, exploitative, dehumanizing, and environmentally destructive old ones.

6. Spiritual discourses (whether orthodox, indigenous, or "New Age") give us the tools to "power up" our social and ecological change activity, particularly if we apply these tools to collective and not just individual change.

7. All forms of spirituality have something to offer, and womanists creatively combine them in ways that "feel right" and prove effective. The universal/ cosmic/Divine Source insures the integrity of this process.

8. Spiritual activism is a distinct form of social–ecological movement praxis that involves the application of mystical, metaphysical, spiritual, or religious tools to social, political, economic, or environmental–ecological problems. These tools are energy-moving mechanisms that operate on a different dimension than materialistic social and ecological change strategies.

9. Human beings are energy transforming machines, that is, we are capable of transmuting any quality of energy into any other quality of energy—and to claim and refine this power is the "next level" of social–ecological change praxis. By transforming the energies that create violence, oppression, ecological destruction, and the "isms," we get rid of them by removing their energetic substrate. There are ways to learn how to do this more consciously and effectively.

10. The best site to make change, to transform energy, and conduct interventions is the site called "everyday life," because everyday life is the most basic locale where consciousness is produced, reinforced, and reified.

11. "Everyday people" are geniuses at making change and we are all everyday people. While this may sound like a paradox, deeper reflection proves that it is not.

12. The most basic social–ecological tool for transformation is LOVE. Love is a particular energy vibration that resonates at the level of our highest and best selves and society. More than just a feeling, it is a technology of change.

13. Women of African descent named, defined, and refined womanism, but now it is a gift to all humanity. The soul of womanism is universal, cosmic, and Divine.

Having offered this understanding of the womanist idea, this account of its deep architecture, as well as its far-reaching potential, I now invite others to contribute to the conversation. In honor of my mother, who bore me and raised me—the original womanist prototype in my life, mother of five, civil rights activist, peace activist, philosopher, and artist—I end by presenting one of her favorite quotes, which she repeated frequently while I was growing up and continued to repeat even after I was grown, with her favorite section emphasized:

> He finds that the question is not whether man returns to religion and believes in God but whether he *lives love and thinks truth*. If he does so the symbol systems he uses are of secondary importance. If he does not they are of no importance.—Erich Fromm[1]

Thank you, Mom, for making it plain and keeping my vision broad.

NOTES

CHAPTER 1

An earlier version of this essay appeared on www.radicalscholar.com on December 31, 2006. See http://www.radicalscholar.com/articles/publish/editorial/Luxocracy_Rule_By_Light.shtml.

1. Ayi Kwei Armah, from a lecture titled "Awakening," accessed October 25, 2010. www.youtube.com/watch?v=6irUySQK5jI.
2. The term *lifesystem* was coined by Baruti KMT, personal communication, March 2004.
3. The Pew Forum on Religion and Public Life, "U.S. Religious Landscape Survey," accessed July 8, 2009, http://religions.pewforum.org/reports.
4. I am reminded of a quote by thirteenth century Japanese Zen Master Dogen, who stated, "Gaining enlightenment is like the moon reflected on the water. The moon doesn't get wet; the water isn't broken. Although its light is broad and great, the moon is reflected even in a puddle an inch wide. The whole moon and the whole sky are reflected in one dew-drop on the grass." July 2 entry, *Wisdom of the East 2009 Calendar* (Riverside, NJ: Andrews McMeel, 2008).
5. Decimus Iunius Iuvenalis, known in English as Juvenal, accessed July 8, 2009, http://en.wikipedia.org/wiki/Juvenal.
6. Bahá'u'lláh, *Gleanings from the Writings of Baha'u'llah* (Wilmette, IL: Baha'i Publishing Trust, 1990), 259–60. This passage was written in the 1800s and the word *man* means *human* here; the word *mankind* here means *humanity*.
7. See Paulo Freire, *Pedagogy of the Oppressed* (New York: Continuum, 1971).
8. See John White, interview, *What Is Enlightenment?* magazine (Spring/Summer 2001), www.wie.org/j19/white.asp. See also Edward Bruce Bynum, *The African Unconscious: Roots of Ancient Mysticism and Modern Psychology* (New York: Teacher's College Press, 1999).
9. See Thich Nhat Hanh, *Interbeing: Fourteen Guidelines for Engaged Buddhism* Berkeley, CA: Parallax Press, 1987), for a fuller discussion of the concept of interbeing.
10. Akasha Gloria Hull, *Soul Talk: The New Spirituality of African American Women* (Rochester, VT: Inner Traditions, 2001); Beverly Guy-Sheftall, ed., *Words of Fire: An Anthology of African American Feminist Thought* (New York: New Press, 1995); M. Jacqui Alexander, *Pedagogies of Crossing: Meditations on Feminism, Sexual Politics, Memory, and the Sacred* (Durham, NC: Duke University Press, 2005).
11. *Livingkind* is a term coined by Taliba Sikudhani Olugbala. See Layli Phillips, ed. *The Womanist Reader* (New York: Routledge, 2006), xxvi.

12. For an overview of these terminologies and their variations, see Gregg Braden et al., *The Mystery of 2012: Predictions, Prophesies, and Possibilities* (Boulder, CO: Sounds True, 2007).

13. The term *noosphere*, which means "the sphere of human thought" (compare with atmosphere or biosphere) was coined by Vladimir Vernadsky and developed further by Pierre Teilhard de Chardin. The idea that the noosphere is in the process of formation at this time has been discussed by authors such as José Aguelles, John White, and others. For a historical overview of this idea, see, accessed July 8, 2009, http://en.wikipedia.org/wiki/Noosphere.

14. John S. Mbiti., *African Religions and Philosophy* (London: Heinemann, 1969). See also Peter J. Paris, *The Spirituality of African Peoples: The Search for a Common Moral Discourse* (Minneapolis, MN: Fortress Press, 1995).

15. I am indebted to Patricia Hill Collins for the "ethics of care" terminology, as outlined in her book *Black Feminist Thought* (1991; repr., New York: Routledge, 2001). I am indebted to Abraham Maslow for the wording of "self-actualization," as introduced in his book, *Toward a Psychology of Being,* 2nd ed. (New York: Van Nostrand, 1968). In this text, I extend both of these terminologies beyond their original meanings by placing them in dynamic synthesis.

16. Faye V. Harrison, "Introduction: Expanding the Discourse on 'Race'," *American Anthropologist* 100, no. 1 (1997), 609–31.

17. Asa G. Hilliard III, *SBA: The Reawakening of the African Mind* (Gainesville, FL: Makare, 1997).

18. Gloria E. Anzaldúa , *Interviews/Entrevistas*, ed.Ana Louise Keating (New York: Routledge, 2000).

19. Barbara A. Holmes, *Race and the Cosmos: An Invitation to View the World Differently* (Harrisburg, PA: Trinity Press International, 2002).

20. "Svalbard Global Seed Vault," n.d., accessed June 6, 2008, http://en.wikipedia.org/wiki/Svalbard_Global_Seed_Vault.

21. Chela Sandoval, *Methodology of the Oppressed* (Minneapolis: University of Minnesota Press, 2000).

CHAPTER 2

A much earlier version of this paper was presented at the Black Feminisms conference hosted by The Graduate Center of the City University of New York, March 12, 2004.

1. Alice Walker, "Coming Apart," in *Take Back the Night,* ed. Laura Lederer (New York: Bantam, 1979), 84–93. See also Walker, *In Search of Our Mothers' Gardens: Womanist Prose* (San Diego, CA: Harcourt Brace Jovanovich, 1983), which contains both Walker's essay "Gifts of Power: The Writings of Rebecca Jackson," originally published in 1981 in *The Black Scholar,* and her famous dictionary style definition of *womanist.*

2. Chikwenye Okonjo Ogunyemi, "Womanism: The Dynamics of the Contemporary Black Female Novel in English," *Signs: Journal of Women in Culture and Society* 11 (1985), 63–80. See also Ogunyemi's monograph, *Africa Wo/Man Palava: The Nigerian Novel*

by Women (Chicago: University of Chicago Press, 1996). Ogunyemi is interviewed by Susan Arndt in "African Gender Trouble and African Womanism: An Interview with Chikwenye Ogunyemi and Wanjira Muthoni," *Signs: Journal of Women in Culture and Society* 25, no. 3 (2000), 709–26; the original interview took place in 1997.

3. Clenora Hudson-Weems, *Africana Womanism: Reclaiming Ourselves* (Troy, MI: Bedford, 1993).

4. For a discussion of this progression, see Melanie L. Harris, "Third Wave Womanism: Expanding Womanist Discourse, Making Room for Our Children," in *Gifts of Virtue, Alice Walker, and Womanist Ethics* (New York: Palgrave Macmillan, 2010), 125–38. See also Monica A. Coleman, ed., *Third Wave Womanist Religious Thought* (Minneapolis, MN: Fortress Press, 2012. See also the theology articles in Phillips, *The Womanist Reader* (New York: Routledge, 2006).

5. Phillips, *Womanist Reader*. This volume inadvertently omitted womanist articles in the fields of ecology and disability studies that had been published between 1979 and 2004. The book did not address womanism in pop culture.

6. Alice Walker, "Coming Apart," in *Womanist Reader,* ed. Layli Phillips (New York: Routledge, 2006), 3–11: all quotations from this story that appear in this chapter come from that edition (emphasis in original).

7. Alice Walker, "Gifts of Power," in *The Womanist Reader*, ed. Layli Phillips (New York: Routledge, 2006), 12–18 (emphasis in original).

8. Gloria Wekker, "Mati-ism and Black Lesbianism: Two Idealtypical Expressions of Female Homosexuality in Black Communities of the Diaspora," *Journal of Homosexuality* 24, no. 3/4 (1993):

9. Alice Walker, Preface to *In Search of Our Mothers' Gardens*, in *The Womanist Reader*, ed. Layli Phillips (New York: Routledge, 2006), 19: all quotations from this definition that appear in this chapter come from this source (emphasis in original).

10. This is why we find a variety of people of different political stripes saying, from the 1980s onward, "I'm a womanist but not a feminist."

11. Melanie L. Harris, "'A Womanist Story': Alice Walker's Moral Biography," in *Gifts of Virtue, Alice Walker, and Womanist Ethics* (New York: Palgrave Macmillan, 2010), 15–48.

12. Ogunyemi, "Womanism," in *The Womanist Reader,* ed. Layli Phillips (*Signs,*1985; repr., New York: Routledge, 2006), 21–36 (emphasis is in the original, except where noted).

13. See Susan Arndt, "African Gender Trouble and African Womanism: An Interview with Chikwenye Ogunyemi and Wanjira Muthoni," *Signs: Journal of Women in Culture and Society* 25 (2000), 709–26; the original interview took place in 1997.

14. Molara Ogundipe-Leslie, "Stiwanism: Feminism in an African Context," in *Re-creating Ourselves: African Women and Critical Transformations* (Trenton, NJ: Africa World Press, 1994).

15. Catherine Acholonu, *Motherism: The Afrocentric Alternative to Feminism* (Owerri, Nigeria: Afa, 1995).

16. Mary E. Modupe Kolawole, *Womanism and African Gender Consciousness* (Trenton, NJ: Africa World Press, 1997).

17. For an overview of these perspectives, see Chidi Maduka, "Feminism, Womanism, and Motherism in African Literary Discourse," n.d., accessed December 29, 2010, www.uni-leipzig.de/~ecas2009/index.php?option=com_docman&task=doc_down load&gid=1568&Itemid=24 motherism.

NOTES

18. Chikwenye Okonjo Ogunyemi, *Africa Wo/Man Palava: The Nigerian Novel by Women* (Chicago: University of Chicago Press, 1996). See especially the first section, "Kwenu: A Vernacular Theory," 17–127.

19. In a similar vein, Diedre L. Badejo presents an in-depth treatment of the Orisa Osun in her very fine text, *Osun Seegesi: The Elegant Deity of Wealth, Power and Femininity* (Trenton, NJ: Africa World Press, 1996), in which she references womanism occasionally. This book should be read as supporting, if not elaborating, Ogunyemi's case for Osun's centrality to the womanist idea.

20. Clenora Hudson-Weems's article, "Cultural and Agenda Conflicts in Academia: Critical Issues for Africana Women's Studies," in *The Womanist Reader*, ed. Layli Phillips (New York: Routledge, 2006), 21–36 (emphasis in original, except where noted).

21. It is interesting to note that, in an afterword to her 1993 book, Hudson-Weems encourages white women to identify with their specific ethnicities (e.g., Italian, German, French, and develop womanisms of their own). In so doing, she makes a clear case that womanism is for everybody and that the recovery of cultural heritage and cultural wisdom is central to the womanist enterprise.

22. See, for example, Angela Y. Davis's treatment of this topic in *Women, Race and Class* (New York: Vintage), 1981.

23. See for example, the collection of articles addressing this topic in Kum-Kum Bhavnani, ed., *Feminism and "Race"* (Oxford: Oxford University Press, 2001).

24. Looking deeply at this argument, I might take a different tack, namely that certain Black women do not view sexism as less important (i.e., "affecting only half the race"), but rather read certain kinds of relationships, situations, and events as "not sexist" that others (e.g., white or even Black feminists) would read as "sexist." This thought occurred to me after a lengthy thesis defense on the topic of African American Sunni Muslimahs (see Lisa Renae Frazier, *Power and Surrender: African American Sunni Women and Embodied Agency*, Atlanta, Georgia: The Digital Archive at Georgia State University, Women's Studies Theses No. 15, 2009), many of whom seemingly argued for the egalitarian and liberatory nature of such things as polygamy and strict gender roles on a particular kind of ontological basis that holds gender as an inalterable category of ultimate reality (which overlays material/historical reality). This relates to West African diunitalism and diarchy, as well as some other metaphysical discussions that are beyond the scope of this chapter.

25. These two terms, *Afrocentric* and *Africentric*, reference two distinct intellectual strands within the Africana studies discipline. A discussion of their nuances is beyond the scope of this chapter; however, their distinctions relate more to who has participated in their articulations and where these articulations have taken place than to major conceptual or philosophical differences. Both are African centered and Black nationalist in flavor, with varying degrees of support for Black separatism or at least self-sufficiency. Collectively, they differ also from what might be called an African perspective, based on perspectives generated by people born and raised on the African continent. Within African studies, there are also three distinct strands, more or less characterized as the white Africanists, the Black Africanists, and the postcolonialists. A fourth, connecting, and sometimes marginalized group is the Egyptologists (which also have a Black and a non-Black strand, the latter often referring to ancient Egypt as KMT), which is more or less a global intellectual community that is not confined to academia. Another such community is the Pan-Africanists, who also interweave throughout all of the above-mentioned groups. While this note *grossly* oversimplifies the "African related" field of knowledge, I present

it to facilitate the most nascent awareness for those who are unfamiliar with one of the many important realms in which womanists circulate, gathering important information and inspiration which is then applied to both gender and humanitarian concerns.

26. A *partial* list of people I would include in this ancestral history of the womanist idea are: Maria W. Stewart (orator), Harriet Tubman (freedom fighter), Sojourner Truth (orator and suffragist), Frances E. W. Harper (poet), Milla Granson (educator), Harriet Powers (quilter), Rebecca Cox Jackson (Shaker eldress), Callie House (reparations activist), Maggie Lena Walker (banker and community leader), Anna Julia Cooper (educator), Claudia Jones (socialist activist), Ida B. Wells (journalist and antilynching activist), Madame Tinubu (businesswoman), Funmilayo Ransome-Kuti (educator and political leader), Mary McLeod Bethune (educator), Elizabeth Ross Haynes (social worker), Zora Neale Hurston (anthropologist and writer), Julia Constancia Burgos Garcia (poet), Fannie Lou Hamer (voting rights activist), Johnnie Tillmon (welfare rights activist), and Shirley Chisholm (U.S. representative and presidential candidate). This list would also include some men, such as Frederick Douglass (abolitionist), Martin Delaney (abolitionist), and W. E. B. DuBois (sociologist and educator).

27. See Carlos Castaneda, *The Active Side of Infinity* (New York: HarperCollins, 1998). I learned about the "foreign installation" from one of my spiritual teachers, Baba Charles Finch III, MD, who is an expert on Castaneda's work and includes it in his Complementary and Alternative Medicine course, which I sat in on at Morehouse School of Medicine during Spring 2007.

CHAPTER 3

1. Dictionary definitions of the term *worldview*, translated from the German *Weltanschauung*, accessed May 27, 2008, http://www.answers.com/worldview&r=67.

2. Linda James Myers, *Understanding an Afrocentric Worldview: Introduction to Optimal Psychology* (Dubuque, IA: Kendall/Hunt (1988, reprinted 1993). See also, Linda James Myers, "Expanding the Psychology of Knowledge Optimally: The Importance of Worldview Revisited," in *Black Psychology*, 3rd ed., ed. Reginald L. Jones (Oakland, CA: Cobb & Henry, 1991), 15–32.

3. La *facultad* and *conocimientos* are terms used by Gloria Anzaldúa, see *Interviews/Entrevistas*, ed., AnaLouise Keating (New York: Routledge, 2000), 122–24, 177–78, respectively.

4. This focus on essence is not the same as philosophical essentialism because spirit in the womanist sense is dynamic rather than static (as would be noumena in philosophical essentialism or pure rationalism). At the same time, this womanist essentialism challenges but does not completely contradict social constructionism, insofar as the dynamism of spirit is constantly in a constructive process that is not completely determined by or reducible to human activity.

5. See David Bohm, *Wholeness and the Implicate Order* (New York: Routledge, 1996).

6. Barbara A. Holmes, *Race and the Cosmos: An Invitation to View the World Differently* (Harrisburg, PA: Trinity Press International, 2002), 147–48.

7. This language follows Charles S. Finch III's interpretive discussion of Carlos Castenada's work, "Journey to Infinity: The Magic of Humanness" (unpublished lecture, January 17, 2007). Finch writes on African and comparative cosmology in such books as *Echoes*

of the Old Darkland: Themes from the African Eden (Decatur, GA: Khenti, 1991) and *Star of Deep Beginnings: The Genesis of African Science and Technology* (Decatur, GA: Khenti, 1998). An introduction to Castaneda's work on Yaqui cosmology can be found in his book *The Teachings of Don Juan: A Yaqui Way of Knowledge* (New York: Ballantine Books, 1968; repr. Berkeley: University of California Press, 1998); however, see *The Active Side of Infinity* (New York: HarperPerennial, 1998) for a deeper exploration of his concept of Infinity.

8. Melanie L. Harris, "Womanist Humanism: A New Hermeneutic," in *Deeper Shades of Purple: Womanism in Religion and Society*, ed. Stacey M. Floyd-Thomas (New York: New York University Press, 2006), 211–25.

9. In this chapter, and in this book as a whole, I distinguish between "self," which is our everyday, mundane self, and "Self," which references our Higher Self. The two are related, intertwined, and, in many respects, the same entity; however, I use "Self" for emphasis when I wish to remind readers that I am generally speaking to the cultivation of the Higher Self; that is, the self that aligns with Innate Divinity, through the vehicle of the everyday self. When I use the word self, I may be incorporating meanings in which both "self" and "Self" are merged, so the reader must simply rely on contextual clues and the general intent of this book. A full discussion of the Self/self distinction is beyond the scope of this book. However, in general, I capitalize words when I am intending to emphasize the Divine significance of something (e.g., Spirit vs. spirit, Light vs. light, etc.)

10. See Jeff Schmidt's *Disciplined Minds: A Critical Look at Salaried Professionals and the Soul-Battering System that Shapes Their Lives* (Lanham, MD: Rowman & Littlefield, 2000) for a provocative treatment of this topic.

11. See, for instance, Keating, *Interviews/Entrevistas*, or Akasha Gloria Hull's *Soul Talk*, or even the case of Rebecca Jackson in Alice Walker's essay "Gifts of Power: The Writings of Rebecca Jackson," *The Black Scholar*, 1981, 64–67; see also chap. 5, this volume.

12. See Chela Sandoval's discussion of revolutionary love in *Methodology of the Oppressed* (Minneapolis: University of Minnesota Press, 2000).

13. See, for instance, Luisah Teish's classic discussions of Afro-diasporic traditional spiritual magic in *Jambalaya: The Natural Woman's Book of Personal Charms and Practical Rituals* (New York: HarperCollins, 1985); and M. Jacqui Alexander's more recent meditations on Yoruba/Ifa priesthood in *Pedagogies of Crossing: Meditations on Feminism, Sexual Politics, Memory, and the Sacred* (Durham, NC: Duke University Press, 2005). Although both writers identify themselves as Black feminists rather than womanists, their commentaries on spirituality exemplify womanist sensibilities.

14. See, for example, Alice Walker's various writings on Buddhism as well as her ethnogenic experiments. I would also place works by Gloria Anzaldúa, such as *Borderlands/La Frontera: The New Mestiza* (San Francisco: Aunt Lute, 1986), *Interviews/Entrevistas*, as well as her essay, "now let us shift ... the path of conocimiento ... inner work, public acts," in *This Bridge We Call Home: Radical Visions for Transformation*, ed. Gloria Anzaldúa and AnaLouise Keating (New York: Routledge, 2002), in this category.

15. See, for instance, novels such as Gloria Naylor's *Mama Day* (Boston: Ticknor & Fields, 1988), Amy Tan's *The Kitchen God's Wife* (New York: G. P. Putnam's Sons, 1991), and *The Bonesetter's Daughter* (New York: Putnam Adult, 2001). Julie Dash's film *Daughters of the Dust* (New York: Kino International, 1991), DVD.1991) and Julia Kwan's film *Eve and the Fire Horse* ((Toronto, Canada: Red Storm Productions, 2005), DVD, 2005) could also be included in this category.

16. See, for instance, texts as diverse as Barbara A. Holmes's academic *Race and the Cosmos: An Invitation to View the World Differently* (Norcross, GA: Trinity Press, 2002); Akasha Gloria Hull's interview study, *Soul Talk: The New Spirituality of African American Women* (Rochester, VT: Inner Traditions, 2001); Pregs Govender's political memoir *Love and Courage: A Story of Insubordination* (Johannesburg, SA: Jacana Media, 2008); Diane Kennedy Pike's spiritual memoir *My Journey into Self* (Binghamton, NY: LP Publications, 1979); and Immaculée Ilibagiza's popular nonfiction memoir, *Left to Tell: Discovering God Amidst the Rwandan Holocaust* (Carlsbad, CA: Hay House, 2006).

17. The old name for the Book of Humanity is the Book of Man, which means knowledge of the world through knowledge of self, based on the Hermetic principle. The new name, Book of Humanity, is designed to be gender-neutral or gender-encompassing. This term was presented to me by one of my spiritual teachers, Will Coleman, PhD. Both of these terms refer to metaphysical principles and are not actual books per se.

18. The Book of Nature is a contrastive to the Book of Humanity. Like the Book of Humanity, the Book of Nature is a metaphysical principle and not an actual book per se. From a Hermetic perspective, the assumption is that "As within" corresponds with the Book of Humanity and "So without" corresponds with the Book of Nature. The other part of this principle is vertical rather than horizontal: "So below" also corresponds with the Book of Humanity, while "As above" corresponds with the Divine (Invisible) Realm. This is one meaning of the cross: "As above, so below"—vertical dimension; "As within, so without"—horizontal dimension. The human being is at the point of intersection.

19. The concept of Ntuology (Ntu means "spirit of God") was developed by Edwin J. Nichols in, "The Philosophical Aspects of Cultural Differences" (paper presented at the World Psychiatric Association conference, Ibadan, Nigeria, November 10, 1976). It was subsequently cited by a number of Afrocentric psychologists, most notably Linda James Myers, *Understanding an Afrocentric Worldview* (Dubuque, IA: Kendall/Hunt, 1993. See also n. 65 in the following anonymous document, accessed December 26, 2010, http://rvh. socialwork.dal.ca/07%20Project%20Resources/Theoretical%20Context/endnotes. htm. Finally, see also, Ferdinand Mutaawe Kasozi, *Introduction to an African Philosophy: The Ntu'ology of the Baganda* (Freiburg, Germany: Verlag Karl Alber, 2011).

20. See Linda James Myers's article, "Expanding the Psychology of Knowledge Optimally: The Importance of World View Revisited," in *Black Psychology*, 3rd ed., ed. Reginald L. Jones (Oakland, CA: Cobb & Henry, 1991), 19.

21. With my coauthor Marla R. Stewart, I have written briefly on this topic in "'I Am Just So Glad You Are Alive': New Perspectives on Non-traditional, Non-Conforming, and Transgressive Expressions of Gender, Sexuality, and Race among African Americans," *Journal of African American Studies*, 12, no. 4 (2008): 378–400.

22. Patricia Hill Collins, *Black Feminist Thought: Knowledge, Consciousness, and the Politics of Empowerment* (New York: Routledge, 2001), 265.

23. Ibid.

24. See Ignacio Martín-Baró, *Writings for a Liberation Psychology* (Cambridge, MA: Harvard University Press, 1994).

25. Buddhist nun Pema Chodrön does a good job of explaining *metta* and *bodhicitta* in her book *When Things Fall Apart: Heart Advice for Difficult Times* (Boston: Shambhala, 1997). Alice Walker discusses *metta* at length in her book *We Are the Ones We Have Been Waiting For: Light in a Time of Darkness: Meditations* (New York: New Press, 2006).

26. It should be noted that numerous authors have speculated that the species Homo sapiens is currently rapidly evolving into a new species. This new species, variously labeled Homo illuminatus or Homo noeticus (see chapter 1), is presumed to be characterized by a higher level of consciousness or a higher vibrational rate, the normalization of abilities that are currently considered superhuman, paranormal, or psychic, as well as ascension into a peaceful and highly advanced form of social organization in which the oneness of humanity is universally recognized or the species is able to function as a unified organism.

27. For a different perspective, see Ceanne DeRohan, *Right Use of Will* (LaGrange, GA: Four Winds, 1986). This author presents a channeled alternate cosmology about the human race, namely, that the current human race is a type of hybrid. Yet another interesting perspective is presented in Jane Roberts's channeled Seth series, which is mentioned by Anzaldúa in Keating, *Interviews/Entrevistas*. Sample texts include *The Seth Material* (Cutchogue, NY: Buccaneer Books, 1970) and *Seth Speaks: The Eternal Validity of the Soul* (San Rafael, CA: Amber-Allen, 1994). Seth articulates a perspective that human beings are "entities" comprised of multiple versions of self coexisting relatively simultaneously in parallel universes.

28. Taliba Olugbala also goes by the name Jonelle Renée Shields.

29. Sandoval, *Methodology of the Oppressed*.

30. See my introduction, "Womanism: On Its Own," *The Womanist Reader*, ed. Layli Phillips (New York: Routledge, 2006), xxv.

31. Walker, *In Search of Our Mothers' Gardens: Womanist Prose* (San Diego, CA: Harcourt Brace Jovanovich, 1983), xi.

32. This refers to a term coined by quantum physicist John Hagelin to refer to the common substrate of the cosmos. See his book *Manual for a Perfect Government* (Fairfield, IA: Maharishi University of Management Press, 1998) for an accessible discussion of this theory.

33. Regarding nature-based recreation, see Audrey Peterman and Frank Peterman, *Legacy on the Land: A Black Couple Discovers Our National Inheritance and Tells Why Every American Should Care* (Atlanta, GA: Earthwise Productions, 2009).

34. It is beyond the scope of this chapter to address the semantic issues surrounding the term nature. I acknowledge that the term nature has historically implied a dichotomous split between humans and the environment; however, I reject this connotation in favor of the view that humans and nature exist in diunital relation. That is, they are conceptually separable but functionally integrated and coextensive.

35. Collins, *Black Feminist Thought*, 262–65.

36. Chikwenye Okonjo Ogunyemi, *Africa Wo/Man Palava: The Nigerian Novel by Women* (Chicago: University of Chicago Press, 1996), 45–61.

37. See Peter Tompkins and Christopher Bird, *The Secret Life of Plants* (New York: Harper & Row, 1973) for an unparalleled, in-depth treatment of this topic from the perspective of flora. There is also a related film by the same name, directed by Walon Green (1979). See also Robert A. Voeks, *Sacred Leaves of Candomblé: African Magic, Medicine, and Religion in Brazil* (Austin: University of Texas Press, 1997).

38. See, for example, Thich Nhat Hanh's "Five Mindfulness Trainings," http://www.plumvillage.org, that extend rights of existence and protection to the mineral world and treats minerals as beings along with humans, animals, and plants.

39. bell hooks, "Simple Living: An Antidote to Hedonistic Materialism," in *Black Genius: African American Solutions to African American Problems,* ed. Walter Mosley, Manthia Diawara, Clyde Taylor, and Regina Austin (New York: Norton, 1999), 124–44.

40. This is Wayne Dyer's paraphrase of Patanjali that appears in his book *The Power of Intention* (Carlsbad, CA: Hay House, 2004). See also *The Yoga Sutras of Patanjali: The Book of the Spiritual Man,* trans. Charles Johnston, (New York: The Quarterly Book Department,1912) or *The Yoga Sutras of Patanjali,* trans. Alistair Shearer (New York: Bell Tower/Sacred Teachings, 1982).

41. See Ayi Kwei Armah, *KMT: In the House of Life—An Epistemic Novel* (Popenguine, Senegal: Per Ankh, 2002) for a treatment of this topic. See also George G. M. James, *Stolen Legacy* (San Francisco: Julian Richardson Associates, 1988).

42. Sometimes referred to as the Akashic Records. For an overview, see "Akashic Records," *Wikipedia,* accessed December 26, 2010, http://en.wikipedia.org/wiki/Akashic_records.

43. Monica A. Coleman, *Making a Way Out of No Way: A Womanist Theology* (Minneapolis: Fortress Press, 2008), 101.

44. Chela Sandoval, *Methodology of the Oppressed,* 139–57.

45. Audre Lorde, "Uses of the Erotic: The Erotic as Power," in Sister Outsider: Essays and Speeches (Berkeley, CA: Crossing Press, 1984).

CHAPTER 4

1. This quote is a signature quote of an organization called The Intenders of the Highest Good, cofounded by Tony Burroughs and Tina Stober, which emphasizes the role of inspiration and visualization in making change, see accessed April 26, 2007, www.intenders.org.

2. See Kelly Brown Douglas, "Twenty Years a Womanist," in *Deeper Shades of Purple: Womanism in Religion and Society,* ed. Stacey M. Floyd-Thomas (New York: New York University Press, 2006), 153.

3. Layli Phillips, "Womanism: On Its Own," in *The Womanist Reader,* ed. Layli Phillips (New York: Routledge, 2006), xxix–xxx.

4. See Norman W. Walker, *The Natural Way to Vibrant Health* (Prescott, AZ: Norwalk Press, 1972), 2.

5. See Norman W. Walker, *Become Younger* (1949; repr., Prescott, AZ: Norwalk Press, 1995), 3.

6. I am reminded of a frequent saying by the late Dr. Asa G. Hilliard III, "If you go with the rhythm of life, you're at ease; if you go against the rhythm of life, you're at dis-ease, thereby creating disease." Personal communication, February 2006.

7. One book that elaborates on such a perspective is Donna Eden, *Energy Medicine* (New York: Jeremy P. Tarcher/Putnam, 1998). Another is Carolyn Myss, *Anatomy of the Spirit: The Seven Stages of Power and Healing* (New York: Crown, 1996).

8. See Linda James Myers, "Expanding the Psychology of Knowledge Optimally: The Importance of World View Revisited," in *Black Psychology,* 3rd ed. Reginald L. Jones (Oakland, CA: Cobb & Henry, 1991), 19. See also Linda James Myers, *Understanding an Afrocentric World View: Introduction to Optimal Psychology* (Dubuque, IA: Kendall/Hunt, 1988), 48.

9. Hermes Mercurius Trismegistus, *Divine Pymander* (1871; repr., Yogi Publication Society, n.d.), 21.
10. As mentioned previously, throughout *The Womanist Idea*, the term *Self* is generally used to indicate this "higher octave" aspect of the person, while *self* is generally used to indicate our more mundane aspect. However, Self and self overlap to such an extent that the distinction is sometimes hard to make.
11. Phillips, *The Womanist Reader*, xxviii.
12. And, ultimately, life in the higher realms, presumed to be human destiny. Cf. the discussion of *homo illuminatus* and *homo noeticus* in chap. 1; however, also note that, metaphysically, this discussion extends beyond the consideration of life on Earth to encompass life after death and states of incarnation "higher" than the kind that is typical on Earth.
13. There is a related concept in Vedic science, as evidenced by statements such as this one by Vincent J. Daczynski, author of *Paranormal Phenomenon: Amazing Human Abilities* (self-published e-Book, 2004): "The Universe is not material after all. It is a projection of consciousness. Siddhi powers are gained by bringing one's awareness to causation, where the mind is most powerful and where the laws of nature reside. One can then create extraordinary outcomes in the projected so-called 'material world.' A God-realized yogi's mind is expanded whereby his awareness is always established at the source of causation. For such a yogi all the laws of nature reside within his conscious mind. He is one with nature. All of nature is his nature. Therefore, he always has the laws of nature at his command," accessed June 2, 2008, http://www.amazingabilities.com/amaze4a.html. For information on the siddhi powers, see http://en.wikipedia.org/wiki/Siddhi. Daczynski continues, "Quantum mechanics, an aspect of modern physics, identifies a field of life called the unified field, or ground state, which is the fundamental nonchanging field of life. It is eternal, unbounded, beyond space and time, wherein are contained all possibilities. It is the unmanifested field of pure potentiality from where all force and matter fields emerge. If you have this you have everything," accessed June 2, 2008, http://www.amazingabilities.com/amaze8a.html. Through spiritual activities, womanists seek to align with this field of creative possibility (by whatever name it may be called) and use it for both self-development and positive social change.
14. Phillips, *Womanist Reader*, xxvii. See also, Sandoval, *Methodology of the Oppressed*, 6.
15. These phrasings come from Alice Walker's definition of "womanist" in the preface of *In Search of Our Mothers' Gardens: Womanist Prose* (San Diego, CA: Harcourt Brace Jovanovich, 1983), xi–xii, see Phillips, *Womanist Reader*, 19.
16. For an overview of intersectionality that includes many of the foundational authors, see Michelle Tracy Berger and Kathleen Guidroz, ed., *The Intersectional Approach: Transforming the Academy through Race, Class, and Gender* (Durham: University of North Carolina Press, 2009). For some older texts that were particularly influential on my thinking, see Beverly Guy-Sheftall, ed., *Words of Fire: An Anthology of African American Feminist Thought* (New York: New Press, 1995); Beverly Smith, ed., *Home Girls: A Black Feminist Anthology* (New York: Kitchen Table: Women of Color Press, 1982); Gloria T. Hull, Patricia Bell Scott, and Barbara Smith, ed., *All the Women Are White, All the Blacks Are Men, But Some of Us Are Brave: Black Women's Studies* (New York: Feminist Press, 1981); Cherríe Moraga and Gloria Anzaldúa, ed., *This Bridge Called My Back: Writings by Radical Women of Color* (New York: Kitchen Table: Women of Color Press, 1981). See also Gloria Anzaldúa and AnaLouise Keating, ed., *This Bridge We Call Home: Radical Visions for Transformation* (New York: Routledge, 2002).

17. Anzaldúa and Keating, *This Bridge We Call Home,* xxvii.
18. Paramhansa Yogananda discusses this in *Autobiography of Yogi* (Philosophical Library, 1946–2005; repr., Nevada City, CA: Crystal Clarity).
19. Jacob H. Carruthers, *MDW NTR: Divine Speech, A Historiographical Reflection on African Deep Thought from the Time of the Pharaohs to the Present* (London: Karnak House, 1995).
20. Ronnie Hartfield, "Nommo," in *The Encyclopedia of Chicago,* accessed September 20, 2010, http://www.encyclopedia.chicagohistory.org/pages/894.html. Akasha Gloria Hull, *Soul Talk: The New Spirituality of African American Women* (Rochester, VT: Inner Traditions, 2001), writes that *Nommo* is "the power of the word and the receiving ear" (126). For more on *Nommo,* see the chapter on Wangari Maathai (this volume).
21. Clenora Hudson-Weems discusses the concept of *Nommo* as self-naming extensively in her book, *Africana Womanism: Reclaiming Ourselves* (New York: Bedford, 1993).
22. This was taught to me by my Kabbalah teacher, Will Coleman, PhD, during a Spring 2006 community course on Kabbalah and the Tree of Life.
23. John Hagelin, *Manual for a Perfect Government* (Fairfield, IA: Maharishi School of Management Press, 1998), 40–70.
24. For example, see U. S. Andersen, *Three Magic Words* (Chatsworth, CA: Wilshire Book Company, 1977).
25. Thich Nhat Hanh, "Five Mindfulness Trainings Certificate," n.d., http://www.plumvillage.org. But see also Thich Nhat Hanh, *Interbeing: Fourteen Guidelines for Engaged Buddhism* (Berkeley, CA: Parallax, 1987).
26. See Kola Abimbola, *Yoruba Culture: A Philosophical Account* (Birmingham, UK: Iroko Academic Publishers, 2006); Wande Abimbola, *Ifa Will Mend Our Broken World: Thoughts on Yoruba Religion and Culture in Africa and the Diaspora* (Roxbury, MA: Aim Books, 1997); Jacob H. Carruthers, *MDW NTR: Divine Speech, A Historiographical Reflection on African Deep Thought from the Time of the Pharaohs to the Present* (London: Karnak House, 1995); E. Bolaji Idowu, *Olodumare: God in Yoruba Belief* (1962; repr., New York: Wazobia, 1994); Kimbwandende Kia Bunseki Fu-Kiau, *African Cosmology of the Bantu-Kongo: Principles of Life and Living* (New York: Athelia Henrietta Press, 2001); Hassimi Oumarou Maïga, *Balancing Written History with Oral Tradition: The Legacy of the Songhoy People* (New York: Routledge, 2010); Malidoma Patrice Somé, *Of Water and the Spirit: Ritual, Magic, and Initiation in the Life of an African Shaman* (New York: Arkana, 1994).
27. The thread of this metaphor can be followed through sources as diverse as the naming of Kitchen Table: Women of Color Press in the 1970s to Barbara and Beverly Smith's "Across the Kitchen Table: A Sister to Sister Dialogue," in *This Bridge Called My Back: Writings by Radical Women of Color* in 1981, to Olga Idriss Davis's more recent scholarship, "In the Kitchen: Transforming the Academy through Safe Spaces of Resistance," *Western Journal of Communications* 63 (1999): 364–81, note. 1.
28. Phillips, *Womanist Reader,* xxvii.
29. Alice Walker, *In Search of Our Mothers' Gardens: Womanist Prose* (San Diego, CA: Harcourt Brace Jovanovich, 1983), xi–xii.
30. Chikwenye Okonjo Ogunyemi, *Africa Wo/Man Palava: The Nigerian Novel by Women* (Chicago: University of Chicago, 1996), 26.
31. Phillips, *Womanist Reader,* xxviii.

32. Ogunyemi, *Africa Wo/Man Palava,* 21–61.

33. Tamara Beauboeuf-LaFontant, "A Womanist Experience of Caring: Understanding the Pedagogy of Exemplary Black Women Teachers in *The Womanist Reader,* ed. Layli Phillips (New York: Routledge, 2006), 280–95.

34. Mercy Amba Oduyoye, *Daughters of Anowa: African Women and Patriarchy* (Maryknoll, NY: Orbis, 1995). See also Diedre L. Badejo, "Gender, Power and African Feminist Theory," in *Osun Seegesi: The Elegant Deity of Wealth, Power and Femininity* (Lawrenceville, NJ: Africa World Press, 1996), 175–86.

35. Shamara Shantu Riley, 234, quoting Ann Snitow, "A Gender Diary," in *Conflicts in Feminism,* ed. Marianne Hirsch and Evelyn Fox Keller (New York: Routledge, 1990), 9–43; see especially 20–21, "Motherists and Feminists."

36. Catherine Obianuju Acholonu, *Motherism: The Afrocentric Alternative* (Owerri, Nigeria: Afa, 1995), 3.

37. Susan Arndt, "African Gender Trouble and African Womanism: An Interview with Chikwenye Ogunyemi and Wanjira Muthoni, *Signs: Journal of Women in Culture and Society,* 25, no. 3 (2000): 709–726.

38. Earle Waugh, "The United States," in *Encyclopedia of Women and Islamic Cultures: Family, Law, and Politics,* ed. Suad Joseph and Afsaneh Najmabadi (Leiden, the Netherlands: Brill Academic, 2005), 169.

39. Edward Bruce Bynum, *The African Unconscious: Roots of Ancient Mysticism and Modern Psychology* (New York: Teacher's College Press, 1999).

40. Chidi Maduka, "Feminism, Womanism, and Motherism in African Literary Discourse," n.d., 14, accessed December 29, 2010, www.uni-leipzig.de/~ecas2009/index. php?option=com_docman&task=doc_download&gid=1568&Itemid=24 motherism.

41. Phillips, *Womanist Reader,* xxix (brackets added).

42. Phillips, *The Womanist Reader,* p. xxviii

43. Emory Bogardus's famous "Social Distance Scale" from the 1930s, subsequently revised and updated by numerous other researchers, captures these sentiments well. See Emory S. Bogardus, "A Social Distance Scale," *Sociology and Social Research,* 17 (1933), 265-271. See also Carolyn A. Owen, Howard C. Eisner, and Thomas R. McFaul, "A Half Century of Social Distance Research: National Replication of the Bogardus Studies," *Sociology and Social Research,* 66:1 (1981), 80-98.

44. Walker, *In Search of Our Mothers,* xi.

45. Phillips, *Womanist Reader,* xxviii–xxix.

46. See the Karamah website, www.Karamah.org. Karamah authored a statement about Islamic womanism, accessed March 29, 2007, http://www.karamah.org/news_womens_ conference.htm; however, it is no longer available online. Other references to womanism can be found in Azizah Y. al-Hibri's writings and speeches, such as "The Qu'ranic Worldview: A Womanist Perspective" (speech delivered at Rice University's Baker Institute, April 21, 2003). See also Earl Waugh, "The United States," in *Encyclopedia of Women and Islamic Cultures: Family, Law, and Politics,* ed. Suad Joseph and Afsaneh Najmabadi (Leiden, the Netherlands: Brill Academic, 2005), 167–70.

47. Phillips, *The Womanist Reader,* pp. xxviii–xxix.

48. E-mail exchange with "Nate," March 29, 2007.

49. For the radio interview, see, accessed March 29, 2007, http://www.npr.org/ templates/story/story.php?storyId=6646568. For another story about Rich-

ard Cizik, accessed March 29, 2007, see also http://baptistmessenger.com/story/E20D0D1E15F7C5084984F09223B46824

50. See, accessed March 29, 2007, http://www.karamah.org/news_womens_conference.htm. See also, accessed March 29, 2007, http://webcast.rice.edu/speeches/20030421alhibri.html.

51. Ibid.

52. E-mail from Layli Phillips to Susannah Bartlow, April 28, 2008.

53. Ibid.

54. E-mail from Susannah Bartlow to Layli Phillips, April 28, 2008.

55. E-mail to from Layli Phillips to Susannah Bartlow, April 28, 2008.

56. Reproduced by permission of Susannah Bartlow.

57. Sandoval, *Methodology of the Oppressed,* 27–31, 58–64.

58. Ibid., 104–5.

59. Ibid., 34, 36, 73.

60. Mary Jo McConahay, "Newtown Florist Club," Marguerite Casey Foundation Grantee Profiles, accessed April 16, 2007,.http://www.caseygrants.org/pages/stories/stories_popup_newtown.asp.

61. McConahay, ibid.

62. Ibid.

63. Newtown Florist Club official website, accessed December 29, 2010,.www.newtownfloristclub.org.

64. Ellen Griffith Spear, "The Newtown Story: One Community's Fight for Environmental Justice," *Southern Changes Magazine* 20, no. 4 (1998): 12–15, accessed December 29, 2010, http://www.newtownfloristclub.org/2/index.php?option=com_content&view=article&id=47:qthe-newtown-storyq-by-ellen-griffith-spears&catid=1:latest-news.

65. McConahay, "Newtown Florist Club."

66. From an interview with Jossy Eyre, PBS News Hour, accessed December 29, 2010, http://www.pbs.org/newshour/video/module.html?mod=0&pkg=17122008&seg=4.

67. Women's Bean Project, accessed December 29, 2010, http://www.womensbeanproject.com/whatwedo.html.

68. Ibid.

69. Ibid.

70. All information in this paragraph comes from a 2006 online interview with Dee Dee Chamblee and is paraphrased from my interview notes.

71. Dee Dee Chamblee, personal communication, 2005.

72. "Womanist Party of India," accessed December 30, 2010, http://en.wikipedia.org/wiki/Womanist_Party_of_India.

73. "The New Amazons," *Calcutta Telegraph,* August 15, 2004, accessed December 30, 2010, http://www.telegraphindia.com/1040815/asp/look/story_3622999.asp.

74. Ibid.

75. Geeta Seshu, "Bar Girls Seek Rights," *Boloji.com,* September 6, 2004, accessed December 30, 2010, http://cms.boloji.com/index.cfm?md=Content&sd=Articles&ArticleID=6103.

76. "The New Amazons."

77. Walker, *In Search of Our Mothers,* p. xi.

78. Ibid.

CHAPTER 5

An earlier version of this paper was presented at Sarah Lawrence College, Bronxville, New York, February 2007.

1. Gary Gutting, "Michel Foucault," in *The Stanford Encyclopedia of Philosophy*, ed. Edward N. Zalta, accessed April 1, 2008, http://plato.stanford.edu/archives/fall2003/entries/foucault/.

2. My first introduction to the term *spiritual activism* came in a public lecture on womanism delivered by AnaLouise Keating in Spring 2000 at the University of Georgia.

3. Layli Phillips, ed., *The Womanist Reader* (New York: Routledge, 2006), xxv.

4. Arguably, the womanist idea goes back into prehistory. See such texts as Erich Neumann, *The Great Mother: An Analysis of the Archetype,* trans. Ralph Manheim, ed. Patricia Managham (1955; repr., Princeton, NJ: Princeton University Press, 1963); Neumann, *Goddesses in World Culture* (Westport, CT: Praeger, 2010); and even Ffiona Morgan, *Daughters of the Moon Tarot* (1984; repr., New York: Hyperion Books for Children 1991). We can identify elements of womanist thought and praxis anywhere that women's power, divinity, and community leadership shape social reality and community survival.

5. My father, Duane Dean Dumbleton, had a master's degree in East Asian studies and an EdD in social science education with an emphasis on anthropology and Native American studies. In addition to teaching standard anthropology courses, he was well known for a regular course on world religions. An active Baha'i teacher and leader, he maintained an extensive collection of religious texts (sacred and academic) from multiple traditions around the world. I grew up with these and his commentary. My mother, Mary Nellenore Worthy Dumbleton, majored in philosophy and also studied philosophy at the graduate level. A master at the art of skeptical inquiry, she frequently raised questions about the nature of given knowledge, particularly religiously based knowledge, and embodied the Baha'i principle of "independent investigation of truth." She maintained an extensive collection of original philosophical texts, commentaries, and, interestingly, how-to manuals of varying kinds (a fact that will become important in a later chapter). With these parents, you can imagine what dinner table conversations were like as I was growing up!

6. See "Psyche," in The *Oxford Unabridged Dictionary of the English Language*, which traces its etymology to the idea of Soul.

7. Patricia Hill Collins, *Fighting Words: Black Women and the Search for Justice* (Minneapolis: University of Minnesota Press, 1998), 245, cited in *Interviews/Entrevistas,* ed. AnaLouise Keating (New York: Routledge, 2000), 15.

8. Judylyn S. Ryan, *Spirituality as Ideology in Black Women's Film and Literature* (Charlottesville: University of Virginia Press, 2005), 2.

9. Ibid., 2, 11, and 18, respectively.

10. Leela Fernandes, from *Transforming Feminist Practice: Non-Violence, Social Justice and the Possibilities of a Spiritualized Feminism* (San Francisco: Aunt Lute, 2003), 10, cited in Keating, *EntreMundos/AmongWorlds: New Perspectives on Gloria Anzaldúa* (New York: Palgrave Macmillan, 2005), 253.

11. The Pew Forum on Religion and Public Life, "U.S. Religious Landscape Survey," accessed July 8, 2009 http://religions.pewforum.org/reports.

12. As with many of my spiritual teachers, the information conveyed was in oral rather than written form. This is in keeping with the classical structure of mystical instruction and knowledge transmission.

13. *Ma'afa* is the Afrocentric term for the cultural and spiritual dislocation of the transatlantic slave trade. It means, literally, "disaster" or "great tragedy," and is derived from Swahili.

14. *Daughters of the Dust,* directed by Julie Dash (New York: Kino International, 1995), DVD. See also Barbara McCaskill and Layli Phillips, "'We Are All Good Woman!': A Womanist Critique of the Current Feminist Conflict," in *"Bad Girls"/"Good Girls": Women, Sex, and Power in the Nineties,* ed. Nan Bauer Maglin and Donna Perry (Piscataway, NJ: Rutgers University Press, 1996), 106–122.

15. Derrick Lanois, *A Silent and Dignified Army: Prince Hall Affiliated Freemasonry, Gender and Human Rights in the South, 1900-1970,* Unpublished manuscript, Department of History, Georgia State University, Atlanta, Georgia.

16. See, for instance, Idries Shah, *The Sufis* (1971; repr., Garden City, NY: Anchor Books, 1964), 205–215.

17. Laverne Gyant, "The Missing Link: Women in Black/Africana Studies," in *Out of the Revolution: The Development of Africana Studies,* ed. Delores P. Aldridge and Carlene Young (Lanham, MD: Lexington Press, 2002), 178.

18. For example, see, Cheikh Anta Diop, *The African Origin of Civilization: Myth or Reality* (Chicago: Lawrence Hill, 1974); Yosef ben-Jochannan, *Black Man of the Nile* (Baltimore: Black Classic Press, 1989); Ivan van Sertima, *They Came Before Columbus: The African Presence in Ancient America* (New York: Random House, 1976); John Henrik Clarke, *Africa at the Crossroads: African World Revolution* (Lawrenceville, NJ: Africa World Press, 1992); Carter G. Woodson, *The Negro in Our History* (1922; repr., Washington, DC: Associated Publishers, 1941); Jacob Carruthers, *MDW NTR: Divine Speech—A Historiographical Reflection of African Deep Thought from the Time of the Pharaohs to the Present* (London: Karnak House, 1995); Charles Finch, *Echoes of the Old Darkland: Themes from the African Eden* (Decatur, GA: Khenti, 1991) and *Star of Deep Beginnings: The Genesis of African Science and Technology* (Decatur, GA: Khenti, 1998); LaVerne Gyant, "The Missing Link: Women in Black/Africana Studies," in *Out of the Revolution: The Development of Africana Studies,* ed. Delores P. Aldridge and Carlene Young (Lanham, MD: Lexington Press, 2002), 177–90. Regarding *Plessy v. Ferguson,* see Lee D. Baker, *From Savage to Negro: Anthropology and the Construction of Race, 1896-1954* (Berkeley: University of California Press, 1997).

19. Joseph-Antenor Firmin, *The Equality of the Human Races,* trans. Asselin Charles (1896; repr., New York: Garland, 2000), 252. Carolyn Fleuhr-Lobban, "Introduction," in Joseph-Antenor Firmin, *The Equality of the Human Races.* Fleuhr-Lobban is responsible for the recovery of this text on the suggestion of one of her Haitian students.

20. Anna Julia Cooper, *A Voice from the South* (1892; repr., New York: Oxford University Press, 1988).

21. Maria W. Stewart, "An Address Delivered at the African Masonic Hall," in *Maria W. Stewart: America's First Black Woman Political Writer,* ed. Marilyn Richardson (Bloomington: Indiana University Press, 1987), 56–64.

22. Ayi Kwei Armah, *KMT: In the House of Life* (Popenguine, Senegal: Per Ankh, 2002). For a nonfictional text with similar resonance, see Bika Reed, trans., *Rebel in the Soul* (1978;

repr., Rochester, VT: Inner Traditions International, 1997), a translation of and commentary on Berlin Papyrus 3024 (BCE 2500–1991) by a female scholar.

23. Examples include Freemasonry (including Prince Hall Freemasonry) and Rosicrucianism. As with any major thought community, there are numerous branches and subgroups. See, for example, Jeremy Harwood, *The Freemasons* (London: Hermes House, 2006), a "coffee table book" treatment of the Craft, or W. L. Wilmshurst, *The Meaning of Masonry* (New York: Barnes & Noble Books, 1999), a mass-market reproduction of a 1922 "layman's treatment" of Freemasonry. See also KMTically influenced esoteric texts available in the public domain, such as *The Kybalion* (1912; repr., Yogi Publication Society, 1940) by Three Initiates, and *Divine Pymander* (Yogi Publication Society, n.d.), a compilation of translated texts attributed to Hermes Mercurius Trismegistus and edited by Paschal Beverly Randolph (original publication date: 1871). Interestingly, this latter text contains a frontispiece that reads, "The Best Woman,—maiden, wife, or widow,—on earth, whatever be her race, age, or clime; whoever she is, and wherever she be; rich or poor, in palace, cot, or hovel, This Master Work of the Ages is reverently, lovingly dedicated by the editor."

24. Sylvia Ardyn Boone, *Radiance from the Waters: Ideals of Feminine Beauty in Mende Art* (New Haven, CT: Yale University Press, 1986).

25. Paula J. Giddings, *When and Where I Enter: The Impact of Black Women on Race and Sex in America* (New York: HarperCollins, 1984).

26. Bennetta Jules-Rosette, "Women in Indigenous African Cults and Churches," in *The Black Women Cross-Culturally,* ed. Filomina Chioma Steady (1981; repr., Rochester, VT: Schenkman Books, 1985), 185–207.

27. For an in-depth treatment, see Melanie L. Harris, *Gifts of Virtue, Alice Walker, and Womanist Ethics* (New York: Palgrave Macmillan, 2010).

28. See the following nonfiction works by Alice Walker: *In Search of Our Mothers' Gardens: Womanist Prose* (New York: Harcourt Brace Jovanovich, 1983); *Living by the Word* (New York: Harcourt Brace, 1988); *Anything We Love Can Be Saved: A Writer's Activism* (New York: Ballantine, 1997); and *We Are the Ones We Have Been Waiting For: Light in a Time of Darkness* (New York: New Press, 2006).

29. We also know it because Luisah Teish's work is explicitly spiritual.

30. For an excellent literary critical treatment of this text through a womanist lens, see Susannah Bartlow, "Now Is the Time to Open Your Heart: A Womanist Reading" (paper presented at Gender Across Borders III: Research Transformations, SUNY-Buffalo, April 4–5, 2008).

31. Chela Sandoval, *Methodology of the Oppressed* (Minneapolis: University of Minnesota Press, 2000).

32. Osun is also treated extensively in Deidre L. Badejo, *Osun Seegesi: Elegant Deity of Wealth, Power and Femininity* (Lawrenceville, NJ: Africa World Press, 1996) and Shani Settles, "The Sweet Fire of Honey: Womanist Visions of Osun as a Methodology of Emancipation," in *Deeper Shades of Purple: Womanism in Religion and Society,* ed. Stacey M. Floyd-Thomas (New York: New York University Press, 2006), 191–206.

33. Chikwenye Okonjo Ogunyemi, *Africa Wo/Man Palava: The Nigerian Novel by Women* (Chicago: University of Chicago Press, 1996), 17–127.

34. Ibid., 97. All quotes in this paragraph are on this page.

35. Ibid., 22.

36. Ibid., 21–22.

37. Settles, "Sweet Fire of Honey."
38. I am reminded here of the work of Gary Lemons, especially *Black Male Outsider: Teaching as a Pro-Feminist Man: A Memoir* (Albany, NY: SUNY Press, 2008).
39. Phillips, *The Womanist Reader*, xxviii.
40. Ibid.
41. Ibid., xxviii.
42. Akasha Gloria Hull, *Soul Talk: The New Spirituality of African American Women* (Rochester, VT: Inner Traditions, 2001), 29 (emphasis added).
43. Ibid., 44.
44. Ibid., 7 (emphasis in original).
45. Ibid., 93.
46. Ibid., 218.
47. Ibid., 219.
48. Ibid., 100.
49. Ibid., 99.
50. Ibid., 99.
51. The distinction between *bhakti* and *gnani/jnani* paths is discussed in Paramhansa Yogananda, *Autobiography of a Yogi* (Philosophical Library, 1946–2005; repr., Nevada City, CA: Crystal Clarity, 1947).
52. Marcia Masino, *Easy Tarot Guide* (Epping, NH: ACS, 1987), p. 173. This symbolism also appears in Gerd Ziegler's *Tarot: Mirror of the Soul* (New York: Samuel Weiser, 1988) and other sources.
53. Such bookstores have been instrumental in my own spiritual education. For example, I must credit the Shrine of the Black Madonna Bookstore, the former Oasis Bookstore, African Djeli (now online), and, especially, House of Khamit—all of Atlanta, Georgia.
54. Ibid., 164.
55. Ibid., 242.
56. See Stanlie M. James and Abena P. A. Busia, ed., *Theorizing Black Feminisms: The Visionary Pragmatism of Black Women* (New York: Routledge, 1993) on the subject of "visionary pragmatism" in Africana women's thought and praxis.
57. For more on African cosmology and spirituality, see John S. Mbiti, *African Religions and Philosophy* (London: Heinemann, 1971); Peter J. Paris, *The Spirituality of African Peoples: The Search for a Common Moral Discourse* (Minneapolis, MN: Fortress Press, 1998); Kimbwandende Kia Bunseki Fu-Kiau, *Tying the Spiritual Knot: African Cosmology of the Bantu-Kongo: Principles of Life and Living* (1980; repr., New York: Athelia Henrietta Press, 2001); Hassimi Oumarou Maïga, *Balancing Written History with Oral Tradition: The Legacy of the Songhoy People* (New York: Routledge, 2010); Malidoma Patrice Somé, *Of Water and the Spirit* (New York: Penguin, 1995); Sonbonfu Somé, *The Spirit of Intimacy: Ancient African Teachings in the Ways of Relationships* (New York: HarperCollins, 2000).
58. M. Jacqui Alexander, "Pedagogies of the Sacred: Making the Invisible Tangible," in *Pedagogies of Crossing: Meditations on Feminism, Sexual Politics, Memory, and the Sacred* (Durham, NC: Duke University Press, 2005).
59. Ibid., 293–94.
60. Ibid., 294.
61. Ibid.

62. Gloria Anzaldúa, *Interviews/Entrevistas*, ed. Ana Louise Keating (New York: Routledge, 2000). 17. Here she discusses the risks of talking about "wild stuff" in one's academic writing. She says, "I think it's time for these ideas to be in print."

63. Ibid., 7.

64. Ibid., 96.

65. Ibid., 48–53.

66. Ibid., 54.

67. Ibid., 18–19.

68. Ibid., 10.

69. Ibid., 60.

70. Barbara A. Holmes, *Race and the Cosmos: An Invitation to View the World Differently* (Trinity Press International, 2002).

71. Ibid., 3–4.

72. Ibid., 16.

73. Ibid., 112.

74. Ibid., 145–46. In this passage, she is making a direct allusion to the work of quantum physicist David Bohm, including his *Wholeness and the Implicate Order* (New York: Routledge, 1996) and his work with B. J. Hiley, *The Undivided Universe* (New York: Routledge, 1993).

75. Ibid., 83–88. However, see also Charles S. Finch III, *The Star of Deep Beginnings: The Genesis of African Science and Technology* (1998; repr., Decatur, GA: Khenti, 2001) and *Echoes of the Old Darkland: Themes from the African Eden* (1991; repr., Decatur, GA: Khenti, 1999), as well as Marcel Griaule, *Tales of Ogotemmeli: An Introduction to Dogon Religious Ideas* (New York: Oxford University Press, 1975) and (with G. Dieterlen) *The Pale Fox* (Chino Valley, AZ: Continuum Foundation, Afrikan World Book Distributor, 1986). Previously cited texts by Malidoma Patrice Somé, *Of Water and the Spirit*; Hassimi Oumarou Maïga, *Balancing Written History,* and Kimbwandende Kia Bunseki Fu-Kiau, *Tying the Spiritual Knot,* already mentioned, also address this theme. Strangely enough, a segment on Dogon cosmology vis-à-vis Sirius B also appears almost randomly within the film The Secret Life of Plants, directed by Walon Green (Los Angeles, CA: Paramount Pictures, 1979), DVD.

76. A detailed African astrological/astronomical perspective on the Age of Aquarius is presented by Charles S. Finch III, in both *Echoes of the Old Darkland: Themes from the African Eden* (115–28) and *The Star of Deep Beginnings: The Genesis of African Science and Technology* (167–202). For a Kabbalistic perspective, see Philip S. Berg, *Astrology: The Star Connection* (New York: Research Centre of Kabbalah International, 1986), 34–45, 176.

77. Alice Walker, *In Search of Our Mothers' Gardens: Womanist Prose* (San Diego, CA: Harcourt Brace Jovanovich, 1983), xi. Reprinted in Layli Phillips, ed., *The Womanist Reader* (New York: Routledge, 2006), 19.

78. Ines Hernandez-Avila, "Tierra Tremenda: The Earth's Agony and Ecstacy in the Work of Gloria Anzaldúa"; AnaLouise Keating, *EntreMundos/AmongWorlds: New Perspectives on Gloria Anzaldúa* (New York: Palgrave Macmillan, 2005), 240.

79. "I AM the organizing principle of my life" is an affirmation I created to affirm my own and others' right and power to synthesize and unify diverse and competing influences on thought, feeling, identity, or philosophy, into a whole that makes sense *to us.* I often share this affirmation with friends or students who are feeling confused about compet-

ing perspectives or pieces of information and who are struggling to "make sense of it all." It is a reminder that *we* are the sense-makers. Stated differently, it is a mantra for self-authorship.

CHAPTER 6

An earlier version of this paper was presented at the United by Faith: Building a Better Future for Women and Girls summit held in Dallas, Texas, hosted by the Women's Funding Network, January 2010.

1. Judylyn S. Ryan, *Spirituality as Ideology in Black Women's Film and Literature* (Charlottesville: University of Virginia Press, 2005), 11, 16–18.
2. Ibid., 18.
3. Katharine Rhodes Henderson, *God's Troublemakers: How Women of Faith Are Changing the World* (New York: Continuum: 2006). All quotes are from the book jacket flaps, hardcover edition.
4. The Sister Fund, *Healers of Our Time: Women, Faith, and Justice: A Mapping Report* (New York: The Sister Fund, 2008).
5. Paul Hawken, *Blessed Unrest: How the Largest Social Movement in the World Came into Being and Why No One Saw It Coming* (New York: Viking, 2007). Note that current editions of this book display a different subtitle.
6. The Center for Contemplative Mind in Society, *The Activist's Ally: Contemplative Tools for Social Change* (Northampton, MA: The Center for Contemplative Mind in Society, 2007). Quotes are from chap. 1 (n.p.).
7. Womanism does not exclude the possibility that human consciousness may eventually extend beyond Earth to encompass what some have called galactic consciousness or even cosmic consciousness. Planet Earth is simply the most obvious horizon at this juncture in history.
8. See Luisah Teish's book, *Jambalaya: The Natural Woman's Book of Personal Charms and Practical Rituals* (San Francisco: Harper, 1985). See also Chikwenye Okonjo Ogunyemi's *Africa Wo/Man Palava: The Nigerian Novel by Women* (Chicago: University of Chicago Press, 1996), particularly the sections about Osun and juju.
9. See such texts as Donna Eden's *Energy Medicine* (New York: Tarcher/Putnam, 1998), Richard Gerber's *Vibrational Medicine* (Rochester, VT: Bear, 2001), and *Quantum Healing* by Deepak Chopra (New York: Bantam, 1989).
10. See Chela Sandoval's *Methodology of the Oppressed* (Minneapolis: University of Minnesota Press, 2000).
11. Phillips, *The Womanist Reader* (New York: Routledge), xx.
12. Akasha Gloria Hull, *Soul Talk: The New Spirituality of African American Women* (Rochester, VT: Inner Traditions, 2001), 188.
13 AnaLouise Keating, *EntreMundos/AmongWorlds: New Perspectives on Gloria Anzaldúa* (New York: Palgrave Macmillan, 2005), 242.
14. AnaLouise Keating, ed., *Interviews/Entrevistas* (New York: Routledge), 178.
15. Gloria Anzaldúa, "now let us shift ... the path of conocimiento ... inner work, public acts," in *This Bridge We Call Home: Radical Visions for Transformation*, ed. Gloria Anzaldúa and AnaLouise Keating (New York: Routledge, 2002), 572–73.

16. Keating, *Interviews/Entrevistas*, 178.
17. See Idries Shah, *The Sufis* (1964; repr., Garden City, NY: Anchor Books, 1971).
18. Gloria Anzaldúa writes, for instance: "It's a matter of the vibration of consciousness: The vibration of the consciousness of that plant over there is different from that of a towel and different from that of a person," *Interviews/Entrevistas*, 119. Also, "matter is divine also." See p. 103.
19. Lynne M. McTaggart, *The Intention Experiment: Using Your Thoughts to Change Your Life and the World*. (New York: Free Press, 2007).
20. David R. Hawkins, *Power vs. Force: The Hidden Determinants of Human Behavior* (1995; Carlsbad, CA: Hay House, 2002), 68–69, 75–102.
21. See Bynum, *The African Unconscious: Roots of Ancient Mysticism and Modern Psychology* (New York: Teacher's College Press, 1999), 127–48.
22. Gloria E. Anzaldúa (in *Interviews/Entrevistas*, New York: Routledge, 2000), and Analouise Keating (in *EntreMundos/Between Worlds: New Perspectives on Gloria Anzaldúa*, New York: Palgrave Macmillan, 2005), Akasha Gloria Hull (in *Soul Talk: The New Spirituality of African American Women*, Rochester, VT: Inner Traditions, 2001), and Barbara A. Holmes (in *Race and the Cosmos: An Invitation to View the World Differently*, Harrisburg, PA: Trinity Press International, 2002) all reference Rupert Sheldrake. David R. Hawkins discusses Sheldrake's work at length in his own *Power vs. Force: The Hidden Determinants of Human Behavior* (Carlsbad, CA: Hay House, 2002). See Rupert Sheldrake, *The Presence of the Past: Morphic Resonance and the Habits of Nature* (South Paris, ME: Park Street Press, 1995) and *A New Science of Life: The Hypothesis of Formative Causation* (London: Blond and Briggs, 1981).
23. David R. Hawkins has written, "Man [sic] thinks he lives by virtue of the forces he can control, but in fact, he's governed by power from unrevealed sources, power over which he has *no* control. Because power is effortless, it goes unseen and unsuspected. Force is experienced through the senses; power can be recognized only through inner awareness. Man is immobilized in his present condition by his alignment with enormously powerful attractor energy patterns, which he himself unconsciously sets in motion" 37. Anzaldúa makes a similar comment in *Interviews/Entrevistas*: "[W]hatever takes your energy and attention enthralls you, enslaves you" (76). I agree with Hawkins's distinction between power and force, however, I disagree with him that we have no control. My contention is that once we learn about these dynamics, we can consciously participate in them. This is the essence of Divine creativity, indeed, the essence of applied mysticism and applied metaphysics.
24. Anzaldúa, Keating, Hull, and Holmes in the works mentioned above (Note 22) all reference David Bohm as well. David R. Hawkins also mentions his work in the text cited in Note 22. See David Bohm, *Wholeness and the Implicate Order* (1980; repr., New York: Routledge, 1996). Keating writes this in a footnote: "For recent developments in quantum physics and other branches of science, see Barabási; Bohm; Macy; Sheldrake; Watts; and Wolf." Keating, *EntreMundos/AmongWorlds: New Perspectives on Gloria Anzaldúa* (New York: Palgrave Macmillan, 2005), 253, n.
25. John Hagelin, *Manual for a Perfect Government: How to Harness the Laws of Nature to Bring Maximum Success to Governmental Administration* (Fairfield, IA: Maharishi University of Management Press, 1998), 71–109. That mathematical formula obtained by these researchers is the square root of 1% of the population of interest. This formula yields the number of advanced meditators that must be assembled for group

meditation in order to influence a targeted phenomenon within the defined locale or population. See this text for more information about how "advanced meditator" is defined; however, based on Hawkins's formulation of "Levels of Consciousness," such an advanced meditator would need to be one whose vibrational power averages out at the higher end of this scale. TM and other traditions maintain that regular, trained meditation practice is a vibration raising activity that has enduring effects on the individual (as well as the communities and environments surrounding that individual).

26. Masaru Emoto, *The Hidden Messages in Water* (Hillsboro, OR: Beyond Words, 2004).

27. Gloria Anzaldúa, *Interviews/Entrevistas*, 178.

28. Ibid., 101.

29. Anzaldúa makes frequent references to these methods in her writings as well. She discusses them primarily from her own experience of engaging in them, and their impact on her health and consciousness.

30. The bridge metaphor is common in Anzaldúa's writings. She often uses the Spanish term *el puente*. See especially *Interviews/Entrevistas*, 550–551, 557, 567.

31. Will Coleman notes that, spatially, these worlds are not arranged in a linear hierarchy. Rather, they are dimensional, vibrational spheres that are "deep within as well as up." Personal communication, December 2010.

32. Anzaldúa, "now let us shift," 571.

33. Here I am pointing to the notion of "another world is possible," not to one of the Four Worlds of Kabbalah.

34. For one concise esoteric treatment of natural/universal law, see *The Kybalion* by Three Initiates (1912; repr., Yogi Publication Society, 1940).

35. Diedre L. Badejo, *Osun Seegesi: Elegant Deity of Wealth, Power and Femininity* (Lawrenceville, NJ: Africa World Press, 1996), confirms this tendency toward mistranslation, stating: "Although frequently translated as 'witches' in English, the negative connotation of that word misses the essence of the *ajé* in Yoruba cosmology. My informant explained that everyone has her/his own power that can be used for good or evil. So it is with the *ajé* who are an embodiment of power and an expression of the matrix of potentiality from which that power emanates. *Osun* as *orisa* remains a benefactor to humanity; as leader of the *ajé*, she protects the covenants that seal the positive and/or negative actions of the *ajé*. Her role is 'to know and keep' the secret of the covenants and to provide, through *Ifá* and/or *mérindínlógún* divination, the requisite material offering that release those seals. Rather than confront she facilitates the reversal of negative power" (77–78).

36. Kola Abimbola, *Yoruba Culture: A Philosophical Account* (Birmingham, UK: Iroko, 2006),49–50.

37. E. Bolaji Idowu, *Olodumare: God in Yoruba Belief* (1962; repr., New York: Wazobia, 1994).

38. See Will Coleman, *Tribal Talk: Black Theology, Hermeneutics, and African/American Ways of "Telling the Story"* (Philadelphia: Pennsylvania State University Press, 2000), 3–30.

39. Will Coleman has stated: "Think about Ifa as a form of West Afrikan Kabbalah. The reason that human agency is so important is because the universe is dialogical; i.e., it encourages 'spiritual activism' as an ongoing unfoldment of its own destiny." Personal communication, December 25, 2010.

40. This word *placation* is used by Starhawk in her introduction to Luisah Teish's *Jambalaya: The Natural Woman's Book of Personal Charms and Practical Rituals* (San Francisco: Harper), xvii, as a clarifying synonym for "sacrifice" in Voudou. She also uses the word *offering*.

41. Patanjali's original yoga sutras were written down in Sanskrit. The Sanskrit record has been translated numerous times by many different translators. The one I resonate with most and cite here is *The Yoga Sutras of Patanjali,* trans. and with introduction, Alistair Shearer (New York: Bell Tower, 1982), in its Sacred Teachings series.

42. Ibid., 90.

43. Ibid., 91.

44. Ibid.

45. Thich Nhat Hanh, *Interbeing: Fourteen Guidelines for Engaged Buddhism, Third Edition.* (1987; repr., Berkeley, CA: Parallax Press, 1998).See also Thich Nhat Hanh's *The Five Mindfulness Trainings,* http://www.plumvillage.org. This document is received as a certificate upon completion of the first level of training with the European Institute of Applied Buddhism at the Plum Village Practice Center in France, however, it has been reprinted in a variety of places and periodically gets updated. I received such a certificate on June 14, 2009.

46. Keating, *EntreMundos/AmongWorlds,* 249–52.

47. Pema Chodron, *When Things Fall Apart: Heart Advice for Difficult Times.* (Boston: Shambhala, 2000), 88.

48. Alice Walker, "Suffering Too Insignificant for the Majority to See," *Shambhala Sun* (May 2007), accessed October 25, 2010, www.shambhalasun.com/index.php?option=com_content&task=view&id=3093&Itemid=0.

49. Ibid. This quote is excerpted by Alice Walker from Winson Hudson and Constance Curry, *Mississippi Harmony: Memoirs of a Freedom Fighter.*

50. Dalai Lama and Daniel Goleman, ed., *Destructive Emotions: How Can We Overcome Them?* (New York: Bantam, 2003), 82–83.

51. Ibid., 83–84.

52. The spiritual activist women we studied through a womanist lens were Sister Chan Khong (a Buddhist from Vietnam/France), Immaculee Ilibagiza (an evangelical Christian from Rwanda), Pregs Govender (a nonreligious meditator from South Africa), Kiran Bedi (a Buddhist from India), and Wangari Maathai (a Christian from Kenya who also incorporated African traditional religion and ecospirituality in her work).

CHAPTER 7

I am thankful to Sister Chan Khong for her feedback on this chapter, as well as to Sister An Nghiem for her generous assistance in facilitating our communication.

1. In Vietnamese culture, the family name comes first and the given name comes last. Thus, Sister Chan Khong's family name is Cao and her given name was Phuong, pronounced "Fung." Although she did not take on the name Chan Khong until she was ordained, for consistency, I refer to her as Chan Khong throughout this text.

2. Alice Walker, *In Search of Our Mothers' Gardens: Womanist Prose* (San Diego, CA: Harcourt Brace Jovanovich, 1983), xi.

3. Sister Chan Khong, *Learning True Love: Practicing Buddhism in a Time of War* (Berkeley, CA: Parallax Press, 2007), 5.

4. Ibid.

5. Ibid., 13.

6. Ibid., 14.

7. I am reminded of my own observations of missionaries in Liberia, where oftentimes the social change work and direct service that secular progressive activists and theorists only talk about is actually getting done on the ground, and in a loving spirit, even if evangelical. This is a paradoxical contrast to the way I was taught to think of missionaries (based on nineteenth century models and earlier) that emphasized introduction of the Bible as a way of mental colonization meant to smooth the path for economic, political, and military colonization by people of European nationality. My own first-hand observation leads me to the conclusion that missionary work in the world today is more complex than is typically acknowledged or discussed in "progressive" circles.

8. Ibid., 14.

9. Ibid., 15.

10. Ibid, 15–16.

11. "Thich" and "Thay" are different titles for a monk. "Thich" means "formally ordained monk" (Shakyamuni tradition) and is the more formal title, while "Thay" means "teacher" and is the more informal title. Almost all Vietnamese monks have one or the other of these titles in front of their monastic name. Students of Thich Nhat Hanh are permitted to refer to him as Thay.

12. Bodhicitta (also spelled bodhichitta) is "the desire to attain complete enlightenment in order to be of benefit to all sentient beings," see, accessed June 15, 2008, www.wikipedia. ord/wiki/Bodhicitta. Shantideva, eighth century Buddhist master, has written: "In brief, you should know that bodhichitta has two types: The mind that observes enlightenment and aspires, and the mind that observes enlightenment and engages." The first type is considered bookish and less effectual, while the second type is considered truly helpful to the suffering masses. See Shantideva's *Guide to the Bodhisattva's Way of Life*, trans. Neil Elliott under the guidance of Geshe Kelsang Gyatso (Glen Spey, NY: Tharpa, 2002),. Chan Khong's "engaged" bodhicitta can be considered to be of the second type.

13. Neil Elliott describes Avalokitesvara (also spelled Avalokiteshvara) as "the embodiment of the compassion of all the Buddhas," ibid., 196. In Chan Khong's text, the name is generally spelled as Avalokitesvara, and in this chapter, I have exclusively used this spelling.

14. For a reference on "engaged" Buddhism, see Thich Nhat Hanh, *Interbeing: Fourteen Guidelines for Engaged Buddhism* (Berkeley, CA: Parallax Press, 1993); Chan Khong, *Learning True Love*, chap. 8.

15. Chan Khong, *Learning True Love*, 67–68.

16. David R. Hawkins, *Power vs. Force: The Hidden Determinants of Human Behavior* (Carlsbad, CA: Hay House, 2002).

17. Chan Khong, *Learning True Love*, 191.

18. Interbeing, *Tiep Hien* in Vietnamese, is a term coined by Thich Nhat Hanh in 1966 to refer to the fundamental interconnectedness and interdependence of all things. In *Cultivating the Mind of Love* (Berkeley, CA: Parallax Press, 1996), he wrote, "Looking at anything, we can see the nature of interbeing. A self is not possible without non-self elements. Looking deeply at any one thing, we see the whole cosmos. The one is made of the many ." His followers often use related phrases, such as "We inter-are."

19. Chan Khong, *Learning True Love*, 89–90.
20. Ibid., 105–6.
21. AnaLouise Keating, *Teaching Transformation: Transcultural Classroom Dialogues* (New York: Palgrave, 2007), 1. See also, M. Jacqui Alexander, "Remembering *This Bridge*, Remembering Ourselves: Yearning, Memory, and Desire," in *This Bridge We Call Home,* ed. Gloria E. Anzaldúa and AnaLouise Keating (New York: Routledge, 2000), 85.
22. Ibid.
23. A similar perspective is tacitly conveyed in Barbara A. Holmes's text, *Race and the Cosmos* (Harrisburg, PA: Trinity Press, 2002) where she links the concept of the Unified Field from quantum physics to the eradication of racism and other "isms" based on social difference.
24. The "thirteen cedars" were a group of young activist students who worked with Thay Nhat Hanh on "renewing Buddhism" in Vietnam during the 1960s. This mixed-gender group formed out of an intensive study group led by Thay, which was comprised of his most devoted and enthusiastic students. Chan Khong was one of the original "thirteen cedars." The meaning of the term *cedars* in this context is parallel to the meaning of the term *pillars* in Western contexts. Their renewal of Buddhism revolved around linking Buddhist spiritual principles to social work and social change activism, particularly in the areas of relief to the poor, rural development, education, day care, health care, gender equality, and peace. The "cedars" ultimately grew to about 800 in number as increasing numbers of students were attracted to the cause.
25. The "Pioneer Villages" were a project spearheaded by Chan Khong and other "cedars" to create intentional communities in the jungles of Vietnam, based on a government program that allowed indigent people to acquire land for free so long as they would clear and develop it into farmland. Chan Khong and others would take 20 to 30 families at a time and create communities that allowed families to become economically self-sufficient and to collaborate in the provision of other social services, such as schools and day care centers. It is not clear whether these communities were long-lived.
26. See, for example, Natalie Wendt, "Nuns, Invisibility, and the Question of Buddhist Activism," *Tikkun Daily*, July 23, 2010, accessed December 24, 2010, http://www.tikkun.org/tikkundaily/2010/07/23/nuns-invisibility-and-the-question-of-buddhist-activism/. . See also "Buddhism in Thailand: A Report on the Struggle for Women to Be Ordained in the Theravada Buddhist Tradition," Association for Women's Rights in Development (AWID), December 2, 2008, accessed December 24, 2010, http://www.awid.org/eng/Issues-and-Analysis/Library/Buddhism-in-Thailand-a-report-on-the-struggle-for-women-to-be-ordained-in-the-Theravada-Buddhist-tradition.
27. Sister Chan Khong, *Learning True Love*, 26–27.
28. See "Tet Offensive," Wikipedia, accessed December 22, 2010, http://en.wikipedia.org/wiki/Tet_Offensive.
29. Chan Khong, *Learning True Love,* 108.
30. Ibid.
31. Ibid., 109.
32. Ibid., 109–110.
33. Ibid., 113.
34. Ibid., 114.
35. Ibid., 121.

36. Ibid., 122.
37. Ibid., 151.
38. Ibid., 164.
39. Ibid., 171.
40. Ibid., 187.
41. Ibid., 192.
42. Ibid.
43. Ibid., 216–17.
44. In fact, female monastics outnumber male monastics at Plum Village. While most originate from Vietnam, there are many Europeans and people of other nationalities, including some African Americans.
45. Chan Khong, *Learning True Love*, 231.
46. Ibid., 232.
47. Ibid., 235–36.
48. Ibid., 239.
49. Ibid. Others have also attached honorifics and other terms of respect to her name since this time to reflect the deepening of her commitment and the elevation of her status.
50. Chan Khong, *Learning True Love*, 276–77.
51. This is a direct transcription of my notes from a scheduled one-on-one meeting with Sister Chan Khong, who was taking a certain number of 30-minute appointments per day with retreatants who requested them. Although I did not date my entry because it was in a different notebook from my regular journal, it occurred toward the end of my visit, which spanned June 11 to 21, 2009. In the meeting, I told her about the Contemplative Practice Fellowship that had made it possible for me to visit Plum Village as well as the course I was developing on womanist approaches to spiritual activism. The notes were written out in full immediately after our meeting, when my memory was fresh, as I did not want to write while she was talking. Thus, while these notes are not a word-for-word transcription of what she said, they do capture the substance of her comments and the flow of her explanations chronologically and in great detail, without interpretive additions as such from me. At the end of our meeting, she signed my copy of her memoir.

CHAPTER 8

1. A well-documented list of estimates of the death toll can be found in Wikipedia's article on the Rwandan genocide, accessed November 28, 2010, http://en.wikipedia.org/wiki/Rwandan_Genocide.
2. Marianne Williamson, *A Return to Love: Reflections on the Principles in* a Course in Miracles (New York: HarperCollins, 1992).
3. See books such as Antoinette Bosco's *Radical Forgiveness* (Maryknoll, NY: Orbis, 2009) and Colin Tipping's *Radical Forgiveness: A Revolutionary Five-Stage Process to Heal Relationships, Let Go of Anger and Blame, Find Peace in Any Situation* (Louisville, CO: Sounds True, 2009).
4. Wikipedia article on the film *Hotel Rwanda,* directed by Terry George (Los Angeles, CA: United Artists, 2004), DVD, accessed December 6, 2010, en.wikipedia.org/wiki/Hotel_Rwanda.

5. See David Patrick, "Yesterday's News? Western Press Coverage of the Rwandan Geno-cide" (paper presented at the Centre for the Study of Genocide and Mass Violence, University of Sheffield, Sheffield, UK, October 23, 2009), accessed December 5, 2010, www.genocidecentre.dept.shef.ac.uk/documents/Paper%20-%20David%20Patrick%202.pdf.

6. See Lee D. Baker, *From Savage to Negro: Anthropology and the Construction of Race, 1896–1954* (Berkeley: University of California Press, 1998).

7. The film *Hotel Rwanda* has been characterized by various critics and commentators as the "African *Schindler's List*." See Patrick, "Yesterday's News," and, especially, Claudia Puig, "Haunting 'Hotel Rwanda,'" *USA Today,* December 21, 2004.

8. Samantha Powers, "Bystanders to Genocide," *The Atlantic,* September 2001, accessed December 6, 2010, http://www.theatlantic.com/magazine/archive/2001/09/bystand-ers-to-genocide/4571/., See also, accessed November 28, 2010, http://en.wikipedia.org/wiki/Rwandan_Genocide. For the complete text of the "Clinton apology," see, accessed December 6, 2010, www.cbsnews.com/stories/1998/03/25/world/main5798.shtml

9. See Stephanie McCrummen, "Women Run the Show in a Recovering Rwanda," *Washington Post,* October 27, 2008, accessed December 6, 2010, www.washingtonpost.com/wp-dyn/content/article/2008/10/26/AR2008102602197.html. See also "In a World First, Women in the Majority in Rwanda Legislature," AFP/Google News, September 18, 2008, accessed December 6, 2010, afp.google.com/article/ALeqM5hy YDRUBoyMv4qslVEi1H43kUVtEA.

10. Immaculée Ilibagiza, *Left to Tell: Discovering God Amidst the Rwandan Holocaust* (Carlsbad, CA: Hay House, 2006), 15.

11. Ibid., 19.

12. Ibid., 20.

13. Ibid. This young man later broke her heart when, upon being allowed by Pastor Murinzi to see Immaculée in the bathroom, remarked, "I can't believe how skinny you are, Immaculée! You look like a bag of bones!" (119), and "Well ... you don't have that great body anymore, but you still look good. I've been praying you'd still be alive and that no one had raped you. And here you are, alive and unraped!" (120). He made no attempt to rescue or even help her, despite the fact that he stayed in Pastor Murinzi's house for a period of time and even played basketball outside the bathroom window. Later, he also said, "Well, I know one thing—there are no other men looking at you, and that's one less thing for me to worry about, right?" (121) As Immaculée wrote, "With those words, John killed any love left between us" (121).

14. Ibid., 33.

15. Vibrational entrainment is the act of causing others to come into emotional or cognitive alignment with one's own emotional state or thoughts (see the chap. 6, this volume).

16. Ilibagiza, *Left to Tell,* 78 (emphasis in original).

17. Ibid., 79 (emphasis in original).

18. Ibid., 81.

19. Synchronicity, "an acausal connecting principle," see C. G. Jung, *Synchronicity: An Acausal Connecting Principle* (Princeton, NJ: Bollingen, 1973) for a definition.

20. Gregg Braden, *The Isaiah Effect: Decoding the Lost Science of Prayer and Prophecy* (New York: Random House, 2000); Braden, *Secrets of the Lost Mode of Prayer: The Hidden Power of Beauty, Blessing, Wisdom, and Hurt* (Carlsbad, CA: Hay House, 2006).

21. Ilibagiza, *Left to Tell,* 118.

22 ."Faith" as it is used here corresponds to the "strength and quality of feeling" dimension described in Gregg Braden's research on prayer, hence its putative ability to "move mountains." Rather than a purely allegorical or metaphorical saying, this passage from the Bible is, from this perspective, a set of alchemical instructions.

23. Ilibagiza, *Left to Tell*, 130–31.

24. Ibid., 170.

25. The similarity between Immaculeé's action here and the Buddhist practice of loving-kindness meditation (*metta* meditation, *tonglen*, etc.) should be noted.

26. Ilibagiza, *Left to Tell*, 171–72.

27. In *The Isaiah Effect*, Gregg Braden argues that the "lost language of prayer" is actually deep human feeling, that is, wordless gut level emotion, which communicates energetically with the Universe by setting resonant causal chains into motion, thus producing effects such as "answered prayer." Within this schematic, prayers that are words only are completely ineffectual, whereas even wordless feelings can function as prayers. Strong feelings plus detailed words expressing the desired outcome are the most efficacious combination. According to Braden, this idea is not his own, but occurs in old esoteric writings, such as the Nag Hammadi, some of which have found expression in the Biblical book of Isaiah.

28. Ilibagiza, *Left to Tell*, 172–74.

29. In all probability, Aloise's powerful, high-vibrating temperament also played a role in these outcomes.

30. Ilibagiza, *Left to Tell*, 201–2.

31. Ibid, 203–4.

32. Ibid., 144.

33. Alister Shearer, trans., *The Yoga Sutras of Patanjali* (New York: Bell Tower, 1982), 109. This verse is built upon the Sanskrit word *ahimsa*, which we are familiar with as "nonviolence" through the activist praxis of Mahatma Gandhi.

34. See, for example, Wikipedia's overview, "Genocides in History," accessed December 6, 2010, en.wikipedia.org/wiki/Genocides_in_history.

35. The allusion to Shaun Monson's controversial documentary *Earthlings* (Burbank, CA: Nation Earth, 2005), which examines human treatment of animals, is intentional, insofar as a nonspeciesist perspective on genocide would consider human slaughter of animals as yet another manifestation of the human genocidal thoughtform. I neither advocate nor reject this perspective; however, I consider the question important and compelling. The womanist value of "reverence for livingkind" would tend to support the notion that any form of exploitative, wholesale killing of *any* species (particularly that which is predicated on alienated relations between killer and killed) should be abandoned. Indeed, arguably this is a plank of ecowomanism. As for the current chapter, it is a fascinating coincidence that Joaquin Phoenix, who narrated *Earthlings*, is also one of the stars in *Hotel Rwanda*.

36. Ilibagiza, *Left to Tell*, mentions this in her memoir, 86.

37. For the full text of this resolution, see, accessed December 6, 2010, www.un.org/events/res_1325e.pdf.

38. A note of caution here: As Chela Sandoval argues in *Methodology of the Oppressed* (Minneapolis: University of Minnesota Press, 2000), powerful social change methodologies are ethically neutral and can be deployed for good or ill; what makes them positive/justice-oriented is an additional trait, a kind of moral compass or "ethical technology,"

which Sandoval names "democratics." The term *democratics* expresses an explicit commitment to the well-being of the whole, to the upending of violent and exploitative practices and mindframes, to egalitarianism, and to the decolonization of the mind and culture. This theme pervades the book, but especially see 2, 61, 62, 114, and 181.

39. Ilibagiza, *Left to Tell*, 190.

40. Ultimately, the answers she came to were not unlike Sister Chan Khong's realization that "Man is not the enemy" and that "There is only one side—the human side." See previous chapter.

41. Meaning here "transcending intellectual knowledge," not "super smart."

42. Sandoval, *Methodology of the Oppressed*, 81. Here, sign-reading is named as "*la facultad*" and Gloria Anzaldúa is quoted epigraphically: "*La facultad* is the capacity to see in surface phenomena the meaning of deeper realities, to see the deep structure below the surface."

43. 'Abdu'l-Bahá, *Selections from the Writings of 'Abdu'l-Bahá* (Wilmette, IL: Baha'i Publishing Trust, 1978), 247. In this same passage, 'Abdu'l-Bahá identifies five "teachings for the prevention of war," which include (a) "the independent investigation of truth," (b) "the oneness of mankind," (c) upholding religion that "engender[s] love" and putting aside religion that "engender[s] ... malevolence and hate,"(d) "universal peace," and (e) "the equality of men and women and the equal sharing of all rights" (248–49). 'Abdu'l-Bahá also argues for the establishment of a "Supreme Tribunal"—"representative of all governments and peoples" to which "questions both national and international must be referred." "Should any government of people disobey, let the whole world arise against that government or people," he states. This passage, written sometime between 1909 and 1916, anticipates such later supranational governance organizations as the League of Nations, the United Nations, the International Court of Justice (ICJ), and the International Criminal Court (ICC).

44. See also James Allen, *As a Man Thinketh* (Chicago: Cornerstone,1902), This is a canonical text of New Thought, which has influenced the evolution of the "creative visualization" and "positive thinking" movements from the early 20th century to present.

45. See Colin Tipping, *Radical Forgiveness: Making Room for the Miracle* (Burlington, ONT: Quest, 2002) and *Radical Forgiveness: A Revolutionary Five-Stage Process to Heal Relationships, Let Go of Anger and Blame, Find Peace in Any Situation* (Louisville, CO: Sounds True, 2009). See also, Eileen Borris-Dunchunstang, *Finding Forgiveness: A 7-Step Program for Letting Go of Anger and Bitterness* (New York: McGraw-Hill, 2009).

46. A discussion of the ways in which this perspective intersects with discourses about reincarnation is beyond the scope of this chapter. However, see Shantideva, below. Consider also Thich Nhat Hanh's comment on reincarnation that appears in a footnote in Sister Chan Khong's book, Learning True Love (Berkeley, CA: Paralax, 2007). "If there is no self, who is going to be reborn?" (134).

47. This idea is elegantly expressed in a passage from sixth century Buddhist master Shantideva's poem, *Guide to the Bodhisattva's Way of Life,* trans. Neil Elliott under the guidance of Venerable Geshe Kelsang Gyatso (Glen Spey, NY: Tharpa, 2002), 86):

> Those who cause me suffering
> Are like Buddhas bestowing their blessings.
> Since they lead me to liberating paths,
> Why should I get angry with them?

"Don't they obstruct your virtuous practice?"
No! There is no virtuous practice greater than patience;
Therefore, I will never get angry
With those who cause me suffering.

If, because of my own shortcomings,
I do not practise patience with my enemy,
It is not he, but I, who prevent me from practising patience,
The cause of accumulating merit.

My enemy is the cause of my accumulating the merit of patience
Because without him there is no patience to practise,
Whereas with him there is.
So how does he obstruct my virtuous practise?

A beggar is not an obstacle
To people practising giving
Any more than an Abbot is an obstacle
To those wishing to ordain.

Indeed, there are many beggars in this world,
But people who harm me are extremely rare.
In fact, if I had not inflicted harm on other in the past,
There would be no one to inflict harm on me now!

48. For an excellent treatment of peace-building, see Sharon D. Welch's *Real Peace, Real Security: The Challenges of Global Citizenship* (Minneapolis: Fortress Press, 2008).
49. "What Would Jesus Do?" accessed December 6, 2010, en.wikipedia.org/wiki/What_would_Jesus_do%3F.
50. Wikipedia, "What Would Jesus Do?"
51. While the terms *evangelical, charismatic,* and *fundamentalist* do not all mean the same thing, they functionally overlap within Christianity. It is not my intent to conflate these terms but, rather, to address all of them at their points of convergence.

CHAPTER 9

1. Kiran Bedi, *It's Always Possible: One Woman's Transformation of India's Prison System* (1998; repr., Honesdale, PA: Himalayan Institute Press, 2002), 69.
2. Bedi, *It's Always Possible,* 144. (Note: This book has been published under several other titles, including *I Dare!: It's Always Possible*; *It's Always Possible: One Woman's Transformation of Tihar Jail*; and *It's Always Possible: Transforming One of the Largest Prisons in the World.*)
3. "As the first woman to go through police training, Kiran was quickly accepted by her male co-trainees because of her celebrity status, which had put her on the sports pages regularly from the age of fourteen. She was already familiar to them as a national tennis

champion known for her stamina and tenacity." This quote comes from Kiran Bedi's official Ramon Magsaysay Award Biography, accessed December 7, 2010, http://www.rmaf. org.ph/Awardees/Biography/BiographyBediKir.htm. Unless otherwise noted, all quotes and details in this biographical section come from this biography. Although many other sources were consulted, most reference this biography.

4. Ibid.
5. Ibid.
6. See Wikipedia's article on Kiran Bedi, accessed December 7, 2010, http://en.wikipedia. org/wiki/Kiran_Bedi.
7. Ramon Magsaysay Award Biography.
8. She also cross-trained in hurdles, long jump, and marathon running.
9. For this she earned the humorous nickname "Crane Bedi." This anecdote easily establishes Kiran Bedi's womanist credentials as an "outrageous, audacious, courageous" persona. See Tinku Ray, "First Female Police Officer Quits," BBC News, Delhi, November 27, 2007, accessed December 7, 2010, http://news.bbc.co.uk/2/hi/south_asia/7115753. stm, which opines, "She has become a well-recognized face, as much for her outspokenness as for her career successes."
10. Ramon Magsaysay Award Biography. As this article states, "[h]er lack of interest in "playing the game," within a service in which professionalism has been replaced by favoritism, has been costly both professionally and personally."
11. Ibid.
12. Wikipedia, http://en.wikipedia.org/wiki/Kiran_Bedi. Despite an extensive search of other sources containing this same reference, I have been unable to find the name of the degree-granting institution.
13. A partial list of these awards includes: President's Gallantry Award (1979), Women of the Year Award (1980), Asia Region Award for Drug Prevention and Control (1991), Ramon Magsaysay Award for Government Service (1994), Mahila Shiromani Award (1995), Father Machismo Humanitarian Award (1995), Lion of the Year (1995), Joseph Beuys Award (1997), ACCU-IEF Award (1998), Pride of India (1999), Serge Sotiroff Award (UNCDP) (1999), Bharat Gaurav Award (1999), Morrison Tom Gitchoff Award (2001), Woman of the Year Award (2002), UN Medal (2004), Mother Teresa Memorial National Award for Social Justice (2005), FICCI Award (2005), Transformative Leadership in the Indian Police Service Award (2006), Suryadatta National Award (2007), Amity Woman Achiever for Social Justice Award (2007), and Star Parivar Award for Most Damdar Sadasya (2010). See http://kiranbedi.com/recognition.htm.
14. At least two sources report that Bedi submitted her request for resignation after being passed over in favor of a junior male colleague for the prestigious post of Delhi Police Commissioner. See Ray, "First Female Police Officer Quits," and CNN-IBN, "Kiran Bedi Quits Police Force, Takes Voluntary Retirement," November 27, 2007, accessed December 7, 2010, ibnlive.in.com/news/kiran-bedi-quits-police-force-takes-voluntary-retirement/53100-3.html.
15. See www.Navjyoti.org.in.
16. See www.IndiaVisionFoundation.org and also www.SaferIndia.com.
17. View Kiran Bedi's blog, "Crane Bedi," at accessed December 7, 2010, www.kiran-bedi. blogspot.com/; *Doing Time, Doing Vipassana*, directed by Eilona Ariel,and Ayelet Menahemi (Tel Aviv, Israel: Karuna Films, 1997), DVD; *Yes Madam, Sir*, directed by Megan Doneman (Queensland, Australia: Sojourn Films, 2008), DVD.

18. Bedi, *It's Always Possible*, 8–10.
19. "Power over" is hierarchical power, assertive and forceful. "Power with" is collaborative power, inviting and immanent. Historically, "power over" has been considered a masculinist modality, while "power with" is often painted as a feminist (or feminine) innovation. For a discussion of the difference between "power over" and "power with," see Audre Lorde, *Sister Outsider: Essays and Speeches* (Berkeley, CA: Crossing Press, 1984).
20. The terms *punctum* (point) and *aporia* (opening) as theoretical constructs used to denote moments of extraordinary potential for radical social change appear in Chela Sandoval's book, *Methodology of the Oppressed* (Minneapolis: University of Minnesota Press, 2000). Additionally, I further develop these concepts within my article with Shomari Olugbala, "Fighting in He(r) Heels: Sylvia Rivera, Stonewall, Civil Rights, and Liberation," in *The Human Tradition and the Civil Rights Movement, 1865–1980*, ed. Susan Glisson (Lanham, MD: Rowman and Littlefield, 2006), 309–334.
21. See Zimbardo prison study and cite classic psych article on learned helplessness.
22. From an interview with *Life Positive* magazine, accessed December 7, 2010, http://www.lifepositive.com/Mind/ethics-and-values/ethics/kiran-bedi.asp.
23. Ibid., 141.
24. Ibid., 16.
25. Ibid., 22.
26. "DIY" is an acronym standing for "do it yourself," made popular during the punk rock era by anarchist youth who sought to live freely off the excesses of mainstream consumer society. Over time, the term *DIY* itself, with its irreverent yet resourceful connotations, permeated the mainstream.
27. Bedi, *It's Always Possible*, 156.
28. Ibid., 159.
29. Ibid., 24.
30. Ibid., 24.
31. To incentivize the new doctors, Bedi instituted an attractive, even if modest, benefits package that included transportation, better administrative facilities, risk allowance, and reimbursement of telephone expenses. See Bedi, *It's Always Possible*, 227.
32. See chap. 1, this volume, on health empowerment.
33. One article reports that Kiran Bedi declared Tihar a no-smoking zone. See Ramon Magsaysay Award Biography.
34. Bedi, *It's Always Possible*, 192–93.
35. Ibid., 193.
36. See the international home page of vipassana meditation as taught by S. N. Goenka and his students, accessed December 8, 2010, www.dhamma.org/.
37. See "The Art of Living" (a talk by S. N. Goenka), accessed December 8, 2010, www.dhamma.org/en/art.shtml.
38. Ibid.
39. See, for example, the 2008 film *Dhamma Brothers* , directed by Jenny Phillips, which examines the use of vipassana meditation in an Alabama maximum-security prison.
40. These techniques are underrecognized in the academic field of social movement studies as well as in the arena of progressive/left grassroots activism. These techniques are not, however, underrecognized in the areas wherein they have historically predominated, such as in religious communities (sanghas, monasteries, cloisters, etc.) and spiritually oriented/faith-based lay social change communities. It is important to remember that

these techniques can be used by people on the right or on the left, even for people with humanitarian or misanthropic objectives, however, the ethical compass of democratics (see Sandoval, *Methodology of the Oppressed*), ensures their application toward altruistic, egalitarian, liberatory, and healing-oriented ends.

41. Bedi, *It's Always Possible*, 196.
42. Ibid., 197.
43. Ibid., 198.
44. Ibid., 133.
45. Ibid., 142.
46. Ibid., 189.
47. Ibid., 190.
48. Ibid.
49. Ibid., 141.
50. An interesting historical comparison exists between Kiran Bedi's ideas about "moral education" and the "mental hygiene" ideas of mid-twentieth century African American women such as Mamie Phipps Clark, whose social activist praxis also demonstrates womanist features.
51. A good discussion of this "third way" concept appears throughout Chela Sandoval's *Methodology of the Oppressed*, see, in particular, 4, 154–57, 186–87 (n. 9).
52. See Hayden White, "Writing in the Middle Voice," *Stanford Literature Review* 9, no. 2 (1992): 179–87. See also Judith Butler's *Excitable Speech: A Politics of the Performative* (New York: Routledge, 1997).
53. Bedi, *It's Always Possible*, 165.
54. Ibid.
55. Ibid., 168–69.
56. Ibid., p. 178.
57. See Ignacio Martín-Baró's *Writings for a Liberation Psychology* (Cambridge, MA: Harvard University Press, 1994). Martín-Baró's liberation psychology adapts liberation theology, such as that of Oscar Romero or Gustavo Gutierrez, to social psychology and focuses on how psychologists can help society bring about justice and human well-being by creating just social institutions that in turn facilitate optimal psychological well-being and nonoppressive social behavior in people. I have also written two unpublished papers on this topic that apply the principles of liberation psychology, ecologically considered, to lifespan human development vis-à-vis the idea of optimal human development.
58. I am borrowing Paulo Freire's terminology here. Full humanization is that which enables people to live up to their human potential. Thus, it is a concept closely aligned with that of self-actualization. Full humanization is what institutions (are made to) do to facilitate people's self-actualization, the latter being a self-initiated process. See Freire, *Pedagogy of the Oppressed* (New York: Continuum, 1971).
59. Bedi, *It's Always Possible*, 51.
60. Ibid., elsewhere in the text she coins the phrase "Rakshak se shikshak" ("From protector to educator)," see 134.
61. Ibid., 126.
62. Ibid., 136.
63. Ibid., 165. This is a repeat of the same quote used in an earlier section of this chapter.

64. Ibid., 116.

65. Ibid., 180.

66. Ibid., 295.

67. Ramon Magsaysay Award Biography.

68. Freire, *Pedagogy of the Oppressed*.

69. See also, *In Pursuit of Excellence*, a management book popular during the 1970s that advocates "management by walking around"—a method my late father, Duane Dean Dumbleton, a beloved community college president, favored to great effect. I thank Willis J. Potts, Jr., Chair of the Board of Regents of the University System of Georgia, for bringing this connection to my attention (see Terry Orlick, *In Pursuit of Excellence* (Champaign, IL: Human Kinetics).

70. Bedi, *It's Always Possible*, 116, 127.

71. Ibid., 142. Sister Max Mathews, an African American Buddhist nun who did extensive economic development work with the women of Tihar Jail and is cited in *It's Always Possible*, also said this of Kiran Bedi: "She was talking to them [the women on the women's ward] as a mother, as she always did," 251. Other journalists in the text offer similar observations.

72. Tamara Beauboeuf-Lafontant, "A Womanist Experience of Caring: Understanding the Pedagogy of Exemplary Black Women Teachers," *The Womanist Reader,* ed. Layli Phillips (*The Urban Review*, 2002; repr., Routledge, 2006), 280–95.

73. Chogyam Trungpa, *Shambhala: The Sacred Path of the Warrior* (Boston: Shambhala, 1984).

74. Chikwenye Okonjo Ogunyemi, *Africa Wo/Man Palava: The Nigerian Novel by Women* (Chicago: University of Chicago Press, 1996), 45–61. Diedre Badejo also discusses the figure of the Iyalode in her book *Osun Seegesi: The Elegant Deity of Wealth, Power, and Femininity* (Trenton, NJ: Africa World Press, 1996), specifically the chapter titled "Gender, Power, and African Feminist Theory" (175–86). See also Catherine Obianuju Acholonu's work, *Motherism: An Afrocentric Alternative to Feminism* (Abuja, Nigeria: Afa, 1995).

75. Ogunyemi, *Africa Wo/Man Palava,* 45.

76. Ibid., 46.

77. Ibid., 48.

78. Sandoval, *Methodology of the Oppressed,* 141; Doneman, *Yes Madam, Sir.* DVD.

79. Ibid., 4, 139–57.

80. In *It's Always Possible*, Kiran Bedi includes an Epilogue called "Ten Years Later: Life After Tihar." This epilogue includes her own commentary plus a series of interviews with former Tihar inmates conducted by social activist Ruzbeh Bharucha. Many of the former inmates interviewed by Bharucha indicate that Kiran Bedi's programs left a lasting, positive impression on them and changed their lives favorably in the long term. The previously cited Ramon Magsaysay Award Biography, however, suggests that Kiran Bedi's departure was a cause for despair among those inmates who remained behind. See Magsaysay Award Biogaphy, 34, accessed December 7, 2010.

81. Laurie Patton, personal communication, Spring 2008. See also the Ramon Magsaysay Award Biography, 34.

82. Bedi, *It's Always Possible,* 285–86.

CHAPTER 10

1. Pregs Govender, "South Africa: Secrecy as a Weapon of Oppression," *Pazambuka News*, September 23, 2010, accessed December 11, 2010, www.pambazuka.org/en/category/features/67154; reposted at http://www.africafocus.org/docs10/med1010b.php.
2. Pregs Govender, *Love and Courage: A Story of Insubordination* (Johannesburg, SA: Jacana Media, 2007), 5.
3. My personal notes taken at the IFUN workshop (in an entry dated September 9, 2007) record Pregs Govender as making this statement.
4. Ibid., 206–210, 234–35. Pregs Govender's political courage on this vote can be compared with U.S. Congresswoman Barbara Lee's solo vote against President George W. Bush's war in Afghanistan in 2001.
5. See, both accessed December 10, 2010, http://www.net-workingwomen.com/category_list.php?categoryid=424; and http://www.un.org/ga/president/61/follow-up/thematic-gender/pgovender.shtml.
6. Wording courtesy of Pregaluxmi Govender's biography for the "Price Check Panel" of the AIDS 2010 Gender Costing campaign launch sponsored by AIDS-Free World, accessed December 10, 2010, http://www.aidsfreeworld.org/Our-Issues/Politics-of-Funding/READ-an-AIDSFree-World-letter-LISTEN-to-the-AIDS-2010-Gender-Costing-campaign-launch.aspx.
7. See the panel's 2008 report, "Protecting Dignity: An Agenda for Human Rights," accessed December 10, 2010, http://www.udhr60.ch/agenda/ENG-%20agenda_print.pdf.
8. Ibid., 137. My notes from IFUN on September 25, 2007, say, "Her [Pregs Govender's] struggle is with being propped up in the media as a leader, as someone above others, etc. She refuses to be personally profiled."
9. For example, she writes, "In the meeting, I steadfastly refused to be derailed by this emotional outburst [of the minister to whom she reported] and continued raising the issues we had come to see him about. I had spent years trying to learn how to stay centred and 'meet both praise and insult with equanimity'—although I know it's something I need to practice for the rest of my life"(174).
10. Ibid., 23.
11. Ibid., 44.
12. Ibid,. 41.
13. Ibid.
14. Ibid., 41–42.
15. Ibid., 41.
16. Ibid., 43.
17. Ibid.
18. Ibid., 46.
19. Ibid., 128–29, 217–18. See also "Farewell Speech by Pregs Govender, Chairperson of the Joint Monitoring Committee on the Improvement of the Quality of Life and Status of Women," *Agenda*, no. 52 (2002): 98. (*Agenda* is a South African feminist journal).
20. Ibid., 48.
21. Ibid., 50.
22. Ibid.

23. Ibid., 51.
24. Ibid., 53.
25. Ibid., 54.
26. Ibid., 63, 65.
27. Ibid., 66. She was vindicated years later by a friend who remarked, "You work harder than most women I know, yet you spend much more time with your children than many women who are housewives" (113). Pregs also wrote, "My children sustained my spirit in many ways" (114). She credits her regular yoga practice with helping her parent, particularly through the most difficult times (116–17).
28. Ibid., 117.
29. Ibid., 67.
30. Ibid., 84–89. See also 180.
31. Ibid., 92.
32. Patrick Burnett, "Pregs Govender and the Politics of Disobedience," *West Cape News*, December 15, 2008, accessed December 15, 2010, http://westcapenews.com/?p=554.
33. What she also learned is that, often, the problems lay more readily with the "middle management" of the organizations rather than the highest levels of command.
34. Govender, "Farewell Speech," 127.
35. She writes, "In 1994 I had felt a distinct ambivalence about formal political power and being a parliamentarian. Yet in Madiba's parliament I had enjoyed working closely with other insubordinate women of the ANC to push the boundaries of policy and institutional change," ibid., 184, and see also 141. By the time Nelson Mandela's successor, Thabo Mbeki, was elected, the tide began to turn and Pregs's feelings about participation within the halls of power began to sour (199).
36. Ibid., p. 135.
37. Pregs Govender, personal communication, January 14, 2011.
38. By "unauthorized" here, I primarily mean energy transformation activities and techniques, such as would be associated with mystical, metaphysical, and esoteric practice (regardless of tradition of origin), not what might be called normative religious participation such as church attendance, mosque attendance, synagogue attendance, or participation in public festivals.
39. This topic is treated extensively, albeit without the use of this "closet" terminology, in Akasha Gloria Hull's book, *Soul Talk: The New Spirituality of African American Women* (Rochester, VT: Inner Traditions International, 2001). I also encountered this sentiment in a lecture by M. Jacqui Alexander at the National Black Arts Festival, in which she "came out" as an initiated Voudou Priestess. This issue is treated in her book *Pedagogies of Crossing: Meditations on Feminism, Sexual Politics, Memory, and the Sacred* (Durham, NC: Duke University Press, 2005), chap. 7, "Pedagogies of the Sacred: Making the Invisible Tangible."
40. Govender, "Farewell Speech," 135–36.
41. It bears noting that charisma is basically a form of personality-based energy work.
42. Govender, "Farewell Speech," 147, 163.
43. Ibid., p. 185.
44. In one section, she writes, "Five years later he [Thabo Mbeki] became president and inherited a democracy plagued by the militarised, violent and poverty-ridden legacy of apartheid, which globalisation had compounded. But the 'people of the rainbow' were

expected to continue being the 'miracle nation.'" (185). The quoted material within the quote refers to Nelson Mandela's 1994 inauguration speech.

45. Ibid., 149.
46. Ibid., 165.
47. Ibid.
48. Ibid., 167.
49. Ibid.
50. Ibid.
51. Ibid., 197–98.
52. Ibid., 199.
53. Ibid.
54. All of these quotes come from my IFUN journal in an entry dated "Day 9," which was September 25, 2007.
55. Ibid., 203–4.
56. Ibid., 206.
57. This scientific approach has been fruitfully utilized by mindfulness researchers and teachers such as Jon Kabat-Zinn. See his *Wherever You Go, There You Are: Mindfulness Meditation in Everyday Life* (New York: Hyperion, 1994).
58. Gloria Anzaldúa refers to this as "yoga of the body" and writes, "'Yoga of the body' has to do with flexibility and fluidity—going beyond physical boundaries. It has to do with extending beyond limitations." *Interviews/Entrevistas*, ed. Ana Louise Keating (New York: Routledge, 2000), 77, 99.
59. For references on the energy body/ies, see Donna Eden's *Energy Medicine* (New York: Tarcher/Putnam, 1998), Richard Gerber's *Vibrational Medicine* (Rochester, VT: Bear, 2001), and *Quantum Healing* by Deepak Chopra (New York: Bantam, 1989).
60. Pregs Govender, personal communication, January 14, 2011.
61. Govender, *Love and Courage*, p. 8.
62. Personal notes from my IFUN journal dated September 19, 2007. Other quotes in this paragraph also come from that entry.
63. Govender, "Farewell Speech," 96. While she uses the word *feminist* here, I also see parallels to a womanist perspective.
64. Alice Walker, "Coming Apart," in The Womanist Reader, ed. Layli Phillips (Bantam, 1979; repr., New York: Routledge, 2006), 3–11.
65. Alice Walker, Preface, *In Search of Our Mothers' Gardens: Womanist Prose,* in *The Womanist Reader*, ed. Layli Phillips (Harcourt Brace Jovanovich, 1983; repr., New York: Routledge, 2006), 19.
66. Mercy Amba Oduyoye, *Daughters of Anowa: African Women and Patriarchy* (Maryknoll, NY: Orbis, 1995), 10.
67. Ibid, 29.
68. Marianne Williamson, *A Return to Love* (New York: HarperCollins, 1992), chap. 7, sect. 3.
69. Govender, *Love and Courage*, 138–39. I again make the comparison here to Sister Chan Khong's "Man is not our enemy" remarks.
70. Ibid., 228. Here, Mandela is addressing the International AIDS Conference.
71. Pregs Govender, "When 'Traditional Values' Are a Stick to Beat Women," *South Africa Times*, February 28, 2010,, accessed December 11, 2010www.timeslive.co.za/opinion/editorials/article329381.ece.

72. From my personal IFUN notes, dated September 24, 2007.
73. Govender, *Love and Courage*, 88.
74. Pregs Govender, personal communication, January 14, 2011 (emphasis added).
75. Ibid., September 19, 2007.
76. Govender, *Love and Courage*, 7–8.

CHAPTER 11

1. *Taking Root: The Vision of Wangari Maathai*, directed by Lisa Merton and Alan Dater (Marlboro, VT: Marlboro Arts, 2008), DVD.
2. Wangari Maathai, "A Winning Partnership," *The Guardian* (online), October 11, 2008, accessed December 19, 2010, http://www.guardian.co.uk/commentisfree/2008/oct/11/blackhistorymonth-race2. See also Maathai, *Unbowed: A Memoir* (New York: Anchor Books, 2007), 73–78.
3. The date of Wangari Muta Maathai's PhD conferral is 1971. Even though the University College of Nairobi became the University of Nairobi in 1970, she was "grandfathered in," obtaining her degree under the old institutional moniker.
4. Maathai, *Unbowed*, 113.
5. Ibid., 106.
6. Ibid., 151.
7. Ibid., 147.
8. Ibid., 163.
9. Ibid., 130.
10. Chikwenye Okonjo Ogunyemi, *Africa Wo/Man Palava: The Nigerian Novel by Women* (Chicago: University of Chicago Press, 1996), 26.
11. Maathai, *Unbowed*, 52.
12. Ibid., 5.
13. Ibid., 3–4.
14. Ibid., 5.
15. Ibid., 37.
16. This scenery is beautifully depicted in the documentary film, *Taking Root*,(2008) including one of the DVD bonus segments titled "Wangari: The Early Years." This film is directed by Lisa Merton and Alan Dater and is available from www.takingrootfilm.com.
17. As I use the word *nature* in this chapter or anywhere in this book, I am aware of debates about "the nature of 'nature,'" particularly as they pertain to the critique that the term *nature* is dualizing. Although I agree with this critique, preferring more integrative understandings such as those embodied in neologisms like *livingkind*, for the sake of simplicity and ease of communication, I resort to using the word *nature* with its slippery, lay meaning in this text.
18. Ibid., 45.
19. Ibid., 45–46. See also *Taking Root*, the DVD bonus feature titled "The Green Belt Movement: Environmental Conservation and Tree Planting."
20. Wangari Maathai, from an interview in *Taking Root* (00:33:35).
21. Ibid., 121–22.

22. This viewpoint is elaborated on in Shamara Shantu Riley's article, "Ecology is a Sistah's Issue Too: The Politics of Emergent Afrocentric Womanism," in *Readings in Ecology and Feminist Theology*, ed. Mary Heather MacKinnon and Moni McIntyre (Lanham, MD: Rowman and Littlefield, 1995), 216–17.
23. Cf. Linda James Myers's discussion of Afrocentric vs. Eurocentric worldviews in her book, *Understanding an Afrocentric World View: Introduction to an Optimal Psychology* (Dubuque, IA: Kendall/Hunt, 1993/1998).
24. Ibid., 81–82.
25. Ibid., 90. Wangari Maathai offers an extended anecdote about her invitation to a Nation of Islam meeting and its impact on her religious and political thinking. She also discusses the inspirational impact of the U.S. civil rights movement on Kenyan nationalists, particularly those who came up with the idea that later became known as the Kennedy Airlift.
26. Maathai, *The Green Belt Movement*, 91.
27. Maathai, *Unbowed*, 109.
28. This interpretation was explored in-depth during a semester-long class with one of my spiritual teachers, Dr. Will Coleman, who is a multilingual Biblical scholar, Kabbalist, and esotericist.
29. Mark I. Wallace, "Sacred-Land Theology: Green Spirit, Deconstruction, and the Question of Idolatry in Contemporary Earthen Christianity," in *Ecospirit: Religions and Philosophies for the Earth*, ed. Laurel Kearns and Catherine Keller (New York: Fordham University Press, 2007), 291–92.
30. Ibid., 293.
31. *Taking Root* [01:09:28].
32. Wangari Maathai, "The Cracked Mirror," *Resurgence,* November 11, 2004, accessed January 14, 2011, http://www.greenbeltmovement.org/a.php?id=28.
33. Maathai, *Unbowed*, 165.
34. This speech is captured on film in *Taking Root* (01:17:00).
35. Wallace,"Sacred-Land Theology," 130.
36. Wangari Maathai, *The Green Belt Movement: Sharing the Approach and the Experience* (1985; repr., Brooklyn, NY: Lantern Books, 2006), 20–22 (reduced font size and brackets original in indented section).
37. For an overview, see Okwui Enwezor, *The Short Century: Independence and Liberation Movements in Africa, 1945–1994* (New York: Prestel, 2001).
38. See Maulana Karenga, *Introduction to Black Studies* (1968; repr., Timbuktu, Mali: University of Sankore Press, 2002). The Nguzo Saba are: Umoja (unity), Kujichagulia (self-determination), Ujima (collective work and responsibility), Ujamaa (cooperative economics), Nia (purpose), Kuumba (creativity), and Imani (faith). See also "Kwanzaa," accessed December 22, 2010, http://en.wikipedia.org/wiki/Kwanzaa.
39. Maathai, *Unbowed*, 131.
40. Ibid. Men of the Trees actively participated in her second tree planting.
41. Ibid., 173.
42. Maathai, *The Green Belt Movement*, 47–49. This education program later expanded to neighboring African countries under the auspices of "Pan-African Training Workshops," see 54.
43. Maathai, *Unbowed*, 179–80.
44. Ibid., 173.
45. Ibid.

46. This dialogue is colorfully brought to life in the documentary *Taking Root*, as well as three of its DVD bonus features, including "Civic and Environmental Education Workshops (CEE)," "Food Security: CEE Workshop," and "The 'Hut Tax': CEE Workshop."
47. Maathai, *Unbowed*, 139–63. But see also 184–276. Various passages from *Unbowed* appear in the film *Taking Root* as videotaped interview segments.
48. Ibid., 177.
49. Ibid., 227. It should be noted that from 1978 to 2002, Kenya's President Daniel arap Moi, who succeeded Jomo Kenyatta upon his death in office, was Wangari Maathai's chief political nemesis and, according to her account, directly or indirectly the orchestrator of many of her political difficulties and obstructions. He was succeeded by Mwai Kibaki in 2002, whose administration was much more hospitable to the activities of the Green Belt Movement.
50. Ibid., 248.
51. *Taking Root* [30:35]. Note: This is a translation found in the subtitles, as she is speaking Kikuyu in this segment of the film.
52. Riley cites Ann Snitow on the definition of motherism: "Motherists are women who, for various reasons, 'identify themselves not as feminists but as militant mothers, fighting together for survival.'" Snitow, 1989, 48, is cited, although the reference is not provided in the text. See, however, Ann Snitow, "A Gender Diary," in *Conflicts in Feminism*, ed. Marianne Hirsch and Evelyn Fox Keller (New York: Routledge, 1990), 9–43. The quote cited by Riley falls on 20–21.
53. Ogunyemi, *Africa Wo/Man Palava*, 53.
54. Maathai, *Unbowed*, 217.
55. Combahee River Collective, "The Combahee River Collective Statement," in *Home Girls: A Black Feminist Anthology* ed. Barbara Smith (New York: Kitchen Table: Women of Color Press), 272.
56. "Satyagraha," Wikipedia article, accessed December 22, 2010).http://en.wikipedia.org/wiki/Satyagraha.
57. Walker, Preface , *In Search of Our Mothers' Gardens: Womanist Prose*, in *The Womanist Reader*, ed. Layli Phillips (Harcourt Brace Jovanovich, 1983; repr., New York: Routledge, 2006), 19.
58. Ogunyemi, *Africa Wo/Man Palava*, 53-54.
59. Wole Soyinka, quoted in Cheryl Johnson-Odim and Nina Emma Mba, *For Women and the Nation: Funmilayo Ransome-Kuti of Nigeria* (Chicago: University of Illinois Press, 1997), 66.
60. Maathai, *Unbowed*, p. 287.
61. Ibid., 175.
62. Ibid., 294.
63. Shamara Shantu Riley, "Ecology Is a Sistah's Issue Too: The Politics of Emergent Afrocentric Womanism," in *Readings in Ecology and Feminist Theology*, ed. Mary Heather MacKinnon and Moni McIntyre (Lanham, MD: Rowman and Littlefield, 1995), 215.
64. Ibid., 224. Note that the "both/and" language also invokes the Black feminist theory of Patricia Hill Collins. See her *Black Feminist Thought: Knowledge, Consciousness, and the Politics of Empowerment*, 10th anniv. ed. (New York: Routledge, 2001).
65. Riley, "Ecology," 224.
66. Ibid. See also Luisah Teish, *Jambalaya: The Natural Woman's Book of Personal Charms and Practical Rituals* (New York: HarperCollins, 1985), 61, for the original citation.

67. Riley, "Ecology," 224. Here she is directly quoting Jahn, 1961, 105. Although no complete citation is given, she is presumably quoting from Jahnheinz Jahn's book, *Muntu: An Outline of the New African Culture* (New York: Grove Press, 1961).
68. See "Nommo," accessed December 20, 2010, http://www.encyclopedia.chicagohistory.org/pages/894.html. This reference reflects the Bantu usage. In the Dogon context, the Nommo are deities or ancestral figures associated with the Sirius star system. A Google search on "Nommo" will turn up several websites on this topic. See, for instance, accessed December 20, 2010, http://en.wikipedia.org/wiki/Nommo.
69. Clenora Hudson-Weems, "Nommo: Self-naming, Self-Definition and the History of Africana Womanism," in *Africana Womanism, and Race and Gender in the Presidential Candidacy of Barack Obama* (Bloomington, IN: AuthorHouse, 2008), 29, 34, 35. Portions of this chapter appeared previously in Hudson-Weems debut text, *Africana Womanism: Reclaiming Ourselves* (Troy, MI: Bedford Publishers, 1993).
70. Ogunyemi, *Africa Wo/Man Palava,* 22.
71. Riley, "Ecology," 224.
72. Ibid.
73. Ibid. See also Luisah Teish, *Jambalaya,* 63, for the original citation. Note that this "power with" formulation is reminiscent of Audre Lorde's discussion of power in "Uses of the Erotic: The Erotic as Power" in her book *Sister Outsider: Essays and Speeches* (Berkeley, CA: Crossing Press, 1984).
74. Riley, "Ecology," 224.
75. Ibid., 225.
76. Pamela A. Smith, "Green Lap, Brown Embrace, Blue Body: The Ecospirituality of Alice Walker," *Cross-Currents 48* (1998/1999), 471–87, accessed December 20, 2010, http://www.crosscurrents.org/walkereco.htm.
77. Alice Walker, *Living by the Word* (San Diego, CA: Harcourt Brace Jovanovich, 1988), 147. Cited by Smith, "Green Lap," no page number.
78. Alice Walker, *Anything We Love Can Be Saved: A Writer's Activism* (New York: Random House, 1997), 44. Cited by Pamela A. Smith, "Green Lap," no page number.
79. Melanie L. Harris, *Gifts of Virtue, Alice Walker, and Womanist Ethics* (New York: Palgrave Macmillan, 2010).
80. Ibid., 17.
81. Ibid.
82. Ibid., 60, 67.
83. Ibid., 114.
84. Ibid., 67.
85. See Elsa Barkley Brown, "Womanist Consciousness: Maggie Lena Walker and the Independent Order of Saint Luke," in *The Womanist Reader,* ed. Layli Phillips (*Signs,*1989; repr., New York: Routledge, 2006), 173–92. See also Mary Frances Berry, *My Face Is Black Is True: Callie House and the Struggle for Ex-Slave Reparations* (New York: Knopf, 2005), and Cheryl Johnson-Odim and Nina Emma Mba, *For Women and the Nation: Funmilayo Ransome-Kuti of Nigeria* (Chicago: University of Illinois Press, 1997).
86. Maathai, *Unbowed,* 172.
87. Xiumei Pu, "Nature, Sexuality, and Spirituality: A Womanist Reading of Di Mu (Earth Mother) and Di Mu Jing (Songs of Earth Mother) in China," in *Ain't I a Womanist, Too? Third Wave Womanist Religious Thought,* ed. Monica A. Coleman (Minneapolis, MN: Fortress, forthcoming).

88. Pu, ibid., 2.
89. Nonlocal consciousness is evident in psychic phenomena (ESP, telepathy, clairvoyance, clairaudience, telekinesis, etc.), as well as the direct knowledge that is sometimes obtained through meditation or other spiritual practices, as well as through such phenomena as the Akashic records, in which the history of the entire universe is said to be stored.
90. A fascinating episode in *Taking Root* involves Wangari Maathai addressing a military garrison and encouraging them to plant trees around the base in order to augment their efforts to protect the land that is Kenya. She states, "I'm really trying to encourage the military to establish forests around their barracks. It is very important for the soldiers to understand that, even as they march with their guns, the land is being stolen away by and unseen enemy" (01:14:55). As the film goes on to portray, that "unseen enemy" is soil erosion caused by deforestation. She concludes, "I want them to ... protect the land from that enemy, too, by planting trees ..." (01:15:15). Her willingness to bring her message to the military, despite her pacifist belief system, is further evidence of the "nonideological," love-based character of womanism, the womanist idea, and womanist activism: Be where you are and just do it.
91. Maathai, *Unbowed*, 5–6.
92. Ibid., 285. See also *The Green Belt Movement*, 51–54, 120–21.
93. Ibid., 262, 274.
94. There's a popular feminist slogan, often appearing on buttons or bumper stickers, originating from the 1970s that says "Sexism-Racism-Classism-_____ Recognize the Connections" (various versions fill in the last blank with anti-Semitism, homophobia, etc.). The point here is to always include the environment in this equation, whether ecological destruction, environmental exploitation, or Earth injustice, regardless of which social "isms" are included.
95. Margot Adler, "Preface," *Drawing Down the Moon: Witches, Druids, Goddess Worshippers, and Other Pagans in America Today,* rev. ed. (1979; repr., New York: Penguin Compass, 1986), accessed December 22, 2010, http://xixiant.tripod.com/text.html#preface. Interestingly, this influential "breakout" book on women and neopaganism was published the same year as the first publication to use the term *womanist*, namely, Alice Walker's short story, "Coming Apart." Elsewhere in this same preface, Margot Adler also writes, "The world is holy. Nature is holy. The body is holy. Sexuality is holy. The mind is holy. The imagination is holy. You are holy. A spiritual path that is not stagnant ultimately leads one to the understanding of one's own divine nature."

CHAPTER 12

A much earlier draft of this chapter was presented at a one-year anniversary memorial service, organized by Aliyah's friends and sponsored by the Office of President Debora Spar, held at Barnard College, New York on November 20, 2010, which would have been Aliyah's 24th birthday.

1. The source of this quote is an "Eastern Wisdom" quote-of-the-day calendar given to me as a Christmas gift by my friend Katina Grays. This was the daily quote for November 11, the day I learned of my daughter's death.

2. Gloria Anzaldúa, "now let us shift ... the path of conocimiento ... inner work, public acts," in *This Bridge We Call Home: Radical Visions for Transformation*, ed. Gloria Anzaldúa and AnaLouise Keating (New York: Routledge, 2002), 540.
3. Ibid., 541.
4. Ibid.
5. In fairness, she did have a few flaws—she was quite messy and frequently late for things, both a cause of ongoing struggle between us. "Life's gonna teach you if you don't listen to me," I used to say.
6. Jeremiah 1:4-5, *New Revised Standard Version*.
7. One thing that the coroner (or was it the police detective) said that sticks out in my mind is that they were able to rule out foul play by where Aliyah had landed on the asphalt. When a person simply falls or is pushed, they said, they land close to the building; when they are trying to fly, they land far from the building. She landed quite far, almost making it to the adjacent building.
8. Aishwarya Bhatt, "Sophia Stewart Wins Copyright Infringement Case," *Thaindian News*, November 11, 2009, accessed December 31, 2010, http://www.thaindian.com/ newsportal/entertainment/sophia-stewart-wins-the-matrix-copyright-infringement-case_100273392.html.
9. As the police informed us, neither was her iPod. She had taken it with her to the rooftop. Her music of choice in the weeks before the jump had been Jimi Hendrix. Apparently the device still worked after being recovered.
10. Bahá'u'lláh, *The Hidden Words of Bahá'u'lláh* (Chandigarh, India: Carmel, 2002), no. 32 from the Arabic, 17.
11. Anzaldúa, "now let us shift," 551. This quote comes from the section labeled "2. the Coatlicue state ... desconocimiento and the cost of knowing."
12. When Aliyah was growing up, the Marvel Comics character known as Storm, an African woman with long silver hair who could fly and control the weather, was one of her heroines.
13. Sushila Blackman, *Graceful Exits: How Great Beings Die—Death Stories of Hindu, Tibetan, Buddhist, and Zen Masters* (Boston: Shambhala, 2005), 44.
14. And maybe, also, somehow, the mortician made that smile on her face using mortuary secrets. Who knows.
15. This poem appears in Aliyah's journal, dated June 27, 2009. It was written during the solo portion of a group vision quest rites of passage program that Aliyah participated in during June 2009, in the Inyo Mountains of eastern California.
16. The diary offers two versions of this verse. Here is the second: "Gaze once more upon the twilit horizon./Part your lips and breathe our name./Follow us to the Starbound procession/from whence you came."
17. In *Jambalaya*, Luisah Teish discusses dreams as a site for communication with ancestors (see 98–99). Remarkably, the night after reading this, I had a dream about Aliyah after many, many months of not dreaming about her, in which I happened upon her unexpectedly and said, "Is it really you?" to which she replied, with a knowing smile, "Yes, it's really me."
18. Diedre Badejo briefly discusses the issue of premature death (death prior to elderhood, particularly of children) in her book, *Osun Seegesi: The Elegant Deity of Wealth, Power, and Femininity*. Trenton, NJ: Africa World Press, 1996). On p. 68, she explains that, in the Yoruba view, premature death can cause cosmic imbalance, and that child death alone

does not necessarily elevate one to the role of venerable ancestor. This has, of course, left me with questions. *Abiku* is the name for a child with a spirit that is barely hanging on in this world (see Ogunyemi, *Africa Wo/Man Palava*, 61–74 on this theme), and the mother of an *abiku* child spends all her time trying to keep the child alive, to the neglect of others. I don't think this was the case with Aliyah, as she was very life-filled until the very moment of transition and, additionally, at 22, she was on the brink between childhood and adulthood. I do not know what the Yoruba view is of death among young people of this age group.

19. Brian Weiss, *Many Lives, Many Masters: The True Story of a Prominent Psychiatrist, His Young Patient, and the Past-Life Therapy That Changed Their Lives* (Whitby, ON: Fireside, 1988) and *Same Soul, Many Bodies: Discovering the Healing Power of Future Lives Through Progression Therapy* (New York: Free Press, 2005).

20. Most notable is the research of Ian Stevenson of the University of Virginia. See, for instance, his *Children Who Remember Previous Lives* (Charlottesville: University of Virginia Press, 1987).

21. Paramhansa Yogananda discusses several such Ascended Masters in his book, *Autobiography of a Yogi*, including his own teacher, Sri Yukteswar, who became one during Paramhansa's lifetime and continued to communicate with him from "across the veil." Ascended Masters are also given prominence in Theosophy and various initiatic traditions. See Paramhansa Yogananda, *Autobiography of a Yogi* (New York: Philosophical Library, 1946, repr. Nevada City, CA: Crystal Clarity Publishers, 2005).

22. Edward Hoffman mentions the Lamed-Vov—the 36 concealed righteous ones—in his divinatory text, *The Kabbalah Deck: Pathway to the Soul* (San Francisco: Chronicle Books, 2000), 38. The description of them in other places is similar to the description of other kinds of high-vibrating beings who silently or quietly "hold the world together" with their powerful good energy.

23. Within this framework, disembodied beings, such as angels, Archangels, bodhisattvas, dakinis, buddhas, etc., exist at a level of consciousness above 1,000. This is why the scale does not end with 1,000; rather, 1,000 is designed to mark the point at which the density of physical embodiment on Earth ceases to be possible.

24. Aliyah listed this as one of her favorite quotes on her Facebook page. It is one of Coleman Barks's translations. See Coleman Barks, trans., *The Essential Rumi* (New York: Quality Paperback Book Club, 1995).

EPILOGUE

1. Erich Fromm, *Psychoanalysis and Religion* (New Haven, CT: Yale University Press, 1959), 9.

BIBLIOGRAPHY

BOOKS

'Abdu'l-Bahá. *Selections from the Writings of 'Abdu'l-Bahá*. Wilmette, IL: Baha'i Publishing Trust, 1978.

Abimbola, Kola. *Yoruba Culture: A Philosophical Account*. Birmingham, UK: Iroko Academic, 2006.

Abimbola, Wande. *Ifa Will Mend Our Broken World: Thoughts on Yoruba Religion and Culture in Africa and the Diaspora*. Roxbury, MA: Aim Books, 1997.

Acholonu, Catherine Obianuju. *Motherism: The Afrocentric Alternative*. Abuja, Nigeria: Afa, 1995.

Adler, Margot. *Drawing Down the Moon: Witches, Druids, Goddess Worshippers, and Other Pagans in America Today*. rev. ed. New York: Penguin, 1986.

Alexander, M. Jacqui. *Pedagogies of Crossing: Meditations on Feminism, Sexual Politics, Memory, and the Sacred*. Durham, NC: Duke University Press, 2005.

Allen, James. *As a Man Thinketh*. New York: Tarcher, 2008. First published in 1902.

Andersen, Uell S. *Three Magic Words*. Chatsworth, CA: Wilshire Book, 1977.

Anzaldúa, Gloria E. *Borderlands/La Frontera: The New Mestiza*. San Francisco: Aunt Lute, 1986.

———, AnaLouise Keating, ed., *This Bridge We Call Home: Radical Visions for Transformation*. New York: Routledge, 2002.

Armah, Ayi Kwei. *KMT: In the House of Life—An Epistemic Novel*. Popenguine, Senegal: Per Ankh, 2002.

Badejo, Diedre L. *Osun Seegesi: The Elegant Deity of Wealth, Power and Femininity*. Trenton, NJ: Africa World Press, 1996.

Bahá'u'lláh. *The Hidden Words of Bahá'u'lláh*. Wilmette, IL: Baha'i Publishing Trust, 1954.

———. *The Hidden Words of Bahá'u'lláh*. Chandigarh, India: Carmel 2002.

Baker, Lee D. *From Savage to Negro: Anthropology and the Construction of Race, 1896–1954*. Berkeley: University of California Press, 1997.

Barks, Coleman, trans. *The Essential Rumi*. New York: HarperOne, 2004.

Bedi, Kiran. *It's Always Possible: One Woman's Transformation of India's Prison System*. Honesdale, PA: Himalayan Institute Press, 2002.

ben-Jochannan, Yosef. *Black Man of the Nile and His Family*. Baltimore: Black Classic Press, 1989. Berg, Philip S. *Astrology: The Star Connection*. New York: Research Centre of Kabbalah International, 1986.

Berger, Michelle Tracy, and Kathleen Guidroz, eds. *The Intersectional Approach: Transforming the Academy through Race, Class, and Gender*. Chapel Hill: University of North Carolina Press, 2009.

Berry, Mary Frances. *My Face Is Black Is True: Callie House and the Struggle for Ex-Slave Reparations.* New York: Knopf, 2005.

Blackman, Sushila. *Graceful Exits: How Great Beings Die—Death Stories of Hindu, Tibetan, Buddhist, and Zen Masters.* Boston: Shambhala, 2005.

Bohm, David. *Wholeness and the Implicate Order.* New York: Routledge, 1996.

Bohm, David, and Basil J. Hiley. *The Undivided Universe.* New York: Routledge, 1993.

Boone, Sylvia Ardyn. *Radiance from the Waters: Ideals of Feminine Beauty in Mende Art.* New Haven, CT: Yale University Press, 1986.

Borris-Dunchunstang, Eileen. *Finding Forgiveness: A 7-Step Program for Letting Go of Anger and Bitterness.* New York: McGraw-Hill, 2009.

Bosco, Antoinette. *Radical Forgiveness.* Maryknoll, NY: Orbis, 2009.

Braden, Gregg. *The Isaiah Effect: Decoding the Lost Science of Prayer and Prophecy.* New York: Random House, 2000.

———. *Secrets of the Lost Mode of Prayer: The Hidden Power of Beauty, Blessing, Wisdom, and Hurt.* Carlsbad, CA: Hay House, 2006.

Braden, Gregg, Peter Russell, Daniel Pinchbeck, Joanna R. Macy, and John Major Jenkins. *2012: Predictions, Prophecies, Possibilities.* Louisville, CO: Sounds True, 2007.

Butler, Judith. *Excitable Speech: A Politics of the Performative.* New York: Routledge, 1997.

Bynum, Edward Bruce. *The African Unconscious: Roots of Ancient Mysticism and Modern Psychology.* New York: Teachers College Press, 1999.

Carruthers, Jacob H. *MDW NTR: Divine Speech, A Historiographical Reflection on African Deep Thought from the Time of the Pharaohs to the Present.* London: Karnak House, 1995.

Castaneda, Carlos. *The Teachings of Don Juan: A Yaqui Way of Knowledge.* Berkeley: University of California Press, 1969.

———. *The Power of Silence.* New York: Washington Square Press, 1987.

———. *The Active Side of Infinity.* New York: HarperCollins, 1998.

Chan Khong, Sister. *Learning True Love: Practicing Buddhism in a Time of War.* Berkeley, CA: Parallax Press, 2007.

Chodrön, Pema. *When Things Fall Apart: Heart Advice for Difficult Times.* Boston: Shambhala, 1997.

Chopra, Deepak. *Quantum Healing.* New York, Bantam, 1989.

Clarke, John Henrik. *Africa at the Crossroads: African World Revolution.* Trenton, NJ: Africa World Press, 1992.

Coleman, Monica A. *Making a Way Out of No Way: A Womanist Theology.* Minneapolis: Fortress Press, 2008.

———. ed. *Ain't I a Womanist, Too?: Third Wave Womanist Religious Thought.* Minneapolis: Fortress Press, forthcoming.

Coleman, Will. *Tribal Talk: Black Theology, Hermeneutics, and African/American Ways of "Telling the Story."* University Park: Pennsylvania State University Press, 2000.

Collins, Patricia Hill. *Black Feminist Thought: Knowledge, Consciousness, and the Politics of Empowerment,* 2nd ed. New York: Routledge, 2001).

———. *Fighting Words: Black Women and the Search for Justice.* Minneapolis: University of Minnesota Press, 1998.

Cooper, Anna Julia. *A Voice from the South.* New York: Oxford University Press, 1988. Originally published in 1892.

Daczynski, Vincent J. *Paranormal Phenomenon: Amazing Human Abilities.* Self-published e-Book, 2004.

Dalai Lama, and Daniel Goleman, ed. *Destructive Emotions: How Can We Overcome Them?* New York: Bantam, 2003.

DeRohan, Ceanne. *Right Use of Will: Healing and Evolving the Emotional Body.* Santa Fe, NM: Four Winds, 1986.

Diop, Cheikh Anta. *The African Origin of Civilization: Myth or Reality.* Chicago: Lawrence Hill, 1974.

Dyer, Wayne. *The Power of Intention.* Carlsbad, CA: Hay House, 2004.

Eden, Donna. *Energy Medicine.* New York: Tarcher, 1998.

Emoto, Masaru. *The Hidden Messages in Water.* Hillsboro, OR: Beyond Words, 2004.

Enwezor, Okwui, ed. *The Short Century: Independence and Liberation Movements in Africa, 1945–1994.* New York: Prestel, 2001.

Fernandes, Leela. *Transforming Feminist Practice: Non-Violence, Social Justice and the Possibilities of a Spiritualized Feminism.* San Francisco: Aunt Lute, 2003.

Finch, Charles S. III. *Echoes of the Old Darkland: Themes from the African Eden.* Decatur, GA: Khenti, 1991.

———. *Star of Deep Beginnings: The Genesis of African Science and Technology.* Decatur, GA: Khenti, 1998.

Firmin, Joseph-Antenor. *The Equality of the Human Races.* Translated by Asselin Charles. New York: Garland, 2000. Originally published (in French) in 1896.

Floyd-Thomas, Stacey M., ed. *Deeper Shades of Purple: Womanism in Religion and Society.* New York: New York University Press, 2006.

Freire, Paulo. *Pedagogy of the Oppressed.* New York: Continuum, 1971.

Fromm, Erich. *Psychoanalysis and Religion.* New Haven, CT: Yale University Press, 1959.

Fu-Kiau, Kimbwandende Kia Bunseki. *African Cosmology of the Bantu-Kongo: Principles of Life and Living.* Brooklyn, NY: Athelia Henrietta Press, 2001.

Gerber, Richard. *Vibrational Medicine.* Rochester, VT: Bear, 2001.

Giddings, Paula J. *When and Where I Enter: The Impact of Black Women on Race and Sex in America.* New York: HarperCollins, 1984.

Govender, Pregs. *Love and Courage: A Story of Insubordination.* Johannesburg, SA: Jacana, 2008.

Griaule, Marcel. *Conversations with Ogotemmêli: An Introduction to Dogon Religious Ideas.* Oxford: Oxford University Press, 1965.

———, Germaine Dieterlen. *The Pale Fox.* Translated by Stephen C. Infantino. Chino Valley, AZ: Continuum Foundation, 1986.

Gutierrez, Gustavo. *A Theology of Liberation: History, Politics, and Salvation.* Maryknoll, NY: Orbis, 1988.

Guy-Sheftall, Beverly, ed. *Words of Fire: An Anthology of African American Feminist Thought.* New York: New Press, 1995.

Hagelin, John. *Manual for a Perfect Government.* Fairfield, IA: Maharishi University of Management Press, 1998.

Harris, Melanie L. *Gifts of Virtue, Alice Walker, and Womanist Ethics.* New York: Palgrave Macmillan, 2010.

Harwood, Jeremy. *The Freemasons.* London: Hermes House, 2006.

Hawkins, David R. *Power vs. Force: The Hidden Determinants of Human Behavior.* Carlsbad, CA: Hay House, 2002.

Hilliard, Asa G. III. *SBA: The Reawakening of the African Mind.* Gainesville, FL: Makare, 1997.

Holmes, Barbara A. *Race and the Cosmos: An Invitation to View the World Differently.* Harrisburg, PA: Trinity Press International, 2002.

Hudson, Winson, and Constance Curry. *Mississippi Harmony: Memoirs of a Freedom Fighter.* New York: Palgrave Macmillan, 2002.

Hudson-Weems, Clenora. *Africana Womanism: Reclaiming Ourselves.* Troy, MI: Bedford Publishers, 1993.

Hull, Akasha Gloria. *Soul Talk: The New Spirituality of African American Women.* Rochester, VT: Inner Traditions, 2001.

Hull, Gloria T., Patricia Bell Scott, and Barbara Smith, eds. *All the Women Are White, All the Blacks Are Men, But Some of Us Are Brave: Black Women's Studies.* New York: Feminist Press, 1981.

Idowu, E. *Bolaji. Olodumare: God in Yoruba Belief.* New York: Wazobia, 1994. Originally published in 1962.

Ilibagiza, Immaculée. *Left to Tell: Discovering God Amidst the Rwandan Holocaust.* Carlsbad, CA: Hay House, 2006.

Jahn, Jahnheinz. *Muntu: An Outline of the New African Culture.* New York: Grove Press, 1961.

Javane, Faith, and Dusty Bunker. *Numerology and the Divine Triangle.* Atglen, PA: Schiffer, 1979.

Johnson-Odim, Cheryl, and Nina Emma Mba. *For Women and the Nation: Funmilayo Ransome-Kuti of Nigeria.* Chicago: University of Illinois Press, 1997.

Johnston, Charles, trans. *The Yoga Sutras of Patanjali.* Public domain book. Originally published in 1912.

Jung, Carl G. *Synchronicity: An Acausal Connecting Principle.* Princeton, NJ: Bollingen, 1973.

Kabat-Zinn, Jon. *Wherever You Go, There You Are: Mindfulness Meditation in Everyday Life* (New York: Hyperion, 1994).

Karenga, Maulana. *Introduction to Black Studies.* Los Angeles: University of Sankore Press, 2002. Originally published in 1968.

Kasozi, Ferdinand Mutaawe. *Introduction to an African Philosophy: The Ntu'ology of the Baganda.* Freiburg, Germany: Verlag Karl Alber, 2011.

Keating, AnaLouise, ed. *Gloria E. Anzaldúa: Interviews/Entrevistas.* New York: Routledge, 2000.

———. *Teaching Transformation: Transcultural Classroom Dialogues.* New York: Palgrave, 2007.

Lemons, Gary. *Black Male Outsider: Teaching as a Pro-Feminist Man: A Memoir.* Albany, NY: SUNY Press, 2008.

Lorde, Audre. *Sister Outsider: Essays and Speeches.* Berkeley, CA: Crossing Press, 1984.

Maathai, Wangari. *The Green Belt Movement: Sharing the Approach and the Experience.* New York: Lantern Books, 2006. Originally published in 1985.

———. *Unbowed: A Memoir.* New York: Anchor Books, 2007.

Maïga, Hassimi Oumarou. *Balancing Written History with Oral Tradition: The Legacy of the Songhoy People.* New York: Routledge, 2010.

Managham, Patricia, ed. *Goddesses in World Culture.* Santa Barbara, CA: Praeger, 2010.

Martín-Baró, Ignacio. *Writings for a Liberation Psychology.* Cambridge, MA: Harvard University Press, 1994.

Masino, Marcia. *Easy Tarot Guide.* San Diego, CA: ACS, 1987.

Maslow, Abraham. *Toward a Psychology of Being,* 2nd ed. New York: D. van Nostrand, 1968.

Mbiti, John S. *African Religions and Philosophy*. London: Heinemann, 1969.

McTaggart, Lynne M. *The Intention Experiment: Using Your Thoughts to Change Your Life and the World*. New York: Free Press, 2007.

Moraga, Cherríe, and Gloria Anzaldúa, eds. *This Bridge Called My Back: Writings by Radical Women of Color*. New York: Kitchen Table: Women of Color Press, 1981.

Morgan, Ffiona. *Daughters of the Moon Tarot*. Graton, CA: Daughters of the Moon, 1991.

Myers, Linda James. *Understanding an Afrocentric Worldview: Introduction to Optimal Psychology*. Dubuque, IA: Kendall/Hunt, 1993.

Myss, Carolyn. *Anatomy of the Spirit: The Seven Stages of Power and Healing*. New York: Crown, 1996.

Naylor, Gloria. *Mama Day*. Boston: Ticknor & Fields, 1988.

Neumann, Erich. *The Great Mother: An Analysis of the Archetype*. Translated by Ralph Manheim. Princeton, NJ: Princeton University Press, 1963.

Oduyoye, Mercy Amba. *Daughters of Anowa: African Women and Patriarchy*. Maryknoll, NY: Orbis, 1995.

Ogunyemi, Chikwenye Okonjo. *Africa Wo/Man Palava: The Nigerian Novel by Women*. Chicago: University of Chicago Press, 1996.

Paris, Peter J. *The Spirituality of African Peoples: The Search for a Common Moral Discourse*. Minneapolis: Fortress Press, 1995.

Peterman, Audrey, and Frank Peterman. *Legacy on the Land: A Black Couple Discovers Our National Inheritance and Tells Why Every American Should Care*. Atlanta, GA: Earthwise, 2009.

Peters, Thomas J., and Robert H. Waterman Jr. *In Search of Excellence: Lessons from America's Best Companies*. New York: Warner, 1982.

Peterson, Christopher, Steven F. Maier, and Martin E. P. Seligman. *Learned Helplessness: A Theory for the Age of Personal Control*. New York: Oxford University Press, 1995.

Phillips, Layli, ed. *The Womanist Reader*. New York: Routledge, 2006.

Pike, Diane Kennedy. *My Journey into Self*. Binghamton, NY: LP, 1979.

Randolph, Paschal Beverly, ed. *Hermes Mercurius Trismegistus: His Divine Pymander, also The Asiatic Mystery, The Smaragdine Table and the Song of Brahm*. Des Plaines, IL: Yogi Publication Society, n.d. Originally published in 1871.

Reed, Bika, trans. *Rebel in the Soul*. Rochester, VT: Inner Traditions International, 1997.

Roberts, Jane. *The Seth Material*. Cutchogue, NY: Buccaneer Books, 1970.

———. *Seth Speaks: The Eternal Validity of the Soul*. San Rafael, CA: Amber-Allen, 1994.

Ryan, Judylyn S. *Spirituality as Ideology in Black Women's Film and Literature*. Charlottesville: University of Virginia Press, 2005.

Sandoval, Chela. *Methodology of the Oppressed*. Minneapolis: University of Minnesota Press, 2000.

Schmidt, Jeff. *Disciplined Minds: A Critical Look at Salaried Professionals and the Soul-Battering System That Shapes Their Lives*. Lanham, MD: Rowman and Littlefield, 2000.

Shah, Idries. *The Sufis*. Garden City, NY: Anchor Books, 1971.

Shantideva. *Guide to the Bodhisattva's Way of Life*. Translated by Neil Elliott with Geshe Kelsang Gyatso. Ulverston, UK: Tharpa, 2002.

Shearer, Alistair, trans. *The Yoga Sutras of Patanjali*. New York: Bell Tower, 1982.

Sheldrake, Rupert. *A New Science of Life: The Hypothesis of Morphic Resonance*. London: Blond & Briggs, 1981.

——. *The Presence of the Past: Morphic Resonance and the Habits of Nature.* Rochester, VT: Park Street Press, 1995.

Smith, Beverly, ed. *Home Girls: A Black Feminist Anthology.* New York: Kitchen Table: Women of Color Press, 1982.

Somé, Malidoma Patrice. *Of Water and the Spirit: Ritual, Magic, and Initiation in the Life of an African Shaman.* New York: Arkana, 1994.

Somé, Sonbonfu. *The Spirit of Intimacy: Ancient African Teachings in the Ways of Relationships.* New York: Harper, 2000.

Stevenson, Ian. *Children Who Remember Previous Lives.* Charlottesville: University of Virginia Press, 1987.

Tan, Amy. *The Kitchen God's Wife.* New York: Putnam, 1991.

——. *The Bonesetter's Daughter.* New York: Putnam, 2001.

Teish, Luisah. *Jambalaya: The Natural Woman's Book of Personal Charms and Practical Rituals.* New York: HarperCollins, 1985.

Thich Nhat Hanh. *Interbeing: Fourteen Guidelines for Engaged Buddhism.* Berkeley, CA: Parallax Press, 1987.

——. *Cultivating the Mind of Love.* Berkeley, CA: Parallax Press, 1996.

Three Initiates. *The Kybalion.* Chicago: Yogi Publication Society, 1940. Originally published in 1912.

Tipping, Colin. *Radical Forgiveness: A Revolutionary Five-Stage Process to Heal Relationships, Let Go of Anger and Blame, Find Peace in Any Situation.* Louisville, CO: Sounds True, 2009.

Tompkins, Peter, and Christopher Bird. *The Secret Life of Plants.* New York: Harper & Row, 1973.

Trungpa, Chogyam. *Shambhala: The Sacred Path of the Warrior.* Boston: Shambhala, 1984.

van Sertima, Ivan. *They Came Before Columbus: The African Presence in Ancient America.* New York: Random House, 1976.

Voeks, Robert A. *Sacred Leaves of Candomblé: African Magic, Medicine, and Religion in Brazil.* Austin: University of Texas Press, 1997.

Walker, Alice. *In Search of Our Mothers' Gardens: Womanist Prose.* San Diego, CA: Harcourt Brace Jovanovich, 1983.

Walker, Alice. *Living by the Word.* New York: Harcourt Brace, 1988.

——. *Anything We Love Can Be Saved: A Writer's Activism.* New York: Ballantine, 1997.

——. *We Are the Ones We Have Been Waiting For: Light in a Time of Darkness: Meditations.* New York: New Press, 2006.

Walker, Norman W. *The Natural Way to Vibrant Health.* Prescott, AZ: Norwalk Press, 1972.

——. *Become Younger.* Prescott, AZ: Norwalk Press, 1995. Originally published in 1949.

Weiss, Brian. *Many Lives, Many Masters: The True Story of a Prominent Psychiatrist, His Young Patients, and the Past-Life Therapy That Changed Their Lives.* New York: Fireside, 1988.

——. *Same Soul, Many Bodies: Discovering the Healing Power of Future Lives Through Progression Therapy.* New York: Free Press, 2005.

Welch, Sharon D. *Real Peace, Real Security: The Challenges of Global Citizenship.* Minneapolis: Fortress Press, 2008.

Westfield, N. Lynne. *Dear Sisters: A Womanist Practice of Hospitality.* Cleveland, OH: Pilgrim Press, 2001.

Williamson, Marianne. *A Return to Love: Reflections on the Principles in* A Course In Miracles. New York: HarperCollins, 1992.

Wilmshurst, Walter Leslie. *The Meaning of Masonry*. New York: Barnes & Noble Books, 1999. Originally published in 1922.

Woodson, Carter G. *The Negro in Our History*. Washington, DC: Associated Publishers, 1941. Originally published in 1922.

Yogananda, Paramhansa. *Autobiography of Yogi*. Nevada City, CA: Crystal Clarity, 2005. Originally published in 1946.

Zimbardo, Philip. *The Lucifer Effect: Understanding How Good People Turn Evil*. New York: Random House, 2008.

BOOK CHAPTERS AND JOURNAL ARTICLES

Alexander, M. Jacqui. "Remembering *This Bridge*, Remembering Ourselves: Yearning, Memory, and Desire." In *This Bridge We Call Home*, edited by Gloria E. Anzaldua and AnaLouise Keating. New York: Routledge, 2000.

Anzaldúa, Gloria E. "now let us shift ... the path of conocimiento ... inner work, public acts." In *This Bridge We Call Home: Radical Visions for Transformation*, edited by Gloria E. Anzaldúa and AnaLouise Keating, New York: Routledge, 2002.

Arndt, Susan. "African Gender Trouble and African Womanism: An Interview with Chikwenye Ogunyemi and Wanjira Muthoni." *Signs: Journal of Women in Culture and Society* 25 (2000).

Beauboeuf-LaFontant, Tamara. "A Womanist Experience of Caring: Understanding the Pedagogy of Exemplary Black Women Teachers." *The Urban Review*, 34 (2002), 71–86. Reprinted in *The Womanist Reader*,. edited by Layli Phillips, 280–95. New York: Routledge, 2006. .

Brown, Elsa Barkley. "Womanist Consciousness: Maggie Lena Walker and the Independent Order of Saint Luke."

Reprinted in *The Womanist Reader*, edited by Layli Phillips, 173–92. New York: Routledge, 2006. First published in *Signs: Journal of Women in Culture and Society* 14 (1989), 610–33.

Combahee River Collective, "The Combahee River Collective Statement." In *Home Girls: A Black Feminist Anthology*, edited by Barbara Smith. 272–82.New York: Kitchen Table: Women of Color Press, 1983.

Davis, Olga Idriss. "In the Kitchen: Transforming the Academy through Safe Spaces of Resistance." *Western Journal of Communications* 63 (1999): 364–81.

Douglas, Kelly Brown. "Twenty Years a Womanist." In *Deeper Shades of Purple: Womanism in Religion and Society*, edited by Stacey M. Floyd-Thomas. New York: New York University Press, 2006, 145–57.

Govender, Pregs. "Farewell Speech by Pregs Govender, Chairperson of the Joint Monitoring Committee on the Improvement of the Quality of Life and Status of Women." *Agenda*, no. 52 (2002): 95–98.

Gyant, Laverne. "The Missing Link: Women in Black/Africana Studies." In *Out of the Revolution: The Development of Africana Studies*, edited by Delores P. Aldridge and Carlene Young, 177–90. Lanham, MD: Lexington Books, 2002,

Harris, Melanie L. "Womanist Humanism: A New Hermeneutic." In *Deeper Shades of Purple: Womanism in Religion and Society*, edited by Stacey M. Floyd-Thomas. New York: New York University Press, 2006, 211–25.

Harrison, Faye V. "Introduction: Expanding the Discourse on 'Race'." *American Anthropologist* 100, no. 1(1997), 609–31.

Hernández-Ávila, Inés. "Tierra Tremenda: The Earth's Agony and Ecstacy in the Work of Gloria Anzaldúa." In *EntreMundos/AmongWorlds: New Perspectives on Gloria Anzaldúa,* edited by AnaLouise Keating, 233–40. New York: Palgrave Macmillan, 2005.

hooks, bell. "Simple Living: An Antidote to Hedonistic Materialism." In *Black Genius: African American Solutions to African American Problems,* edited by Walter Mosley, Manthia Diawara, Clyde Taylor, and Regina Austin, 124–44. New York: Norton, 1999.,

Hudson-Weems, Clenora. "Nommo: Self-naming, Self-definition and the History of Africana Womanism." In *Africana Womanism, and Race and Gender in the Presidential Candidacy of Barack Obama.* AuthorHouse, 2008.

Jules-Rosette, Bennetta. "Women in Indigenous African Cults and Churches." In *The Black Women Cross-Culturally,* edited by Filomina Chioma Steady, 185–207. Rochester, VT: Schenkman Books, 1985. First published 1981.

Keating, AnaLouise. "Risking the Personal." In *Gloria E. Anzaldúa: Interviews/Entrevistas,* edited by AnaLouise Keating, 1–15. New York: Routledge, 2000.

Lorde, Audre. "Uses of the Erotic: The Erotic as Power." In *Sister Outsider: Essays and Speeches.* Berkeley, CA: Crossing Press, 1984.

McCaskill, Barbara, and Layli Phillips. "'We Are All Good Woman!': A Womanist Critique of the Current Feminist Conflict." In *"Bad Girls"/"Good Girls": Women, Sex, and Power in the Nineties,* edited by Nan Bauer Maglin and Donna Perry,106–122. New Brunswick, NJ: Rutgers University Press, 1996.

Myers, Linda James. "Expanding the Psychology of Knowledge Optimally: The Importance of Worldview Revisited." In *Black Psychology.* 3rd ed., edited by Reginald L. Jones, Oakland, CA: Cobb and Henry, 1991.

Ogunyemi, Chikwenye Okonjo. "Womanism: The Dynamics of the Contemporary Black Female Novel in English." *Signs: Journal of Women in Culture and Society* 11 (1985).

Phillips, Layli. "Mamie Phipps Clark." In *Notable American Women,* Vol. 5, edited by Susan Ware, 125–26. Cambridge, MA: Harvard University Press, 2005.

———. Shomari Olugbala. "Fighting in He(r) Heels: Sylvia Rivera, Stonewall, Civil Rights, and Liberation." In *The Human Tradition and the Civil Rights Movement, 1865–1980,* edited by Susan Glisson, Lanham, MD: Rowman & Littlefield, 2006.

———. Marla R. Stewart. "'I Am Just So Glad You Are Alive': New Perspectives on Non-Traditional, Non-conforming, and Transgressive Expressions of Gender, Sexuality, and Race among African Americans." *Journal of African American Studies* 12: 378–400.

Pu, Xiumei. "Nature, Sexuality, and Spirituality: A Womanist Reading of Di Mu (Earth Mother) and Di Mu Jing (Songs of Earth Mother) in China." In *Ain't I a Womanist, Too? Third Wave Womanist Religious Thought,* edited by Monica A. Coleman (Minneapolis: Fortress, forthcoming).

Riley, Shamara Shantu. "Ecology is a Sistah's Issue Too: The Politics of Emergent Afrocentric Womanism." In *Readings in Ecology and Feminist Theology,* edited by Mary Heather MacKinnon and Moni McIntyre, 216–17. Lanham, MD: Rowman and Littlefield, 1995).

Settles, Shani. "The Sweet Fire of Honey: Womanist Visions of Osun as a Methodology of Emancipation." In *Deeper Shades of Purple: Womanism in Religion and Society,* edited by Stacey M. Floyd-Thomas, 191–206. New York: New York University Press, 2006. .

Sheldrake, Rupert. *A New Science of Life: The Hypothesis of Formative Causation* (London: Blond and Briggs, 1981).

Smith, Barbara, and Beverly Smith, "Across the Kitchen Table: A Sister to Sister Dialogue." In *This Bridge Called My Back: Writings by Radical Women of Color*, edited by Cherríe Moraga and Gloria Anzaldúa, New York: Kitchen Table, Women of Color Press, 1981, 113–27.

Smith, Pamela A. "Green Lap, Brown Embrace, Blue Body: The Ecospirituality of Alice Walker." *Cross-Currents* 48 (1998/1999): 471–87.

Stewart, Maria W. "An Address Delivered At the African Masonic Hall." In *Maria W. Stewart: America's First Black Woman Political Writer*, edited by Marilyn Richardson, 56–64. Bloomington: Indiana University Press, 1987.

Walker, Alice. "Coming Apart." In *Take Back the Night*, edited by Laura Lederer. New York: Bantam, 1979, 84–93.

———. "Suffering Too Insignificant for the Majority to See." *Shambhala Sun* (May 2007), 50–57.

Wallace, Mark I. "Sacred-Land Theology: Green Spirit, Deconstruction, and the Question of Idolatry in Contemporary Earthen Christianity." In *Ecospirit: Religions and Philosophies for the Earth*, edited by Laurel Kearns and Catherine Keller, 291–314. New York: Fordham University Press, 2007,

Waugh, Earle. "The United States." In, *Encyclopedia of Women and Islamic Cultures: Family, Law, and Politics*, edited by Suad Joseph and Afsaneh Najmabadi, 167–70. Leiden, the Netherlands: Brill Academic, 2005.

White, Hayden. "Writing in the Middle Voice," *Stanford Literature Review* 9, no. 2 (1992).

FILMS

Ayi Kwei Armah. "Awakening." Videotaped lecture. www.youtube.com/watch?v=6irUySQK5jI (accessed October 25, 2010).

Ariel, Eilona, and Ayelet Menahemi, directors. DVD. *Doing Time, Doing Vipassana*. Tel Aviv, Israel: Karuna Films, 1997.

Dash, Julie, director. *Daughters of the Dust*. DVD. New York: Kino International, 1991.

Doneman, Megan, director. *Yes Madam, Sir*. DVD. Queensland, Australia: Sojourn Films, 2008.

George, Terry, director. *Hotel Rwanda*. DVD. Los Angeles, CA: United Artists, 2004.

Green, Walon, director. *The Secret Life of Plants*. DVD. Los Angeles, CA: Paramount Pictures, 1979.

Kwan, Julia, director. *Eve and the Fire Horse*. DVD. Toronto, Canada: Red Storm Productions, 2005.

Merton, Lisa, and Alan Dater, director. *Taking Root: The Vision of Wangari Maathai*. DVD. Marlboro, VT: Marlboro Arts, 2008.

Monson, Shaun, director. *Earthlings*. DVD. Burbank, CA: Nation Earth, 2005.

ONLINE PUBLICATIONS

AFP/Google News. "In a World First, Women in the Majority in Rwanda Legislature" (September 18, 2008). Accessed December 6, 2010. afp.google.com/article/ALeqM5hyYDRUBoyMv4qslVEi1H43kUVtEA.

AIDS-Free World. "Pregaluxmi Govender." Accessed December 10, 2010. http://www.aidsfreeworld.org/Our-Issues/Politics-of-Funding/READ-an-AIDSFree-World-letter-LIS-TEN-to-the-AIDS-2010-Gender-Costing-campaign-launch.aspx.

Association for Women's Rights in Development (AWID). "Buddhism in Thailand: A Report on the Struggle for Women to be Ordained in the Theravada Buddhist Tradition" (December 2, 2008). Accessed December 24, 2010. http://www.awid.org/eng/Issues-and-Analysis/Library/Buddhism-in-Thailand-a-report-on-the-struggle-for-women-to-be-ordained-in-the-Theravada-Buddhist-tradition.

Bedi, Kiran. Interview. *Life Positive* magazine, n.d. Accessed December 7, 2010. http://www.lifepositive.com/Mind/ethics-and-values/ethics/kiran-bedi.asp.

Bhatt, Aishwarya. "Sophia Stewart Wins Copyright Infringement Case." *Thaindian News* (November 11, 2009). Accessed December 31, 2010. http://www.thaindian.com/newsportal/entertainment/sophia-stewart-wins-the-matrix-copyright-infringement-case_100273392.html.

Burnett, Patrick. "Pregs Govender and the Politics of Disobedience," *West Cape News* (December 15, 2008). Accessed December 15, 2010. http://westcapenews.com/?p=554.

CNN-IBN. "Kiran Bedi Quits Police Force, Takes Voluntary Retirement" (November 27, 2007). Accessed December 7, 2010. ibnlive.in.com/news/kiran-bedi-quits-police-force-takes-voluntary-retirement/53100-3.html,

Goenka, S. N. "The Art of Living." www.dhamma.org/en/art.shtml. Accessed December 8, 2010.

Govender, Pregs. "When 'Traditional Values' Are a Stick to Beat Women." *South Africa Times* (February 28, 2010). Accessed December 11, 2010. www.timeslive.co.za/opinion/editorials/article329381.ece

———. "South Africa: Secrecy as a Weapon of Oppression." *Pazambuka News* (September 23, 2010). Accessed Decmber 11, 2010. www.pambazuka.org/en/category/features/67154 and reposted at http://www.africafocus.org/docs10/med1010b.php.

Gutting, Gary. "Michel Foucault." In *The Stanford Encyclopedia of Philosophy*. Fall 2003 ed., edited by Edward N. Zalta. Accessed February 6, 2008.http://plato.stanford.edu/archives/fall2003/entries/foucault/

Hamilton, Craig. "Toward Homo Noeticus: An Interview with John White." *What Is Enlightenment?* (Spring/Summer 2001). Accessed December 1, 2006. www.wie.org/j19/white.asp

Maathai, Wangari. "A Winning Partnership," *The Guardian* (October 11, 2008). Accessed December 19, 2010. http://www.guardian.co.uk/commentisfree/2008/oct/11/black historymonth-race2

Maduka, Chidi. "Feminism, Womanism, and Motherism in African Literary Discourse," n.d., Accessed December 29, 2010.www.uni-leipzig.de/~ecas2009/index. php?option=com_docman&task=doc_download&gid=1568&Itemid=24motherism

McCrummen, Stephanie. "Women Run the Show in a Recovering Rwanda," *Washington Post* (October 27, 2008). Accessed December 5, 2010.http://www.washingtonpost.com/wp-dyn/content/article/2008/10/26/AR2008102602197.html

"Nommo," *Encyclopedia of Chicago.* Accessed December 20, 2010. http://www.encyclopedia.chicagohistory.org/pages/894.html

Panel of Eminent Persons. "Protecting Dignity: An Agenda for Human Rights." Accessed December 10, 2010. http://www.udhr60.ch/agenda/ENG-%20agenda_print.pdf

Patrick, David. "Yesterday's News? Western Press Coverage of the Rwandan Genocide" (paper presented at the Centre for the Study of Genocide and Mass Violence, University of Sheffield, Sheffield, UK, October 23, 2009). Accessed December 5, 2010. www.genocidecentre.dept.shef.ac.uk/documents/Paper%20-%20David%20Patrick%202.pdf.

The Pew Forum on Religion and Public Life. "U.S. Religious Landscape Survey." Accessed July 8, 2009. http://religions.pewforum.org/reports.

Powers, Samantha. "Bystanders to Genocide," *The Atlantic* (September, 2001). Accessed December 5, 2010. http://www.theatlantic.com/magazine/archive/2001/09/bystanders-to-genocide/4571/.

Puig, Claudia. "Haunting 'Hotel Rwanda.'" *USA Today* (December 21, 2004). Accessed December 5, 2010. http://www.usatoday.com/life/movies/reviews/2004-12-21-hotel-rwanda_x.htm.

Ramon Magsaysay Award. "Kiran Bedi." Accessed December 7, 2010. http://www.rmaf.org.ph/Awardees/Biography/BiographyBediKir.htm.

Ray, Tinku. "First Female Police Officer Quits," BBC News, Delhi (November 27, 2007). Accessed December 7, 2010. http://news.bbc.co.uk/2/hi/south_asia/7115753.stm.

Wendt, Natalie. "Nuns, Invisibility, and the Question of Buddhist Activism," *Tikkun Daily* (July 23, 2010). Accessed December 30, 2010. http://www.tikkun.org/tikkundaily/2010/07/23/nuns-invisibility-and-the-question-of-buddhist-activism/.

Wikipedia. "Satyagraha." Accessed December 22, 2010.http://en.wikipedia.org/wiki/Satyagraha.

OTHER RESOURCES

Bartlow, Susannah. "*Now Is the Time to Open Your Heart*: A Womanist Reading" (paper presented at the Gender Across Borders III: Research Transformations Conference, SUNY Buffalo, Buffalo, New York, April 5, 2008).

Finch, Charles S., III. "Journey to Infinity: The Magic of Humanness" (class lecture, Morehouse School of Medicine, Atlanta, Georgia, January 17, 2007).

al-Hibri, Azizah Y. "The Qu'ranic Worldview: A Womanist Perspective" (lecture, Baker Institute, Rice University, Houston, Texas, April 21, 2003).

Lanois, Derrick. *A Silent and Dignified Army: Prince Hall Associated Freemasonry, Gender and Human Rights in the South, 1900-1970.* Doctoral dissertation (in progress). Department of History, Georgia State University, Atlanta, Georgia.

Nichols, Edwin J. "The Philosophical Aspects of Cultural Differences" (unpublished manuscript. World Psychiatric Association Conference, Ibadan, Nigeria, November 10, 1976).

Thich Nhat Hanh, "Five Mindfulness Trainings Certificate," n.d.

Wisdom of the East 2009 Calendar. Riverside, NJ: Andrews McMeel, 2008.

INDEX